Research Methods in Health Care

Milbank Resource Books

David P. Willis, *Series Editor*

Research Methods in Health Care

A SELECTION OF ARTICLES FROM THE
MILBANK MEMORIAL FUND QUARTERLY

Edited by John B. McKinlay

Published for the Milbank Memorial Fund
by PRODIST   New York   1973

PRODIST

a division of

Neale Watson Academic Publications, Inc.

156 Fifth Avenue

New York, N. Y. 10010

© 1973 Milbank Memorial Fund

ISBN 0-88202-051-X

Library of Congress Catalog Card Number 73-17177

Manufactured in U.S.A.

Foreword to the Milbank Resource Books

Since 1923, the Milbank Memorial Fund has published a *Quarterly* journal in response to the premise that "the lack of application of knowledge which is in the possession of experts . . . is about the most difficult thing with which the world has to contend." This early statement of purpose, somewhat disarming in its simplicity and hopefulness, is even now characterized by an essential wisdom. Eminent scholars in a range of fields dealing with the health of the public have responded generously over the past 50 years, making the *Quarterly* a notable forum and repository of knowledge. More recently, teachers, researchers, policymakers, public administrators, and especially students, have had to contend with an even more elemental difficulty, i.e. gaining convenient access to the rich resources contained in these 50 volumes.

Many of these articles are widely recognized as classic statements. Their seminal significance makes them as viable as they are venerable. In response to continuing requests for accessibility and economy, the Milbank Memorial Fund is undertaking to republish selected papers as Resource Books.

A venture of this nature has limitations which must be faced with cautious confidence. In order to expedite publication, articles in this series are drawn exclusively from the universe of the *Quarterly*. Nevertheless, the broad range of topics addressed over the years presents an extraordinary diversity from which to select. A number of selections were originally contributed several years ago, and no pretense is made for their being either the last word or even the latest word in their substantive content. T. S. Eliot, when asked why one should read earlier writers since we now know so much more than they did, replied, "Precisely, and they are that which we know." The reader is reminded that all of the authors represented here have progressed in their thinking and have advanced their subsequent work in other journals and books.

Milbank Resource Books are envisaged as introductory readers for students with varied interests in the organization and delivery of health services. In selecting articles for individual volumes, the respective editors attempt to balance general theoretical concerns or overall principles with illustrative practical examples. The division of each volume into different sections advances this perspective.

It is planned to keep this series active and responsive to changing needs. Suggestions for future volumes will be welcome.

Contents

STATISTICAL TECHNIQUES
FOR DESIGN AND ANALYSIS

Introduction

The last few decades have seen rapid technological developments in methods for handling large data sets, increased availability of suitable sampling frames in the general population, and the development of more sophisticated statistical methods for design and analysis. As a consequence, research methods in the field of health care have expanded from the somewhat restrictive use of existing hospital or other vital records. In collecting data on human populations, three general methods are commonly available: existing records, cross-sectional surveys, and longitudinal "panel" studies.

As a source of data, existing records have many known limitations. Hospital and other medical records, with few exceptions, are maintained primarily for administrative rather than research purposes. Not only does this result in the omission of relevant information (such as some key measure of socio-economic status), but the quality of the information which is gathered is generally not closely monitored.

Cross-sectional studies or surveys, while able to compensate for some of the major inadequacies of existing records, fail to resolve the problem of retrospectivity. Unless the subject of research is confined to the brief period of the survey itself, memory errors are always present. However, methods for minimizing such errors have been and are still being developed, including modifications to questionnaires and alternative forms of data analysis. Moreover, the cross-sectional study has proved to be a relatively inexpensive method for obtaining considerable information. Included in this general group is a class of studies usually termed "retrospective." Although memory errors are a major problem in this type of study, as with most cross-sectional designs, the term "retrospective" refers rather to the type of inferences being made. The researcher is required to argue from a known effect to an hypothesized cause which may have occurred many years previously. Classic examples of such designs may be found in the many epidemiological investigations of the etiology of cancer of the lung and of the cervix uteri.

The third and most recently developed design is the longitudinal or "panel" study. An alternative term for this type of design, "prospective," is the antithesis of retrospective in that it indicates that inferences are from an hypothesized cause to a possible future effect. The best known prospective study of heart disease, established two decades ago in Framingham, Massachusetts, is a good example of this type of design. Such investigations, however, have been few, since generally large samples, repeated interviewing over many years, and high attrition rates involve problems of high costs. Cost reduction would make the panel study a feasible alternative to the cross-sectional surveys, especially as the memory problem would be absent or minimal, and the inferences more conclusive.

This volume embraces all three designs as well as the different stages of research: planning, data collection, and analysis. Given the diversity of the papers and a preponderance of reports based on actual research experience, the material is organized according to the three research stages rather than types of design.

The first part of this volume contains a series of papers on the planning and design of investigations in the health field. The two introductory papers reflect the major concerns in this area— the study of human beings and the study of service systems. The next four papers treat aspects of design in a general fashion; specific examples follow. The last two selections, in particular, are concerned with the study of service systems.

Part two is specifically devoted to the major method of data collection in studies of human populations: the interview. The emphasis is on sources of error or variation in response rates, beginning with a useful comparison of methods employed in two similar surveys and the effects of these methods on the analysis. The remaining papers are devoted to methodological contributions on the design of health surveys.

The third part presents statistical methods of analysis applicable in health research but not generally available in standard textbooks of statistics, demography, or epidemiology.

The ordering of this volume follows quite naturally the stages in any investigation. It is hoped that this sequence will aid the reader to gain insight into a range of methodological problems in health care research.

JOHN B. McKINLAY, PH.D.
Department of Sociology
Boston University

The Design and

Planning of Studies

RESEARCH TECHNIQUES IN THE STUDY OF HUMAN BEINGS

William G. Cochran[1]

WHEN Dr. Boudreau invited me to speak tonight, he happened to mention some of the hopes expressed by Dr. Sydenstricker when the Milbank Memorial Fund's division of research was established in 1929. I was struck by one phrase which Dr. Sydenstricker used: he referred to "the possibility of including social data in the domain of scientific research." This phrase set me to trying to sort out my impressions of the quantitative study of human beings as a supposed branch of science. How well is it progressing relative to other branches of science?

Consequently, I would like to present a few of these impressions, with particular reference to the tools of measurement and the general methods of investigation that have been developed.

The claims of the study of social data to be regarded as a branch of science were examined in the 1830's. The occasion was an application made to the British Association for the Advancement of Science to form a section in statistics. In those days, statistical data dealt largely with economic or social matters. The Association appointed a committee to report on the application, and one of its tasks was to consider whether statistics *was* a branch of science. The committee's verdict is interesting. So long as statistics confined itself to the collection, tabulation, and orderly presentation of data, that was science. But if statistics were to concern itself with the interpretation of economic and social data, that would be argumentation, with passions and politics entering, and that was not science. In the picturesque language of the committee, the interpretation of such data could not be allowed as a branch of science, "lest we admit the foul demon of discord into the Eden of philosophy."

The same point of view was maintained a few years later

---

[1] Professor of Biostatistics, The Johns Hopkins University.

3

when a statistical society (which became the Royal Statistical Society) was formed in London. The Committee's verdict was in fact embodied in the motto of the new society. This motto consisted of a fat sheaf of wheat, representing the abundant harvest of data that has been collected and tidily arranged. Around the motto was an ornamental ribbon, like the ribbon worn by Miss Atlantic City in the Beauty contests. But in place of the words "Miss Atlantic City" was the Latin motto "Aliis exterendum"—"Let others thrash it out." I am slightly embarrassed that the statisticians should have started their organized career by timidly proclaiming to the world what they will *not* do. The motto is also curious in that the chairman at the early meetings in which statistical organization was discussed was a man well-known to some of you, by the name of Thomas Malthus. It is true that he left much material for others to thrash out, but he did a certain amount of "thrashing out" himself.

Since I shall speak from the viewpoint of the statistician—I can't help it—I must first say a little about statisticians and their relations to scientists. The statistician has long been known as a person who handles data, and the scientist tends to think of seeing a statistician when he has some problem in the analysis of his data. In earlier days, this happened mostly when something had gone wrong with the experiment or survey—or more accurately when the scientist realized that something had gone wrong. As a result, statisticians used to see a sorry collection of the wrecks of research projects.

Now it is a hard fact, which the statistician and the scientist both had to learn, that little could be done to get these wrecks floating again. Usually, some error in the way in which the data were collected made it impossible to draw sound conclusions, manipulate them how you will. This led to two developments. The statistician began to advise scientists to come and see him at the beginning of an investigation—to make him, as it were, an accessory before the fact. Also, the statisticians began to study the process of collecting data in order to learn

4

what procedures and precautions were necessary to ensure that sound conclusions *could* be drawn at the end.

The result is that, at present, the role played by the statistician in the planning of research is often that of verifying that the scientific methodology is sound and sometimes even that of supplying the scientific methodology. Of course, the statistician has other duties. He helps with the arithmetic, tells where the decimal point goes, and he may supply technical formulas from statistical theory, but these are often secondary contributions. Perhaps the statistician's role as a consultant in scientific methods is temporary, because one would expect scientists to perform this function themselves. Indeed, there are signs of a trend in this direction. A few years ago, a conference with a physician about the testing of new drugs on hospital patients seemed to be mainly a matter of trying to wheedle or cajole the physician into taking some precautions that he regarded as a nuisance and as unnecessary. Now he is often found insisting on these precautions himself before the statistician can open his mouth, and the statistician's contribution is to nod his head in agreement at diplomatic intervals. In time, the doctors may decide that they don't need this yes-man.

While it lasts, this role requires close and friendly cooperation between statisticians and research workers. In statistical training centers, something is done to teach young statisticians how to get along with scientists. While in the presence of a number of distinguished scientists, I would like to give a few hints on how to get along with statisticians. In any extensive discussion of a statistical problem, some wag is likely to repeat the old chestnut about the three kinds of lies: "lies, damn lies, and statistics." If you feel an urge to give birth to this witticism, please remember that it is not new, and it was not funny when it was new. The statistician also gets tired of hearing the scientist say "Of course, I am no statistician," in a tone of voice which implies that he is mentioning one of his most sterling virtues. If you *are* no statistician, this fact will probably reveal itself in the course of the conversation, and if you must tell us about it, please do so with an apologetic air. Remember also that the statistician is a poor marriage risk, and may be suffering from marital strains. The reason for this is that the statistician has to cultivate a dislike for imprecise statements, and the person most likely to be making imprecise statements in his vicinity is his unfortunate wife. Statisticians' wives have not, thank goodness, formed an international union, but if they do, the first plank in its platform will be to stop their husbands from being so persnickety.

Tools of Measurement

The consulting statistician has a fascinating opportunity to learn something about the triumphs and the difficulties of research in different branches of science. He begins to wonder why some branches are forging ahead in an exciting way, while others seem to be creeping. Among the numerous factors that influence the rate of progress of scientific research, two of the most important are the tools of measurement that the research worker has at his disposal and the general methods of investigation available to him.

I shall use the phrase "tools of measurement" in a broad sense, to cover both the range of phenomena that can be measured and the precision of the measuring devices. It can be argued that the available tools of measurement are the most important single factor in determining the rate of progress in a field of research. I do not wish to build up this argument, but one example may be quoted from physics. Towards the end of the last century, the laws of physics seemed to have reached a pinnacle. They were of high accuracy, of immense scope, and were pleasing to common sense. Then improvements in measurement were made that enabled very minute bodies as well as very distant bodies to be more accurately studied. Large cracks appeared in the edifice of physical theory, and to the rescue the physicists had to bring in the revolutionary ideas of quantum mechanics and the theory of relativity. To judge from

6

their difficulties in understanding these concepts and in reconciling them with simple common sense ideas, they must have felt at times as if they had brought in the Marx brothers to repair the building.

The importance that is rightly attached to an improvement in measuring technique is illustrated by the recent award of the Nobel prize in medicine to Dr. Enders and his associates. Their contribution was to grow poliomyelitis virus in tissue culture, and other workers helped to perfect the technique. What does this mean to research in the field? In measuring virus concentrations in specimens from suspected polio cases, as many tests can now be made from the kidneys of a discarded monkey as required 600 monkeys previously. The monkey can be dispensed with entirely, by use of the Hela human cancer cells. Experiments that were impossible can now be done in a week. After a development of this type, any area of research can expect to take great strides forward.

A second impression about measurement techniques is that one never knows where the next advance is coming from. Often it does not come from the field of work that desperately needs the advance. The anthropologists, after measuring skulls from every angle with admirable zeal, have to thank the geneticists for blood group methods that for some purposes are much more reliable. The paleontologists were presented with a new and independent method of dating fossils—radioactive carbon—by the physicists. The electron microscope is a godsend to the manufacturers of paint. And so on.

In the study of human beings many of the problems of measurement are formidable. Not only have we to measure fairly concrete attributes like the state of disease in the individual, (which the doctors will assure us is not easy to measure well) but we need to classify and if possible to measure many things that are hard enough to define in the first place, like motives, morale, intentions, feelings of stress. This means a vast undertaking that has had to start from the ground with rude homemade tools. Thus far, for want of anything better in sight, we

7

have obtained our raw data mainly from what the individual tells us. And the recording instrument has usually been another individual.

We are having to learn about the idiosyncrasies of the human being as a reporter. On the whole, he is surprisingly cooperative, and his good nature in taking up his time to talk to us is heartwarming. He is, in fact, a little too friendly, and will sometimes give the kind of answers which he thinks we would like to have. He is anxious to put on a good front: his statement about the amount he paid for his present car is not entirely to be trusted, and his plans for buying all sorts of expensive gadgets in the future are still less so. On the other hand, he can shut up like a clam. At the end of the war, I helped to gather some data from a carefully selected sample of the German civilian population. According to our results, the Nazi party was one of the world's most exclusive clubs. He is loyal to those whom he likes. The English, in their industrial mortality statistics, were puzzled by the fact that the death rate for the drivers of railway engines (i.e. the locomotive engineers) was above the national average, while that for the man with the apparently less healthy job of stoking the coal furnace was well below. The explanation was that father, after a life of service as stoker, was often posthumously promoted by mother to the position of engine driver on the death certificate.

The recording device—the interviewer—is not perfect either. A quotation from Bertrand Russell, although rather overdrawn, illustrates this point. He is writing about studies of learning in animals. "The animals that have been carefully observed have all displayed the national characteristics of the observer. Animals studied by Americans rush about frantically, with an incredible display of hustle and pep, and at last achieve the desired result by chance. Animals observed by Germans sit still and think, and at last evolve the solution out of their inner consciousness. To the plain man, such as the present writer, this situation is discouraging."

As instances of the amount that has to be learned in order to make the best use of human beings as reporters and recorders, the following are some, but by no means all, of the questions that arise in the planning of morbidity surveys in which the data are obtained by interviews in the home. Over what period of time can the subject remember episodes of illness? What types of illness are easily remembered and accurately reported, and what types are poorly reported? What aids to memory are worth while? How well does the housewife remember and report illnesses of other members of the family? To what extent can the reports be used for a diagnostic classification of the illnesses? How much is gained by checking the reports with physicians who have attended the families? How do lay interviewers compare in effectiveness with public health nurses or medical students? How much information can be picked up at a second visit that was missed at the first? Since a substantial amount of experience has been accumulated for morbidity surveys, at least partial answers can be given to these questions. In other words, something is now known about the precision and the limitations of this type of measuring tool, and about good and bad ways of applying it. Research on more difficult concepts like attitudes and sources of motivation will in time have to answer an analogous list of questions about the interviewer-respondent relationship.

Social scientists are attacking vigorously the fascinating problems involved in devising ways of classifying and measuring what might be called, for want of better words, the strengths and directions of opinions, attitudes, and feelings. They are making surprisingly early use of quantitative scales, with an implied continuum in the background, and have shown ingenuity in constructing methods for testing the internal consistency of the scale and for checking how well the scaled results can be reproduced from a second examination of the same group of people. The criticism has been made, with some justification, that these scales may deceive research workers into thinking that they have measured some rather intangible quantity that they are nowhere in sight of measuring. I don't think that the difficulty arises from the use of quantitative scales themselves: the dangers in pushing this process too fast do not seem to me great. It would be well, however, to be cautious and humble in making claims about what we have measured. Until we are very sure of our ground, use of long Greek names for the things measured might be preferable, rather than claiming to have measured, say, the strength of maternal affection.

GENERAL METHODS OF INVESTIGATION

Methods of investigation in scientific research can be classified roughly into three types, which may be called chance observations, planned observations, and experiments.

Chance Observations. Something unusual strikes the curiosity of an alert scientist, and off he goes into a chain of speculation and then into action. Many of you have heard Sir Alexander Fleming's account of the beginnings of his discovery of penicillin. He happened to notice an unusual contamination from the air of some plates lying in his laboratory. The contribution of chance observations to progress in science must be very great. Last week I was talking to a productive scientist who had had occasion to review carefully his work during the past fifteen years. He remarked that, to his surprise, all his most important discoveries had arisen in unexpected deviations from his main path of research. None of them would have appeared in that anathema of the modern scientist—the "Statement of work to be done during the next fiscal year."

Planned Observations. Here the scientist knows what he is after—he knows the questions to which he would like answers —and he maps out a plan of observation which he hopes will provide the answers. Some of the current investigations of the relation between smoking and cancer of the lung are of this type. In the British Medical Research Council's study, all the British doctors were asked three years ago to fill out a questionnaire giving their ages and their recent smoking habits. The rest of the study is just a matter of waiting until a reasonable proportion have died, and then examining whether the death

10

rate and the causes of death are related to smoking habits. Doctors present many advantages for this kind of study: they are likely to cooperate, it is relatively easy to find out if they have died, and when they do die there is reason to believe that the cause of death will be more accurately known than for laymen.

Experiments. The word "experiment" has a very broad meaning both in common speech and among scientists. For my present purpose I would like to restrict it to situations in which we are able to *interfere* with nature. In this sense, the essence of an experiment is that we deliberately apply certain chosen procedures for the purpose of measuring their effects. The power of experimentation in speeding up progress in science is tremendous. It has two strong advantages over the observational method. It enables us to select for investigation the factor or factors that will be most informative, whereas with observations, we are restricted to those factors that nature is kind enough to give us the opportunity to observe. The experiment is also the surest method of working out the causal relations that underlie the associations which we observe. With the observational method, the step from correlation to causation is often hazardous and uncertain. For instance, even if several studies in different countries should reach the common conclusion that the death rate from cancer of the lung increases steadily as the amount of smoking increases, the objection will be made (in fact, it has already been made) that this is not a cause and effect relationship, because of the alternative possibility that the kinds of men who smoke heavily are unusually susceptible to cancer of the lung, and would be so even if they did not smoke. Whatever our opinions about the plausibility of this explanation, it is hard to devise an observational study that will clearly support or rebut it. If experimentation were possible, the issue could be cleared up much more easily.

In the study of human beings we are groping our way around among these general methodologies, trying to find which ones pay off best in results. Thus far, observational methods have been used to a large extent, since opportunities for experimentation appear limited.

In particular, we are having to learn how much can be obtained from past data, originally gathered for some other purpose, for example, in connection with the adminstration of a program. Since the data are already there, the method is much speedier than a fresh start would be. In cost, it may mean the difference between $5,000 and $150,000. Although the past data are seldom what we would like to have if we were doing the job anew, yet often there are masses of it, and perhaps it will be possible to select what we need.

Although it is difficult to generalize, experience with past data has been disappointing. It has often given a confused picture from which no clear leads can be drawn, and it has sometimes given leads that turned out to be the wrong ones. The main difficulties appear to be that the definitions used in the data are not rigorous and clear-cut enough for scientific investigations, and that the effects that we wish to study are inextricably tangled up with other effects. Some of my own disappointments with past data remind me of a statement made by Available Jones in the Little Abner comic strip. Available Jones makes his living in part by giving advice. He has two kinds of advice, the 10-cent and the 50-cent kind. Of the 10-cent kind, he says (after some modifications of his spelling): "For 10 cents, I barely listens—in fact I yawns in your face, and the cheap advice you gets will do you more harm than good."

In many human studies, workers are realizing that they must face the long and hard business of planning new observations in order to obtain the 50-cent advice. I do not mean, however, to condemn the use of past data in any outright manner: if a few factors predominate, this should be revealed, and very often, past data are all that we have. Moreover, I owe my first post, in the depression, mainly to the fact that my employers had a large batch of past data which were regarded as a potential mine of information. They hired me to dig it out. I dug furiously, but I doubt whether they received their money's worth. Fortunately, my salary was so low that this moral problem caused me no loss of sleep.

In new studies, we are having to learn how much ground can be covered, that is, how many different questions can be investigated in a single study. At the moment, the lesson seems to be not to be too ambitious. This can be illustrated with respect to one approach to exploratory studies that might be called the method of casting the net widely, if you happen to like it, or the method of shooting blindly in all directions, if you don't happen to like it. Suppose that there is some phenomenon about which not much is known, and we are trying to discover which factors or variables have the most predominant influence on it, or are at least most clearly associated with it. It seems rational to write down all the factors that are likely to have an influence on the phenomenon, include them in the study, and rely on statistical techniques, particularly those of multiple classification or regression, to reveal the most important ones. I know of no one as clever as the social scientist at writing down a ten-page list of factors that might influence any given phenomenon. For the relatively poor results given by this method, the statisticians may be partly to blame, because they may have oversold the power of statistical techniques to unscramble an omelet. If nature mixes things up thoroughly, as she sometimes seems to do, statistical methods will not sort them out very well. Indeed, the more factors that are included in the study, that is, the more painstaking the scientist is, the harder it becomes to disentangle all their effects. Many studies now go to the opposite extreme, concentrating on learning something about a single factor, such as differences between premature and normal children, or between public and slum housing. This means slow progress, and perhaps with more experience some intermediate method will prove rewarding.

Social scientists are having to learn how to observe the same people over a period of years, as in the study of chronic diseases or of the effects of administrative programs. Such studies are

13

expensive and hazardous, because it is difficult to foresee the contingencies that may arise to plague us. For one thing, the human subjects won't stay where they are: off they go to Portland or Honolulu, and if we cannot find means to keep observing them, the group under study dwindles year by year to a remnant consisting of the most settled families. Sometimes it is the scientist who is off to Rangoon or Monte Carlo. My guess would be that we now know how to observe groups for as long as three years, and perhaps for as long as five years: beyond that, there are too few successfully completed studies to be able to say that the technique has been mastered.

In such long-term studies the subjects are sometimes influenced by the fact that they are being studied, in a way that vitiates the purposes of the study. I have heard of farm management studies of poor farmers where the list of questions opened the eyes of some of the farmers to financial opportunities that had never occurred to them. In a few years, these farmers were offering the interviewers jobs. In the British study of smoking and cancer, the Medical Research Council's scientists became alarmed at the number of doctors who replied to the original questionnaire by saying "I have been smoking twenty cigarettes a day, but after reading this questionnaire I have given up smoking for ever."

These long-term studies require, for their direction, a type of scientist who is quite different from the "ivory tower" concept of a scientist. He must be able to assemble a team of workers and to maintain good relations among them: he must obtain the cooperation of various administrators and their agencies, and must handle a considerable amount of paper work. Scientific competence alone does not guarantee success in this type of research: some scientists are too shy, and others too quarrelsome, to meet the requirements.

Social scientists are also having to learn to exercise the kind of ingenuity that is delightful when it comes off. Nature occasionally provides golden opportunities to study some group that will be particularly revealing, as with identical twins who have been reared under different circumstances, or with groups of people who have been long isolated. Ingenuity may also enable us to take the difficult step from correlation to causation. If we have established correlation between two variables A and B in an observational study, we may *think* that A is the cause of B, but nobody saw the murder committed, and the evidence pointing to A as the culprit is only circumstantial. But if by ingenuity we can build up a series of separate pieces of evidence, all pointing to A, it becomes harder and harder to think of an alternative hypothesis that will explain them all away simultaneously. In this connection the social scientist has to use the methods of the detective, the good criminal lawyer, and even the man who is trying to prove that Bacon wrote Shakespeare.

As I have indicated, the use of the more powerful method of experimentation has been small. The obstacles with human subjects are obvious. Yet with persistence and tact, the difficulties can sometimes be overcome, and it may be that experimentation will come to play a more important role than it now does. In medical research on the prevention and cure of disease, some notable successes have been scored by experimentation, and experiments are now being attempted that would, I believe, have been considered impossible a few years ago. The main problem is to secure the tightness of control that is essential for a good experiment, without relaxing the ethical requirement that the welfare of the patient is the paramount consideration.

The trial of the polio vaccine conducted this summer is an example. In some of the states, this trial was made by a method that I would describe as observational, but in others, involving hundreds of thousands of children, the trial was a genuine experiment. The children were divided into two groups at random. Those in one group received, at intervals, three shots of the vaccine. Those in the other group received in the same way three shots of an inert substance that is expected to have no effect. No one in the areas concerned knows which child received vaccine and which control. This, in fact, is known to

15

very few persons, and it will not be revealed until necessary in the final stages of the analysis.

A second example is an international cooperative experiment on drugs for the treatment of leprosy, conducted under the leadership of the Leonard Wood Memorial, that was an organizational masterpiece. The same six drugs were tested at the same time in three different institutions, with uniform methods of measuring and recording the dermatological, neurological and bacteriological progress of the patients, and with random allotments of patients to drugs. One institution was in Japan, one in the Philippines, and one in Pretoria, South Africa. In fact, the chief barrier to progress in this line of research is probably a deficiency in tools of measurement. Since no experimental animal has been found in which leprosy can be studied in the laboratory, it is difficult to obtain clues as to the most promising types of drug to test in the future.

SUMMARY

The quantitative study of human beings, particularly in their social aspects, is a young field. Because of the multitude of critical problems in human relations facing the world today, research workers are trying to obtain helpful answers on practical questions with rather crude tools of measurement and none too powerful methods of investigation.

In hazarding a few suggestions about the use of resources in this area of research, I should make it clear that I have not surveyed the present use of resources in any adequate way. It may be that my suggestions are already being prosecuted as vigorously as seems worth while.

The field needs to devote ample resources to improving its tools of measurement. This is best done by workers who do not have to produce answers to practical questions at the same time. Raymond Pearl used to urge biologists to stop beating their breasts about the difficulty of doing accurate work in biology. If the biologists would devote as much brains, energy and care to refining their measurements as the physicists do, he

16

claimed that they would obtain as accurate results. Although I think he promised too much, the amount of research that physicists devote to measuring devices as such is impressive, and the returns are equally so. In the social sciences, the work of the psychometricians in the construction of scales is a good beginning. I have heard some hard words about the Rorschach test, but both orthodox and unorthodox methods of measurement should be developed and tried.

Experimentation (in the sense in which I have used it) needs to be exploited as much as possible. The question: "Why can't I do an experiment?" is always worth asking, even if it sounds unrealistic. There may be many opportunities for simple experiments using students as volunteers. A colleague, one of the few men still working on the discouraging task of producing a vaccine for the common cold, finds his volunteer subjects among the convicts.

A balance should be retained between studying what people say they will do and studying what they actually do. Here there is perhaps a contrast between economics and sociology. The economist has kept a close eye on what people do, but has tended to rely on armchair reasoning to uncover the motives for their actions, to the neglect of attempts to study motives independently. The sociologists have been enterprising in tackling the difficult task of studying motives, but they need also to be constantly checking reported motivations against actions.

In addition to scientists engaged in large-scale studies, the field needs a supply of those German animals (in the quotation from Russell) who sit still and think. These might be younger scientists with steady incomes, but with restricted research budgets.

Finally, the field needs to keep strong lines of communication with other branches of science, and particularly with biology, and to recruit some of its research workers from these other branches. For certain research problems, the "interview" method of obtaining data is likely to prove inadequate, and progress may have to await new measuring techniques that are

17

adapted from developments outside of social science. The need for links with biology is obvious: man is biological as well as social; moreover, although biology has access to more powerful and flexible research techniques than social science, many of the problems are the same.

In conclusion, I hope that my comments have not sounded pessimistic. If there is one lesson to be learned from the history of science, it is that the optimists are always right, except that they should have been more optimistic.

RESEARCH PROBLEMS IN EVALUATION
OF HEALTH SERVICE DEMONSTRATIONS

EDGAR F. BORGATTA

Research problems in evaluative research are not unique to the health services or health service demonstration programs; rather, they recur in the many circumstances where programs operate manifestly to improve existing conditions, or where efforts are being made to prevent or stop deterioration of existing conditions.

In society many things are done with the intention of bringing about changes, and some of these are relatively simple to evaluate. That is, success may be relatively clear and agreed upon, and the methods utilized for bringing about the change may be accepted by all concerned. An implicit utility theory says that things that work will be retained in society. Stated somewhat backwards: just how some discoveries occurred and came into play is sometimes difficult to understand, because they appear to be so wise in their structure and so effective in their consequences. This, as a retrospective judgment, is sometimes called the "wisdom" of the system.

When a new program is initiated, lack of success may also at times be clear. That, of course, is most obvious not only when no change occurs in the direction intended, but when some worsening of the situation occurs. Where a program may have been initiated in response to a felt need, and the need was clear and obvious, lack of improvement may be equally obvious.

Between the clear successes and the clear failures lie many degrees of ambiguity as to what the results are. Whether something is or is not maintained as a service, then, may be a matter of values other than those that are ostensibly related to the goal to be achieved. If success may be the case, for example, but doubt remains, the possible positive value may be worth keeping if the cost is not considered excessive. The value of life, for example, may itself he held as precious, depending on the circumstances.

Care must be taken, however, not to assume that matters of utility as measured by cost in money—or some other form of relative value— are always the bases for maintaining ways of behaving in societies. Even a peripheral contact with the comparative study of cultures will indicate that accepted ways of doing things do not necessarily exist because of some "rational" basis or because they are effective for particular purposes. Maintaining ways of behaving must often be described as an end in itself, which is to say that no rational way of explaining the behavior is uncovered. Expressed another way, people accept "things" with which they are familiar and, in fact, value what is familiar to them and has previously been accepted by them.

The references to normative forms of behavior in society have been relatively abstract to this point, but the relevance here must be obvious. Professions have norms that may not have a rational basis. How these arise is not at issue here, but many mechanisms may exist to generate forms of behavior of this type. For example, people have within themselves a tendency to rationalize from their own experience, and this, of course, is a fine art in some professions. If the case is sufficiently well dramatized, its relevance and importance may not be seriously questioned. Similarly, with tendencies that are called bureaucratization, institutionalization and so forth, processes once established tend to be maintained by the authority systems in which they reside. Thus, many things may exist where success or failure of the intended actions is not at all clear, yet authority, convention and other forces may tend to keep them as they are.

Concern with evaluation is not new, and presumably concern with effectiveness is something that has existed as long as people have tried to change situations or otherwise find out what were the fruits of their efforts. Scientific concern with program evaluation may be of more recent vintage, as general programs of amelioration of health and other social conditions appear to be associated with the greater value on human life and welfare that is identifiable with recent generations. But, in general, programs for amelioration have existed for a long time, and essentially when conditions are bad enough and social conscience is brought into play, both the need and the potential for

20

improvement may lead to the development of a program designed to be corrective. Most programs that receive systematic attention for evaluation occur in the context of correcting an existing situation. Preventive programs are even of a more recent vintage and, essentially, to exist they require more general theories of cause and effect than do corrective programs.

WHAT IS TO BE EVALUATED

Evaluation research requires a clear statement of what is to be evaluated. In the health services, such a clear statement may be available and often contrasts with many other areas which have more implicit values of what is good. In theory at least, some medical disorder is undesirable, and eliminating or diminishing the problem in society is appropriate. Thus, for example, most persons may agree that to reduce the amount of tuberculosis in the community, to eradicate a particular communicable disease, or to reduce suffering from some disorder is important. However, developing programs for these purposes is not a simple matter, even with reasonable agreement as to what the appropriate condition in society should be. For example, although the community may agree that a concerted effort should be made to eliminate tuberculosis, the question of cost to produce a really effective program may become a serious issue.

Certainly, an effective method of controlling tuberculosis is to have all persons undergo appropriate medical diagnostic tests on a regular basis. How can that be done, however, in a society in which compulsion for such matters is found objectionable? Compulsion may be possible in certain circumstances, as, for example, when chest x-rays are required of all teachers in a state, with the rationale that these persons have contact with children and young adults and could conceivably infect them. The rationale may be extended to food and other services, but the segment of the population that becomes involved may be relatively limited.

With groups where compulsion is possible, evaluation may have a peculiar meaning. For example, what is to be evaluated under such circumstances? Whether or not people conform? Whether the tests are effective in detecting existing cases of tuberculosis? Whether the children and young adults in schools are appropriately protected? Under such circumstances evaluation research may not be at all appropriate, except in examining the intent of the program and its

21

correspondence in fact. If no cases of tuberculosis are uncovered by the routine tests, the justification for the tests would be difficult to make. On the other hand, if a few cases are located, this may be sufficient in the value system of those who are concerned to warrant perpetuation of the system. In other words, under circumstances of compulsion and presumed 100 per cent participation, questions of evaluation may concern merely the appropriateness of assumptions relative to the medical diagnostic procedures involved. If the effectiveness of the program is being tested in a medical sense, questioning the validity of the procedure would be difficult unless ultimately more accurate diagnostic tests are carried out with segments of the population which allow additional case finding.

With no compulsion or less compulsion programs of evaluation may have different meanings. For example, regarding tuberculosis, questions may be raised about the extent of coverage of the relevant group and the possible selective factors that may arise. In the total population, for example, something is known about the groups most likely to have tuberculosis. Questions may be phrased around whether or not these groups are involved in the program, and if so to what degree. Effectiveness of a program may be stated not in how well the disease is uncovered among those who arrive for chest x-rays, but in the extent to which the project includes the relevant groups in the population. Depending upon rational persuasion rather than compulsion, such projects may often actually involve just those segments of the population that least need to be pursued. Those who are more educated and those who are most concerned with their health, possibly, are most likely to cooperate with such programs on a voluntary basis. On the other hand, those who are relatively ignorant of their limitations, particularly with regard to health, may not cooperate at all. Such groups may believe, for example, that if one is ill, one would know about it, and only then would a chest x-ray be appropriate. Thus, programs may be devised specifically to involve such segments of the population which are most difficult to reach. An evaluation of health services in such cases deals very little with the medical aspects of the problem, but rather emphasizes the effectiveness of the program as a piece of social engineering.

What is to be evaluated is not always clear. If a new program is being initiated, grandiose, general values may be stated initially. The implementation, however, may be a homely set of procedures. When testing for the effectiveness of the program, which of the values involved is to be examined? The broadly stated ones or specific ones that may not correspond very clearly to the broad program? What is the criterion of success? The problem in attempting to answer this is that the relationship of the goals involved in a program to what is considered success may be very complex. Evaluation of the situation by those who are conducting the program may involve many factors other than the intended changes. For example, if the staff derives satisfaction (not to mention income) from the program, that may influence their view of it. Even though the program may not effectively treat the disorder, the attention may appease those who are suffering. And, if it does not appease them, it may appease their relatives.

OBJECTIVITY IN SCIENCE

All science requires objectivity, but this goal may be achieved more easily in some circumstances than in others. Particularly in evaluative research, many factors may exist which will work against the actual application of evaluative research on the one hand, and may also provide rationalizations before and after the fact as to why evaluative research may neither be applicable nor useful. In other words, many values in the system may deny the feasibility of evaluative research on the one hand, and, on the other hand, if carried out and negative results are encountered, reasons are provided for discounting the negative findings.[1]

A few of the rationalizations that may occur could be mentioned to set the stage:

1. The effects of the program are long-range, thus the consequences cannot be measured in the immediate future.
2. The effects are general rather than specific, thus no single criterion can be utilized to evaluate the program, and, indeed, even using many measures would not really get at complex general consequences intended.
3. The effects are small, but important, thus cannot be measured effectively because instruments are not sufficiently sensitive.
4. The effects are subtle, and circumstances may not be ordered appropriately to get at the qualities that are being changed. The measurement would disturb the processes involved.
5. Experimental manipulation cannot be carried out because to withhold treatment from some persons would not be fair.

These rationalizations, of course, are relatively difficult to apply if medical criteria of success and failure in a discrete disorder are utilized. However, most evaluation research with demonstration programs in the health services is concerned with the impact on the community rather than with controlled experimentation under laboratory conditions, and these kinds of advance rationalizations may be feasible.

The fact that in health service demonstration programs medical diagnostic or treatment procedures are involved becomes a major rationalization for not becoming seriously involved in evaluation research. After all, the diagnostic utility of the x-ray, the pill, the innoculation and so forth is demonstrated. What is the point of evaluating a demonstration program that uses such dependable medical procedures?

Rationalization of negative findings after the fact, assuming an adequate research design, are possibly even more plentiful. A few of these are listed here:

1. The effectiveness of the program cannot really be judged because those who could most use the services did not participate.

2. Some of the persons who received the services improved greatly. Clearly, some of the persons who recovered could not have done so if they had not received attention.

3. Some of the persons who most needed the program were actually in the control group.

4. The fact that no difference was found between the persons receiving services and those not receiving services clearly indicates that the program was not sufficiently intensive. More of the services are obviously required.

5. Persons in the control group received other kinds of attention.

Of course, the previous list of rationalizations "before the fact" also applies in retrospect. Many other rationalizations are provided, of course, including indicating that the particular agency or program used was not really the best or the most modern or the most something else.

In this connection, response to evaluation research sometimes is peculiar. For example, scientists ordinarily do not define what the programs will be, although they may consult on design of programs. In evaluation research, the concern of the scientist should be with whether or not the program brings into effect the consequences intended. However, in circumstances where the evaluation research

24

leads to negative findings, the scientist very often is placed in a position of apologizing about the lack of positive findings. The failure of the program is associated with the inability of the evaluation research to demonstrate the change.

CONFLICTING GOALS

Although certain circumstances render the goals of a program clear and well-defined, some goals within the program will conflict, and the goals of the program may well conflict with those of groups to which the program is directed. The problem of goals and values may be discussed more generally to show how they complicate evaluation.

In the minds of the social engineers who devise a program, the intentions and the definition of expected good may be relatively clear. They may be less clear, and indeed denied by others. For example, if a program designed to improve the social welfare and health of families involves contraceptive information, segments of the population may be aligned directly in opposition to the values of the program.

A program of dissemination of birth control information is a viable type within society, but some approaches to health and family planning are totally rejected and in fact are illegal. In Japan, abortion has been legalized, and for the lower classes has been the means for family planning and control. Medically speaking, the operation has become highly routine and under the best conditions involves little danger. The use of abortion has been relatively effective, and at this stage a transition is being noted in Japan such that preventive contraceptive procedures are becoming effective substitutes for the corrective abortions. That is, family planning and control have become possible and meaningful through legalized abortions and the value of these has been translated into preventive procedures. Thus, a short-term goal of family planning moves directly into a longer-term goal of family planning. No conflict of values manifestly exists between these goals in Japan. However, in the United States, abortion is illegal, and in many instances programs of contraception and information dissemination are opposed vehemently. The goal of an agency or program, thus, may be at variance with the goals of the population or a significant segment of the population they are supposed to serve, not because of disagreement on certain overriding general values, such as family planning, but because the effective implementation of the goal conflicts with other values.

As noted, conflict can occur between long-term and short-term goals. General community goals may conflict with goals that are appropriate for some families, and what may be good for families may not be good for particular types of individuals. Different subgroups may have different goals. Goals may be explicit and salient in one case and implicit, but equally salient in another case. The intended services may be directed to a set of values associated with a class of people, and thus may be incomprehensible and irrelevant to those of another class.

Science cannot determine the wisdom of any particular goal unless the goal is stated as a means to another goal. An intended program may be inappropriate to realize a particular goal, but scientific analysis or research may uncover the misdirection. Thus, science is directed toward increasing knowledge about the correspondence between intended goals and actual consequences of types of action. Science asks such questions as: By undertaking such and such a program, does the health of the population improve? In the long run, by taking a given course of action, do certain conditions of the poor improve?

Programs are initiated for many different reasons, other than those manifestly given as goals, as already implied when agencies and programs were said to have many different goals. The fact that some agreement can be found on the undesirability of a particular condition does not necessarily mean that it can be resolved. Evaluative research is not designed to solve a problem, but merely to examine whether a procedure which is being utilized to solve it actually works. In this circumstance, recognition must be given to the notion that many things are not done with a clear expectation that they will lead to positive results. When looking at the condition of the poor, the deprived or the unhealthy, the inclination of many is to say, "We must do something now." That does not mean that in fact something can be done within the ken of the relevant sciences. Or, as with the case of legalizing abortions in this country, obvious and viable solutions may be excluded.

EXPERIMENTAL DESIGNS AND EVALUATIVE RESEARCH

Whether one is dealing with health service demonstration programs or any other program of change, inferences about effectiveness can be made only to the extent that appropriate control group design is implied in the study. The classic design involves an experimental group and a control group, and a comparison of these after the program has been applied. In theory, if the assumption can be made that the groups were initially equivalent, no "before" measures are necessary, and the simple "after" comparison, will suffice. Variation in the experimental design can go in two directions. Either loosening the design to make it more applicable, but with greater dependence on assumptions about equivalence of the experimental group and the control group; or making it more rigorous if equivalence must be demonstrated before the program has been put into effect. These differences in experimental designs will be examined with reference to demonstration programs.[2]

Rigorous Designs

If the design utilized is the simple one of comparing experimental and control groups only after the program has been carried out, the most that can be indicated is that some difference does exist between the experimental group and the control group. But any of a number of alternatives may lead to the condition of the difference. For example, the difference may occur because the experimental group has improved faster than the control group, which also improved. The difference may be that the control group deteriorated, while the experimental group did not. Or, the difference might be that the control group deteriorated faster than the experimental group. In such a design, the relative advantage associated with the program (and the experimental group) cannot be judged unless some specific knowledge is available about the "before" condition of the two groups. Of course, still other factors may lead to the result. Although experimental and control groups were supposedly selected to be exactly equivalent in the "before" condition, they were not.

To be exactly equivalent in the "before" condition ordinarily requires some notion of random selection. If random selection is applied, in theory the experimental group and control group are both drawn from the same population. Selection of persons for the two groups is carried out in such a way that each person, and each combination of persons, has the same probability of being selected. As science becomes more rigorous, equivalence must be demonstrated rather than assumed. Demonstration usually consists of comparing the experimental and the control groups before the experiment on those variables considered to be relevant to the criterion that will be used to measure the change. Thus, the utilization of measurement before the experiment serves two purposes. First, it permits demonstration that the

27

experimental and the control groups are equivalent to begin with, and second, it provides the reference point for change.

In the actual design of experiments many other factors become involved, and these may require introduction of additional control groups. For example, perhaps the program could be judged more effective after the classical design of before and after measurement, using an experimental and control group, and the assessment could be fallacious. Interaction may occur between the program and the "before" testing in such a way that the combination leads to improvement, while in the absence of the "before" measurements, it might not. For example, utilizing the "before" measurements might make the persons receiving the program aware of matters to which they should attend and conscious of a need to change which becomes even more evident as they participate in the program. Thus, the experimental design may be made more complicated by adding two additional groups not to receive the "before" test, selected on the same bases as the two groups that will be given the "before" test. Examination of the four groups after the program has been applied should indicate that those who received the program are different from those who did not, whether a "before" test was given or not. If results indicate a difference in improvement for the two groups which received the program, this may indicate something more about how the program should be carried out. As indicated in the example, developing salience for the program through "before" testing may have some additional effect on the program itself.

When designing a program under circumstances where costs are a serious problem, the cost factors may alter the pattern of experimental design in allocating sample sizes. For example, if the method of assessing the relevant criterion is relatively cheap, control groups of larger size than the experimental groups may be used, although selection must be maintained on the random basis required of any experiment. However, if, as is often the case, the sampling procedures are relatively expensive, then the most efficient design is probably one in which the experimental and control groups are of the same size.

What is meant by random selection? Random selection means that a person has the same probability as every other person of being selected, and every combination of persons has the same probability of being selected. That means, of course, that an experimental group and control group must be chosen at the same stage. An experimental group, for example, cannot be chosen from those who arrive requesting services if a control group is to be selected from the population at large. These two groups would differ radically in the sense that one is seeking attention and the other is not. Thus, equivalence relative to the program could not under any circumstances be judged as existing. Random selection, in this case, would occur only if the experimental and control groups were both chosen from persons requesting services, or from the general population (and then some procedures would be implied for bringing those selected as the experimental group in for the services).

Additional comments may apply on the question of sampling. If particular variables are relevant to the response of the program, the sample may be stratified on these variables, essentially matching the two samples on these variables and doing random assignment within each of the cells involved in the stratification. However, selection must be from the same population. For example, stratifying on I.Q., but selecting the experimental sample from middle and upper class children in a test of "ability to absorb additional instruction" might lead to fallacious results. If I.Q. test performance bears some relationship to class differences, possibly persons in the lower classes are being selected who have more "native" intelligence than the middle or upper class group, thus the design would be contaminated. If large sample sizes are utilized, control for equivalence through stratification may be less necessary. The sensitivity with which matching is carried out must be related to the nature of the program that is being tested.

The problem of *post hoc* matching of persons in groups that have not been selected at random from the population may be illustrated easily. For example, suppose that the effects of a program on the poor is to be examined. Two communities are selected, one that is almost entirely Negro and one that is almost entirely white. Now, the question is one of how the effectiveness of a program could be tested if it were carried out in one of these communities and not in the other, say under circumstances where a special program directed to the improvement of conditions for Negroes is initiated, and where the white community is going to be used as a "control." Matching persons on the characteristic of being poor to have equivalent groups will raise thorny questions. The poor whites, for example, may have incomes of 3000 dollars per year per family. In the population at large, these may be the most deprived whites. By contrast, in the Negro community families at that economic level may not be relatively the most deprived. Thus, the first question is: Does matching on income mean matching on poorness?

Additional problems, of course, are encountered at the same time. For example, although Negroes of an income level may be reasonably prosperous relative to other Negroes, educationally they may still be inferior to the whites of equivalent income, who are relatively poor among the whites. Clearly, when such problems may be anticipated by attempting to compare groups that are quite different in what appears to be a cultural sense, all sorts of difficulties may be encountered if one is made the control for the other, even with *post hoc* matching. Thus, controls, groups or comparison groups should be chosen to be equivalent or similar on general grounds, and matching *post hoc* will not be satisfactory unless this is the case. Although statistical techniques can account for initial differences of groups in part, the cultural differences cannot be taken into account by the analysis of covariance or any other statistical maneuvering.

The idea that a control group is randomly selected by employing two groups, such as two neighborhoods, using one as an experimental group and the other as a control group, is only as good as the initial matching of the neighborhoods. Since people ordinarily select neighborhoods to live in, selective factors may be involved that are of great importance. If one compares different groups, and they are selected as groups initially, the sample size for the experiment may not be the number of persons in each group, but instead may be one (1) for the experimental group and one (1) for the comparison group.

Assuming that technical and cost factors are not a problem, in theory the most refined experiment will involve matching each person in each experimental group with each person in each control group, but the selection of the matched persons would be at random, with regard to which group they are assigned. Thus, even under the condition of maximum stratification, the requirement of random selection for experimental groups and control groups persists. Maximum stratification and matching is desirable if one is concerned that two groups may not be equivalent, even though they have similar marginal distributions of relevant characteristics. For example, two groups having approximately the same distribution in age and sex may actually differ; one group may have more older females and the other group more older males. Thus differences in the average and other statistical characteristics of samples may be eliminated without actually developing exactly equivalent experimental and control groups.

Some limitations involved in the research designs should be pointed out that may have little to do with the formal structuring of experimental designs as indicated thus far. Some of these will be relatively simple, but in fact may be forgotten in establishing demonstration programs in the health services, as they often are in other areas. For example, samples must be selected in such a way that they have a potential for change. In some types of services that are provided, of course, clients are brought to the attention of the organization when they are in an acute condition, possibly as bad as they can be and still be ambulatory. Under these circumstances, of course, considerable latitude for improvement, and thus an appropriate circumstance for applying a program, may exist. On the other hand, because people are arriving in an acute condition, most would improve, and the effect of a program may be difficult to demonstrate on the grounds that the spontaneous remission rate, or improvement by contact with ordinary aspects of society, may be as large as that under a planned program. Under such circumstances concern with "regression effects" is most important.[3] By contrast, some difficulty could arise if one is dealing with a preventative program under circumstances when most persons are in good health. The health habits of this population would be sufficient to maintain good health, and further improvement in the maintenance of good health may be difficult to demonstrate. Some thought must be given, explicitly, to outlining exactly what kind of improvement the demonstration program should make, and the feasibility with the selected population must be well established.

Before moving on to a discussion of some looser designs in evaluation research, the importance of defining what the program is that is being evaluated should be emphasized, particularly through the specification of the control group. For example, if the health service involved is a sheltered workshop for the rehabilitation of tuberculosis patients, the program may involve immediate location of the individuals when discharged from the hospital, introduction into the workshop program, medical, psychiatric and social work attention, removal of the client from his family for ten or more hours a day, support financially at a given level, etc. The control group might be selected at the same time, at the point of entry for the experimental group, and the control group might receive no attention directly. Then, the finding, if positive effects are demonstrated, would be that the program is better than no attention or such attention as might incidentally be found in the open community. This leaves totally unanswered many additional questions, such as what would have been the result if only the financial support had been provided for the experimental group. Would the experimental group have done as well merely with this support as with the entire program? Would the experimental group have done as well with only the medical attention provided? Obviously, such questions cannot be answered without devising an experiment in which many subgroups of attention are defined, in which case one is not only testing the effectiveness of a program, but its component parts. A program may turn out to be effective only when all its parts are involved, but it may also turn out that only a few of the parts contribute to the improvement of the clients, or that only one of the parts might be effective in this sense. Thus, the medical, psychiatric and social work attention given could conceivably be irrelevant, and merely the enforced routine of work and rest could be the important aspect of the program. Even if that were the finding it does not mean that the medical, psychiatric and social work aspects of a program would be eliminated. It might emphasize the fact that only one aspect of the program had been evaluated, mainly what was being done for the rehabilitation of the clients. Other aspects, such as the feeling that the program is worthwhile among the donors and benefactors of the program, was not tested. Their opinions of the effectiveness of the program could well be raised if medical, psychiatric, and social work help is given, independently of whether it does any good for the patients.

Looser Designs

To this point, the development of experimental design under conditions of considerable rigor has been emphasized. Implicitly, limitations to interpretation when the designs are not carried out have been emphasized. A few directions in which the designs may be loosened or relaxed should now be indicated on the assumption that rough measures may be sufficient and that judging equivalence is feasible. The main relaxation that is carried out is the utilization of the group that receives the health service demonstration program as its own control. The assumption is that the sample, group or community to which the program is directed is operating at a known level. Then, when the program is introduced, if it does have a significant change, it will be of sufficient magnitude that the contrast between the condition after the program and that before the program will be easily visible.

In medical practice such designs are frequent. Drugs are introduced and rates of disease or disorder are examined to see if significant changes have occurred. Serious problems often arise, of course, with this design. The program may not be what caused the change in rates, but the change could be associated with other historical changes occurring at the same time. Sanitary conditions, control of pollution or other major circumstances may be changing at the same time that the drugs are being introduced. Or diagnostic procedures are becoming more accurate, and may show that conditions normally associated with the disorder are attributable to some other condition. The existence of a program in a community may cause other self-conscious interests with matters of health. But, additional factors may be involved that are associated with change in time. For example, resistance and immunities may be developing in the population, the population characteristics may be changing, either through migration or maturation, etc.

When less than full controls in experimental design are utilized, the key to drawing appropriate conclusions centers on raising questions about alternative explanations for changes that are observed. Systematically, alternative hypotheses must be raised, and, for the original hypothesis to be maintained, the alternatives must be adequately answered and eliminated.

Under the concept of demonstration programs, whether they be in the health services or in welfare, emphasis is placed on the exemplary application of a service that is assumed already to be effective. In theory, the demonstration indicates feasibility and resolves technical and administrative problems in such a way as to indicate how appropriate services may be provided. Under such conditions the use of controlled experiments is relatively unlikely, and effectiveness is more likely to be judged on some intuitive basis. Demonstration programs, thus, frequently are not initiated in a way in which they can be evaluated in any scientific sense. But, to be evaluated some analogy to controlled experimentation must be made.

That, of course, leads to one alternative to experimentation; that is, the systematic study of communities to find situations which are analogous with regard to important social characteristics of population, and where programs do or do not exist. Great care must be used in such comparative research, but if the unit of study is taken as the community rather than the individuals within it, a considerable amount of information could be garnered. This is particularly the case if a substantial number of alternatives exist, and if enthusiasm of communities and of staff may be expected for each of the alternatives. However, even here, care must be used in interpreting what is an effective program and what is not. Each, in its own way, may be providing some relevant services for the community.

Evaluation in other fields is no less difficult than with health services. For example, graduate school departments are constantly re-examining their criteria for a program of study leading to the Ph.D. Such a revision was recently made in the sociology department at Wisconsin, which is composed of a substantial number of younger staff members. Before proceeding with the discussion of the proposed new program each of the younger staff members was asked to describe the program under which he was trained. After the many reports were given the chairman concluded that by witness of the presence of all these young men, obviously quite different programs could produce excellent Ph.D's.

THE PROGRAM AS EXPERIMENTAL MANIPULATION

If attention is now given to the type of demonstration program being utilized, additional cautions arise as to how results of an evaluation study are to be interpreted. First, a prime difficulty that is encountered is in detaching the program, in its technical or professional specification, from other effects or circumstances. For example, often a program is introduced into a community at the request of some segment of the community. Thus, receptivity for the program may be established before the program is introduced, and for all practical purposes the community may have oriented itself to making a success of the program, independently of what the program involves in terms of technical or professional manipulations. Certainly, the success of the program could not be contributed to its specified procedures, and then be expected to work in another community where such local response is not a precursor.

Equally important, very often programs are initiated by individuals who have great confidence in them. In this case, professionals and nonprofessionals working together may develop such a level of enthusiasm that they, with charisma, may carry the program independently of what it is. This is sometimes called the pioneering effect, and a program that has been successful with such staffing will not necessarily be equally successful when introduced into other locations by staff who view the program more phlegmatically and with less enthusiasm.

The above comments suggest that either enthusiasm of the staff or the receptivity of the community may make a program successful, when its procedures may not be effective as such. Further, both these factors may lead to a favorable evaluation of the program, independently of whether it has been effective or not. Under such circumstances, each program must be viewed as a single case. Viewed comparatively, health service demonstration programs that are judged successful may well be those in which program directors and staff are enthusiastic and devoted and where the communities have been oriented in a receptive and equally enthusiastic way. What, then, would be the way of making inferences about the program itself? The question must be raised about the relevance of the program itself if the application of programs is to occur under less ideal conditions.

Aspects of evaluation under such circumstances often stimulate researchers to raise questions in such a way that they have policy or other implications. Having some knowledge of the areas involved, scientists may suggest that appropriate measures are not being taken. For example, if one is interested in control of veneral disease, the question of appropriateness of a program designed to cure when symptoms are already visible may be questionable. What is the rational basis for the program in terms of what is known about control of the disease? The public health service may be interested in controlling the disease, but in the willingness to actually bring it under control the community at large may not cooperate in procedures that would have higher likelihood of success. Is the community willing to have realistic sex education in the schools, common availability of prophylactic devices in all public locations and so forth? At this stage the answer is usually no. Bringing into effect these more direct and possibly more efficient procedures conflicts with other values in this society.

Here again the question of conflict of values returns. Health service demonstration programs ordinarily are concerned with attempts at providing services, and the evaluation of the medical aspects of the services may not be in question. What may be central to the program is the social engineering that brings the medical services to the proper clients. But values may apply in the situation that appears to be "irrational," and the procedures may be ineffective for various reasons as previously noted. Appropriate procedures may not be possible and ostensibly appropriate procedures may be thwarted. The process of providing the program may have a higher net survival value in the community than value measured in terms of intended consequences.

With regard to the evaluation of demonstration programs, the tendency is to move out of the arena of direct evaluation unless the program itself is designed as an experimental procedure. Questions of evaluation ask whether the program is an appropriate one for the population, and answers have to be given on bases other than those which

35

involve scientific knowledge. Dependence increases on what is called analysis, which in fact boils down to opinion on the part of experts, some of whom may actually be quite wise. They may raise questions, for example, about the appropriateness of a program for a given population, assuming considerable knowledge of the cultural aspects of the population and its limitations. Further, a fair amount of experience may suggest the limitations of generalization of programs in communities other than the ones where the health service demonstration was carried out. Such experience, for example, may militate for the development of very simple programs and procedures that require little involvement on the part of the population to which they are directed, and where the effects are reasonably easily demonstrable. Appropriateness of a program may depend entirely on its ability to operate under the worst conditions rather than under the optimal conditions usually defined in demonstration programs. Of course, these comments are relevant whether or not a control group design or a historical descriptive case analysis is carried out.

REFERENCES

[1] For another consideration of such factors in the area of psychotherapy see, Borgatta, Edgar F., Research, Pure and Applied, *Group Psychotherapy*, 8, 263–277, 1955. In the area of criminology, another such list was prepared. *See*, Cressey, Donald R., The Nature and Effectiveness of Correctional Techniques, *Law and Contemporary Problems*, 23, 754–771, 1958.

[2] In the area of educational research, considerable attention has been given recently to questions of experimental designs in terms of the array of both "true" experiments and "quasi" experiments. Although designed for another area of concern, persons interested in evaluation research will profit from reading the following. Campbell, Donald T. and Stanley, Julian C., Experimental and Quasi-Experimental Designs for Research on Teaching, *in* Gage, N. L. (Editor), HANDBOOK OF RESEARCH ON TEACHING, Chicago, Rand McNally & Co., 1963, pp. 171–246.

[3] The problem of "regression effects" in research that is less than experimental in design is enormous and presents itself in many ways. One brief but dramatic exercise shows how strong such effects are when a program is directed toward cases arriving in an acute condition, with a before and after design, but with no control group. *See,* Borgatta, Edgar F., Demonstration of Genuine Placebo Change, *Psychological Reports,* 64, 645–646, 1964. The problem of improvement when apparently irrelevant attention is given is frequently encountered in the literature under the consideration of "placebo reactors." That is a misnomer, for if persons are indeed reacting to the placebo, then it should be viewed as a (or another) change agent; it is not irrelevant. The reader may be interested in examining the kinds of statement that can be made in the absence of demonstrated effectiveness of a program, or, in fact, in the absence of even the test of effectiveness. *See,* Borgatta, Edgar F., The New Principle of Psychotherapy, *Journal of Clinical Psychology,* 15, 330–334, 1959.

RESEARCH USES OF VITAL RECORDS IN VITAL STATISTICS SURVEYS

Monroe G. Sirken

Introduction

I T is not an easy matter to keep well informed about recent technological developments involving research applications of vital records. One factor is the substantial increase in the research uses that have been made of these records in recent years. Another factor is that, customarily, matters pertaining to technology and methodology get considerably less attention than is given to the substantive findings of research projects. The net result is that the research potential of vital records, in terms of existing methodology and technology, is not being fully exploited.

The existence of a typology or index of research uses that have been made of vital records and a bibliography of published reports describing research applications would probably help to disseminate information about technical developments in this field. Preparation of these reference materials is, however, a task beyond the scope of this paper. Rather, this presentation is limited to some major types of research applica-

---

This article is a revision of a paper presented at the 90th Annual Meeting of the American Public Health Association, Miami, Florida, October 16, 1962.

tions of statistics that have been derived from vital statistics surveys conducted by the National Vital Statistics Division (NVSD).

First, it is necessary to briefly summarize the scope, objectives and methodology of the NVSD program for vital statistics surveys. Subsequently, research applications which have been made of statistics derived from these surveys will be discussed.

Survey Program of the NVSD

The basic objective of the NVSD survey program is to produce vital statistics which will contribute to the fund of basic data required by the National Center for Health Statistics in its program for developing a national intelligence system with respect to the character and dynamics of health problems, their trends and implications.

The program for vital statistics surveys originated about six years ago. The survey program was conceived as a stage in the evolutionary development of the registration system for producing national vital statistics. (9, 10, 11, 12) The surveys are linked to the registration system and seek to supplement the limited information reported about vital events on vital records. The basic methodology of the survey program at the present is the "followback survey linked to vital records." Three essential features of the methodology are:

1. Selection of a probability sample of vital events from files of vital records or from files of punch cards representing these records.

2. Conduct of surveys in which the mail questionnaire is the principal data collection method and persons and institutions identified on the vital records are the primary sources of information.

3. Derivation of unbiased national and regional statistics and estimation of the sampling and nonsampling errors of these statistics.

Until fairly recently, there were two parts to the NVSD vital

40

statistics survey program. One part involved conducting the *ad hoc* surveys on a contractual basis for agencies both within and outside the Department of Health, Education, and Welfare. In the other part of the program, developmental studies were undertaken in order to improve the survey technology of the existing program and to explore and develop new survey methodology.

In 1961, the scope of the survey program was expanded to include a national mortality survey based on a sample of one out of every 330 registered deaths in the nation, or about 5,000 deaths annually. The survey program will be expanded again in 1963 to include a national natality sample survey. This survey will be based on a sample of one out of every 1,000 registered births, or about 4,300 births annually. The sample designs of both surveys will not change from year to year, and in this sense, the surveys will be continuing, but the content of the surveys will be developed on a topical basis and periodically the survey topic will be changed. Essentially, these two continuing surveys will serve as the mechanisms for conducting a series of special studies so that over the years a wide variety of national multipurpose mortality and natality statistics will be collected (8).

Uses of Survey Data

The national mortality and natality surveys will enlarge the scope of vital statistics by supplementing items of information reported on the vital records with the information about the vital event which have never been obtained and most likely could not be obtained on the vital records themselves. This is probably the most important use of the survey data. The 1962 national mortality survey, for example, will produce estimates of differential utilization of hospitals and institutions in the last year of life according to socio-economic status of the decedent. Data collected in these surveys have served also as a basis for evaluating the quality of the information reported on the vital records. This is another important use of the survey data. For example, the results of diagnostic tests reported by physicians who certified death records in the Pennsylvania Mortality Survey produced statistics on the quality of diagnostic information supporting the causes of death. (7)

In some applications, the survey data provide only part of the information needed in the research project, and the estimates derived from the vital statistics surveys are combined with estimates derived from other sources. These uses of survey data are less well known than those mentioned above. Research problems have arisen which necessitated combining the estimates derived from mortality surveys conducted by the NVSD with estimates derived from another source. The other source has been either a population survey, a health survey, or a record matching study. Each of these is briefly described below.

POPULATION SURVEYS

Estimation of specific death rates for the general population presents a difficult problem when the mortality data are not available from the death records and the population data are not available from the census. Recently, a sample survey methodology was developed to cope with this problem. The methodology, which produces unbiased estimates of specific mortality rates, involves conducting two sample surveys. One of these, a survey linked to the death record, provides unbiased estimates of the numerators of the rates. The other, a survey of the corresponding population at risk, provides unbiased estimates of the denominators of the rates.

This "dual sampling" methodology was applied in a national lung cancer epidemiological study (4) sponsored by the National Cancer Institute. The objective of the study was to obtain national estimates of lung cancer death rates specific for age, smoking habits and residence history. The mortality estimates, required for the numerators of these rates, were produced by a national lung cancer mortality survey in which information pertaining to cigarette smoking habits and residence histories were collected from family informants for a national sample of lung cancer deaths that occurred during 1958. To obtain the estimates required for the denominators of the lung cancer mortality rates, arrangements were made with the Bureau of the Census to obtain comparable information on smoking habits and lifetime residences for a sample of the national population included in the Current Population Survey. (1)

HEALTH SURVEYS

Currently, national estimates of the annual volume of hospital utilization are based on data obtained in household interviews conducted weekly by the Health Interview Survey (HIS) of the National Health Survey Division. (13) The interviews obtain information on hospital utilization by each resident member of the household during a reference period of specified duration preceding the week of the interview. The household interviews do not, however, obtain information on hospital utilization by the persons who would have been residents of the household except for the fact that they died during the reference period. Thus, the estimates derived from the health survey relate only to that portion of the population at risk that survived the reference period and were alive at the time of the interview. To obtain estimates of the volume of hospital utilization by the entire population, the estimates derived from the HIS have to be supplemented by estimates of hospital utilization by persons who died during the reference period.

In 1958, the National Health Survey Program arranged for the NVSD to develop and test a method of estimation and data collection to fill the gap in hospitalization data. The procedure developed makes use of information about hospital utilization in the last year of life. (14) A method for collecting these data by means of surveys linked to the death record was demonstrated in a pilot study conducted in the Middle Atlantic

States and, subsequently, the methodology was applied in the 1961 National Mortality Survey.

RECORD MATCHING STUDIES

By matching death certificates for persons who died after the Decennial Census to their census enumeration schedules, the information about the decedent reported on the death record is supplemented by the demographic and socioeconomic information about the decedent and other persons in his household collected in the census. The major technical difficulty with this methodology for expanding mortality statistics has been the limited success of the matching operation. Past efforts (3, 5) at matching death and census records have been uniformly unsuccessful in locating the census schedule for about one-fifth of the decedents. Lack of census information for a proportion of decedents represented by a nonmatch rate of this size would produce potentially biased results that could scarcely be tolerated in most studies.

In a recent study of social and economic differentials in mortality (6) that involved matching 340,000 death certificates for persons who died in the 4-month period May to August, 1960 with the 1960 census schedules, the matching problem was resolved by conducting a mortality survey in which the census information was collected for a subsample of about 10,000 decedents. The mortality survey was conducted in advance of the operation for matching death certificates with census schedules in order to avoid the risks of delaying data collection operations. Consequently, of the 10,000 decedents in the survey, it is expected that for about one-fifth, or 2,000 decedents, the death certificates will not be matched with census schedules; and for about four-fifths, the match will be successful. The survey information collected for the former group will provide estimates of the census characteristics of decedents whose death certificates will not be matched with census schedules. The survey information collected for the latter group will be compared with the respective information

44

reported on the census schedules, thus providing a statisical basis for assessing the validity of the estimating procedure making use of survey data in lieu of census data for the unmatched cases.

Conclusions

The effective dissemination of today's flood of technical information presents a serious problem in virtually all branches of science and technology. (12) There is a need, I believe, for more effective dissemination of information concerning recent technological and methodological developments involving research applications of vital records. In this connection, several types of research applications of statistics derived from sample surveys linked to death records were described in this report.

Undoubtedly, more effective dissemination of technical information on research uses of vital records would further stimulate methodological developments along these lines, and I believe that these innovations are long overdue. Recent developments, particularly in data collection methods, in other fields of health statistics appear to have surpassed those in vital statistics. This, I believe, is one of the reasons why vital statistics have lagged behind other types of health statistics in recent years. Thus, whereas a few years ago, mortality statistics were virtually the only regularly available national morbidity statistics, at the present time more is known about the morbidity and medical care experience of the general population than is known about the terminal experience of the population prior to death.

The initial objective in developing the methodology referred to in this report as "surveys linked to the death record" was to expand national mortality statistics to include the terminal morbidity and medical care experience and other related health and behavioral experiences that are not reported on the death certificate. The other types of research applications of data derived from these surveys, presented in this report, represent unexpected dividends on the original investment in methodological research.

45

REFERENCES

1. Bureau of the Census: CONCEPTS AND METHODS USED IN THE CURRENT EMPLOYMENT AND UNEMPLOYMENT STATISTICS PREPARED BY THE BUREAU OF THE CENSUS. [Series P-23, No. 5], May, 1958.

2. Gray, Dwight E.: Information and Research-Blood Relatives or In-laws? *Science,* July 1962, 137: 263–266.

3. Guralnick, Lillian, and Nam, Charles B.: Census-NOVS Study of Death Certificates Matched to Census Records. The Milbank Memorial Fund *Quarterly,* April, 1959, xxxvii, (2): 144–153.

4. Haenszel, William, Loveland, Donald B. and Sirken, Monroe G.: Lung-Cancer Mortality as Related to Residence and Smoking Histories. I. White Males. *Journal of the National Cancer Institute,* April 1962, 28(4): 947–1001.

5. Kaplan, David L., Parkhurst, Elizabeth and Whelpton, Pascal K.: The Comparability of Reports on Occupation From Vital Records and the 1950 Census. *Vital Statistics-Special Reports,* June 1961, 53(1).

6. Kitagawa, Evelyn M., and Hauser, Philip M.: Methods Used in a Current Study of Social and Economic Differentials in Mortality *in* EMERGING TECHNIQUES IN POPULATION RESEARCH. New York, Milbank Memorial Fund, 1963, pp.

7. Moriyama, Iwao M., Baum, William S., Haenszel, William M., and Mattison, Berwyn F.: Inquiry into Diagnostic Evidence Supporting Medical Certifications of Death. *American Journal of Public Health,* October, 1958, 48(10): 1376–1387.

8. National Vital Statistics Division: Sample Survey Program of the National Vital Statistics Division. *Proceedings of the Ninth Conference on Records and Statistics,* June 1962. Washington, D. C.

9. Sirken Monroe G., and Brown, Morton L.: Quality of Data Elicited by Successive Mailings in Mail Surveys. *Proceedings of the Social Statistics Section,* 1962, American Statistical Association. [To be published.]

10. Sirken, Monroe G. and Dunn, Halbert L.: Expanding and Improving Vital Statistics, *Public Health Reports,* June 1958, 73(6): 537–540.

11. Sirken, Monroe G., Pifer, James W. and Brown, Morton L.: Design of Surveys Linked to Death Records. National Vital Statistics Division, Washington, D. C., September 1962.

12. ———————: Survey Procedures for Supplementing Mortality Statistics, *American Journal of Public Health,* November 1960, 50(11): 1753–1764.

13. U.S. National Health Survey: Hospital Discharges and Length of Stay: Short-stay Hospitals, United States, 1958–1960. *Health Statistics,* [Series B-No. 32], April, 1962.

14. U.S. National Health Survey: Hospital Utilization in the Last Year of Life. *Health Statistics,* [Series D-No. 3], January, 1961.

THE DETERMINATION OF VITAL RATES
IN THE ABSENCE OF REGISTRATION DATA

ANSLEY J. COALE

Some 45 to 66 per cent of the world's population still lives in areas in which births, deaths and marriages are so incompletely recorded that vital rates based on registered data are virtually useless (the wide range between the two figures of 45 and 66 per cent is caused by uncertainty about the state of vital statistics in mainland China). For some time to come, knowledge of vital rates for much of the world's population will be based on special procedures of estimation.

The past twenty years have seen the development and application of a variety of procedures that with varying degrees of success have yielded estimates of birth and death rates. The literature on estimation has become substantial, and as the co-author of a manual published by the UN on methods of estimation, and as a teacher who devotes the better part of the spring term in a graduate course to teaching procedures of this sort to his students, I find it an embarrassing assignment to compress useful information on the topic in a short paper.

I shall try to achieve the necessary compression by attempting, in most instances, little more than an enumeration of the procedures that have been developed, with at most an indication of the principles upon which the methods of estimation are based, and the kinds of data that they require. Anyone wanting to learn how to prepare estimates will have to look beyond this paper, beginning with the references provided in the footnotes.

RECORDING OF EVENTS BY TWO INDEPENDENT PROCEDURES IN A SAMPLE OF AREAS

A method of great potential usefulness whose effectiveness is not, however, fully proved is to obtain current statistics of vital events by an intensive effort covering a representative sample of the population. The sample design typically includes a stratified sample of villages to represent the rural population, and a sample of blocks to represent the urban.

A key feature of the better designed of such projects is the use of two independent sets of records of the events. In Pakistan, where so far as I know the first such experiment was initiated, special registrars residing in the villages (the schoolteacher or some other educated person was usually selected) were utilized to maintain a continuous record of vital events. The second system of recording was by means of periodic surveys in which households in the sample areas were asked about the events that had occurred in the preceding six months. In Turkey the two sources of information are two independent surveys, one survey conducted monthly, and the other at intervals of every six months by more highly trained interviewers. The important feature of a dual system is that individual events recorded in one system are verified (or an omission detected) by an event-by-event match of the records. Such individual matches make it possible to detect omissions in both systems, in contrast to an aggregate comparison of the number of recorded births or deaths, which merely indicates which is more nearly complete. A scheme of this sort has been initiated in India on a gradually expanding basis, and also employed in Thailand and Liberia. The accuracy achieved by this approach must still be considered uncertain because of the difficulties of being sure that the two records do or do not pertain to the same event, and because of the administrative problems of maintaining independence of the two systems of recording, and of preventing deterioration in the quality of the records as the project continues for a long time.

A manual examining dual record systems in detail is to be published by the Population Council.[1]

METHODS OF ESTIMATING FERTILITY
FROM CENSUS AND SURVEY DATA

*Age-Specific Fertility Rates from Retrospective Data
of High Quality*

Suppose that every woman in a large representative sample in a closed population supplied accurate information about the date of her birth, the date of her marriage, the date of the birth of each of the children that she had ever borne and the date of its death if it had not survived until the present. On the usually justifiable assumption that the fertility experience of women who have died does not differ enough from those who have survived to cause serious inaccuracies in estimation, the data that we have just supposed collectable would provide the basis for determining the past age-specific fertility rates for each cohort of women in the population. The limit on the number of years for which estimates could be extended into the past would be the highest age (say 60 or 65) at which women can be expected to supply accurate data genuinely representative of the cohort. Rearrangement of the cohort rates would provide the means of constructing age-specific fertility schedules by period for each of the past 15 or 20 years.

On the basis of knowledge merely of the current age of each woman, it is a simple matter to determine how many person-years she contributed to each five-year age-interval above age 15, and how many person-years she contributed to what age interval in specific time intervals in the past. In other words, for each woman it is a simple matter to calculate her contribution to the denominator of past age-specific fertility rates, and equally simple to record the births that she supplied to enter the numerator of such rates.

Most demographers with experience in the use of census data from countries that lack vital statistics would be skeptical about the possibility of obtaining full and accurate data of the sort required. In many populations most respondents cannot supply a usable answer to a question about date of birth or chronologic age for themselves or for their children. Also, it is well known that older women tend to omit some of the children they have borne in response to a question about the number of live births they have experienced. However, a number of demographers, especially Donald Bogue, a major developer and advocate of this approach, argue that the construction of a detailed history of a woman's marriage and individual birth record makes it possible for a well-educated and highly trained enumerator to correct errors in age, age at marriage, timing of births and so forth, initially reported. The interviewer makes use of such clues as improbably long interbirth intervals, or inconsistency between the reported date of birth of a child and his present age, especially if he is seen by the interviewer. Carefully taken surveys in which a well-qualified interviewer devotes as much as half an hour to the completion of an individual fertility history can produce surprisingly high quality data, not only for the past two or three years, but even for the past decade or so, thus making it possible to establish recent trends as well as current levels of fertility. Donald and Elizabeth Bogue have prepared a manual on this technique,

including a questionnaire, instructions for coding and computer programs for tabulation and analysis.[2]

To my knowledge at least, experience with such detailed fertility
histories is not yet sufficient to judge under what circumstances they
provide information to support estimates of fertility levels and trends.

Fertility from Tabulations of Own Children by Age, and by Age of Mother[3]

If most young children live with their own mothers, data approx-
imating those obtained in the special fertility survey described above
could be extracted by merely making a special tabulation from a census
in which each household is identified and relationship to the head of
the household is recorded. The first step is to infer whether each child
is the own child of a woman in the household. The inference is based
on the relation to the head of the household—based on the fact that
the child is the child of the head of the household and the woman is
his wife, and the head of the household has been married only once.
In most countries a very high proportion of children under five are
"own children," and in many the proportion remains high to age ten
or beyond.

Korea is a country in which such data can be used to very good
effect. The proportion of own children is very high up to age ten, and
in the Korean census of 1966 age was determined by responses to a
question about the year of birth. In common with other people of a
culture related to the Chinese, each Korean, whether literate or not,
knows beyond a doubt the year in which he was born. Consequently
age distributions based on responses to such a question in Korea are
virtually free of error.

By making allowance for mortality and for the small proportion of
children who are not own children it is possible to estimate the numerator of age-specific fertility rates by single years of age during the past
ten years, and by allowing for mortality among women to estimate the
denominators of such age-specific fertility rates. In Korea, estimates of
child mortality can be derived from data internal to the census by an
adaptation of a method described below. Application of the procedure
to the 1966 census by Lee Jay Cho has produced a set of ten single-
year age-specific fertility schedules of impressive internal consistency
and plausibility. Before long the validity of these estimates can be
further checked by applying the procedures to tabulations from the

1970 census from which estimates of five or six overlapping years can be derived.

Unfortunately, full usefulness of data on own children tabulated by age of child and age of mother depends on a census free of substantial differential underenumeration by age and with accurate age reporting.

Fertility Based Wholly or Partly on Data on Parity
(or the Total Number of Children Ever Born)

Many censuses and surveys in the past have included a question on the number of live births each woman has experienced during her lifetime. This information in itself is a summary measure of the average fertility of each cohort—a partial measure for the cohorts still in the childbearing years, and a measure of total fertility of those that have passed the last age of childbearing. It is, of course, an indication of the average fertility only of the surviving members of the cohort, but in fact the effect of differential mortality between the relatively fertile and the relatively infertile is minor, even in populations with high death rates.

It is commonly observed in censuses in less-developed countries that older women give deficient responses to a question about parity, understating the number of children they have ever borne. It seems unlikely that in fact women have forgotten the births that have occurred to them, and more likely that the deficient answers are a result of a misunderstanding of the question. One source of misunderstanding is children who have grown up and left home may not be considered as "children." If three questions about parity were asked instead of one, this deficiency could be greatly reduced, if not eliminated. The three questions are:

1. How many children has this woman ever borne who are still living with her?

2. How many children has the woman ever borne who are now living elsewhere?

3. How many children has this woman ever borne who have died?

Asking the three questions makes it clear to the respondent that she is not to omit children who have died or moved away.

In a population subject to essentially constant fertility in the recent past, the rising curve of average parity with age at a given moment in time found in a census or survey approximates the history of rising

51

parity of each cohort. Average parity (or average number of children ever born) at a given age for a cohort is the sum of the age-specific fertility rates from the earliest age of childbearing to the given age. Therefore, if fertility in the population has been approximately constant, age-specific fertility can be estimated by taking differences between values of average parity at consecutive ages recorded in a census. For this method of calculation to yield accurate rates, the reporting of age and parity must be extraordinarily accurate, and fertility must have been extraordinarily stable. The same principle of determining age-specific fertility by taking differences in average parity at different ages can be applied to data tabulated by five-year age intervals. Curvilinearity in the typical schedule of fertility implies that simple differencing of average values of parity for consecutive five-year age intervals would yield poor estimates of age-specific fertility, and also estimates for unconventional age intervals (from 17.5 to 22.5 years, for example). Some form of curve fitting is called for.

The requirement that fertility schedules be stable over time is a severe limitation on the usefulness of tabulations of parity as a means of estimating the current or recent schedule of fertility. However, the fact that average parity at a given age is the cumulation of the age-specific fertility rates experienced up to that age by the cohort in question can sometimes be used to determine the completeness of birth registration and to provide a correction factor to adjust registered births for omissions. Age-specific fertility rates for each cohort calculated from births registered by age are cumulated to determine what average parity should be reported at each age in a census or survey, if registration were complete. The ratio of reported average parity to cumulated fertility can then be used as an indication of the degree of omission from the register and as an adjustment factor to apply to registered births. This procedure can be employed even when only one question on children ever borne has been asked and when, in consequence, the parity reported by older women tends toward understatement. It can be assumed that the parity reported by younger women (for example under age 25) will be virtually free of such omissions, and the estimation of incompleteness of registration and the adjustment for incompleteness can be based on the experience of these younger women.

William Brass has developed and made extensive use of the estimation of fertility from two sets of data collected in a single survey. One set of data is parity reported by age, and the other consists of responses to a question about whether each woman bore a child during the preceding year, tabulated by age. If the responses to the latter question were accurate, they would provide the basis for a straightforward calculation of an age-specific fertility schedule. However, there is a tendency in many populations for either under-reporting or over-reporting the number of births in the preceding year, and Brass suggests that the reason is typically a misperception of the duration of the reference period (one year), so that women on average report births perhaps for the preceding eight months, or perhaps for the preceding 15 months. If such a tendency in a given survey is approximately uniform for women of different ages, the age-specific fertility rates determined on the basis of responses to this question can be treated as systematic underestimates or overestimates of the true age-specific fertility rates; the degree of underestimation or overestimation being determined by comparing the cumulated age-specific fertility rates up to age 20 to 25 or 25 to 30 with the average parity reported by women at these ages. This procedure is valid only if the fertility schedules of young women have been stable over the preceding few years.[4]

The Brass method of estimating fertility just briefly described and the analogous procedure utilizing registered births do not work well when the ages reported in censuses or surveys are subject to massive and systematic misstatements. The Brass methods failed to give usable results when applied to a number of African censuses or surveys, but appear to be potentially useful in Latin America, where age misreporting is less severe.

Inferring Fertility from an Age Distribution

In a closed population the number of births during any time period in the recent past can be estimated by calculating the number of births that would have been required to provide the number of survivors at the appropriate age interval recorded in a census or survey. Thus, the number of persons at ages 15 to 20 divided by the appropriate survival factor provides an estimate of the number of births 15 to 20 years ago. The size of the population at the appropriate time in the past can be estimated from the average rate of increase of the population over the appropriate time interval, and by this kind of reverse projection the birth rate in the past can be approximated. In our hypothetical example it would also be possible to project in reverse the number of women now aged 30 to 60 to estimate how many there were at ages 15 to 45 fifteen years ago, and by a parallel calculation to determine how many there were 15 to 45 twenty years ago; and the average of these two values would be the approximate number of women 15 to 45 during the time interval 15 to 20 years in the past. Thus, a general fertility rate for the past could be estimated. For accuracy such forms of estimation require an accurately recorded age distribution and valid estimates of mortality during the recent past.

When fertility and mortality have been constant for the past 25 or 30 years the age distribution would closely approximate the stable age-distribution, and the estimates of fertility derived from different age-segments of the population should be the same. Thus approximation to a stable form makes it possible to construct much more robust estimates (valid, for example, even when ages are only approximately recorded) and also makes it possible to infer the true age structure of the population more exactly than by mechanical techniques of smoothing. The application of the techniques of analysis associated with stable populations when fertility and mortality have been constant, and of the so-called quasistable techniques when fertility has been constant and mortality declining would take too long to describe, even in the succinct form of summary being attempted here, and I shall say no more about it.[5]

ESTIMATING MORTALITY FROM DATA OBTAINED IN CENSUSES AND SURVEYS

The estimation of mortality in the absence of reasonably complete registration of deaths is greatly facilitated by a strong tendency for death rates at different ages in a given population to be intercorrelated. The intercorrelation arises from the fact that the mortality risks to which a population is subject depend upon the general living conditions and upon the state of development of public health facilities, environmental sanitation and curative medicine. In general, mortality rates at any age will be high when these conditions are adverse, and low when these conditions are favorable. Consequently, in a population in which the mortality rates of people in their fifties are among the highest in the world, one can confidently anticipate that infant mortality rates are also near the upper end of the world scale. If the interrelations among mortality rates at different ages were perfect, one would need only know the mortality rates at one age to obtain good estimates of the mortality rates at all other ages. In fact, the relations among mortality risks at different ages are not this narrow.

The tendency for age-specific death rates at different ages to be related has been expressed in a form useful for estimation by the preparation of "model life tables." The first set of these tables published and widely utilized was prepared by the Population Division of the United Nations. Subsequently model tables have been published by the Office of Population Research and by the Institut National d'Études Démographiques.[6] The later sets of model life tables embody variations in the age structure of mortality at the same overall level, but still make it possible to approximate a full schedule of mortality at all ages from fragmentary information.

In trying to estimate the mortality schedule that a given population is subject to in the absence of direct data, one is typically faced with uncertainty as to the detailed interrelations of mortality rates at different ages. Thus there are different model life tables with the same mortality rate at a particular age, or with a different overall index of mortality such as the average duration of life. In estimating mortality for a population without valid records, there are often inadequate clues for choosing which of the various possible model life tables is the appropriate one. The most important difference in the interrelations of mortality rates in different populations is different relationships between child mortality on the one hand and adult mortality on the other. Populations with the same expectation of life at age five may have widely different expectations of life at birth because of a tendency for unusually high infant and child mortality or for unusually low infant and child mortality to be associated with a given mortality above age five. This fact implies that it is useful to have separate direct evidence bearing on infant and child mortality on the one hand, and on mortality at ages above five on the other. Procedures have been devised for extracting such evidence from data collected in censuses or surveys.

ESTIMATION OF MORTALITY BY FORWARD PROJECTION[7]

Suppose two censuses are taken with an intercensal interval of ten years, and that each census records the number of persons in each five-year age-interval for each sex. The number of persons over ten in the later census constitute (in the absence of international migration) the survivors of those who were enumerated in the earlier census. If the mortality to which the population has been subject may be assumed to belong to a particular family of model life tables, one can determine the level of mortality within the family by projecting the population at each age from the earlier to the later date using alternative levels of mortality from the lowest to the highest that might conceivably characterize the population in question, and by selecting (using linear interpolation) that level of mortality that produces a projected population over age ten exactly matching the recorded population over age ten (such a projection can be made separately for each sex). The level of mortality estimated in this way may be biased by a tendency for relative undercount or overcount of the population under age ten, caused, for example, by a misstatement of age that transfers adolescents above ten to the five to nine age interval. Another estimate of mortality can be obtained by finding what level produces the recorded population over 15 in the later census by the projection of the population over five and the earlier. In fact, it is evident that a series of estimates of the level of mortality can be obtained by seeing what level matches the recorded population over ten, over 15, over 20 and so forth. The median of the first nine estimates of level obtained in this way provides a plausible summary estimate. If different assumptions are made about the age pattern of mortality to which the population is subject (i.e., if different families of model life tables are considered), it is found that an index of overall mortality above age five, such as the expectation of life at age five, is much the same. However, the mortality under age five ascribed to the population by assuming that its experience belongs to a family of model life tables is widely different depending upon which family is assumed. In short, forward projection provides what appears to be a valid estimate of adult mortality, but gives only an indirect and not very robust estimate of child mortality.

The technique of forward projection is applicable only if international migration is negligible or is of moderate volume and can be accurately estimated. Even in a closed population, if the completeness of coverage of the two censuses utilized is different, the difference in coverage is equivalent to an understatement or overstatement of the number of deaths to which the population had been subject.

ESTIMATION OF MORTALITY IN INFANCY AND CHILDHOOD FROM DATA ON NUMBER OF CHILDREN EVER BORNE AND NUMBER OF CHILDREN SURVIVING[8]

Consider a cohort of women whose ages fall in a particular span, say 20 to 25 at the time of the census. If we knew the age-specific fertility to which the cohort had been subject, we could readily determine the time-distribution of the births that the women had experienced in the past, and therefore could also determine the age distribution that the children they had borne would have in the absence of mortality. Finally, if for each age up to that of the oldest child we knew the cumulative probability of death to which the children had been subject, we could calculate the proportion of the children the women had ever borne who would be dead at the time of the census. In fact, the proportion dead is merely the cumulative product of the proportion of children at each age (in the absence of mortality) and the proportion dying from birth to that age. With the given time distribution of births in the past there would be a one-to-one correspondence between the proportion of the children ever borne who were dead at the time of the census and the level of mortality to which the children had been subject, assuming their mortality experience to conform to a family of model life tables. In fact, for a given age-specific fertility schedule, one can calculate the proportion dead among the children-ever-born to women in a particular age interval for each level of mortality in a family of model life tables. Conversely then, always assuming the age-specific fertility schedule to be known, knowledge of the proportion dead among the children-ever-borne to women in a particular age interval makes it possible to determine the level of mortality to which the children have been subject.

In general, the age-specific fertility schedule to which a cohort has been subject is not known. However, William Brass had the ingenuity and insight to propose that the general structure of the age-specific fertility schedule can be inferred from the way in which average parity rises with age. If average parity is tabulated by five-year age intervals, the most reliable basis for determining the level of mortality from the proportion dead among children-ever-born to women is the ratio of average parity at age 20 to 25 to average parity at 25 to 30.

This procedure determines the level of mortality for childhood ages only; specifically, data on children-ever-born and children surviving for women 20 to 25 provide an estimate of the proportion of children who die before their second birthday, data for women 25 to 30 an estimate of the proportion of children who die before their third birthday, and data for women 30 to 35 from the proportion of children who die before the fifth birthday. The mortality schedules to which the children have in fact been subject extends increasingly into the past as one uses data for older women. Data for women 20 to 25 provide an estimate of average mortality during perhaps the preceding four or five years. This method of estimating child mortality, which has properly enough come to be known as the "Brass Method," is surprisingly exact when applied to data from censuses in advanced countries that also have accurate vital statistics. When applied to data from countries (typically the less developed countries) that do not have vital statistics, it yields estimates of child mortality substantially higher than obtained from direct survey data asking respondents about births and infant deaths during the preceding year. Estimates by the Brass method are clearly the more plausible, partly because it is hard to imagine that these estimates, consistently higher, are an overstatement. If the Brass estimates tended systematically to overstate mortality, the implication would be that women tend to report the children who have died more fully than they did those who survive.

The combination of two consecutive censuses to which forward projection can be applied to determine mortality above age five with questions on children ever borne and number of children surviving to determine childhood mortality is very useful. Such a combination also provides the requisite estimates of mortality needed for reverse projection to estimate fertility from the recorded age distributions. However, forward projection requires two consecutive censuses or surveys of approximately the same quality of coverage, and a closed population.

An additional possibility of estimating adult mortality from a single survey or census is by including a question asking each person whether his own mother and his own father are still alive.

If we assume that the structure of age-specific fertility five years ago is known, we can determine the approximate age distribution of the mothers who gave birth during that year. The product of the proportion of mothers at each age and the proportion dying within five years of that age according to a model life table at a particular level of mortality would, when summed, equal the proportion of maternal orphans among five-year-old children in a population subject to that level of mortality. Thus approximate knowledge of the age-specific fertility schedule is sufficient to determine the proportion of children at each age who would be orphaned at each level of mortality in a family of model life tables. Conversely, the level of mortality can be estimated from the proportion of children at each age who are orphans. Such a procedure has not as yet been widely applied, and it is not yet known what sort of results it might produce.

CONCLUSION

The conscientious reader who has tried to follow the preceding highly condensed description of methods of estimation will realize that there is an extensive battery of procedures by which fertility and mortality can be estimated. Under some circumstances data can be obtained from surveys or censuses that provide excellent and detailed estimates of the recent course of fertility and mortality. Indeed, when it is possible to get full and accurate fertility histories from a large enough sample of women, or when very precise records of age are obtained in a census, age-specific fertility schedules may be constructed for each year in the preceding decade and detailed trends detected in fertility by age. Under such circumstances it is possible to obtain the requisite data for evaluating the impact of a family planning program or to detect the beginning of a modern decline in fertility.

Under less auspicious circumstances, a large demographic survey every five years, including a full battery of questions with regard to children ever borne, and incorporating intensive efforts to obtain more accurate reports of age can yield usable estimates of recent fertility and mortality, certainly of sufficient accuracy to reveal substantial trends.

There is no doubt that in the long run a modernizing country must have complete registration of vital events, and some reason for supposing that the development of a model registration scheme in a representative sample of areas, cross-checked by dual recording, may be a useful way of moving toward a complete registration system. But meanwhile, the incorporation of relevant questions and the preparation of the relevant tabulations from periodic censuses, supplemented by intensive, well designed demographic surveys can provide indispensable data on current levels and current trends in fertility and mortality.

REFERENCES

[1] Marks, E., Seltzer, W. and Krotki, K., POPULATION GROWTH ESTIMATION: A HANDBOOK OF VITAL STATISTICS MEASUREMENT, to be published.

[2] Bogue, D. J. and Bogue, E., A MODEL INTERVIEW FOR FERTILITY RESEARCH AND FAMILY PLANNING EVALUATION, Family Planning Manual No. 3; and TECHNIQUES OF PREGNANCY HISTORY ANALYSIS, Family Planning Manual No. 4, Chicago, Community and Family Study Center, University of Chicago, 1970.

[3] Grabill, W. H. and Cho, L. J., Methodology for the Measurement of Current Fertility from Population Data on Young Children, Demography, 2, 50–73, 1965; Cho, L. J., Recent Changes in Fertility Rates of the Korean Population, Demography, 3, 690–698, 1968.

[4] Brass, W., *et al.*, THE DEMOGRAPHY OF TROPICAL AFRICA, Princeton, Princeton University Press, 1968, Chapter 3; Coale, A. J. and Demeny, P., *Methods of Estimating Basic Demographic Measures from Incomplete Data,* United Nations Manuals on Methods of Estimating Population, Manual IV, New York, United Nations, 1967.

[5] Bougeois-Pichat, J., THE CONCEPT OF A STABLE POPULATION: APPLICATION TO THE STUDY OF COUNTRIES WITH INCOMPLETE DEMOGRAPHIC STATISTICS, New York, United Nations, 1968; Coale, A. J. and Demeny, P., REGIONAL MODEL LIFE TABLES AND STABLE POPULATIONS, Princeton, Princeton University Press, 1966; ————, *Methods of Estimating Basic Demographic Measures from Incomplete Data.*

[6] Ledermann, S., NOUVELLES TABLES-TYPES DE MORTALITÉ, Institut National d'Etudes Démographiques, Travaux et Documents, Paris, Presses Universitaires de France, 1969.

[7] Coale and Demeny, Methods of Estimating Basic Demographic Measures from Incomplete Data, *op. cit.*

[8] Brass, *et al.*, THE DEMOGRAPHY OF TROPICAL AFRICA.

60

THE LONGITUDINAL STUDY OF FAMILIES AS A METHOD OF RESEARCH

JEAN DOWNES[1]

THE peculiar quality of a study of a population of families over a period of years is that it affords the opportunity to obtain information which is dynamic. Thus it is a valuable method suitable for use in many fields.

The growth and decline of the family as a biologic unit can be described. In the field of population, growth is depicted by the number of children born to a given union in relation to the date of marriage and the age of husband or wife. However, the size of the family is dynamic for reasons other than growth. It is subject to depletion over a period of time by death of members, and also to dissolution by divorce or separation from the family of one spouse.

The growth of the family as a social unit can also be described if measurable characteristics of such growth can be developed. Also, the family can be described as an economic unit and since changes in this respect provide fairly objective data, it is possible to note them over a period of time.

In the field of anthropology, Kluckhohn has suggested that contemporaneous observation of persons over a period of time may yield even better and more reliable information concerning culture and personality than is obtained from retrospective life histories (1).

An adequate description of a population of families is more difficult than is a description of a population of persons. The family is complex and is constantly undergoing change. An extreme example of its complexity may be cited. The mobility among a sample of Negro tuberculous households in Upper Harlem, New York, was studied. This investigation included a description of the movement of persons into and out of the households. The households were composed of the immediate

[1] From the Milbank Memorial Fund. This paper was presented at the Annual Conference of The Milbank Memorial Fund, November 14-15, 1951.

family unit, that is, husband, wife and their children, other relatives, and lodgers. Members of the immediate family moved at the rate of 17 per 100 persons per year, other relatives at the rate of 46 per 100 per year, and lodgers in these families moved on the average twice a year; their rate was 196 per 100 persons per year (2).

The longitudinal study of a population composed of families was originated by Sydenstricker. He described the purpose of the study made over a period of twenty-eight months (December, 1921–March, 1924) in Hagerstown, Maryland, as follows: "This record, the first of its kind as far as we are aware, was regarded as desirable in order to give a picture of the sickness *incidence* in a general population over a sufficiently long period of time to distinguish it from sickness prevalence as ascertained at a given instant in time by the cross section method" (3).

In studies of diseases of long duration, Frost introduced a new concept of epidemiology—that studies of such diseases must be carried out over a long period of time (4). For example, it is characteristic of tuberculosis that the time intervening between exposure to infection and the development of clinical symptoms of disease is much longer than in the acute communicable diseases. Persons who have had familial exposure should be followed over a considerable period of years if incidence of disease among them is to be obtained.

It is apparent that the longitudinal observation of families was introduced in order to study disease. As a method of study, however, it has many other potentialities. It can be used in the study of health.

Reed has emphasized the possibility of studying "health" instead of disease provided that suitable gradations or measurements with respect to health can be determined. At the Fund's Annual Conference in 1947, Reed said "A definition of positive health . . . . is a problem calling for research in physiological fields; some of the work being done in geriatrics at the present time will be helpful in this direction, but a real solution will come when we have better concepts and better knowledge of the development of the human being as a functioning organism. Rather than a seeming separation of pediatrics from geriatrics, we need knowledge as to the growth and development of physiological processes as we proceed from infancy to old age. This knowledge may give us some of the yardsticks necessary for an evaluation of 'positive health' and may help us to lay down objectives in this field" (5).

The concept of long-term field studies of the child in his natural environment is fairly new. An important study of this sort is being conducted by Sir James Spence in Newcastle Upon Tyne. The objective of the investigation was to study 1,000 infants from the day of their birth through their 8th year of life. According to Sir James Spence, this study of 1,000 infants inevitably became a study of 1,000 families. The records which are being accumulated show how 1,000 families drawn from all social classes live, how they react to the problems of life, how they avail themselves of the health services, how the children are nurtured in body and mind, what their activities are, and the relation of these to others in the family. This approach to the study of child life holds great promise of valuable results (6).

To return to the use of longitudinal observation of a population as a method of study of disease, I wish to place emphasis upon the unique possibilities which this method affords in the study of chronic conditions. One of these possibilities is the observation of incidence of such diseases in the population. Illnesses of a chronic nature have a low incidence, that is, recognition of newly-diagnosed cases, in comparison with their prevalence at any given time. For example, in the population observed in the Eastern Health District of Baltimore, the annual incidence of new diagnoses of "major chronic" illness was 23.6 per 1,000 person years compared with a prevalence of 178 per 1,000 person years (7). It is apparent that if prevalence is not considered, incidence of new cases alone will not reveal the true state of the population with respect to the presence of chronic disease in it.

The incidence or attack rate of chronic disease, however, is of particular interest to many workers in the field of health and especially to the epidemiologist. Observation of cases from the time of first recognition or first diagnosis enables more accurate study of the course of the disease in time and of the effect of such illness upon the family than is possible from retrospective histories. Furthermore, cases prevalent in the population at a given time cannot be used for this type of study since they represent survivors only. Close observation of a population over a one-year period is not a sufficient time for gauging accurately disease and conditions which develop slowly and occur at a relatively low rate.

INCIDENCE OF CHRONIC CONDITIONS

Data from the morbidity study in the Eastern Health District of Baltimore over the five-year period June, 1938 to May, 1943 are presented to illustrate various ways of expressing incidence.

Briefly, the method of the study was as follows: Families living in thirty-four city blocks were visited at monthly intervals to obtain a record of illness of their members. In seventeen of the thirty-four city blocks the families were visited over a period of five years; in the other seventeen, visiting was continued for three years. Careful inquiry was made concerning members of the family who were in institutions for the mentally ill, for the feeble-minded, for the tuberculous, and for other chronic conditions requiring institutional care.

The instructions for the use of the family visitors contained a list of the more common chronic diseases about which special inquiry was to be made. This special information included data concerning onset of the first symptoms of the disease, their nature and date, the date first diagnosed, and whether the diagnosis was made by a private physician, at a clinic, or at a hospital. Illnesses that were reported as chronic were asked about on each subsequent visit to the family. Inquiry was made concerning the amount of discomfort or disability suffered from the condition since the last visit and the amount and nature of medical care received for it.

64

The causes of chronic illness as reported by the family informants were submitted to attending physicians for confirmation or correction. The cases which had clinic attendance and hospital admissions were also checked against the records of the clinic or hospital where the service was given. The only exception to this procedure was for cases hospitalized outside the City of Baltimore.

The chronic conditions included in this analysis are those classed as "major." They include: heart disease, hypertension or high blood pressure, arthritis, tuberculosis, diabetes, chronic nephritis, rheumatic fever, varicose veins, chronic gall-bladder disease, syphilis, malignant neoplasm, peptic ulcer, toxic goiter, epilepsy, mental deficiency, psychoses and psychoneuroses, and other important but relatively rare conditions, such as Parkinson's disease, cerebral palsy, and multiple sclerosis.

When a population of families is first surveyed for illness the chronic diseases usually form the major proportion of the total illnesses present at that time. In the study in the Eastern Health District of Baltimore, from 60 to 70 per cent of the total illnesses reported as present at the time of the first visit were those of a chronic nature. These were all conditions which had their onset prior to observation of the family and cannot be considered as incident within the period of observation. Information concerning the presence of persons in the population with chronic disease which had its onset before observation makes it possible to separate these persons from those at risk of development of such conditions during subsequent observation. Thus we have two classes of population—those who reported the presence of chronic illness and those who considered themselves as free from a chronic condition at that time. There are also two classes of families—those in which one or more persons were reported to have a chronic illness and those which reported their members as having no chronic condition.

This fact should be stressed. Incidence of chronic disease as expressed in this analysis is the incidence of a new or first diagnosis or report of such disease in the observed population at risk. Quite different results would no doubt be obtained if all persons in the sample population had frequent medical examinations to detect the presence of chronic conditions. However, it is believed that incidence which includes only persons sufficiently ill to obtain a diagnosis of the illness has value and in fact it is the only measure of incidence we have at the present time.

The annual incidence of new diagnoses of major chronic disease by type is of interest. Table 1 shows these data for the total sample population in the thirty-four city blocks. The population for this table is composed of 20,832 person years. Heart

Table 1. Annual incidence of new diagnoses of chronic disease.

Diagnosis Class	Rate Per 1,000 Population (20,832 Person Years)
Total	23.6
1. Arthritis	4.6
2. Heart Disease	5.1
3. Hypertensive Vascular Disease and Arteriosclerosis	3.3
4. Psychoneurosis and Nervousness	2.2
5. Rheumatic Fever	1.2
6. Varicose Veins	0.6
7. Gall-Bladder Disease	1.1
8. Diabetes	0.5
9. Mental Deficiency	0.0
10. Psychosis	0.4
11. Tuberculosis	0.9
12. Syphilis	0.3
13. Neoplasm (Malignant)	1.2
14. Peptic Ulcer	0.5
15. Goiter (Toxic)	0.1
16. Other Chronic Diseases	1.8

disease, type No. 2 on the table, occurred most frequently. If all circulatory disease be considered, types 2 and 3, the rate was 8 per 1,000 per year, a rate almost double that for arthritis. The incidence of new cases of psychoneurosis and nervousness was 2 per 1,000 per year. Rheumatic fever, type No. 5, and malignant neoplasm, type No. 13, had an annual frequency of slightly more than 1 per 1,000 person years.

One interesting point brought out by this table is the fact that, excepting arthritis and psychoneurosis and nervousness, the leading chronic illnesses which appear in incidence of new cases are also leading causes of death.

During the first year of the study there was in the seven-

66

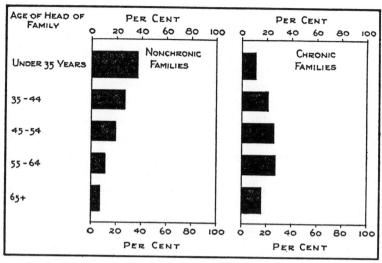

Fig. 1. Distribution of "nonchronic" and "chronic" families according to the age of the head of the family.

teen city blocks observed for five years a total of 951 families. These families must have been observed two months or longer to be included in the study. 305 or 32 per cent were classed as "chronic families," that is, families in which one or more members reported the presence of a major chronic condition. Figure 1 shows the distribution of the families according to the age of the head. The left-hand side of the chart shows the "nonchronic" families and the right-hand side those which reported one or more cases of chronic illness when first observed. There is a striking difference between the two groups. The majority of the "nonchronic" families was in the younger age groups; addition of the first and second bars shown in the chart indicates that in 63 per cent the head of the household was under 45 years of age. In the "chronic" families, only 31 per cent of the families were in these two age groups.

Incidence of Persons With First Diagnosis. One way of presenting incidence of chronic disease in the longitudinal study is to show the annual rate in each year at which persons from the nonchronic population are transferred to the population classed as having chronic disease. These data are based on the seventeen city blocks observed for five years and are shown in Table 2. Here the population (Column 3) is composed of persons who have not had a diagnosis of a major chronic disease or condition. The population is expressed in person years. The rates from the first to the fourth year range from 17 to 22 per 1,000 in the population at risk of such a diagnosis. There was a sharp decline in the fifth year. The incidence of persons newly diagnosed in that year was less than half the rate noted in any of the preceding years. Evidently by the fifth year some selection in the observed population had taken place.

Incidence of New Diagnoses of Chronic Disease. A second way of presenting incidence of chronic disease in the longitudinal study is to show the incidence of new diagnoses of chronic conditions. Here the population at risk includes not only those who were reported as free of any chronic condition but also those who at the beginning of observation were reported to be affected by the presence of chronic illness. The population in the latter group are at risk of developing

Table 2. Incidence of first diagnosis of chronic disease among persons at risk.

STUDY YEAR	ANNUAL RATE PER 1,000 PERSON YEARS	NUMBER OF PERSONS WITH FIRST DIAGNOSIS OF CHRONIC DISEASE	NUMBER OF PERSON YEARS AT RISK
First Study Year (6,1938-5,1939)	20.9	56	2,682
Second Study Year (6,1939-5,1940)	16.9	44	2,600
Third Study Year (6,1940-5,1941)	21.9	55	2,516
Fourth Study Year (6,1941-5,1942)	18.9	45	2,376
Fifth Study Year (6,1942-5,1943)	8.1	18	2,217

a different and unrelated chronic condition. For example, a person with hypertrophic arthritis has the risk of developing heart disease or cancer as do others of the same age and sex in the general population. When the rate of development of arthritis is considered, those known to have arthritis are excluded. This procedure applies to each type of chronic illness.

Table 3 shows the total incidence of new diagnoses (Column 2) and the incidence of new diagnoses among persons previously reported as free of any chronic illness (Column 1). These rates are presented in the same table to illustrate the fact that consideration of all new diagnoses does not distort the incidence rates. The rate of new diagnoses is composed chiefly of instances of persons with a first diagnosis of chronic illness. However, it should be emphasized that incidence among nonchronic persons only does not give a true picture of the incidence of disease when the total community is considered. Here the rates in the first four years range from 22 to 25 per 1,000 person years compared with rates of 17 to 22

Table 3. Incidence of first diagnosis of chronic disease among persons and of new diagnoses.

	RATE PER 1,000 PERSON YEARS		NUMBER	
STUDY YEAR	New Persons With Chronic Disease	New Diagnoses of Chronic Disease	New Persons With Chronic Disease	New Diagnoses of Chronic Disease
First Study Year (6,1938-5,1939)	20.9	22.6	56	68
Second Study Year (6,1939-5,1940)	16.9	21.6	44	63
Third Study Year (6,1940-5,1941)	21.9	25.0	55	71
Fourth Study Year (6,1941-5,1942)	18.9	22.4	45	60
Fifth Study Year (6,1942-5,1943)	8.1	12.3	18	31

per 1,000 person years among those with a first diagnosis of chronic disease.

The consideration of the incidence of new diagnoses, both in the nonchronic and chronic populations is important because, in community planning for adequate facilities for care and treatment of chronic disease, it is advantageous to know the size of the problem in terms of the number of diagnoses rather than solely on the basis of persons affected. For example, the patient with arthritis and hypertensive vascular disease may need treatment for both conditions.

Incidence of Family Units With a First Diagnosis of Chronic Disease. The longitudinal study of families affords a third expression of incidence, that is, the rate at which family units were affected by a first diagnosis of chronic illness in one of their family members. The population at risk is composed of family units reported to be free of chronic illness at the beginning of observation; that is, no member was reported as affected.

Table 4 shows for each study year the per cent of the nonchronic families which had a first diagnosis of chronic disease

Table 4. Per cent of nonchronic families with a first diagnosis of chronic disease in a family member.

Study Year	Number of Families Present in Each Year	Families With First Diagnosis of Chronic Disease in Each Year	Per Cent With First Diagnosis of Chronic Disease in Each Year
First Study Year (6,1938-5,1939)	646	31	4.8
Second Study Year (6,1939-5,1940)	611	23	3.8
Third Study Year (6,1940-5,1941)	562	28	5.0
Fourth Study Year (6,1941-5,1942)	534	24	4.5
Fifth Study Year (6,1942-5,1943)	450	11	2.4

in a family member. The per cent which became affected ranged from 4 to 5 during the first four years of the study.

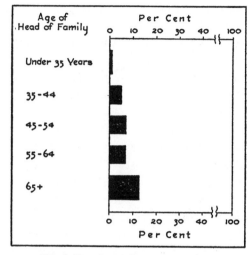

There was a sharp decline in the fifth year. Only 2 per cent of the 450 families observed in that year reported a first diagnosis of chronic illness in one of their family members.

Figure 2 shows for the first study year the per cent of the nonchronic families in each group—according to the age of the head of the family— where during that period a diagnosis of chronic disease was made for the first time. Young families (head under 35 years of age) yielded the smallest proportion, 1 per cent, of their total and those where the head of the family was 65 years of age or older, the highest proportion, 13 per cent. This is as expected. However, it is of interest that from 5 to 7 per cent of the families in the other three age groups had a member who brought them for the first time into the category "chronic disease families." Also, it is noteworthy that no age group was entirely exempt from the risk of producing families with a member who developed a chronic condition to the point that it was reported as illness.

Fig. 2. Per cent of "nonchronic" families, according to the age of the head of the household, where a diagnosis of chronic disease was made for the first time.

In the new chronic families, heart disease was the most frequent diagnosis; those next in order were arthritis, hypertensive vascular disease, rheumatic fever, cancer, and psychoneurosis.

It is certainly apparent that family units with no chronic disease among their members when first observed became

71

affected at a fairly regular rate, year by year. The longitudinal study offers an unusual opportunity to study these families which have been observed with equal care before and after the advent of a diagnosis of chronic disease in one of their members. For example, in 45 per cent of the new chronic families, the head of the household was the patient. It will be of interest to learn the effect of a major illness upon all of these family units and especially those where the patient had a great responsibility in that unit.

The incidence among persons with a first diagnosis of chronic illness, the incidence of total new diagnoses and of new families affected all showed annual rates which were consistent in their general level during the first four years of observation of the population in the seventeen city blocks. None of the variations in incidence noted in that period were statistically significant. The consistency of these rates over a period of time supports the belief that they express a reality, that is, the rate at which persons become so aware of illness that they obtained a diagnosis or reported it as an existing condition.

From the data presented, it is evident that by the fifth year of the study some sort of selection had taken place in the population being observed for illness. There was a significant decline in the incidence of new persons with a first diagnosis or report of chronic disease, and of new diagnoses in the fifth year compared with any previous year. There was also in that year a significant change from the other years with respect to the proportion of families previously classed as nonchronic which for the first time reported a member as having an important chronic illness.

One form of selection may arise from refusal of the family to cooperate in the study. Table 5 shows in each year the per cent of the total families which refused to cooperate. The data are shown for families classed as nonchronic and for those classed as chronic. In both groups of families, refusal to cooperate occurred most frequently in the first study year.

About 5 per cent in each group were lost to the study in that year. The proportion lost to the study declined sharply in the second and third years compared with the first year. In the fourth and fifth years the proportion who wished to be dropped from the study increased and reached the level of the first year. It is important to note that in each year a smaller proportion of the families with chronic disease refused to cooperate than was true of families with no person in them who reported a major chronic condition. The difference between the two groups of families with respect to the proportion which refused cooperation is statistically significant in the third year, in the fourth year, but not in the fifth year.

Table 5. Per cent of families present in each study year which refused to cooperate in the study.

Study Year	Nonchronic Families	Chronic Families
First Study Year (6,1938-5,1939)	5.4	4.9
Second Study Year (6,1939-5,1940)	3.3	1.2
Third Study Year (6,1940-5,1941)	1.8	0.3
Fourth Study Year (6,1941-5,1942)	4.5	1.4
Fifth Study Year (6,1942-5,1943)	5.3	3.6

Some of the other possibilities for the study of chronic illness which the longitudinal observation of a population affords may be mentioned briefly. It is of interest to learn how chronic illness manifests itself over a period of time. Is the risk of disability from chronic disease greatest at the time of first diagnosis and does that risk diminish with time? Persons found to be diabetic and those who have survived their first attack of coronary disease may be cited as those where the risk of disability may decrease with time. What proportion of the total adjust and learn how to live with their chronic conditions? Or is the disease of such a rapidly progressive nature that the risk of disability increases with time? Some types of cancer may illustrate diseases in this

73

category. Also, disabling episodes of chronic illness can be related to the total observed population in order to express the general risk of such illness. It may be that some of these questions cannot be answered in a period so short as five years. However, it will be of interest to explore the possibilities for doing so.

FAMILY PATTERNS OF CHRONIC DISEASE

The study of chronic illness in the Eastern Health District of Baltimore has also made it possible to investigate family patterns of disease. An index case was designated for each family with "major chronic" disease, that is, the index case was the person with a chronic condition which determined the classification of the family. In families where, at the time of first observation, there was more than one living case of "major chronic" disease, the case with the earliest onset was selected as the index person. It was then possible to learn whether other members of the family tended to have the same type of chronic illness as the index case.

During the period of study of the families in the thirty-four city blocks in the Eastern Health District, a total of 828 families reported one or more cases of chronic illness among their members. The shortest possible period of observation of these families was two months and the longest possible period was five years. Excluding the index case, these families contained 2,842 people. The presence of some major chronic condition was reported for 15 per cent of these family members.

To illustrate the family pattern of chronic illness, all families in which there was a person designated as ill because of psychoneurosis or nervousness are compared with the total universe of chronic-disease families. There were 90 such families. The index case in each of these families was an adult 20 years of age or older who was diagnosed as psychoneurotic or who reported chronic nervousness.

It should be explained that patients do not report themselves as having a psychoneurosis. This term is not a part of

74

their vocabulary. They report their illness in terms of complaints or symptoms. The diagnosis "psychoneurosis" comes from the attending physician. Sixty-six of the 90 index cases, or 73 per cent, had such a diagnosis. The remaining 24 patients complained of chronic nervousness but were not seen by a physician because of their complaint.

The complaints of the 66 diagnosed by a physician were as follows:

Nervous with:

Indigestion	Giddiness and dizzy spells
Cardiac symptoms	Stuttering
Menopause	Loss of voice
Low blood pressure	Nervous throat
High blood pressure	Lump in throat
Headache	Melancholy
Shortness of breath and choking	Worry
Weakness and run down	Itching all over

The complaints of the 24 not seen by a physician were similar to those who received a diagnosis.

In a study of the complaint of nervousness and the psychoneuroses in the population of the Eastern Health District, made by Lemkau and his associates, it was concluded that "the lay term nervous is used to cover a multitude of psychiatric conditions, but when treated as a residual group, after the removal of known psychotics and mental defectives, this group corresponds in sex and race distribution patterns to the group of adult cases diagnosed psychoneurosis or as having neurotic traits" (8). This was considered as sufficient reason for including nervous cases in a group called the "adult neurotic group." Therefore, in this analysis the 24 index cases with chronic nervousness were included with the 66 who had the diagnosis psychoneurosis.

This table (Table 6) compares the per cent of persons with specific diagnoses in the 90 families, index case psychoneurosis or chronic nervousness, and those in the total 828 families, the

Diagnosis Class	Index Case Psycho-neurosis (90 Families)	Index Case Major Chronic Condition (828 Families)	Ratio Column 1 Column 2
Total	26.98	14.80	1.82
1. Mental Disorder or Mental Deficiency	3.81	0.32	11.91
2. Mental Retardation	0.32	0.14	2.29
3. Psychoneurosis or "Nervousness"	1.90	1.48	1.28
4. Rheumatic Fever	2.54	1.09	2.33
5. Heart Disaese	4.76	2.64	1.80
6. Hypertensive Vascular Disease and Arteriosclerosis	3.81	1.72	2.22
7. Diabetes	0.63	0.35	1.80
8. Arthritis	2.86	2.67	1.07
9. All Other Chronic Diseases	6.35	4.39	1.45

Table 6. Per cent of persons with a major chronic condition in two groups of families (index cases excluded).

universe from which the 90 families were drawn. Column 3 indicates the ratio of the per cent of persons affected in the families, index case psychoneurosis, to those affected in the total 828 families. All index cases have been excluded from both groups. It certainly is apparent that persons with chronic illness are more highly concentrated in these 90 families than in the total universe of families from which they were drawn. The differences in the per cent affected in these families and in the total 828 families are highly significant.

An examination of the 90 families with regard to socio-economic factors revealed no important difference between them and the 828 families from which they were drawn. They were similar with respect to size, to moving, crowding, income, home ownership, and education of persons 20 years of age and older.

From the etiological point of view, it may be that a concentration of chronic conditions among members of families tends to produce psychoneuroses among some of those not otherwise affected. In other words, the stress upon the family brought about by illness may be so great that responsible members of the family may be affected to the degree that they seek an escape in illness. However, genetic and constitutional factors in these families have not been studied and it may be profitable in future investigations to consider such factors.

One of the most important potentialities of the study of families over a period of time is the determination of a better understanding of family attitudes towards health and towards illness. Late diagnosis of chronic illness is a problem difficult to cope with and we have been prone to consider that it is in great part due to an economic barrier between the patient and the procurement of medical care. However, there are other barriers. The psychological barrier between the knowledge of the presence of symptoms and the procurement of a diagnosis is real, very real. A person may feel under par as to his health but he may wish to avoid as long as possible the knowledge as to why he is not well.

Experiments which are now under way, The Health Insurance Plan of Greater New York and The Family Health Maintenance Plan, will no doubt increase our understanding of family attitudes towards health and sickness. In these experiments the economic barrier to procurement of medical care has been removed and those in charge are doing their utmost to remove the psychological barrier through a campaign of education for better health through use of medical service. Their results will need to be carefully measured. They will be eagerly awaited.

References

1. Kluckhohn, Clyde: Needed Refinements in the Biological Approach: Culture and Personality Proceedings of an Interdisciplinary Conference, held under the auspices of the Viking Fund, November 7–8, 1947. Published by the Viking Fund, 1949, pp. 75–89.

2. Preas, Sally and Downes, Jean: A Study of Mobility Among Tuberculous Households in Upper Harlem. The Milbank Memorial Fund *Quarterly,* January, 1944, xxii, No. 1.

3. Sydenstricker, Edgar: A Study of Illness in a General Population Group. Hagerstown Morbidity Studies, No. 1. The Method of Study and General Results. Public Health *Reports,* September 24, 1926, pp. 2069–2088.

4. Frost, W. H.: Risk of Persons in Familial Contact with Pulmonary Tuberculosis. *American Journal of Public Health,* May, 1933, 23, No. 5.

5. Reed, Lowell J.: Principles Applying to the Collection of Information on Health as Related to Socio-Environmental Factors: BACKGROUNDS OF SOCIAL MEDICINE. Milbank Memorial Fund, 1949.

6. Spence, Sir James Calvert: Family Studies in Preventive Pediatrics. *New England Journal of Medicine,* August 10, 1950, 243, pp. 205–210.

7. Downes, Jean: Cause of Illness Among Males and Females. Milbank Memorial Fund *Quarterly,* October, 1950, xxvii, No. 4.

8. Lemkau, Paul; Tietze, Christopher; and Cooper, Marcia: Complaint of Nervousness and the Psychoneuroses. *American Journal of Orthopsychiatry,* April, 1942, xii, No. 2.

THE RELIABILITY OF LONGITUDINAL SURVEYS

J. W. B. Douglas[1] AND J. M. Blomfield[2]

IN a recent paper on research techniques Cochran[3] makes the following comment on longitudinal surveys: "My guess would be that we now know how to observe groups for as long as three years, and perhaps for as long as five years: beyond that, there are too few successfully completed studies to be able to say that the technique has been mastered." For the past ten years a national sample of children has been kept under observation in Great Britain. Losses have been small and the reliability of the information obtained appears to be high. It therefore seemed of interest to give an account of this sample study; the methods used and the problems encountered are described below.

NATURE OF THE INQUIRY

The original stimulus for the study came from the Royal Commission on Population who wished to have information on the use made of the maternity services and on the costs of child-bearing. A Joint Committee of the Population Investigation Committee and the Royal College of Obstetricians and Gynaecologists was set up in 1945 to collect information about the circumstances and costs of all confinements occurring in Great Britain during the first week of March, 1946. The results of this first inquiry were published in 1948.

At the end of the maternity inquiry we found ourselves in possession of a sample that was fully representative of children from all social groups and from all parts of the country. It was unlikely that the chance of obtaining another such sample would recur in the near future and the Committee decided to use this unique opportunity to observe the health, growth and

[1] Senior Lecturer in Public Health and Social Medicine, University of Edinburgh.
[2] Research Assistant, Population Investigation Committee.
[3] Cochran, William G.: Research Techniques in the Study of Human Beings. The Milbank Memorial Fund *Quarterly* April, 1955, XXXIII, No. 2, pp. 121–136.

development of the group of children. The enthusiastic support given by the Society of Medical Officers of Health and the local authorities made it possible to start a longitudinal inquiry which has continued until the present day, in cooperation with the Institute of Child Health (University of London), and supported by grants from the Nuffield Foundation; the Hospital for Sick Children, Great Ormond Street; the Regional Hospital Boards of Great Britain; and the Ford Foundation.

Limitations of money and staff made it necessary to reduce the size of the original sample. This was done by taking only one-in-four of the children of manual workers and of the self-employed, who comprised 72 per cent of the original maternity survey sample. The full numbers of children in the other occupational groups were retained. The result was that the number of survey children was reduced from 12,930 to 5,386. The numbers in the reduced sample were sufficient for most purposes of statistical analysis, and when required the original sample structure could be regained by suitable "weighting." It should also be mentioned that all twins and all illegitimate children were excluded from the longitudinal inquiry (*see* page 232).

During the first ten years of the inquiry six main sources of information have been used:

Home Visits. The homes have been visited nine times by health visitors or school nurses. The records of these visits describe the changing home background of the families, their increase in size, and their movement upwards or downwards in the social scale. They also give a running record of accidents, major episodes of illness and major disturbances of behaviour. These events can be set against the basic information collected early in the survey on such characteristics as the parents' ages, duration of marriage, and education.

Clinical Examinations. The school doctors have examined the survey children twice (at six and seven years-of-age), using a schedule which asked for both a clinical history and an examination paying particular attention to defects of the special senses and locomotor system and to the condition of the nose and pharynx. In addition, the doctors weighed and measured the children.

80

School Absence Records. A complete record of school absences has been kept by the teachers on special record cards which are changed each year. All prolonged absences (of one week or more) were checked with the mothers in the course of the subsequent home visits.

School Teachers' Questionnaire. At the end of the first year at school, teachers were asked to give information on the type of school and class and on the interest shown by parents in their child's education.

Tests of Mental Ability and School Achievement. Four tests were designed for this inquiry by the National Foundation for Educational Research in England and Wales and given to the children when they were eight years old. There were two tests of reading, one of vocabulary and one picture intelligence test.

Hospital Records. All reported hospital admissions of survey children were checked with the hospitals concerned. The hospital superintendents were asked to state dates of admission and discharge, to give the initial and final diagnoses and to describe the ward layouts and visiting rules.

It will be seen that this inquiry has covered a wide field. In the early years interest was centered on the health and growth of children in relation to their home environment. In later years problems of mental ability and school achievement have become relatively more important.

RETURN OF SURVEY FORMS

It was intended that in each survey all the children should be seen at approximately the same date, but owing to the substantial movement of families and the difficulty in tracing some of them, this could not always be done. A typical pattern of the distribution of interviews is shown in Figure 1 which refers to the visit made in 1950 when the children were $4\frac{1}{4}$ years old.

The major difficulty in this, as in all other visits, was to trace families that had moved to a new authority. Many were found only after several months; for example, in 1950, sixty-nine children were traced only after the cards were punched

81

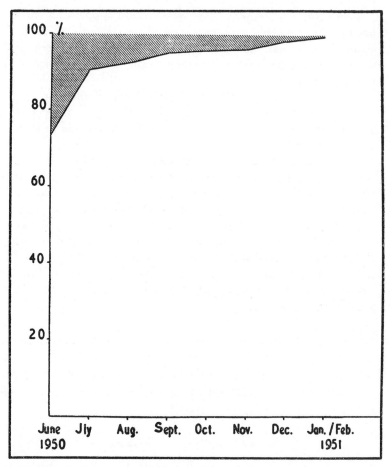

Fig. 1. Rate of return of completed forms in the 1950 survey.

and that part of the survey closed. The missing information for these sixty-nine children was obtained at the next home visit.

The standard of form filling was high, but occasional questions were missed while some of the answers given were inconsistent with information already received. All problems of this type were referred back to the health authorities, who were most helpful. As an example of the help given, the 1950 survey may again be cited. 3,451 answers were queried and all but 207 of them answered satisfactorily.

We shall now consider a number of questions relevant not only to longitudinal investigations, namely:

1. How far, if at all, has the sample been distorted by withdrawals and other losses?

2. What additional distortion would have been suffered if we had been unable to follow our families across local administrative boundaries?

3. What is the reliability of the information given by mothers about their children's health?

1. The Extent and Nature of the Survey Losses

Two types of loss are involved here: that incurred in obtaining the original maternity survey sample in 1946, and that incurred in following up the children since then.

Maternity Survey Losses. At the time of the maternity survey there was no intention of following the children born. Consequently, the losses were greater than would have occurred if, from the start, we had used all the means of tracing children that were applied at later stages of the inquiry.

The original aim was to investigate all births that occurred during the first week of March, 1946, in all parts of England, Wales, and Scotland. We were fortunate in securing the cooperation of 424 out of a total of 458 local authorities responsible for maternity and child welfare at that time. In the thirty-four authorities unable to take part in the survey, 1,300 children were born during the survey week. It is unlikely that any serious bias was introduced by their loss since the thirty-four authorities were evenly distributed over Great Britain and the combined infant mortality rate for 1946 in those authorities was similar to that for the rest of the country.

In addition, 1,443 children were lost in 1946 because their mothers had either refused to give information or had moved since their confinements and could not be traced. The children concerned formed 9.5 per cent of all those born during the survey week in the 424 participating authorities. We were able to obtain details of 425 of the children from the antenatal records, and since 1946 we have traced a further 417, so that we now have information about 58 per cent of the 1,443 missing children.

Losses of illegitimate children were high and, indeed, 34 per cent of all illegitimate births occurring during the survey week were untraced. Because of this, and of the difficulties of keeping in touch with unmarried mothers, no attempt was made to include illegitimate children in the follow-up inquiry.

The losses of legitimate children were unevenly distributed over the occupational groups,[4] being highest among the most prosperous families. In order to judge whether these unequal losses have significantly distorted the structure of the sample we have compared in Table 1 the number of children falling into each occupational group of the maternity survey sample with the number that would have been expected if the losses had been randomly distributed over all occupational groups. The third row of the table shows how far the number of children in each group exceeds or falls below expectation. The differences between the numbers found and the numbers expected in each occupational group are small and the 1946 losses produced no serious bias in the sample.

The stillbirth and neonatal death rates in the survey popu-

Table 1. Number of children enrolled and numbers of children expected in each occupational group in 1946.

	OCCUPATIONAL GROUPS					ALL GROUPS
	Professional and Salaried	Black-Coated	Manual Workers	Agricultural Workers	Own Account and Farmer	
Number Enrolled	1,129	1,443	8,998	571	789	12,930
Number Expected	1,164	1,469	8,931	558	808	12,930
Difference	−35	−26	+67	+13	−19	

$\chi^2 = 2.72$ $n = 5$ $0.8 > P > 0.7$.

[4] For a description of the contents of the occupational groups see MATERNITY IN GREAT BRITAIN, (Oxford University Press, 1948).

84

lation were closely similar to those for Great Britain during 1946. The survey stillbirth rate was 26 per 1,000 total births as compared with the national figure of 28. The survey neonatal death rate was 28 per 1,000 live births as compared with the national figure of 25. Here is further support for the lack of bias in the sample.

Losses from the Longitudinal Survey. We have already mentioned that the size of the longitudinal survey sample was reduced by excluding illegitimate children and twins and by taking a random one-in-four sample of children in two occupational groups—the "manual workers" and the "own account and farmers." The results are shown in Table 2.

It will be seen that there are eleven fewer children in the follow-up survey sample than were expected, a discrepancy that is explained by the exclusion of illegitimate children who had been wrongly coded as legitimate in 1946. At the same time a number of errors in occupational coding were corrected with a consequent small change in the numbers in the five groups.

During the first ten years of the inquiry, twelve contacts were made with the children at home, school or clinic, and on each occasion some of the children were lost. The losses were of two broad types which will be described separately. First, there were the *unavoidable* losses of children who had died or left the country with their parents; secondly, there were the

Table 2. Numbers of children in each occupational group of the follow-up survey sample compared with the numbers expected from the 1946 maternity survey sample after differential sampling.

	OCCUPATIONAL GROUPS					ALL GROUPS
	Professional and Salaried	Black-Coated	Manual Workers	Agricultural Workers	Own Account and Farmer	
Numbers in 1948 Sample	1,075	1,387	2,157	557	210	5,386
Numbers Expected	1,086	1,399	2,168	554	190	5,397

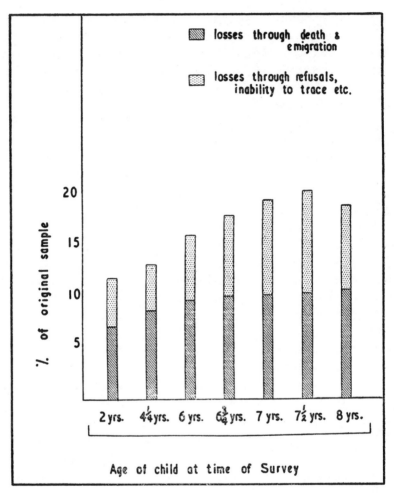

Fig. 2. Losses from the survey sample.

avoidable losses for such reasons as the refusal of a parent to give information or our own failure to trace a child. The first represents a natural decrease in the population, which is not a source of bias, the second needs to be considered more carefully. The proportion of children lost for these two reasons for seven home visits is shown in Figure 2.[5]

[5] Losses from medical examinations, school reports and mental tests were closely similar and need not be shown here.

Unavoidable losses rose steadily from 7.1 per cent at two years-of-age to 10.7 per cent at 8½. In the early years both death and emigration were heavy sources of loss; by 1950, 220 children had died and 240 had emigrated with their families. The loss through emigration was particularly heavy during this early period because of the aftermath of the war. Out of the 240 families lost in this way during the first four years of the survey, 108 were dominion, colonial, or foreign nationals returning to their own countries.

It is likely that many of the families going to the Colonies and all the families going abroad with the Armed Forces will in time return to this country, but no attempt will be made to enrol them again in this survey when they do so. It would be difficult to trace them and, in view of the inevitable gaps in their histories and of the exceptional living conditions abroad, the additional information obtained would hardly justify the expense and effort involved.

Whereas the *unavoidable* losses increased with each successive contact, the *avoidable* losses reached a peak of 10.1 per cent at 7½ years and then declined to 8.3 per cent. This decline reflects the success of efforts to persuade parents who had withdrawn their children to allow them to rejoin. The final figure of 8.3 per cent exaggerates our final loss, since some of the children will be found and included in later surveys when earlier gaps will be filled in. It is probably more realistic to take as completely lost only those children missing in both 1953 and 1954, they amount to 345 or 6.4 per cent of those originally enrolled.

Before discussing any possible distortion of the sample introduced by these losses, it may be of interest to mention that measures have been taken at intervals during the course of the survey to keep alive the interest of those taking part—both the health visitors and the mothers. Two booklets giving a simple account of the more important findings were produced for the health visitors and seem to have been greatly appreciated. In addition, the Committee sent a letter of appreciation

| | PROFES-SIONAL AND SALARIED | BLACK-COATED | MANUAL | | | OWN ACCOUNT AND FARMER | ALL GROUPS |
			Skilled	Semiskilled and Unskilled	Agricultural		
Actual Numbers Enrolled	793	1,136	1,255	593	486	189	4,452
Expected Numbers	823	1,143	1,241	579	476	190	4,452
Difference	−30	−7	+14	+14	+10	−1	nil

Table 3. Number of children in each occupational group enrolled in 1954 compared with the numbers expected assuming no bias.

to each mother after the first eight years and offered a free copy of the health visitors' booklet to those who were interested enough to apply for it. Shortage of funds alone prevented the Committee from doing more in this line, which may contribute materially to the success of a long-term survey.

In October, 1954, after excluding the 345 children (missing in 1953 and 1954) and the children who had died or who had left the country, there were 4,452 still enrolled in the survey. Table 3 shows how their actual distribution by occupation of father differs from that which would be expected on the assumption that the avoidable losses were not biased in respect of this factor.

It will be seen that there is a small deficit in the more prosperous groups and a small excess in the poorer groups. But as tested by X^2 the distribution of observed and expected numbers in these six groups is not significantly different.

Similar calculations are shown in Table 4 after regrouping the children by position in family. Here again, there is no significant difference between the observed and expected distribution.

We may conclude that up until October, 1954, the sample had not become appreciably biased in respect of either occupational groups of the parents or ordinal position of the child in the family. Similar conclusions are reached when other charac-

	First Born	Second or Third Born	Later Born	Total
Actual Numbers Enrolled	1,725	2,065	662	4,452
Expected Numbers	1,739	2,057	656	4,452
Difference	−14	+8	+6	nil

Table 4. Number of children of different ordinal position in family enrolled in 1954 as compared with the number expected assuming no bias.

teristics, such as age of mother or degree of crowding, are examined.

It has been suggested that in long-term studies the very fact of being under observation may introduce a bias. For example, in the present study the more intensive and more frequent medical examinations may have revealed defects that would otherwise have been missed. In order to estimate the extent of this bias we shall examine some 2,000 children who, though born during the survey week, were excluded from the longitudinal study when a one-in-four sample of manual workers' children was taken. By comparing their school health records and records of clinic attendances with those of a matched group of the survey children, we shall be able to see in what ways, if any, the latter have been influenced by being enrolled in the survey.

2. Internal Migration as a Possible Source of Bias

Some of the difficulties in following up our children were caused by a high incidence of movement from one local authority to another. And it is of interest to see how far this inquiry would have been biased if we had been unable to extend the survey across administrative boundaries. Most longitudinal surveys have been limited to a single city and all those moving out have been lost, so that this question has considerable practical importance. The following comments refer to the *internal* movements of the population during the first four years of the present survey: it is not feasible at the moment to give an account of movements in more recent years.

During the first four years nearly half of our survey families had moved from where they were living in March, 1946. Some had moved within local boundaries and others had overstepped them. This is to some extent an artificial distinction since when a town is growing rapidly it will expand beyond its administrative area, but the characteristics of the local and non-local migrants are different and they have accordingly been kept separate in the following discussion.

The period 1946–1950 was in some ways abnormal. Movements of population in part represented a return of those who had migrated during the war. On the other hand, throughout the period there was a shortage of houses, limiting freedom of movement especially in the lower income groups. Local authority housing was mainly available for those who were local inhabitants and families moving across administrative boundaries largely moved to privately owned dwellings. The general effect was to discourage the movement of the poorer families or to direct it to areas in which there were relatives to house them.

Only 55 per cent of our families had remained in the same dwelling between 1946 and 1950 whereas 14 per cent had crossed local administrative boundaries and 31 per cent had moved to another address within the same administrative area.

Table 5. Occupational group of families that did not move and of families making local and nonlocal moves in 1946–1950.

| | | | MOVED | |
OCCUPATIONAL GROUP	TOTAL	NO CHANGE OF ADDRESS PER CENT	Within Local Boundaries Per Cent	Across Local Boundaries Per Cent
Professional and Salaried	865	16.2	14.5	33.3
Black-Coated	1,193	24.3	23.6	31.1
Skilled Manual	1,303	30.4	30.3	18.2
Semiskilled Manual	347	8.8	7.8	3.5
Unskilled Manual	252	5.9	6.8	1.9
Agricultural	497	9.1	14.0	8.7
Own Account and Farmer	211	5.3	3.0	3.3
TOTAL	4,668[a]	100.0	100.0	100.0

[a] This number refers to complete interviews in 1950; that is to say, it excludes all losses through death, emigration, or other causes.

We cannot show the full extent of movement during these years, for change of address was noted only at the time of each survey and some families may have moved more than once in between. Accordingly, in the following discussion we have simply grouped the families into those that *did not move,* those *moving within local boundaries,* and those *crossing local boundaries.* Attention will be drawn to some of the characteristics of each of these groups.

Table 5 gives the social composition of these three groups.

Those that made local moves tended to come from the poorer social groups, especially the unskilled and the agricultural workers. The differences, as compared with families which did not move, are significant, though small.[6] In contrast, the families that moved across local boundaries showed a great excess in the non-manual groups, particularly in the professional and salaried group, whereas those in the manual worker groups, particularly the semiskilled and unskilled, were underrepresented.[7] If all the families that moved across administrative boundaries had been lost and if only the stable families and those making local moves had been retained, the sample would have been heavily biased by the poorer social groups. Instead of an expected total of 710 families of professional and salaried workers remaining in the inquiry there would have been 591, while the number of manual worker families would have been correspondingly increased.

We have next related migration to occupational movement, confining our attention to the two groups of black-coated and skilled manual workers where both upward and downward movements can be clearly distinguished. The results of this analysis are shown in Table 6.

The following statistically significant differences are found: (a) The families that did not move show less occupational mobility than the migrants; (b) families of black-coated workers that make local moves tend to move downwards in the

[6] ($\chi^2 = 32.98$ n = 6 P < 0.001).
[7] Compared with the families that did not move ($\chi^2 = 186$ n = 6 P < 0.001).

occupational scale; (c) families of both occupational groups that have crossed local boundaries show a greater upward mobility and, among the black-coated group, a greater tendency to go into business on their own account. These differences cannot be explained by the younger age structure of the migrant families.

It appears, then, that the families making local moves are on the average poorer and of deteriorating social position, whereas those making non-local moves are more prosperous and are mounting the social ladder.

The migrant families differ from the stable families in other respects. The parents are younger and have a relatively low fertility before removal and a relatively high fertility afterwards. In these respects there is little to distinguish the local from the non-local migrants.

The answer to our question of whether the sample would have been biased if we had been unable to follow our families across local boundaries is thus unequivocal. In these circumstances the survey population would have been progressively denuded of the younger and more rapidly growing families, of those in the upper social groups, and of those who were mount-

Table 6. Occupational mobility (1946–1950) of stable families and of families making local and non-local moves.

	Un-changed Occupa-tional Group Per Cent	Up-ward Mo-bil-ity Per Cent	Down-ward Mo-bil-ity Per Cent	Move to Self-Em-ploy-ment Per Cent	Total Per Cent	No. in Group
Black-Coated Workers						
(No Change of Address)	69.6	13.2	14.0	3.2	100.0	569
(Local Moves)	62.7	12.2	20.5	4.6	100.0	327
(Non-Local Moves)	54.5	23.6	13.8	8.1	100.0	246
Skilled Manual Workers						
(No Change of Address)	78.3	6.3	12.4	3.1	100.1	719
(Local Moves)	74.5	9.1	13.7	2.8	100.1	431
(Non-Local Moves)	63.8	15.8	13.8	6.6	100.0	152

ing the social ladder or setting up in their own businesses. During the survey years the extent of these losses would have been sufficient to make the sample decreasingly representative either of the whole country or of individual social groups, and its value would have been greatly impaired. Accordingly, it is of practical interest to see how far losses of this type can be reduced by extending the area of a survey over several adjacent authorities instead of limiting it to a single one. In Table 7 we consider the case in which the authorities are grouped into regional aggregates.

The table shows the percentage of families moving out of each region during the survey years and the average loss for all regions of 4.4 per cent should be compared with the average loss through movement across local boundaries which is 13.6 per cent. Thus, by choosing regional aggregates rather than individual authorities as the unit of study two-thirds of the losses through migration can be avoided.

The number of individual authorities in each region is large and the question arises whether smaller aggregates of authority could profitably be taken. It was originally expected that the main saving would be achieved when urban authorities were related to their surrounding county areas, but this is not

Table 7. Families moving out of each regional aggregate in 1946–1950.

REGIONAL AGGREGATE	NUMBER OF[1] COOPERATING AUTHORITIES	NUMBER OF CHILDREN IN 1946 WHO WERE STILL SURVIVING AND ENROLLED IN THE SURVEY IN 1950	PER CENT LEAVING[2] REGION 1946–1948
Greater London and South East	27	1,452	3.0
North	51	1,182	4.3
Midlands	27	807	5.4
East	15	247	5.9
South West	8	155	8.2
Wales	16	253	7.3
Scotland	55	572	3.5
ALL PARTS	199	4,668	4.4

[1] Counties, country boroughs and large boroughs only—the smaller authorities that were Maternity and Child Welfare authorities in 1946 are included with the counties.
[2] Adjusted for sampling fraction.

so as the following figures for Northumberland and Durham and their seven contained county boroughs show. The movement from these authorities considered individually was 17.6 per cent whereas the movement from the whole area was 14.6 per cent; that is to say, by including all the nine authorities in a single inquiry, we should have saved only one-fifth of the losses. This is a far smaller saving than would have been achieved if the whole Northern region had been taken, in which case the losses through migration would have been 4.3 per cent or one-quarter of the losses from the individual authorities.

3. The Accuracy of the Information Obtained

Underlying the whole inquiry is the assumption that women will give reliable answers to questions about their homes and families and that they can remember over varying periods of time specified major illnesses and accidents and the approximate dates when they occurred. It is also assumed that the women can answer with reasonable accuracy such questions as when their child first walked alone, when he was immunized, or when he was taken to an infant welfare center. These assumptions are clearly open to question and our object here is to show how far they are justified.

We obtained the following direct checks on our information:

1. Five local maternity and child welfare authorities were visited and the information on immunization and infant welfare center attendance given on the survey forms was checked with that on the local records.

2. The mothers' answers to questions on hospital admissions were checked with the hospitals concerned.

3. An analysis was made of answers given by the same mothers to the same questions in successive surveys.

These checks have so far been applied only to information gathered during the first four years of the survey, when the interviews were most widely spaced and the possibilities of error greatest.

In the succeeding paragraphs it will become clear that no general statement on the accuracy of memory can be made. The memory and placing of events varies with the intensity of their impact and women who remember the precise date of a hospital admission may give the date of an attack of whooping cough with much less accuracy. The important fact is that similar errors are made by women in all occupational groups so that social comparisons of the age incidence of disease may be valid although the errors in each group are large. It is also important that few of the illnesses asked about appear to have been forgotten and that most diagnoses were given correctly.

Accuracy of Information on Infant Welfare Attendances and Diphtheria Immunization. In Table 8 it will be seen that social differences in the use made of welfare centers are as clearly shown from the answers given when there was a two year period of recall, as from those given concurrently. None of the small differences shown in the table is significant.

When the answers given by mothers in five local authority areas were checked against the public health records it was found that the *dates* of 51 per cent of first attendances at welfare centers were given correctly to the nearest week, 32 per cent showed errors of between one and four weeks and 17 per cent showed larger errors. Seven per cent of the mothers said

Table 8. Proportion of mothers making their first attendance at infant welfare centers in the eight weeks following confinement. (Rowntree, 1950 b).

	Per Cent Using Centers in First Eight Weeks					
	Profes- sional and Salaried	Black- Coated	Manual Workers	Agricul- tural Workers	Own Account and Farmer	Total
Maternity Survey (1946)	44.5	62.5	61.5	35.1	39.5	6,469[a]
Follow-up Survey (1948)	49.7	63.9	63.2	34.0	37.8	4,690[b]

[a] In the 1946 maternity survey only approximately half the mothers were asked questions on the use of the infant welfare centers. (*See*, Maternity in Great Britain, p. 4.)

[b] This number excludes all losses during the first two years from death (210 children), emigration (118 children), refusal (56 children), and other causes (215 children), and also 97 children whose mothers were interviewed but failed to answer questions on infant welfare attendance.

| | AGE ON ADMISSION (IN MONTHS) | | | | | TOTAL NUMBER OF CHILDREN |
	0–12	13–24	25–36	37–48	More Than 48	
Mothers	153	127	167	204	12	663
Hospital Records	145	132	166	220	nil	663

Table 9. Comparison of the ages of children when admitted to hospital as recalled by their mothers and as given by the hospital records.

they had attended infant welfare centers when they had not done so. The total *number* of attendances made during the first two years was often incorrectly reported, but in general the number of attendances claimed by a mother was a fair indication of the actual frequency with which she had attended, and when the survey records and the local records were ranked according to the number of attendances in the first year a correlation of +0.69 (n = 92 P < 0.001) was found between the two sets of information.

In the same five authorities the mothers' statements on diphtheria immunization were checked with the health visitors records, and out of 145 answers only two were found to be incorrect (Rowntree 1950 a).

Accuracy of Information on Hospital Admissions. Hospital records were used to check the information given by mothers in respect to 663 hospital admissions during the first four years of life. The ages on admission, as given by the mothers, are compared in Table 9 with the actual ages.

The mothers' reports accurately describe the age distribution of hospital sicknesses in the whole survey population, and the mean reported age on admission (27.4 months) is not significantly different from the true mean age (27.2 months t = 1.53 n = 662 0.2 > P > 0.1).[8] The correlation coefficient relating the ages of admission given by the mothers and by the hospitals is +0.96.

[8] This test was based on the errors made by individual mothers and not on a direct comparison of the two means.

When the period of recall is less than two years there is a slight but not significant understatement of the age on admission. With longer periods of recall the age is significantly overstated,[9] but not so much so that the mothers' estimates of the age distribution of early admissions are seriously distorted. With longer periods of recall the women from the lowest occupational groups are the most likely to make gross errors.

It was expected that women with many children would make larger errors than those with few, but this was not so. Nor can it be shown that the dates of admission are better remembered when the illnesses are serious than when they are slight.

We have also been able to check how accurately the number of days spent in hospital is remembered. While there was a close agreement between the mothers' accounts and the hospital records, (as shown by a correlation coefficient of $+0.94$), there was a consistent tendency to overestimate the length of stay. Thus the actual mean length of stay was 18.0 days whereas the remembered length of stay was 20.7 days.[10] These overestimates were greater when the period of recall was long, when the length of stay was short, and when the mothers belonged to the manual worker group. The errors largely resulted from a tendency to report length of stay in weekly intervals rather than in days.

There is no evidence that mothers who make large errors in recalling age on admission are more likely to make large errors in recalling length of stay. The correlation coefficient relating the size of these two types of error is not significantly different from zero.

Comparing the mothers' statements of reason for admission with the final hospital diagnoses, it was found that only twenty-four were misleading in the sense that they would have led to a different classification of the illnesses concerned if we had used them alone. It is of interest that the majority of these errors were made by the women in the lower groups. Some had given

[9] By 0.63 months $(t = 2.37 \ n = 275, \ 0.02 > P > 0.01)$.
[10] $(t = 2.21 \ n = 1296 \ 0.05 > P > 0.02.)$

the first but not the final diagnosis, for example, a suspected inguinal hernia was reported as such although it was later shown to be a cyst of the spermatic cord. Others mentioned a minor complaint but not a serious complication—for example, a child admitted to hospital with tonsillitis later developed acute nephritis, but only the first was mentioned. In two instances it appears that the mothers were hiding a condition which they considered shameful—a child with congenital syphilis was reported as having a "nervous complaint" and a mentally backward child was labelled "possible infantile paralysis." Finally a mother reported that her child had been in hospital with pneumonia but did not say that the precipitating cause of admission was not this illness but severe erythema following the too enthusiastic application at home of thermogene wool poultices to the chest.

In general, it appears that the mothers have given an accurate account of the hospital admissions of their children and that even if we had had to rely on their memories alone, the reliability of our information on hospital care would still have been high.

How Completely Has Illness Been Reported? In the survey we have only asked about hospital admissions, accidents where the doctor was called in, and the major infectious diseases, and the questions concerned only one child in the family. Even so, a few incidents appear to have been left out; for example, out of 656 accidents to our children between birth and two years forty-six were forgotten or suppressed and only revealed at a later stage of the inquiry. These accidents were all trivial and six of them appear to have resulted from the mothers' own carelessness.

The same questions on incidence asked in successive surveys did not always yield the same results. At two years of age 1,296 children were reported by their mothers to have had either measles or whooping cough or both. But ninety-six mothers failed to recall these illnesses two years later until they were pressed by the health visitors and shown local records. It

Period of Recall	28–33 Months	34–39 Months	40–45 Months	46–51 Months
Age of Child	2 Years to 19 Months Per Cent	18 Months to 13 Months Per Cent	1 year to 7 Months Per Cent	6 Months to 0 Months Per Cent
Proportion of Attacks *Not* Reported in the 1950 Survey (*i.e.* Taken at 4 Years of Age)	11.1	7.6	5.9	3.7

Table 10. Comparison of information on measles and whooping cough given in 1948 and in 1950. Losses with different periods of recall.

is worth noting that the mothers were least likely to forget illnesses that had occurred early in their child's life, as Table 10 shows.

The ages of admission to hospital were also best remembered when they occurred within six months of birth and illnesses in infancy appear to have a greater impact on the memories of mothers.

A further source of error lay in the confusion of the survey child with his sibs. Twelve mothers incorrectly attributed accidents or illnesses to the survey children which had in fact occurred to their brothers or sisters.

None of the sources of error discussed in this section appears to be large enough to have distorted the general pattern of reported illnesses.

Present Aims and Future Development

The main fields of interest in the early years of this study are shown by the titles of the twenty-two publications listed at the end of this paper. In addition, a book on the health, growth and environment of the pre-school child is nearly completed. Particular fields of interest at the present time are as follows:

1. We are in a position to isolate and define groups which fail to use the welfare services even when they are available. And we can also assess the value of these services in terms of the health and growth of the children. The infant welfare services

existing in Great Britain today were, to a considerable extent, designed for the economic environment and standards of education of twenty years ago, and it is administratively important to make an objective assessment of how far they meet our present needs. This, we believe, can be done by using the information provided by this survey.

2. We have a unique opportunity to examine the handicaps suffered by certain groups of children and the extent to which they need special help. The largest group and the one that is administratively the most important is made up of the prematurely-born children, about whose health and development there have been many conflicting reports owing to the difficulty in finding adequate samples of premature children and of mature controls to compare them with. In the present study these sampling difficulties are avoided. All children prematurely born during the survey week have been followed up and compared with a closely matched group of children born at term. Four papers comparing the health, growth, and mental ability of premature children with their controls have been published and in general show the former to be little handicapped, though a small well-defined group made exceptionally low scores in tests of school achievement and mental ability.

3. This study is especially well adapted for getting direct evidence on such problems as whether maternal employment has an adverse effect on the child or whether separation from the mother in infancy leads to later difficulties in emotional adjustment. We have accordingly noted all major periods of separation from the mother and all periods during which she was employed. In addition, we hear of all broken marriages in our sample. A paper describing the incidence of such marriages and examining children from broken homes has already been published.

4. The children in the sample are now approaching the point in their school careers when they take the examination which determines whether they go to a grammar, secondary modern, or technical school. Relatively little is known about the factors affecting achievements in this examination, and we hope to examine the part played by the attitude of the parents, by illness or absence from school, by the size of the class, by the frequency of change of teacher, etc.

There would be no difficulty in following our children through the remainder of their school careers, even into their first jobs and, for the boys, until they have completed their National Service. And there are many questions relating to adolescence and entry into employment which could be answered if the survey were continued. It would also be of value to continue to follow the special groups of premature children, deprived children, bedwetters, etc. In such further investigations the problems involved are not likely to be of the kind referred to by Professor Cochran. As has been shown, all the authorities concerned have been extremely cooperative and continue to be so, while our experience suggests that the mothers of the survey children tend to become more, rather than less, cooperative with time. Moreover, the possible "warping" of the survey children can be tested periodically by drawing upon the children not covered by the continuous survey. The main difficulty as regards the future, is primarily one of finance. So far all our interviewing has been carried out without cost to the Committee, the services of the health visitors, school nurses, and school doctors having been given most generously by these groups, with the enthusiastic consent of their authorities. Nevertheless, substantial costs are involved in maintaining the central organization necessary for keeping in contact with the children and the interviewers, and in tracing migrant families, as well as in the processing and analysis of the data collected. And such costs can only be met by correspondingly substantial grants from Foundations.

Summary

A longitudinal study of the health and development of a national sample of children has been described. Losses during the ten-year period for which the survey has been running were analyzed and it was shown that no significant bias has been introduced into the sample thereby.

Internal migration was discussed and the likelihood of a progressive distortion of the sample in longitudinal studies

101

which do not attempt a national coverage was shown to be considerable. Such distortion could be reduced by covering large regional aggregates instead of a single administrative area.

The reliability of the information given by mothers in answer to questions on their child's health and early history was examined and it was shown that while some events are remembered better than others the errors made are not large enough to lead to an appreciable distortion of the facts.

Acknowledgments

This survey is being made by a Joint Committee of the Institute of Child Health (University of London), the Society of Medical Officers of Health, and the Population Investigation Committee. The chairman of the Committee is Professor James Young; the vice-chairman, Professor A. A. Moncrieff; and the secretary, Professor D. V. Glass. The Nuffield Foundation has financed this inquiry during the pre-school years, and grants for continuing it in the primary school period have been made by the Board of Governors of The Hospital for Sick Children, Great Ormond Street (through the Institute of Child Health); by the Regional Hospital Boards in Great Britain; and by the Ford Foundation.

We wish to thank the chairman and members of the Joint Committee for their help and advice; the Medical Officers of Health, School Medical Officers, and Health Visitors whose generous cooperation made this survey possible, and the mothers in all parts of the country who willingly answered numerous and detailed questions on their children's health.

Papers Giving the Results of the National Survey

I. The Maternity and Child Welfare Services

1. A Survey of Childbearing in Britain. *Population Studies,* 1947, 1, p. 99.

2. Maternity in Great Britain. Oxford University Press, 1948.

3. Douglas, J. W. B., and Rowntree, G.: Supplementary Maternal and Child Health Services. Part I, Postnatal Care—Part II, Nurseries. *Population Studies,* 1949, 3, p. 205.

4. Rowntree, G.: Supplementary Child Health Services. Part III, Infant Welfare Centres. *Population Studies,* 1950, 3, p. 375.

5. Rowntree, G.: Diptheria Immunization in a National Sample of Children Aged Two Years in March 1948. *Monthly Bulletin of the Ministry of Health,* 1950, 9, p. 134.

6. Douglas, J. W. B.: Deux, Enquêtes nationales sur la maternité et la santé de l'enfant en Grande Bretagne. *Population,* 1950, 5, p. 625.

II. The Premature Child

7. Douglas, J. W. B.: Some Factors Associated with Prematurity. *Journal of Obstetrics and Gynaecology of the British Empire,* 1950, 57, p. 143.

8. Douglas, J. W. B.: Birthweight and the History of Breast-feeding. *Lancet,* 1954, ii, p. 685.

9. Douglas, J. W. B., and Mogford, C.: The Health of Premature Children During the First Four Years of Life. *British Medical Journal,* 1953, i, p. 748.

10. Douglas, J. W. B., and Mogford, C.: The Growth of Premature Children. *Archives of Disease in Childhood,* 1953, 28, p. 436.

11. Douglas, J. W. B.: The Age at which Premature Children Walk. *Medical Officer,* 1956, 95, p. 33.

12. Douglas, J. W. B: The Mental Ability of Premature Children. *British Medical Journal,* 1956, i, p. 1210.

III. Morbidity

13. Douglas, J. W. B.: Social Class Differences in Health and Survival During the First Two Years of Life; the Results of a National Survey. *Population Studies,* 1951, 5, p. 35.

14. Douglas, J. W. B.: The Health and Survival of Children in Different Social Classes: the Results of a National Survey. *Lancet,* 1951, ii, p. 440.

15. Rowntree, G.: Accidents Among Children Under Two Years of Age in Great Britain. *Journal of Hygiene,* 1950, 48, p. 323.

16. Rowntree, G.: Accidents Among Young Children. *Monthly Bulletin of the Ministry of Health,* 1951, 10, p. 150.

17. Blomfield, J. M.: An Account of Hospital Admissions in the Pre-School Period. Mimeographed—copies available on application to the Joint Committee.

IV. Miscellaneous

18. Douglas, J. W. B.: The Extent of Breast-Feeding in Great Britain in 1946, with Special Reference to the Health and Survival of Children. *Journal of Obstetrics and Gynaecology of the British Empire,* 1950, 57, p. 336.

19. MacCarthy, D.; Douglas, J. W. B.; and Mogford, C.: Circumcision in a National Sample of Four-Year-Old Children. *British Medical Journal,* 1952, ii, p. 755.

20. Bransby, E. R.; Blomfield, J. M.; and Douglas, J. W. B.: The Prevalence of Bed-Wetting. *Medical Officer,* 1955, 94, p. 5.

21. Blomfield, J. M., and Douglas, J. W. B.: Bed-Wetting. Prevalence Among Children Aged 4–7 Years. *Lancet*, 1956, i, p. 850.

22. Rowntree, G.: Early Childhood in Broken Families. *Population Studies*, 1955, 8, p. 247.

104

METHODOLOGICAL CONSIDERATIONS IN STUDYING PATTERNS OF MEDICAL CARE RELATED TO MENTAL ILLNESS

SAM SHAPIRO

AND

RAYMOND FINK

In spite of the increasing number of studies of mental illness reported in recent years, little work has appeared on how the family physician deals with mental or emotional problems in a non-institutionalized population. This paper examines a number of methodological questions involved in studying the family physician's role in providing medical care for patients who, in his judgment, have a mental, emotional or psychological condition. Some of the problems encountered in a recently completed pilot study on this issue are described, and procedures for dealing with them are presented.

The beginnings of research in this area have been seen in England. Kessel, Shepard, Stein and Fisher[1, 2] have reported approaches taken by them and examined the effects of varying criteria on measurement of psychiatric morbidity in a surburban practice in London. Findings of sufficient interest to continue this type of investigation have also been presented.

Some clues to the role of the family physician in this country in the treatment of mental illness have been provided by a number of extensive studies of mental health. Hollingshead and Redlich,[3] for example, in their New Haven study of social class characteristics of patients receiving psychiatric care report that, among those classified as "neurotics," about half of the upper and middle social class patients were first referred for psychiatric care by a non-psychiatric physician. Presumably many of these were family physicians. Gurin, Veroff and Feld[4] in their book, AMERICANS VIEW THEIR MENTAL HEALTH, revealed that nearly a third of those who have sought help for their emotional problems have turned to physicians.

It is the purpose of the current investigation to examine more closely the function of the family physician in treating mental and emotional problems, largely through the use of direct interviews with both physicians and their patients. Although the study is predominantly methodological, information will also be presented to illustrate the kinds of substantive data that can be gathered through this approach to the study of mental health.

It should be observed that, as used here, the term "family physician" will refer to internists, family physicians and pediatricians. To a great extent those internists and pediatricians included in the study do actually perform in much the same manner as those designated as "family physicians".

METHODOLOGY

Study Setting. This pilot study is being conducted by the Division of Research and Statistics of the Health Insurance Plan of Greater New York. H.I.P. is a prepaid group practice medical care program in the New York City area with about 630,000 members at the time of the study. The plan provides its members with almost the entire range of diagnostic and therapeutic services. Medical care is received from family physicians, internists and other specialists in the medical group center or doctor's office, the patient's home, and in a hospital. Although H.I.P. coverage does not include psychiatric treatment, at each of the 32 medical group centers a psychiatrist is available to whom patients may be referred for consultative or diagnostic purposes.

Employee groups have been the primary source of enrollment, with about 3 in 5 of the members coming into the program through contracts with the official agencies of New York City, including such departments as the Board of Education, Police, Fire and Transit Authority. The largest sources of enrollment next to this group are union health and welfare funds.

Three medical groups were selected for the pilot study. They have a combined enrollment of about 45,000 and cover a wide range of occupational pursuits, educational and income groups. High, average and low utilization of neuro-psychiatric and other physician services are represented by the medical groups in the pilot study.

Study Objectives and Restrictions.   Although designed basically to answer questions related to feasibility and methodology, the study is also aimed at obtaining preliminary information on certain aspects of medical care related to mental illness. These concern such questions as, what is the relative frequency with which, in the judgment of the family physician, mental, emotional or personality disorders are presented by patients seen during the regular course of providing medical care? To what extent are these conditions judged to be transient in nature, and to what extent do they represent more deep-seated disorders? What does the physician consider as the probable future course of his patient's emotional problems, either with or without medical treatment?

Of particular interest were several questions related to patterns of medical care given by family physicians to patients whom they have diagnosed as having some kind of emotional

107

problem. Interest was in a wide range of possible approaches including referrals to psychiatrists and community agencies, prescription of drugs, and discussions with the patient regarding his problem.

It was planned to seek the answers from information available on H.I.P.'s medical records and through interviews with H.I.P. physicians. Other information, significantly related to the study, could best be obtained from the patients themselves. For this purpose the study included interviews with a sample of patients seen by their family physicians. From the patient's point of view we wished to learn the following:

First, in what terms does the patient describe the condition for which he has seen the doctor? From the point of view of medical care and treatment, what does the patient see as having been done for his emotional problems by his family physician? To what extent does the patient follow the physician's suggestions for treatment of his emotional problems? Also, to what extent does the patient turn to non-medical sources for help or advice?

There are other subjects on which it was obvious that the patient would be best informed. Among these was the degree to which the patient felt that the care provided had succeeded in relieving him of his anxieties and the degree to which his emotional problems had interfered with his life activities in the home, on the job, and elsewhere.

The methodology and aims of the pilot study are subject to important limitations. The study, for example, was not directed at validating family physicians' diagnoses of mental or emotional disorders. Rather it was intended to examine the nature and context of these diagnoses. Neither was this a study of physician characteristics as these might relate to a tendency to ascribe to patients a variety of emotional problems. Lastly, we did not seek to examine emotional problems as they occur in the general population, but only as they have come to the attention of the family physician.

The study population imposes additional limitations on this

108

pilot study. The population was limited to patients in three of H.I.P.'s 32 medical groups who were seen by a family physician during the three month period from December 1, 1961 through February 28, 1962. Two other restrictions were placed on the sample of patients to be included in the interview study. They had to be at least 12 years of age, and at the time when they saw their family physician during the three-month period, they had to have been in H.I.P. for at least two years. The latter was designed to increase the likelihood that the patient was known to the physician for a reasonable period of time.

Sample Selection. In selecting the sample of respondents for interview, it was possible to rely upon some of the special advantages offered by H.I.P.'s routine procedure of obtaining doctor reports on patient visits. For each patient visit, the H.I.P. physician fills a line on a routine report form. The patient is identified by name, age and sex. Information is also provided on the patient visit itself. This includes where the visit took place—that is, in the home, office or hospital; the type of service given—whether an operation, examination, or treatment; and the tentative or final diagnosis.

For the purposes of this study, an additional column was provided on the routine report form. He was instructed to enter a check mark in this column if, in his opinion, "a mental, emotional, psychological or personality disorder or disturbance plays a part in the patient's condition,"—and to indicate whether or not he had already entered this as part of his diagnosis.

Three random samples, each of approximately 150 patients, were selected from the medical groups in the study. The first of these was a sample of those patients qualified for the study who were diagnosed by family physicians as having a mental, psychoneurotic or personality disorder. The classification of the diagnosis was based on the W.H.O. International Classification of Diseases. Respondents whose diagnosis was classified under Section V of this coding scheme were included in this first sample. This will be referred to as the neuro-psychiatric or *"N-P diagnosis"* sample.

The second sample was taken from among patients not classified under a Section V diagnosis, but for whom the physician indicated there was an emotional problem associated with the condition for which they had seen him. This group was obtained from the routine report form entries with a check mark in the special column. It is referred to as the *"N-P associated"* sample.

The third sample was taken from among all other patients 12 years of age and over (with at least 2 years of coverage), who saw their family physician in one of the three medical groups during the three month study period.[5] For these respondents there had not been indicated any emotional or neuro-psychiatric problem either through a diagnosis or through a check in the appropriate column. Physicians were further questioned about these patients to determine whether or not some of them had, in fact, exhibited emotional problems either during or before the study period.

Each of the three sample groups of *"NP"* patients could be viewed as implying a different definition of an *N-P* case as arrived at by the family physician. But this was not necessarily the case, and it was indeed one of the purposes of this study to determine how the inclusion or exclusion of one or another group affects study findings.

Interviews with Physicians.   When the sample of patients had been drawn, arrangements were made to interview family physicians about each of the patients included in the sample. The interview with a physician was generally conducted between one and two months after the visit made by the patient, which was optimum considering the lag in gaining access to the the report forms. To maximize the accuracy of the physicians' reports, each was notified in advance of the interview and told the names of the patients about whom questions would be asked. It was requested that the physician have available

110

during the interview the patient's medical chart for easy reference. In nearly every case the physician complied with this request.

Information from the physician about the patient's visit during the study period was obtained on two forms. The first of these, the *Physician's Preliminary Questionnaire* had a two-fold purpose. For the *N-P* diagnosis and the *N-P* associated groups it served to obtain additional information on the nature of the emotional problem indicated for the patient. For the control group, the *Preliminary Questionnaire* was used to identify those patients whom the physician might consider to have an emotional problem, but for whom this had not been reported on the Med 10 reporting forms during the three month study period. The bulk of the information from the physician interview was obtained on the *Main Physician Questionnaire* which inquired into the nature of the *N-P* condition, medical care given, an assessment of its effectivness, etc.

Interviews with Patients. Interviewing of patients in the sample was planned to take place from sixty to ninety days after the patient's study visit to the family physician. Interviews were conducted by personnel who had not had contact with the physicians, and who could not distinguish between *N-P* patients and control patients. For those patients identified as having an emotional problem (further discussed later) the questionnaire then paralleled in content the one used in the physician interview. Social background questions and a number of other questions were asked of all patients.

FINDINGS RELATED TO METHODOLOGY

One of the central purposes of the pilot study was to provide an opportunity to examine closely a number of methodological issues that bear on the design of a full-scale study. In this section, findings related to several of these issues are presented along with an analysis of their significance.

Time Period. The pilot study was restricted to a three month period (December, 1961–February, 1962) primarily because of operational circumstances. While this approach proved satisfactory for the purposes in hand, it imposes restrictions on the ability to generalize from the figures derived for the study period as to what would be found if a full year were covered. This limitation stems in part from the fact that seasonality exerts an influence on the volume of patients seen and on the reasons for patient visits to physicians. Potentially of even greater significance is the fact that doctor visits are not evenly distributed among patients. Since the probability that a patient seen in any time interval is proportionate to the number of months during the year he visits the physician, the shorter the time period under observation, the more heavily loaded is the patient group with comparatively high utilizers.

This issue has been examined on the basis of distributions of patients by number of months during the year in which they are seen and reported by physicians to have an *N-P* or *N-P* associated condition. The results suggest that a three-month period contains a moderate bias of the type mentioned. Leaving aside the effects of seasonality, the pilot study might therefore be expected to provide somewhat higher estimates than a full-year study of the proportions of patients with *N-P* conditions that interfere with certain life activities, the volume and types of medical care obtained for the condition, and other measures related to seriousness of the condition.

Physician Classification of Patients. While the time period of the pilot study is restrictive, the manner in which *N-P* cases were identified is expansive. The three procedures used for identifying patients judged by their family physicians as having an *N-P* problem were intended to provide for study samples of patients with a wide range of emotional problems. For about

112

4 per cent of all patients seen, the physician indicated on the routine report form an *N-P* diagnosis.. For another 4 per cent the physician indicated that the condition was associated with an *N-P* condition. And finally, for 26 per cent of the patients in the control group, the physician reported an *N-P* problem during the interview.

The last two groups served to broaden the base of *N-P* patients, and in so doing may have "softened" the definition of the *N-P* group. In the case of patients with an *N-P* associated condition, we were able to add to the *N-P* cases those patients for whom the physician may have shown some reluctance to classify as having a problem which was predominatly emotional, but for whom he could at least feel that there was some emotional aspect to the patient's complaint. So too was the case with patients in the control group later reported by the physician as having an emotional problem. For these patients, the physician could have indicated an emotional problem manifested either during the study visit, or at *any other* time previous to that visit. And, in fact, in half the cases he said the conditions were presented at a visit prior to the three month study period. (See Appendix for question wording).[6] This "softer" approach to an *N-P* diagnosis may thus have included some patients for whom the *N-P* problem was no longer salient.

Patient Response Rates.   In every case the interview with the family physician regarding a patient preceded the patient interview. At that time the physician was asked to indicate which patients he did not wish interviewed. The number of such patients totaled 5 per cent of the *N-P* diagnosis sample and 2 per cent or less of the other two samples. In most of these instances the physician expressed the belief that an interview might seriously upset the patient, or might create problems in the future between the physician and the patient. But emotional problems were not the only reasons given for not interviewing patients. Some were too ill from other causes to be interviewed.

TABLE 1. PATIENT RESPONSE RATES AND REASONS FOR NON-INTERVIEWS BY PHYSICIAN *N-P* AND CONTROL GROUPS.

	Physician Reports		
	$N\text{-}P^1$ Diagnosis	$N\text{-}P^2$ Associated	[3] Control
Sample Size—(Unweighted)—Number	167	133	159
Per Cent	100	100	100
Interviewed	82	90	92
Not Interviewed—	18	10	8
At Physician's Suggestion	5	2	1
Patient Refusal	5	2	2
Couldn't Locate or Contact	5	4	3
Death, Patient Ill, Other	2	1	2

[1] Sample of patients for whom a diagnostic entry on physician's routine report of medical services was classified as a mental, psychoneurotic, or personality disorder (International Classification of Diseases, rubrics 300–326).
[2] Sample of patients for whom the physician's routine report of medical services indicated the presence of a mental, psychoneurotic or personality disorder associated with some other condition.
[3] Sample of patients seen who did not fall in categories defined in other two columns.

TABLE 2. *N-P* STATUS BASED ON PHYSICIAN AND PATIENT REPORTS

	Physician Reports			
	$N\text{-}P^1$ Diagnosis	$N\text{-}P^2$ Associated	Control $N\text{-}P^3$	Control Non-$N\text{-}P$
Patient Reports				
Sample Size—(Unweighted)	(138)	(121)	(41)	(106)
Weighted[4]—Number	290	265	55	158
Per Cent	100	100	100	100
N-P Condition Discussed with Physician—				
On Study Visit	55	34	14	11
On Previous Visit	18	32	44	20
No *N-P* Condition Discussed	27	34	42	69

[1] and [2] See Table 1.
[3] Patients in sample of control cases for whom the physician at time of interview indicated presence of a "psychological, mental, emotional or personality disorder or condition."
[4] *N-P* diagnosis and *N-P* associated groups are weighted to the total number of cases located in the study period through screening of physician routine reports. The weighted control group is a three per cent sample of patients who do not fall in the other two categories.

The refusal rate among respondents was unusually low. Of the 463 patients in the three original unweighted samples, only 14 or three per cent refused to speak to our interviewers. Here again there were some differences among the three sample groups. Among those with an *N-P* diagnosis, the refusal rate was almost five per cent, while among the *N-P* associated group and the control group, the refusal rates were about two per cent for each. Practically none of the refusals came once the interview was begun, in spite of the sensitive nature of the questions asked the patients. (Table 1)

In addition to the reasons cited for not having interviewed patients, there were the usual circumstances of inability to locate because of address change, illness, etc. These accounted for about 4 per cent of each of the study groups. In all, 87 per cent of those patients included in the original sample were interviewed. The figures for the three sample groups were: 82 per cent for the *N-P* diagnosis group, 90 per cent for the *N-P* associated group and 92 per cent for the control group.

This is viewed as a highly successful field operation. In New York City it is estimated by many researchers that a total loss of at least twenty per cent and a refusal rate in excess of ten per cent should be expected. It is undoubtedly true that by identifying themselves with H.I.P., interviewers reduced much of the resistance frequently encountered among potential respondents. At the same time, however, it should be remembered that about two-thirds of the patients in the sample had been identified by their family physicians as having some kind of emotional problem. That the refusal rate was low even among these patients should be a source of comfort to others interested in the study of mental health.

Patient Reports on N-P Condition. Now what of the patients themselves—what did they have to say about the presence or absence of emotional problems that they might have discussed with their family physician? It should be pointed out that a major objective in the patient interview was to increase the likelihood of having an emotional problem identified by patients for whom the physicians had reported on N-P or N-P associated condition. This was essential since part of the study was expected to focus eventually on such patients, and unless they acknowledged having discussed an emotional problem with the physician, none of the questions related to medical care, assessment of its value, etc., could be asked of them.

The problem was to provide proper means for the patient to make this acknowledgment. It was clearly not possible to inform the patient that he had been described by his physician as having an emotional problem. Instead it was necessary for the patient to provide the information about an emotional problem that would permit further questioning about that problem, and about the care that might have been provided by the physician in question. For this the patient was provided with what was hoped to be ample opportunity and encouragement to report on the discussion of emotional problems with the physician. (See Appendix.)

The first opportunity was provided in a series of questions asking details about the patient's visit to the physician during the study period. If the patient reported in these free-response questions that he went to the physician for an emotional problem, or that the pyhsician told him of or treated him for an emotional problem, he was then skipped to the main part of the questionnaire.

All other patients were asked directly whether the condition for which they visited the physician was "affected by worries, nervousness or tensions". Those who believed there was such a connection were asked if their "worries or nervousness" were discussed with the physician either at the time of the study visit or at some previous visit. A positive reply brought the patient to the main part of the questionnaire to be asked further about the emotional condition.

Finally, those patients who saw no connection between the study visit or the condition for which they had seen the doctor

116

and an emotional problem, were asked two additional questions. The first of these inquired whether or not they had *ever* discussed with the doctor being "worried, upset or nervous" about their health. The second asked about any other worries they might have discussed with the doctor. Again, an affirmative reply brought the patient to the main part of the questionnaire.

The results of this approach were as follows:

First, with regard to those patients who had been diagnosed by their physicians as having an *N-P* problem during the study period (Table 2). Among these patients, 55 per cent reported having discussed their emotional problem during the same visit in which they had received an *N-P* diagnosis from the physician. Another 18 per cent reported that they had discussed an emotional problem with the physician during a visit previous to the study visit. On the other hand, 27 per cent of the physician-designated *N-P* group did not report ever having discussed with their physician this kind of problem or being "nervous" about their health.

Lest it be thought that all of the 27 per cent not reporting an *N-P* condition were concealing this information from the interviewer, it should be pointed out that not all of the patients were necessarily aware that their condition had been diagnosed as one that was primarily emotional. In fact, among the *N-P* diagnosed group, 26 per cent were reported by their physicians as *not* being aware of their emotional problem. About half of these reported no discussion of an emotional problem with their physician.

Next to be considered are those identified on the routine report forms as having an *N-P* associated condition and their reports of whether or not the condition had been discussed with their physician. Among these, about one-third reported having discussed an emotional problem or "nervousness about their health" with their physician at the time of the study visit, while another third said they had had such a discussion during some previous visit. The final third responded in the negative to all

TABLE 3. *N-P* STATUS OF CONTROL GROUP BASED ON PHYSICIAN
AND PATIENT REPORTS.

Sample Size—(Unweighted)	(147)	
Weighted—Number	213	
Per Cent	100	
Physician Reports *N-P* Condition	26	
Patient Reports *N-P* Condition Discussed[1]		15
Patient Reports no *N-P* Condition Discussed		11
Physician Reports No *N-P* Condition	74	
Patient Reports *N-P* Condition Discussed[1]		23
Patient Reports No *N-P* Condition Discussed		51

Note: Table refers to patients in control group interviewed. See footnotes—Tables 1 and 2 for other definitions.
[1] Includes patients who during the interview indicated that they discussed at some time with the physician "worries (in general), nervousness or tensions" or a worry about health, or a specific emotional or psychological condition.

TABLE 4. PATIENT REPORT OF NATURE OF EMOTIONAL PROB-
LEMS DISCUSSED WITH FAMILY PHYSICIAN.

	Physician Reports[1]			
	N-P *Diagnosis*	*N-P* *Associated*	*Control* *N-P*	*Control* *Non-N-P*
Patient Reports				
Sample Size—				
(Unweighted)	(102)	(85)	(23)	(34)
Weighted—Number	211	175	32	49
Total (per cent)	100	100	100	100
Discussed "Nervousness" about Health	18	33	37	49
Discussed other Emotional Problem	82	67	63	51

[1] Includes only patients interviewed who stated they had discussed an emotional problem or health worry with their physician. Patients are retained in the particular *N-P* group in which they were classified on the basis of routine reports and interviews of physicians.

118

inquiries on this issue.

Of perhaps equal interest is what occurred among the control group when they were asked about any discussions they might have had with their family physicians concerning an emotional problem or "nervousnes about their health". It has already been observed that for about one-fourth of the control group, further questioning of the family physician revealed that a previously unreported psychological or emotional problem was manifested at some time by the patient either during or previous to the study visit. Three out of five of these patients (58 per cent) stated that there had been a discussion of emotional problems or "nervousness about health" (14 per cent at the doctor visit during the study period, 44 per cent at an earlier visit).

The picture of the patients' reports is rounded out when the situation is examined for that segment of the control group for which no emotional problem was reported by the physician. Among these patients, 31 per cent indicated that they had discussed with the physician an emotional problem or "nervousness about health" (11 per cent at the doctor visit during the study period, 20 per cent at an earlier visit). Sixty-nine per cent agreed with the physician that there had never been a discussion about this class of problems. (See Table 3 for data regarding both segments of the control group combined.)

In reviewing the correspondence between physician and patient reports of whether or not there was a discussion between them about an emotional problem, the importance of the question on "nervousness" about health can be plainly seen. Correspondence was increased for the groups identified by the physicians on the report forms as having an N-P or N-P associated condition through the addition of the "nervousness about health" series of questions. Here 18 per cent of the N-P cases and 33 per cent of the N-P associated cases would have been missed on the patient screening without these questions. In the control group identified by physicians on interview as having an N-P condition, 37 per cent of these cases would have been

119

missed (Table 4).

On the other hand, as a result of including questions on "nervousness about health", there was a significant decrease in correspondence between physician and patient reports among patients for whom the physician did not indicate an *N-P* condition. Half of these patients who stated that they had discussed an emotional problem with their physician, identified "nervousness about health" as the problem.

It remains a problem for future analysis to determine the nature of differences between those who have identified "nervousness about health" as their problem source and those who identified other problems.

General Findings

The discussion of study findings has until now been concerned primarily with methodological considerations. Although it is frequently difficult to draw a distinction between findings that are "methodological" and those that are "substantive" the balance of the paper focuses on study results which might be considered substantive in character. That the two cannot be completely divorced from each other will be clear as attention is called occasionally to differences among the differently defined *N-P* groups. The data presented are examples of what is being derived in this study from H.I.P. records, and physician and patient interviews, and are descriptive in nature.

Information obtained from physicians and patients about the patients' emotional problems are shown side by side. Data derived from the physician interviews refer to all of the patients who were considered by them to have an *N-P* or *N-P* associated condition. Data obtained from patient interviews refer to patients who were interviewed and who stated that they had an emotional problem or were "nervous" about their health, without regard to the physician information. Thus data presented

120

at this time involve samples of patients that overlap to varying degrees. As discussed earlier, the overlap is considerable among patients screened on the basis of an *N-P* entry on the physicians' routine report forms. The overlap is only moderate for the control group patients. Later there will be available data on the concurrence between physician and patient reports on the variables examined here.

Seriousness of the Problem.   Both physician and patient were asked a number of questions intended to determine the seriousness with which they regard the patients' emotional problems. One of these asked directly, "On the whole, how do you consider these worries (nervousness and tensions)—not so important or rather important?" Physician and patient were also asked questions about the extent to which the patient's problems or "nervousness about health" interfered with his work (or a housewife's work at home), home life, ability to get along with other people, or other activities. Finally, physicians and patients were asked two questions about the course the emotional problem might take in the future—without medical care and with medical care.

Physicians report that they consider as important the emotional problems among half the patients in each of the three *N-P* groups. They also report that for from half to two-thirds of their patients in the *N-P* groups some interference in daily activities was caused by the emotional problems. The degree of interference was judged to be "a great deal" in from a fourth to about a third of the cases seen. (Tables 5, 6 and 7.)

Physicians' prognosis of the future course of the emotional problems with and without medical care tended to vary according to the *N-P* group into which the patient had been classified. For example, physicians thought there would be no improvement with or without medical care, for more than half the *N-P* associated group as compared with a third of the *N-P* diagnosis group. The proportion of patients they thought would improve without any kind of medical care was between 10 and 20 per

| | Physician | | | Patient | | |
	N-P Diagnosis	N-P Associated	Control N-P	N-P Diagnosis	N-P Associated	Control N-P
Sample Size (Unweighted)	(167)	(133)	(44)	(102)	(85)	(57)
Weighted—Number	343	300	60	211	175	81
Per Cent	100[1]	100[1]	100	100	100	100
N-P Condition Not So Important	46	53	58	16	19	20
N-P Condition Rather Important	53	46	42	84	81	80

Note: See previous tables for description of groups.
[1] Includes "No Answers."

| | Physician | | | Patient | | |
	N-P Diagnosis	N-P Associated	Control N-P	N-P Diagnosis	N-P Associated	Control N-P
Sample Size (Unweighted)	(167)	(133)	(44)	(102)	(85)	(57)
Weighted—Number	343	300	60	211	175	81
Per Cent	100	100	100	100	100	100
No. of Activities[1] Interfered with:						
None	33	29	45	41	55	61
One	26	33	23	19	30	19
Two	22	21	22	22	9	14
Three or Four	19	17	10	18	6	6

Note: See previous tables for descriptions of groups.
[1] The four activities are work on the job (or work around the house), family life, getting along with others and a general category for "other" activities.

cent, depending on the *N-P* group (Table 8).

The patients took a somewhat different view of the seriousness of their emotional problems. About 80 per cent of the patients in each of the three *N-P* groups regarded their emotional problem as being somewhat important. On the other hand, only among patients in the *N-P* diagnosis group did as many as half the patients report that their emotional condition interferes with even one of their daily activities. Once again, we find about a fourth to a third who thought that the emotional condition caused "a great deal" of interference in one or more daily activities.

Although four out of five patients thought their emotional condition important they were for the most part optimistic about the prognosis for the condition. In each of the three patient sample groups, about 60 per cent of the patients replied that their condition had either already improved, or that it was likely to improve without any kind of medical care. Less than 20 per cent of the patients in each group thought that future medical care was required for any improvement of their problem, and only about ten per cent thought they might not improve even with medical care.

Physician Reports of Medical Care provided. For the present discussion, there will be considered only three of the possible courses of action that might be taken by the physician for his patient's emotional problem. First, the physician might prescribe drugs for the patient. Secondly, the patient might be referred to an H.I.P. psychiatrist for diagnostic purposes. Finally, the patient might secure treatment by a psychiatrist outside of H.I.P. In the discussion which follows we shall look at the information on these three procedures as they were obtained from the family physician. Doctor-patient discussions, among the most general approaches taken in handling patients' emotional problems, will be taken up in another section.

In comparing the three *N-P* groups it is found that those patients in the *N-P* diagnosis category were more likely than other

TABLE 7. MAXIMUM DEGREE OF INTERFERENCE OF EMOTIONAL
CONDITION WITH ONE OR MORE LIFE ACTIVITIES: RESPONSES OF
PHYSICIANS AND PATIENTS BY *N-P* GROUPS.

	Physician			Patient		
	N-P *Diagnosis*	*N-P* *Associated*	*Control* *N-P*	*N-P* *Diagnosis*	*N-P* *Associated*	*Control* *N-P*
Sample Size						
(Unweighted)	(167)	(133)	(44)	(102)	(85)	(57)
Weighted—Number	343	300	60	211	175	81
Per Cent	100	100	100	100	100	100
Degree of Interference[1]						
A Great Deal	31	25	22	37	26	35
Somewhat	23	27	17	22	21	13
Very Little	13	13	17	10	6	8
Not At All	33	35	45	31	47	45

Note: See previous tables for descriptions of groups.
[1] Rating was obtained from replies to questions on the following activities: work on the job
(or, work around the house); family life; and getting along with others.

TABLE 8. PROGNOSIS FOR FUTURE COURSE OF EMOTIONAL
PROBLEMS WITH AND WITHOUT MEDICAL CARE: RESPONSES OF
PHYSICIANS AND PATIENTS BY *N-P* GROUPS.

	Physician			Patient		
	N-P *Diagnosis*	*N-P* *Associated*	*Control* *N-P*	*N-P* *Diagnosis*	*N-P* *Associated*	*Control* *N-P*
Sample Size						
(Unweighted)	(167)	(133)	(44)	(102)	(85)	(57)
Weighted—Number	343	300	60	211	175	81
Per Cent	100	100	100	100	100	100
Has Already Improved	—	—	—	30	41	49
Will Improve without Medical Care	16	10	22	29	13	11
Would Improve with Medical Care	35	28	25	18	14	16
Will Not Improve with or without Medical Care	32	53	42	11	14	8
Don't Know Whether Will Improve with Medical Care; Other Qualified Comments	17	9	11	12	17	16

Note: See previous tables for descriptions of groups.

124

patients either to have drugs prescribed or to see an H.I.P. or some other psychiatrist (Table 9). Eighty-five per cent of those with an *N-P* diagnosis received either or both kinds of care, compared with 71 per cent of the patients in the *N-P* associated group, and 60 per cent of those *N-P* patients from the control group. Looking more closely at what was done for the patients, we find that the prescribing of drugs was the most commonly followed procedure. About half of the *N-P* diagnosis and *N-P* associated patients received drug prescriptions without any additional referral to or treatment by a psychiatrist. For some patients, referral to or treatment by a psychiatrist accompanied the prescribing of drugs by the family physician. Drugs for their emotional problem and psychiatric care were provided for 22 per cent of the *N-P* diagnosis group, 12 per cent of the *N-P* associated group, and 10 per cent of the *N-P* patients from the control group. Altogether, between twenty and thirty per cent of the patients in each of the three groups were referred to an H.I.P. or non-H.I.P. psychiatrist.

Drugs and referrals to a psychiatrist are not the only courses of action available to a family physician in treating patients. There are non-medical professionals to whom patients may be sent, and in fact 15 per cent of the *N-P* diagnosis and *N-P* associated groups, and 5 per cent of the *N-P* control groups were referred to an H.I.P. social worker or to some social agency.

Helpfulness of Drugs and Discussions. As a final example of the type of information available from this pilot study of physicians and patients, an examination will be made of how two medical procedures were viewed with regard to their effectiveness in treating patients for their emotional problems. Both physicians and patients were asked to rate on a four point scale ranging from "very helpful" through "not at all helpful", the use of drugs for their emotional problems (where these had been prescribed) and the value of discussions between physician and patient (Tables 10 and 11).

In rating drugs in the treatment of patients with emotional

TABLE 9. MEDICAL CARE GIVEN FOR PATIENTS' EMOTIONAL PROBLEMS: RESPONSES OF PHYSICIANS BY *N-P* GROUPS.

	N-P Diagnosis	*N-P* Associated	Control *N-P*
Sample Size—(Unweighted)	(167)	(133)	(44)
Weighted—Number	343	300	60
Per Cent	100	100	100
Neither Drugs nor Psychiatrist	14	29	40
Patient Received Drugs	77	63	40
Received Drugs only	55	51	30
Drugs and H.I.P. Psychiatrist	12	7	3
Drugs; H.I.P. and Non-H.I.P. Psychiatrist	7	3	7
Drugs and Non-H.I.P. Psychiatrist	3	2	—
Patient Referred Only to Psychiatrist	8	8	20
Referred to H.I.P. Psychiatrist	5	4	13
Referred to H.I.P. and Non-H.I.P. Psychiatrist	3	3	—
Referred to Non-H.I.P. Psychiatrist	—	1	7

Note: See previous tables for descriptions of groups.

TABLE 10. HELPFULNESS OF DRUGS IN TREATING PATIENTS' EMOTIONAL PROBLEMS: RESPONSES OF PHYSICIANS AND PATIENTS BY *N-P* GROUPS.

	Physician			Patient		
	N-P Diagnosis	*N-P* Associated	Control *N-P*	*N-P* Diagnosis	*N-P* Associated	Control *N-P*
Sample size						
(Unweighted)	(91)	(80)	(18)	(80)	(56)	(26)
Weighted—Number	265	189	24	161	109	40
Per Cent	100[1]	100[1]	100[1]	100[2]	100[2]	100[2]
Drugs "Very Helpful"	23	11	4	39	54	48
Drugs "Somewhat Helpful"	32	53	63	24	29	35
Drugs "Very Little" or "Not At All Helpful"	26	31	29	33	14	15
Don't Know	19	5	4	—	—	—

[1] Includes physician reports for patients who were prescribed drugs for their emotional problem.
[2] Includes patients who report having received drugs for their emotional condition. Total includes "No Answers."
Note: See previous tables for descriptions of groups.

126

| | Physician | | | Patient | | |
	N-P Diagnosis	N-P Associated	Control N-P	N-P Diagnosis	N-P Associated	Control N-P
Sample size						
(Unweighted)	(167)	(133)	(44)	(102)	(85)	(57)
Weighted—Number	343	300	60	211	175	81
Per Cent	100[1]	100[1]	100[1]	100	100	100
Discussions "Very Helpful"	18	17	22	60	61	55
Discussions "Somewhat Helpful"	36	47	47	25	24	23
Discussion "Very Little" or "Not At All" Helpful"	40	30	15	15	14	22
Don't Know	2	2	7	—	—	—

[1] Includes "No Answers."
Note: See previous tables for descriptions of groups.

problems, physicians found them "very helpful" for about a fourth of the patients in the *N-P* diagnosis goup to whom they had prescribed them, and for a far smaller proportion of patients in the other *N-P* groups. They found talking to the patients "very helpful" in about one in five cases in each of the *N-P* groups.

A sizable proportion of patients, on the other hand, held both the value of drugs and their talks with the physicians in high regard. At least four in ten patients in each of the three *N-P* groups described the drugs they had received as "very helpful." And in contrast to the physicians' views of the effectiveness of doctor-patient discussions, about six patients in ten in each of the three *N-P* groups regarded these talks as "very helpful." It should be noted that some of the differences observed between physcians and patients in the "very helpful" categories may be due to differences in manner of responding. Some studies have observed a tendency for well-educated respondents, as represented here by physicians, to choose less extreme response cate-

127

gories than others who are less well-educated.

The findings just presented are clearly but the beginnings of the analyses possible from the data available in this pilot study. As observed earlier, direct comparisons between physician and patient responses to the same questions have yet to be made; there is available a battery of items used in other studies of mental health against which physicians' judgments will be compared with regard to patients' emotional problems; and cross-analyses among important variables have just begun. Also, a wide range of open-end questions have provided numerous statements from physicians and patients from which hitherto unexamined variables will be examined, and from which it is likely that new hypotheses will be forthcoming.

SUMMARY AND CONCLUSIONS

A pilot study of "Patterns of Medical Care Related to Mental Illness" has been carried out in three medical groups associated with H.I.P., a prepaid, comprehensive medical care program in the New York City area. This paper describes the procedures used, some of the reasoning behind their use, and a number of findings both methodological and substantive.

Three groups of patients seen by the family physicians during the period December, 1961–February, 1962 were studied. Two of these groups were designated as "*N-P* diagnosis" and "*N-P* associated", based on information that appeared on the physicians' routine reports of services rendered. The third group, consisting of a sample of the other patients was designated as the control.

Interviews were held with the family physicians to obtain more information for the first two groups about the mental or emotional problem and medical care prescribed. In the case of the control group, the interview was designed to locate additional patients with emotional problems, and for these the main line of inquiry was pursued. Parallel interviews were conducted with patients in the three study groups.

For methodological purposes, the most significant findings thus far concern the various definitions of "emotional" problems used in screening procedures. The group identified in the physicians' routine reports of services as having a mental or emotional problem is comparatively small (4 per cent of all patients seen). This number is doubled when the report form is the means for identifying an *N-P* associated condition, and is greatly augmented to reach possibly 30 to 35 per cent when the report form is supplemented by an interview which covers mental and emotional problems present at a physician visit during the study period or at any previous visit. This escalation is even more marked in the interviews with patients. To an important extent, this is due to the inclusion of questions regarding worries or nervousness about their health.

Patients identified by their family physicians through different means as having mental or emotional problems were dissimilar in several respects; e.g., in their availability for interviewing, in the physician's view of the future course of the emotional problem, and in the medical care offered by the physician for the problem. At the same time, certain similarities were found among patients with emotional problems located in a different way; e.g., in the physician's view of the importance of the problem, and in the degree of interference caused by the emotional problems in the patient's major life activities.

Differences between patient and physician replies to parallel questions about patients' emotional problems demonstrated the need to interview both groups. There was, for example, a marked difference between them in the assessment of the seriousness of patients' emotional problems and in the prognosis of the future course of these problems.

At this time, it is clear that, with certain modifications, the methodology of the pilot study and the instruments used are suitable for developing a wide range of presently unavailable information on practices of family physicians in handling mental and emotional problems as they meet them.

129

REFERENCES

[1] Shepard, M., Fisher, M., Stein, L., and Kessel, W. I. N.: Psychiatric Morbidity in an Urban Group Practices. *Proceedings of the Royal Society of Medicine*, 1959, 52: 269–274.

[2] Kessel, W. I. N.: Psychiatric Morbidity in a London General Practice. *British Journal of Preventive and Social Medicine*, 1960, 14: 16–22.

[3] Hollingshead, A. B., and Redlich, F. C.: SOCIAL CLASS AND MENTAL ILLNESS. New York, John Wiley and Sons, 1958.

[4] Gurin, G., Veroff, J., and Feld, S.: AMERICANS VIEW THEIR MENTAL HEALTH. New York, Basic Books, 1960.

[5] Each of the three samples was stratified by month, by medical group, and by physician. Differential sampling ratios were used to distribute the interview load over time and place. Close to half of the patients with an *N-P* diagnosis, about half of those with an *N-P* check, and 3 in 100 of all the other patients eligible for selection fell in the three samples.

[6] A detailed examination of the physicians' routine report forms for a full year reveals that 13 per cent of all control group patients had an *N-P* diagnosis or *N-P* associated condition recorded at some time during the nine months preceding the three month study period. Half of these patients were reported by the physicians as having had an emotional problem at the time of the interview; the other half were not so reported.

APPENDIX

SCREENING QUESTIONS USED IN PHYSICIAN AND PATIENT
QUESTIONNAIRES TO DETERMINE N-P STATUS

Physician Questionnaire. The following screening questions were asked physicians about patients in the control group. (The term "condition" refers to the medical condition reported for the patient by the physician on the routine reporting form used by all H.I.P. physicians. "This visit" refers to the study visit during the period from December, 1961–February, 1962.)

A. Is this condition connected in any way with a psychological, mental, emotional, or personality disorder or condition?

...... Yes*

...... No (Skip to B)

B. Did the patient at this visit, present a psychological, mental, emotional or personality disorder or condition not connected with .... (condition)?

...... Yes*

...... No (Skip to C)

C. Has this patient ever presented a mental or emotional condition at any other visit to you?

...... Yes*

...... No (End interview)

Only questions B and C were asked if the physician's routine report form indicated that the patient was seen for a check-up.

NOTE: Patients for whom the physician answered in one of the categories marked with an asterisk (*) were classified as *N-P*. Further questions were asked the physician about these patients' emotional or psychological problems. The interviews were terminated at the points indicated for all other patients.

Patient Questionnaire. The following screeing questions were asked all patients:

2B. What did you see Dr. .... about? (Would you describe the symptoms to me?)

If reason for visit is "check-up", ask:

(1) Was the check-up for a condition already under medical care?

...... Yes (Skip to C)

...... No (Continue)

(2) Did the doctor find something wrong with you through this check-up?

...... Yes

...... No (Skip to Question 5)

C. What did the doctor say it was? (What did he call it? What medical terms did he use,)

F. What has the doctor recommended or said should be done about it?

(If respondent has mentioned an emotional or psychological condition, skip to question 6; (N–P Questions) otherwise continue)

3. Very often conditions for which people see doctors are aggravated or even caused by worries, nervousness, or tensions they have. Now in connection with the (condition) for which you saw Dr. . . . . , how much do you think this condition was affected by worries, nervousness or tension—very much, somewhat, or very little affected?

> . . . . . .Very much affected) Continue with question 4
> . . . . . .Somewhat affected)   "   "   "   "
> . . . . . .Very little affected) Skip to question 5
> . . . . . .Not at all affected)   "   "   "   "

4B. Did you discuss your worries, nervousness or tensions at all with Dr. . . . . at that visit in . . . .?
(month)

> . . . . . .Yes*
> . . . . . .No

4C. What about the times you saw Dr. . . . . before . . . .;
(month)
did you ever discuss with him your being worried or tense?

> . . . . . .Never saw him before
> . . . . . .Yes*
> . . . . . .No (If also "no" to B, skip to Question 27)

5. *For respondents who checked "No" in Question 2B(2), or "Very Little Affected" or "Not at all Affected" in Question 3:*

A. Did you ever discuss being worried, upset or nervous about your health with Dr. . . . .?

> . . . . . .Yes* (Skip to Question 5D)
> . . . . . .No

B. Did you ever discuss being worried, upset or nervous about something besides your health with Dr. . . . .?

. . . . . .Yes*

. . . . . .No (If "No" to *both* 5A and 5B, skip to Question 27)

NOTE: Respondents who replied in answer to Questions 2B, 2C or 2F that they

132

had discussed an emotional or psychological condition with their family physician at the time of the study visit were classified *"N-P."* Those who replied otherwise, but whose answers were classified in one of the categories marked with an asterisk (*) were also classified *"N-P."* Respondents classified *"N-P"* were asked additional questions related to the *"N-P"* condition discussed with the physician. All others were skipped to a later part of the questionnaire to be asked all patients, *"N-P"* and "non-*N-P.*"

ACKNOWLEDGMENTS.

The present study has been a joint effort involving a number of disciplines, the interests of which have been represented by persons who have participated in the planning and execution of the study. We wish to acknowledge the aid and cooperation of the medical groups which participated in this study. These are the Astoria Medical Group, the East Bronx Medical Group and the New York Medical Group. The family physicians, internists and pediatricians deserve a special word of thanks for their forbearance in the face of the exceptional amount of time required for the interview phase of the study. Finally, for their active participation in the design and planning of this study we wish to thank Dr. Jack Elinson of Columbia University School of Public Health and Administrative Medicine, and Dr. Henry Makover of Albert Einstein School of Medicine.

This project was supported in part by research grant MH 09172–02S1, received from the National Institutes of Health, Public Health Service.

133

COLOMBIAN NATIONAL HEALTH SURVEY
PLANNING, METHODS AND OPERATION

PLANNING

MARGARET D. WEST

In September, 1963, a group from the two Americas met in New York, under the sponsorship of the Pan American Health Organization and the Milbank Memorial Fund, to explore ways of making a study of health manpower requirements and resources in a Latin American country. That group discussed many aspects of the health problems of nations—how they can be measured, the relevance of such measurements to health planning and the study of health manpower requirements, and the changes that may prove necessary in medical education to prepare the profession for the tasks ahead.

Basic to the formulation of national health manpower plans, they saw need for the following:[1]

1. A profile of the health of the people, measured in terms of mortality, morbidity and other health indices—all related to demographic characteristics—age, sex, education, economic status and place of residence.

2. A picture of health services currently supplied—the effective demand—including physician visits, hospitalization and other services, again related to demographic data.

3. A picture of unmet health service needs and demands.

4. An inventory of present health manpower resources, estimates of functional productivity and projections of future supply.

5. A parallel picture of supply and utilization of hospitals and other health service facilities.

6. An appraisal of educational resources available and the manpower pool on which they draw.

7. A study of education requirements for the future.

8. An assessment of the economic resources available for health services and education for such services.

9. Establishment of goals for health achievement related to present and projected resources and determination of the manpower requirements for those goals.

The Round Table agreed that such a study, on a pilot basis, should be undertaken in a Latin American country. Within a few months Colombia had been chosen as that country, a decision based in large part on the existence of imaginative leadership in the Colombian Ministry of Health and Colombian Association of Medical Schools, their joint concern about the organization of health services and their demonstrated ability and interest in working closely together.

PRELIMINARIES

In January, 1964, a group visited Colombia to look into the feasibility of making a pilot study on health manpower in that country. Preliminary plans were developed at those meetings for a group of interrelated studies under the co-direction of the Ministry of Health, to be represented by Alfonso Mejia, and the Association of Medical Schools, to be represented by Raul Paredes. These studies were to be undertaken with the participation of the schools of medicine and nursing, the national statistical department, the hospitals and the local health services. More specifically, the Ministry was to have primary responsibility for demographic and mortality studies, a national health survey, studies of nursing resources, health services institution and socioeconomic studies, while the Association of Medical Schools would undertake primary responsibility for studies of medical resources, medical education and nursing education.

The National Health Survey, then, was planned and carried out under the direction of the Ministry of Health, with the very active participation of the seven medical schools of the nation, acting both collectively and individually. It was not an isolated research enterprise, but an integral part of a fairly comprehensive study designed to give a base for planning to meet national health manpower needs.

The design of the present Round Table calls first for the presentation and discussion of methodology of the Colombian national health sur-

136

vey, to be followed by discussion on selected findings and of implications for health planning. This review will be limited, then, to what was done in the Colombian study, and why it was done that way.

Subsequent papers will deal with the general design of the health survey, by Aurelio Pabón; the design and selection of the sample, by Garrie Losee and Luis Carlos Gómez; the household survey, by Aldemar Gómez; and the clinical examination, by Carlos Agualimpia.

MAJOR DECISIONS

The most important decision was that the survey, using probability sampling, should be national in scope. A household interview and a clinical examination were to be included, with a sample of some 10,000 households containing approximately 50,000 members for the interview survey, and a subsample of 5,000 individuals who were selected for clinical examinations.

A second major decision was to use medical students as interviewers for the household survey, and residents in internal medicine and pediatrics as the clinical examiners. That decision was made in part because of the limited availability of well-educated people for purposes of interviewing and, of equal importance, because it was believed that the study would offer a unique opportunity for medical students and young physicians actually to get out into the country and to see what people were like in their homes and what their health problems were in relation to the places in which they lived.

Survey Content

In accordance with the original guidelines, the survey was designed to provide data on the perception of illness, the physical status and the receipt of health services, as well as on education, occupation, dwelling conditions and other social and economic characteristics of the population.

The sample design and the questions included permitted analyses of health characteristics in relation to five major geographic areas of the country, by age group and sex, by urban-rural residence, by economic grouping, by occupation, by educational status. And, uniquely for a population of this size, the study will permit analysis of the relationship between the perception of illness by individuals, their health status as evaluated by physicians with the aid of laboratory findings, and the receipt of health services.

137

Timing

Planning for the health survey was carried out within strictures of time, money and staff. Conversations in Colombia began in January, 1964, and the study was started in July of that year. From the summer of 1964 until the summer of 1965 (the first year), national planning and pretesting took place. The Health Survey itself took place in the second year (summer, 1965, to summer, 1966). The third year (summer, 1966, to the present) was a period of analysis and preliminary presentation of results to national and international audiences. Now the findings are being used as a basis for national health planning by the Ministry of Health, as a basis for program development in schools of medicine by the Association of Medical Schools and for the development of experimentations with new kinds of teams to provide health services to population groups that now suffer from the lack of services.

Budget

The budget available for the national health survey was limited. In terms of experience in the United States, the budget was fantastically low. The total expenditures for the survey were only $168,000 (United States currency). This low expenditure was achieved in part because the time of the medical student interviewers was donated, although the figure does include travel and per diem expenses of those students. Also, the budget does not include some of the contributions of consultant time that were not met through the Colombian budget.

Unit costs for the household interviews have been computed at $8.33 per family, and $1.40 per individual. The cost of the clinical evaluation was $17.80 per individual examined. In terms of cost of the entire universe, the household interview and the clinical evaluation together represent a cost of 0.9 cents for each person in Colombia.

Staffing

Finding and training the staff for the project was a major problem. When the project was officially undertaken, Alfonso Mejia had to find for the central office a director of household interviews, a director of clinical examinations, statisticians, a dentist, health educators, a field operations analyst and other supporting staff. For the field operations each team required a public health physician as supervisor, an environmental sanitation inspector as field administrator, six medical student interviewers, a public health dentist, two examining physicians, residents in internal medicine and pediatrics and two dispensary assistants, a laboratory assistant and a nursing auxiliary. These teams were assembled in a variety of ingenious ways. The public health physicians, sanitation inspectors, dentists and nurse auxiliaries were primarily borrowed from regional and local public health units. The medical students and medical residents were provided by their teaching institution, which awarded the student academic or training credit for the field experience. Because of the difficulty in securing well-qualified laboratory assistants, and because of the need to have the procedures of these workers highly standardized, the Colombia National Institute of Health undertook two training courses, each of four weeks duration, for laboratory assistants. On the completion of these training programs the best students were selected for participation in the field work.

Consultants for the design of the study were drawn in the United States from the Division of Public Health Methods and the National Center for Health Statistics of the Public Health Service, and from the Census Bureau. These included specialists in sample design, schedule design, interviewer training, field staff logistics, household interviewing, clinical examination, data processing and analysis. Physicians from several countries also served as consultants as did the staff of the Pan American Health Organization and the Milbank Memorial Fund.

Study methods

The development of the sample design was a basic problem in a country that did not have a recent census, and in which travel was often difficult. The solution of the problem of sample design was one of the achievements of the study. Forty primary sampling units were selected for interviews and clinical examinations.

The field work was planned to cover two half-samples of the country, the first in the fall of 1965, the second in the winter and spring of 1966. In each of the 40 primary sampling units, an average of about 240 households were interviewed and 130 individuals examined.

The complete operation was pretested in the small town of Fusagasuga and the surrounding countryside and in Bogotá, the national capital. The test was conducted with the participation of the prospective field supervisors, who thus received practical training in field procedures. It tested the feasibility of the local operating procedures, the effectiveness of the survey methods, procedures and techniques and the precision and utility of the information secured.

Field training was related to the calendar of operations and to the needs of the institutions supplying personnel. Thus medical students

139

and certain other staff members received their preliminary orientation and training in their own schools.

In the field four or five teams worked simultaneously, with operations for each team beginning at staggered dates, so that staff from the central office could participate in the preparations at each center. The cycle in each primary sampling unit lasted for about three weeks.

Meeting the time schedule was no easy task. Some of the units could be reached only by airplane. Some were in areas that were not accessible to airplane, but required traveling by jeep over mountain roads. Some interviewers took to horseback, others to canoes. Clinical examination sites had to be found or improvised. Interviewers had first to persuade, and then to arrange for persons selected for the clinical sample to get to the examination center. Thus, major logistical problems were encountered in reaching the units, in conducting interviews and in carrying out the clinical examinations. Ingenuity triumphed.

Near the Ecuadorian border, the sisters of a convent moved out to provide housing for the survey staff. UNICEF loaned cars and the Army loaned helicopters.

For each of the 40 units, segmentation activities and a cartographic review were made one or two months before the beginning of the field work. At that time the environmental sanitation officer subsampled the rural segments of more than 15 dwellings to reduce the number of selections to about ten. Several weeks before the beginning of activities in each of the sampling units an officer from the central office made a visit of from one to three days to establish contact with the local authorities and persons of influence within the community, to explain the program, secure commitments of cooperation and participate in the final field training and practice.

In view of the scarcity of health educators and the newness of the idea of the household and clinical examination it was essential that all participants in the survey engage in continuous educational work. A variety of educational activities were undertaken by the staff to develop public understanding and acceptance of the scope and importance of the survey, and to encourage participation. These included presentation of the survey to many groups in the community, including the mayor and his staff, clergy, school staffs and the press, radio and television. Ingenious special incentives were employed to encourage the participation of individuals selected for clinical examination, which included free transportation and payment of wages lost because of the time required for the examination under certain circumstances, and food sup-

140

plements (CARE packages) were given or medical care was provided to certain individuals. The team also undertook to forward the findings of the clinical examination to physicians or institutions authorized by the patient. Persons who seemed unwilling to participate in the study were given particular attention, not only by the official sources, but also by such methods as having a person who had been examined go back to his own neighborhood and talk to another who had refused examination, to explain to him both what examination entailed and how important it was that each individual participate.

The high response rate—97.2 per cent participation for the household survey and 95.6 per cent for the clinical examination—was a tribute both to the competence and dedication of the staff and to these educational activities.

After three days of preliminaries in each area, household interviews began on the fourth day, and clinical examinations on the seventh, by which time it had been possible to select candidates for the clinical examinations from the household for which interviews had been completed.

The simultaneous scheduling of interviews and clinical examinations facilitated community cooperation, encouraged collaboration among the interview and clinical staff and helped solve the problems arising from procedures requiring two contacts with the patient, such as tuberculin testing. The clinical examination, whenever possible, was established in a hospital or health center, although in some areas the space secured was fairly primitive. Interviewers worked from these same centers, setting forth on foot, by minibus or, in some areas, on horseback, or in a plane, a launch, or even a canoe. Procedures were established to assure that each household and segment was indeed covered and the interviewer did not overlook selected dwellings.

An important aspect of the field operations from the point of view of medical education was the scheduling of clinical epidemiological meetings. These meetings, held in the evenings, gave the field team greater understanding of the operations of the survey, emphasized the social value of preventive medicine in public health, and the usage and advantage of epidemiological methods and were a fine tool to educate medical students in the social aspects of health and disease. One such conference was held in Socorra, a small town reached by a thrilling drive over the high Andes. The case selected for discussion was of a man in his thirties who had leprosy. The young medical student first described the household situation—a household in which the father, a

141

policeman, had three years of education, the mother none; in which the mother had had four pregnancies and several miscarriages in the course of three years; and in which, of the four small children, three had fairly serious physical defects. The clinician then discussed the father's leprosy and some of the familial implications of the clinical findings and the epidemiology of leprosy in Colombia. The whole group of students and clinicians then engaged in an active round-table discussion. It was apparent that these young people never before had such an opportunity to see health problems in a meaningful relationship to a family and the community, as well as in relation to the individual human being. The Colombian medical schools have indicated that the kinds of perception gained by medical students in these field operations are having a substantial effect on the teaching in their institutions.

An important aspect of the methodology of the survey was the way in which the consultants were used. Their availability made it possible to conduct the study in a minimum of time, with a maximum of reliability and usefulness. The effectiveness of the consultants was due not only to their individual specialized knowledge, but no less to: 1. the use of persons with a wide variety of complementary skills, as a group, in a continuing relationship; 2. the arrangement for intermittent visits of consultants for periods of one week to a month, so that it was always clear that the consultants were helpers and not operators; and 3. the scheduling of short visits by members of the Colombian staff to the United States, where they discussed their problems with specialists in the Census Bureau and the National Center for Health Statistics, and where they saw in operation household surveys and clinical examinations of the United States National Health Survey.

The most important problems encountered in the conduct of the study were those related to staffing, which affected planning, the administration, the supervision and the analysis of the study. Some of the problems were inherent in an undertaking with so little lead time, and one with no assurance of job continuity. The lack of a competent full-time data processing specialist to act as advisor to the study and as liaison between the study group and the census organization was a major deficiency in the study. Also evident was the need for a statistical group to give more adequate time to the design of schedules, the formulation of plans for analysis, the development of tabulating plans and specifications and more pretesting and preliminary analysis. The effect of these omissions has been a delay in the analysis and use of much potentially valuable data.

142

In reviewing the whole enterprise, the consultants believe that several important trends have emerged.

1. The large (and successful) ad hoc technical assistance program;
2. Unusually "kibitz-free" project; the major problems were technical ones, as they should be; no interference by administrators, nor serious budget squeezes;
3. Development of the nucleus of a health statistics center in Colombia;
4. Benefits to scientific community of Colombia—a new awareness of surveys as a scientific tool in medical and social fields;
5. The innovations of the sample design—having the clinical sample as a subsample of the household sample was one; another was the use of two half-samples and application of two-stage controlled selection;
6. The carrying out of this complex operation within two years starting with no staff and no organization.

The findings of the National Health Survey are discussed elsewhere from the methodological point of view, but it should be stressed here that the design of the sample and the schedules will permit an analysis of the relationships of the perception of health and disease by the individuals and by physicians aided by laboratory findings, and the receipt of health services in relation to such variables as age, sex, education, economic status, household environment, urbanization and geographic region. Because the survey made use of many of the definitions and procedures of the National Health Survey of the United States, a basis was also provided for comparison of findings in the two countries, as well as in other countries that are using or that may use a similar methodology.

REFERENCES

[1] This section is adapted from Health Manpower and Medical Education in Latin America, *Milbank Memorial Fund Quarterly*, 42, 61–63, January, 1964.

ADMINISTRATION

AURELIO PABON

According to the initial design of the sample, 10,000 families with approximately 50,000 members were to be interviewed from which 5,200 persons would be selected for clinical examination.

Ultimately, 9,797 dwellings were selected. If the 877 empty buildings are excluded, which correspond to families with permanent residence elsewhere, 8,969 dwellings remained with families to be interviewed. Of these, 97.2 per cent were interviewed for a total of 51,473 persons of which 5,258 were selected for the clinical examination, 5,189 appointments were scheduled and 5,127, or 95.6 per cent, actually underwent the examination.

These response rates are high, especially if Colombia's lack of experience with this type of study is considered. The explanation for the high rate lies in the manner in which the investigation was planned and its orientation, factors that depended on those conducting it, the characteristics of the Colombian people and the methods used. The general lines of the procedures followed are reviewed here.

ADMINISTRATIVE ORGANIZATION

The National Health Survey is a part of the larger survey on health manpower and medical education. The survey was administered and organized by the Ministry of Public Health. It sought the maximum utilization of existing resources in health services and medical education institutions.

Two administrative levels developed: central administration and field operations.

144

Central Administration

The personnel of the central office were: The director of the study of Health Manpower in the Ministry; the head of the household interviews, the head of the clinical examination, the chief statistician, a group of statisticians and an analyst for field operations. From time to time, two health educators and two dentists also participated.

The administrative unit planned, administered, directed and supervised. It received technical assistance from other sections of the Ministry of Health, the National Department of Statistics, the universities and different professional associations in the country. It also received international assistance from officials of the Pan American Health Organization, the United States Public Health Service (and its census division) and the Milbank Memorial Fund.

The members of the central team traveled on several occasions to become acquainted with and to observe the development of the National Health Survey of the United States.

Field Operations

Five field teams were organized for the development of the local operations. The teams were composed of persons connected with the health services and the universities and some were commissioned for a specific period of time.

Each team was composed of:

A field supervisor, director of local activities, a task for which a public health physician with experience in the area was chosen.

A public health dentist, who conducted part of the clinical examination and acted as coordinator for the clinical team. This specialist was selected for his administrative experience, availability of time away from his place of work and because of his satisfactory understanding of the completed indices of oral health.

A field administrator, who supervised the administrative aspects of the local unit, a task delegated to a supervisor of environmental health, an official who, because of his occupation, had wide experience especially in rural areas. As far as possible, the administrators were located in geographic regions with which they were already familiar because of their previous experience.

Six interviewers, medical students in their final years of study were chosen for reasons already cited.

Two medical examiners, a job given to a resident in internal medicine and another in pediatrics connected with the medical schools.

145

Three auxiliaries, a nurse, x-ray technician, and laboratory technician.

One receptionist, who was typically a woman from the locale, whose duties were simple and required knowledge of the area and the cultural habits of the people.

PRETEST OF THE METHODOLOGY

Several months before beginning the final field work, the methodology proposed for the development of the study was pretested. The pretest was used to train the field supervisors in the techniques of the interviews and clinical examinations. The supervisors acted as interviewers, participated in the directing of the field operations and contributed to the adjustments and modifications of the original plans.

The pretest permitted verification of the feasibility of the local operation, helped to determine the composition of the clinical team, established the effectiveness of the public relations methods and the efficiency of the field procedures. With the pilot study as a basis, the method for the selection of the local sample was made precise, and certain procedures and questions were modified. Finally, the tabulation and analysis of the data obtained in the interviews and clinical examinations served as a basis for the initial plan of tabulations.

SELECTION AND TRAINING OF PERSONNEL

In the places of employment of personnel who might be eligible to join the field survey team, a general report was given on the principles, objectives and organization of the survey and on the participation that would be expected of each group. When the number of candidates was larger than needed, a selection was made by evaluating the qualities of the candidates emphasizing their availability and interest, good personal relations, experience in handling people and responsibility in faithfully completing their assignments. Criteria were also established for each group based on academic requirements and other conditions.

Central training

Those selected for the field teams attended conferences at medical schools or the Ministry of Public Health to inform them about the principles of the study, its objectives and their specific functions. They were also trained in the detailed methods, techniques and procedures

146

that they would use. During the training, the participants were evaluated and again selected on the basis of their capacities.

Local retraining

In each location, before beginning work, a retraining program was conducted for all the personnel of the team to complement the training they had received initially from the central administrative teams to emphasize the principal aspects of the interview procedure and techniques, and those of the clinical examination; and to provide information about the specific operation in the locale.

EDUCATING AND REPORTING ACTIVITIES

While the health educators were being oriented to work in specific areas, thorough reports on the purposes of the National Health Survey and the Study of Health Manpower were given to the press, radio and television.

Meetings held with different professional associations and other important public groups, at both national and local levels, allowed these groups in turn to inform the community about the purposes and advantages of the study and to solicit and guarantee cooperation from the community.

PRIOR VISITS

Officials from the central office made two such visits to each primary sampling unit with the following purpose:

First, to determine the selected segments of the sample, to elaborate the detailed draft of these, to identify methods of communication and transportation, to advance first contacts with the interviewees and to begin the informational activities.

Second, to provide information, request cooperation, select sites for offices, find quarters for personnel and study means of transportation.

CENTRAL TIMETABLE FOR ACTIVITIES

In working out the timetable consideration was given to distance between work units, the customary means of transportation, weather and local events. In certain places it is impossible to travel during the rainy season, while in others the chief means of transportation is by water. Possible conflict with regional festivals and harvests was taken into consideration.

The limited time of doctors and medical students, who could be separated from their regular work only for relatively short periods of time, also had to be considered. This resulted in the development of a detailed and tightly scheduled timetable which fortunately was filled to the letter. Five teams worked simultaneously, staggering their activities to facilitate supervision.

The operation was carried out between September, 1965, and July, 1966, in three stages separated by the New Year and Holy Week holidays.

LOCAL TIMETABLE FOR ACTIVITIES

The local timetable took into consideration particular circumstances in each location.

Work began with the arrival of the supervisor and field administrator and lasted for three weeks. The interviews were started two to three days before the clinical examinations so that a sufficient number of patients would have been chosen for the examination since they were selected by a special sample system at the same time as the interviews. The examinations were even given on holidays to facilitate the attendance of workers. The simultaneous operation of the household survey and the clinical examination facilitated the cooperation of the community, stimulated the team's spirit and helped to overcome the problems of a procedure that required two contacts with the patient. The activities of the teams were reevaluated daily.

Local resources and available installations and teams were frequently used. However, all measurement instruments for children and adults were installed to obtain uniform results that would be unaffected by the different types of instruments or by their limited local availability.

Other Means of Obtaining Cooperation

All the participating personnel were given instructions about the courteous and considerate treatment of those being interviewed and examined. To avoid delays in assisting the patients, appointments were scheduled and the patients were requested to arrive a half hour before the appointed time. Also, every effort was made to examine patients who arrived at unscheduled times.

148

Employers and teachers were requested to grant permission for their employees and students to attend the examination. In some instances a day's wages was paid.

Vehicles were placed at the disposal of individuals in accordance with distance and common modes of transportation; these included animals, motor vehicles, launches and, in one unit, even airplanes from airports located in rural areas. When public transportation was available, the fare was paid on request.

If in the course of the clinical examination a disease was diagnosed, the patient was given drugs and directed to existing health services for the treatment to be continued. In each case the results of the examination were referred to the doctor or the designated institution.

People with low incomes who attended the clinical examination were given CARE packages of groceries, which stimulated attendance among these groups.

The low "mortality" rate of the samples should be attributed not only to these stimuli, but also to certain characteristics common to the Colombian people, such as an excellent understanding of the goals of the survey, and widespread acceptance of the recommendations of their leaders and authorities. Civil and ecclesiastical authorities, the medical corps and leaders on the national, departmental and municipal levels gave unanimous and decisive support. The general lack of medical attention services made attendance at the medical examinations attractive for many people who had never previously received a thorough physical examination.

DATA PROCESSING

The information collected was periodically sent to the central office by the safest means of transportation. Material was frequently carried by officials of the survey on their trips.

As the information began to arrive from each unit, the books were systematically revised, classified and stored before being submitted to statistical analysis. The material for special examinations (laboratory, x-ray and electrocardiograms) was given to personnel connected with the medical schools and public service laboratories.

The processing of the data by computers loaned by government organizations (DANE, ICSS) and by some private institutions resulted in considerable delays and posed even greater obstacles than the field collection of the information. Inexperience in this field, and the lack of special teams and programmers resulted in underestimating the required time, resources and personnel that were necessary for the analysis of the data.

These difficulties were overcome by the assistance provided by officials of the Pan American Health Organization and the United States National Center for Health Statistics, which conducted some of the final work with its own equipment.

MORTALITY AND MORBIDITY

CARLOS AGUALIMPIA

An objective diagnosis of the health of a population, based on the nature and magnitude of health problems as well as their determinants, constitutes a basic phase in the planning, development and evaluation of health control programs. The solid foundation for such a diagnosis must be based on accurate knowledge about the mortality and morbidity in any nation.

Nevertheless, the mortality rate alone is inadequate to serve as the sole index of a country's health status for the following reasons:

1. It deals only with fatal diseases, minimizing those that are not always lethal, and completely ignoring nonfatal illnesses.

2. It records only the immediate cause of death without considering other circumstances related to the reported cause that also may have contributed to the outcome.

3. Its applicability is reduced as the danger of death from controllable diseases lessens.

4. The reporting of mortality data is often incomplete. Its comprehensiveness varies in the different regions of the country.

5. In each region, for various reasons, the quality of the data is deficient and uneven. For example, according to the study of mortality in Colombia, 40 per cent of the recorded deaths did not have medical certification. Special investigations in two important cities showed that 43 per cent of the diagnoses in doctors' death certificates were incorrect.[3] In 1965, poorly defined or unknown causes of death accounted for 13.5 per cent of all deaths.[2]

151

Specific and specialized studies of morbidity may be useful for a wide variety of purposes, but they do not present a general picture of morbidity in a country since they deal with only local problems, one aspect of morbidity or one group of individuals.

The only general morbidity survey carried out in Colombia has been the National Health Study. From August, 1965, to July, 1966, this program collected information about the health conditions in the nation from a representative sample of the noninstitutionalized population.

The National Health Study is useful for determining the prevalence of health conditions including those afflictions that, in spite of their minimal severity, affect human well-being, reduce work capacity and increase the need for medical attention. The diagnosis of all of the health problems that may coexist in any given moment provides a more complete understanding of the current state of health. The traditional sources of morbidity data are the established national records relating to the population treated by medical services. In Colombia, these sources are chiefly the records of outpatients and hospitalized cases where consultations are reported by the institutions, and the records of communicable diseases, which must be reported. Typically, these sources of information are incomplete and not uniform. Since the information is usually collected without adhering to clearly established standards, curious errors in reporting often occur. For example, in 1965, the total number of deaths from tetanus (1,997) was greater than the number of cases reported by doctors and institutions (754), and the number of deaths from rabies (47)—a 100 per cent fatal disease—was less than the number of cases reported (109). Also the reported cases of malaria and leprosy constituted respectively 62 per cent and 24 per cent of the number of cases recorded in specific campaigns against these diseases. Reported cases of diphtheria and tetanus were one-third of the number of hospital discharges for the same diseases, though notification supposedly includes hospitalized cases.[6]

The population referred to in the systematic registry does not represent the general population of the country, inasmuch as utilization of services is determined by social and personal factors as well as by political administrative decisions, rather than by the volume and acuteness of the health problems. Also, the systematic registry shows the illnesses, but not the people who have them. One person may repeatedly request one or several medical care services and, since all persons do not seek medical services, it is impossible to determine the number of ill people in the general population. This is especially true in Colombia, where

152

the medical care services are concentrated on one-third of the population, who average five medical service requests a year, whereas the remaining 70 per cent of the population does not receive medical care at all in a given year.

On the other hand, the different coverage, which is incomplete and overimposed, and the variation in the data collection methods and diagnostic facilities dictate that the data of the systematic registry cannot be consolidated or compared within the different regions and institutions. Consequently the registries barely show the primary cause for consultation and the age and sex of the patient, which are insufficient to relate the problems to other important variables that define its multiple cause.

The procedures and techniques of the National Health Survey also guaranteed the exactness, uniformity and integrity of the information that was gathered. Factors that might have affected the observations were controlled through the precise definition of criteria, the type and uniformity of the instruments used and the selection, training and supervision of the personnel.

Exact diagnosis also depends on the methods of observation and the technical equipment utilized, but the medical services in Colombia generally lack these methods and facilities.

In 1962, 42 per cent of the nation's institutions did not regularly produce an adequate case history, 64 per cent lacked laboratory facilities, 66 per cent did not use x-ray services and 90 per cent did not use pathological anatomy services.[7] In 1965, only seven per cent of the physicians used even minimum equipment in their professional services.

The National Health Study precisely determined only those illnesses that could be identified with the procedures used. In spite of the fact that the information was collected with standard equipment and fulfilled the basic objectives that had been set, some procedures useful in the identification of certain diseases (e.g., cancer, mental illness) had to be excluded because of the procedural difficulties that could have been involved, the absence of an established methodology for their collective application and the limitations imposed by the examination of groups of volunteers.

The specific objectives and methods of the Colombian National Health Survey are described in other papers in this volume. The study was partly based on previously verified studies conducted in several parts of the world, and in particular drew on the experience of the Health Household Interview survey and the Health Examination Survey in the United States.

The Colombian study, however, has some unusual, distinctive characteristics. These include:

1. It is a pilot experiment, conducted to facilitate the development of this type of study in other Latin American countries. This involved constant efforts to maintain costs at the lowest possible levels and the adaptation of the methods to the circumstances of the country.

2. It was conceived as a special program of limited duration.

3. It made maximum use of the personnel, facilities, installations and equipment already available in the health services and in the sector of medical education.

4. It incorporated auxiliary personnel to conduct some aspects of the clinical examination commensurate with their capacities and level of education.

5. It used field work as a teaching instrument to complete the experiments of the participants in the social and sanitary conditions of the country.

REFERENCES

[1] United States National Committee of Vital and Health Statistics, *Conceptual Problems in Developing an Index of Health,* Public Health Service Publication No. 1,000, Series 2, No. 17, May, 1967.

[2] Pabón R., A., *Estudio de Mortalidad* (Mortality Study), Bogotá, Ministry of Public Health, 1967.

[3] Correa, P., Llanos, G. and Aguilera, B., Estudio sobre causas de muerte de Cali (Studies of Death Causes in Cali), *Medical Antioch,* 14, 359, May, 1964.

[4] Ministry of Public Health, Division of Technical and Auxiliary Services, INFORMACIÓN BÁSICA PARA EL PLAN NACIONAL DE SALUD (Basic information for the National Health Plan), Volume 1, *Morbidity,* Bogotá, 1967.

[5] Ministry of Public Health Section of Life Statistics, *La Encuesta Hospitalaria* (The hospital survey), Bogotá, 1963.

[6] Paredes Manrique, R., Métodos y resultados del Estudio de Recursos Humanos y Educativos en Colombia (Methods and results of the Study of Human and Educational resources in Colombia), presented at the International Conference on Human Resources, Maracay, June, 1967.

[7] General methodological aspects of the National Health Study can be studied in greater detail in Ministry of Public Health, Colombian Association of Medical Faculties (Schools) STUDY OF HUMAN RESOURCES FOR HEALTH AND MEDICAL EDUCATION IN COLOMBIA, Volume 1, METHODOLOGY, Washington, Pan American Health Organization, 1967.

SAMPLING THEORY AND PROCEDURES

GARRIE J. LOSEE

In July, 1965, at a meeting in Bogotá of members of the Ministry of Health and the Colombian Association of Medical Schools, the Minister of Health selected a single number from a table of random numbers, and thus determined the identity of the 40 sample cities and municipios of the Colombian National Health Survey. This was perhaps the most dramatic moment in a series of new, exciting and challenging events which summed together mark a long step forward in scientific investigation in Latin America.

It is doubtful whether any existing set of statistical information on the health and socioeconomic characteristics of the peoples of a Latin American nation can stand up as well to scientific criticism as can this study. That this is so is only partly attributable to the statistical design that will be described here. It is instead largely attributable to the faithful execution of the design.

Criticism of statistical data can be made on several grounds. Good statistical information should be relevant, reliable, accurate and specific. Statistical sampling has developed over the past 30 years to a level of high technical sophistication. The procedure is well established for selecting representative samples of the population to be studied by a sample survey, for forming unbiased estimates and for describing the probable reliability of the estimates derived from the survey. If the need is for information on which to base national health or economic planning, the sample should be a representative sample of all the people of the nation; that is, every person should have a chance of being selected in the sample. In that way every characteristic of the popula-

155

tion will be represented in the results, subject to the limitations of the sample size and, consequently, sampling error. Thus the appropriate proportions of males, females, children, adults, villagers, city dwellers, farmers, unemployed persons and so on are included in the sample.

Information derived from convenient samples such as patients in the hospital in which the researcher works, outpatients of a nearby clinic, the population of several "poor" barrios and a municipio close to a school of public health is frequently relevant in formulating national health policy, but it is not specific to the needs for information on which to base national policy. Information on the extent of internal parasitic infections in Colombia was available prior to the National Health Survey from several such convenient samples. Put together, these sources are at best a patch-quilt of information that could lead to serious consequences if the information were used to formulate national or regional policy of government.

Few purely technical problems were encountered in designing the sample of the Colombian National Health Survey. On the other hand many practical problems were encountered in implementing the survey design, but on the whole these were satisfactorily resolved. In the practice of good sample design no unique method exists for selecting a sample for a particular purpose, although given a certain set of conditions the choice of sampling methods is limited to a few that offer the best *a priori* possibility of providing sufficiently reliable estimates for the purposes of the study at the least possible cost. In the case of national household interview surveys this nearly always leads to the use of multistage cluster samples with stratification of sampling units at the first and often subsequent stages of selection. The use of these techniques in the Colombian National Health Survey is amply described in the accompanying text. Whenever applicable, experience accumulated in developing the present design of the United States National Health Survey was transferred and adapted to Colombia.

At this point it may be well to describe some of the problems faced in 1963, when planning the sample design, which are peculiar to the survey to be conducted in Colombia, their solutions and some of the features of the design that distinguish it from others. First, Colombia is a geographically large country containing vast stretches of sparsely populated territory. Second, at the time when the sample was selected a population census had not been conducted since 1951, and that one with questionable accuracy, although a national population census was conducted in 1964. The accuracy of the 1951 census was question-

156

able because someone remarked, after it was proposed to use its results in designing the current survey, that the 1951 census was not good —and he said that he knew this because he had directed the census operations. Third, because of the terrain, transportation, except by air, is extremely difficult between many sections of the country and in some areas communities are relatively isolated from their neighbors.

In the United States, information is obtained by the National Center for Health Statistics from two separate surveys, the Health Household Interview Survey and the Health Examination Survey. Due to differing cost and variance configurations, the designs of the two surveys are quite different. The Health Household Interview Survey with low unit costs has a large sample of households (about 40,000 annually) in a large sample of places (over 300) throughout the country. On the other hand, for the Health Examination Survey, a relatively small number of adults was examined (6,500) in a small sample of places (42) because unit costs were high.

The first basic decision made in the design of the Colombian National Health Survey was that the primary focus of attention would be on the collection of information from both interviews and examinations to provide a composite picture of an individual's health status, both as he knew it and as it was known through a clinical examination, for a sample of individuals representative of the Colombian population. Drawing largely on the United States experience this decision implied a small sample of places and persons. Since no additional travel costs for interviewers and supervisors was involved, it was possible to provide greater reliability for disability and medical resource utilization data at little extra cost by collecting interview data only for a larger sample of persons than would be both interviewed and examined in each sample place. The design therefore called for interviewing persons in a sample of about 240 households in each of 40 places, either a city or a municipio. A subsample of one out of every ten persons interviewed was selected to receive a clinical examination.

To overcome the limitations described earlier the following features became part of the survey design. Since the intendancies and comisarias accounted for nearly half of the land area of Colombia, but only 1.3 per cent of the population, these extraterritorial zones were excluded from the study. Their exclusion does not create any bias problem since, if included, even extreme variations from the characteristics of the bulk of the population would not have noticeable effect on national averages.

157

Costs involved in travel, both to the areas sampled and within these areas were minimized in the survey design by having a concentrated sample in a small number of places. The sample places were restricted in size to include only a single city or part of a city and in rural areas usually a single municipio.

Increased efficiency of design, that is, greater reliability per unit of investment, can usually be gained at the sample selection stage when the proportion of total population contained in each place is accurately known. Believing that the 1951 Population Census figures no longer represented the current proportion of population in many places, the population estimates of the Ministry of Health based on adjusted population projections were used in assigning proportions of total population to places in the selection. The resulting unbiased estimates of health characteristics were later adjusted according to a ratio estimation technique to conform with 1964 Population Census totals, not known at the selection stage (1964), but available in 1967 at the estimation stage.

Other technical features of the design worthy of note were: 1. the use of controlled selection in selecting sample places; 2. the provision of flexibility in sample size by the division of the total sample into two balanced random subsamples, each having 20 sample places; 3. the use of 1964 census maps and population counts for sample places in selecting clusters of about ten sample households; 4. a simple but efficient method for estimating sampling errors; and 5. a continued awareness of measurement errors as evidenced by a systematic reinterview program, standardized training of interviewers and examining staff and standardized control procedures throughout the data collection and data processing stages.

DESIGN OF THE SAMPLE

LUIS CARLOS GOMEZ

The universe of the National Health Survey was the civilian non-institutional population of the departments—an intermediate political administrative division—whose surface covers 52.7 per cent of the country, but which contained 98.7 per cent of the total population. Because of their low population density (1.3 per cent of the population) and their rudimentary communication, extensive geographical areas of the country (47.3 per cent of the country's surface) did not become part of the sampled universe. The inclusion of this 1.3 per cent of the population would have involved enormous procedural difficulties and a disproportionate increase in the costs.

GENERAL PROCEDURE

The design of the sample was carried out in two stages.

In the first stage 716 primary sample units were defined and grouped into 40 strata. One unit was selected from each stratum.

In the second stage, the selected primary sample units were subdivided into segments of approximately ten dwellings per unit from which 24 were selected. The 960 segments composed the sample for the household interviews. For the clinical examination, a subsample of approximately one of every ten interviewees was taken.

In Table 1, the size of the samples of the National Study of Colombia and the National Health Poll of the United States are compared.

The Primary Sample Units

The primary sample units were composed of municipalities with a

159

TABLE I. COMPARISON OF SAMPLE SIZE, COLOMBIA AND UNITED STATES

| | Colombia | | United States | |
| | | Per Cent of Total | | Per Cent of Total |
	N	Population	N	Population
Total population	18,000,000		18,000,000	
Persons interviewed	52,000	0.3	180,000	0.1
Persons examined:				
Adults	2,600	0.014	7,200	0.006
Children	2,600	0.014	21,600	0.036
Surface covered by the selected prime units.				
Interviews	350/1900	20.0	40/700	6.0
Examinations	40/1900	•2.0	40/700	6.0

In Colombia a person who was interviewed represented 340 of the universe under study, and a person who was examined represented 3,400.

population of more than 5,000 and with an available hospital, health center or other health service. The municipality was selected as the primary sample unit because it is the smallest political-administrative division about which information is available and which offers operative advantages. The limit of 5,000 population was established to guarantee a minimum probability of selection of 0.01 per unit. The existence of a health service was to guarantee facilities for conducting the study.

Cities with fewer than 5,000 inhabitants or without some health service were annexed to the nearest municipality that fulfilled both of these requirements. Since the population of a stratum should be approximately 450,000, the cities that reached or surpassed that limit were considered to have a number of primary sample units proportionate to their population.

Regional and Strata Division

The departments of the country were grouped into four regions to establish the prime units for the presentation of the results in the study, and the calculation of the reliability of the estimates. Each region with a minimum population of three million contains departments with similar ecological characteristics so that regional estimates were sufficiently reliable for the majority of the data.

Bogotá, the capital of the country, because of its special characteristics, was separated as a region to become an individual area of tabulation since this circumstance was considered to compensate for its

160

smaller population. Five tabulation areas were formed for the four regions of the country.

Within each region, the primary sample units were arranged in 40 strata so that they would have the maximum homogeneity among the grouped units and the greatest heterogeneity between one stratum and another from the point of view of the size of population, percentage of urban population and average altitude.

Ten of the strata classified as "Defined" coincide with the prime unit, and therefore had an assured selection. These strata correspond to the prime units in the most populous municipalities of the country. The other 30 "Undefined" strata were formed from the remaining prime units.

Sample of the Prime Unit of the Undefined Strata

A prime unit was selected as the representative of each of the remaining 30 strata. The probability of being selected was proportional to its population within the strata.

The "controlled selection" technique was used in the process. The use of controls increased the probability of selecting preferred combinations of prime units beyond those obtained in the stratified sample without hampering the real probability of each individual unit.

The following control criteria were used:

Groups of departments formed within each tabulation area considering the homogeneity of its socioeconomic and geographic characteristics and a minimum population of 1.3 million.

Index of medical attention services, simultaneously considering the number of beds available per 1,000 inhabitants and the size of the hospitals.

Subdivision of the Sample into Representative Semisamples

The entire sample was subdivided into two semisamples of the 20 most similar sampling units, so that, independently, results that could be generalized to the country might be obtained from them. This necessitated a security mechanism in case the operative contingencies might hamper the development of the study in all of the selected units. On the other hand, the subdivision facilitated the calculation of the validity of the results.

Selection of the Local Sample

The second stage of the design dealt with the procedures that followed the selection of the prime units and that were verified for each one of them.

The organization and treatment of the basic information about dwellings and cartography was somewhat unusual:

1. Dwellings: Information about the number of completed census tickets in the sectors of the 1964 census was obtained for each of the 40 prime units. Since the information refers to buildings and not to dwellings, it was necessary to make the conversion to the latter measurement by applying adjustment factors established by a rapid revision of the coresponding census tickets to each municipal district.

2. Cartography: Cartographic information about Colombia is still general and in some cases deficient and outdated. Only municipal districts fulfilled the requirements necessary for a rapid sample selection. Therefore, all of the selected rural areas had to be visited beforehand to complete the necessary subsamples and complementary cartographic framework that would permit their location at the time of the study. This work, called "segmentation," decisively influenced the general procedure of the study because of its magnitude and importance.

Once the information necessary for the selection was available in an adequate form, it was completed in various steps both at the central level and at the local level.

Procedure at the central level. The number of theoretical segments of an "average size" of ten dwellings was established for each minimum census sector. (The minimum census sectors were established by blocks in municipal districts and in rural zones, by areas of approximately 100 dwellings.) A systematic selection of 24 "size samples" (units of ten dwellings) was made, and the census sectors in which they were located were identified.

In the second step, the selected sectors were outlined on a map of the unit. Those corresponding to municipal districts offered no difficulty and were later ready for a rapid verification in the "segmentation." Those in rural areas were finally subdivided to obtain the smallest geographical unit that could later be easily managed.

Procedure at the local level. The blocks in the municipal districts, and the rural areas selected at the central level were submitted for verification and a complementary cartographic framework immediately prior to the field work. At that time, rural areas of more than 15 dwellings were subdivided to facilitate the later interview. The work was

162

completed at the departmental and local levels by health workers necessarily trained in the territory, with precise written instructions and with adequate supervision by central level officials.

When the segmentation of each unit was completed, all the documents were sent to the central level where they were reproduced or included in the folders of the interviewers.

When the selected municipal sectors had more than 15 dwellings, they were subdivided by the interviewers immediately before beginning the interviews, and under the direction of the field supervisor.

The subsample of persons for the clinical examination was taken while conducting the interviews using a list of persons interviewed to control distribution by age.

Table 2 refers to the selected and covered sample in the household interview and the clinical examination.

REAPPLICATION AND ADJUSTMENT TO THE UNIVERSE

To obtain correct estimates from the sample, it was necessary to inflate or weigh the studied units with the reciprocal of its probability of being selected to recreate the universe, and to adjust the reconstituted universe to the predictions of the 1964 census.

Restitution. Basic weight of inflation. Each family and individual selected for the home interview had a basic weight of about 340, indicating the number of people in the universe represented by one person in the sample, and equal to the reciprocal of his selection probability.

The basic weight of the people selected for the clinical examination

TABLE 2. SELECTED AND COVERED SAMPLE

	Home Interviews			*Clinical Evaluation*	
	N	*Per Cent*		*N*	*Per Cent*
Families selected*	8,920	100.0	Persons selected	5,258	100.0
Families interviewed	8,669	97.2	Persons examined	5,027	95.6
Families not interviewed**	251	2.8	Persons not examined	231	4.4

* 9,798 dwellings were selected of which 878 corresponded to families with permanent residence in another site, vacant houses and other causes; therefore the number of families actually selected was 8,920.

** The 251 families not interviewed are those who refused or who were momentarily or temporarily absent.

163

was equal to their weight in the interview times the reciprocal of the fraction of the subsample. This number fluctuated around 3,400.

Special weight of the subsample. When the segment was subdivided, the dwellings and persons in the sample received another weight or "special weight," which was the reciprocal of the fraction of the subsample. When the number of dwellings was less than anticipated, the weight was calculated from the relation: dwellings found/dwellings anticipated.

Adjustment of coverage. Families selected but not interviewed, and individuals chosen but not examined received a special treatment that consisted of attributing to them the replies of similar families and individuals.

Justification of estimates. The population reconstructed from the sample for the home interview and the subsample for the clinical examination were adjusted to the urban and rural totals for the 1964 census. This adjustment, even if it might slightly slant the results, reduces the variability of the estimates, corrects the lack of coverage for families not located, assures consistent population bases and overcomes the deficiencies of estimated population used in the selection of prime units.

MEASURE OF VARIABILITY

By dealing with a random sample, it is possible to obtain correct estimates of the variability of error in the sample. The variability of the sample, the interviewers or examiners, can be measured as a total, or separately for each one of the components. Nevertheless, the estimate of total variability was used to measure the trustworthiness of the results.

TABLE 3. COMPARISON OF OBSERVED AND EXPECTED RATES AND STANDARD ERRORS

	National			
			Confidence Limits at 95 per cent Level	
	Standard Error	Estimated Rate	Lower	Higher
Expected rate	.009	10.00	8.2	11.8
Obtained rate	.005	10.9	9.8	12.0
	Tabulation Area 4			
Anticipated rate	0.018	10.0	6.4	13.6
Obtained rate	0.012	12.1	9.7	14.6

TABLE 4. DISTRIBUTION BY AGE AND SEX IN THE 1964 CENSUS, HOUSEHOLD INTERVIEW AND CLINICAL EXAMINATION

| | | Men | | | Women | |
Age (in Years)	Census %	Household Interview %	Clinical Examination %	Census %	Household Interview %	Clinical Examination %
0–14	47.9	49.7	50.6	45.4	45.0	45.5
15–44	39.0	36.4	35.2	41.3	39.9	40.2
45 and above	13.1	13.9	14.2	13.3	14.2	14.3

TABLE 5. DISTRIBUTION BY SEX IN THE 1964 CENSUS, HOUSEHOLD INTERVIEWS AND CLINICAL EXAMINATION

	Census %	Household Interview %	Clinical Examination %
Men	49.3	48.3	47.3
Women	50.7	51.7	52.7
Total	100.0	100.0	100.0

The obtained variability is sufficient for the purposes of the study, and somewhat lower than anticipated in the design of the sample.

The difference between the standard errors is important. The national rate obtained for the number of persons incapacitated for two weeks is almost one-half the expected error for any characteristic of similar frequency, as shown in Table 3.

For Tabulation Area 4, whose population is five millon, the difference between the standard errors anticipated and those obtained is still considerable.

REPRESENTATIVENESS OF THE SAMPLE

The design of a sample is efficient insofar as it represents the characteristics of the universe in the combination of unlisted units. Nevertheless, this analysis is practical only for those characteristics about which information already exists in other sources such as the population census or various systematic reports.

Table 4 shows the percentage distribution by age for each sex in the 1964 census, the home interview and the clinical examination.

165

The largest difference, 3.8 per cent between the census and the clinical examination, occurs in the group of men between ages 15 and 44. This is explained by the exclusion of the institutional population from the study and by the size of the interval in the age group. The rest of the differences vary around 0.1 and 2.7 per cent.

The minimal differences between the interviewed and examined population demonstrates the effectiveness of the system adopted for taking the subsample of persons for the clinical examination.

The differences in the percentage distribution according to sex are of even less importance, as seen in Table 5.

APPENDIX

Selection Process for the Sample for the National Health Survey

I. Division of the country into 716 prime sample units.
    Political administrative division and number of units per department.
    Universe: 716 prime sample units in 18 departments; 98.7 per cent of the total population of the country; 52.7 per cent of the total surface.
    Criteria:
    1. political administrative division.
    2. population.
    3. minimal health resources.
    4. accessibility.
    Note: Bogotá, Medellin, Cali, Barranquilla and Bucaramanga were treated independently.

II. Grouping of the prime units into 40 strata.
    Regional division and number of strata per division.
    Criteria:
    1. population of approximately 450,000.
    2. homogeneous characteristics within each stratum: total population, per cent of urban population and average altitude.
    3. combination of prime units from the same region.

III. Selection of 40 prime units, one prime unit per stratum.
    Criteria:
    1. selection controlled by two criteria: groups of departments and index of health services.
    2. probability of selection of each unit, proportional to the volume of population within the stratum.

166

IV. Selection of 960 segments for the home interview. One segment per ten dwellings; 24 segments per unit; 9,600 dwellings = 52,500 persons.
Criteria:
1. proportionality of the number of urban and rural segments established by the size of their populations.
2. systematic selection.

V. Selection of subsample of 5,250 people for the clinical examination. 130 persons per unit, approximately five persons per segment.
Criteria:
1. systematic selection among people who were interviewed.
2. control of the distribution by age.

THE HOUSEHOLD INTERVIEW

ALDEMAR GOMEZ

The National Health Survey not only measured the incidence and prevalence of diagnosed and reported illnesses, but also studied the conditions under which sickness occurs, the social and economic factors related to it and its effects on the individual and the family expressed in terms of incapacity, immobility and economic loss.

The household interview was used as a method to determine these facts. The study unit was the "statistical or epidemiological family" defined as a person or group of persons who share a dwelling and food, thereby forming a unit. This definition groups people who are subjected to similar physical, social, cultural, economic and nutritional influences and to other factors that contribute either to the spread of disease or the maintenance of a state of health.

CONTENT

To determine the content of the interview, it was necessary to consider the general and specific objectives of the study. Only the latter will be mentioned.

1. To determine the attributes that characterize the typical Colombian family, such as its composition, size, level of education, general sanitary conditions of the home and social and economic factors.

2. To discover the state of health reported by the general population by exploring its morbidity and the various ecological factors affecting it.

3. To specify the impact of sickness expressed in terms of costs, incapacity and immobility.

4. To study the sources and attributes of medical care such as its quality, use, methods of financing and payment, costs and attitudes of the family toward health services.

5. To verify the quality of existing statistical data about vital statistics such as numbers of live births, miscarriages and deaths of children under five years of age and to ascertain the general characteristics of pregnancies (number, duration, complications).

Characteristics of the family

Data about the size of the family, the relationship of its members, urban-rural distribution patterns and economic status were studied.

The economic status of the family, although difficult to obtain accurately, is of fundamental importance when this variable is related to other factors that influence the health and well-being of the population.

The information should be given a relative value since factors that hamper an exact collection, such as forgetfulness, badly recorded accounts and cultural factors, may intervene. The belief of a large sector of the population that the information about income would be used for tax purposes or to underrate their apparent social condition also played an important part in the cultural factors mentioned above.

A man's occupation was defined as that activity the person performs by preference and to which he devotes the greatest part of his time. Information about occupation was requested of everyone over six years of age. Paid activity, as well as inactivity, begins to have importance and merit consideration when a person reaches his sixth birthday. Between the ages of six and 14, many children do not attend primary school because their parents are forced to allow them to work so that they may contribute to the income of the family.

The level of education was determined for people over six years of age. Some of the reasons already mentioned in using this age limit for occupations are valid here. Also, it is customary in Colombia to begin primary education at the age of six. The classification into primary, middle, secondary and higher education is based on current norms of the Ministry of Education.

Sanitary conditions of the dwelling

Information obtained during the pretesting of the questionnaire revealed that, in the interview, only information about those character-

169

istics of the building that could directly influence health should be gathered. Information collected included type of building, mode and form of tenancy, water service, waste disposal system and hygienic state.

State of Health

The information obtained about an individual's state of health refers to diseases, dental problems, accidents and injuries reported. Incapacity and immobility produced by these conditions were measured in terms of days in which normal activity was hindered, days in bed and absence from work. Data relating to diseases, accidents and injuries were gathered over a period of two weeks, whereas information about dental problems and chronic illnesses was obtained for a period of aproximately one year. These periods were considered sufficient since the frequency of the occurrences, during those same periods, allowed statistically significant inferences.

Information about those chronic situations and defects that could be reported by the general public without danger of error was obtained. The majority of the reported chronic conditions could be identified during the course of the interview by a general inspection. Except for deafness, asthma and epilepsy or periodic convulsions, which involve a fair amount of subjective evaluation, and which in many cases do not correspond to the real disease, all of the chronic conditions studied are easily identifiable by the general public.

Medical and dental attention

Questions about the sources of medical and dental attention dealt with quality of medical care, its costs and methods of financing. With regard to hospitalization demand, inquiries were made about its frequency, its causes, its costs and the usual forms of payment.

Social Security System

Whether those interviewed were affiliated with or received aid from either public or private social security systems was also determined.

Vital Statistics

Questions were asked about the duration of medical attention during pregnancy, the type of attention received at birth and the proportion of live births and miscarriages. These facts have been related to other attributes of the population such as age, geographic distribution, level of education and economic conditions.

170

Facts related to pregnancy and birth were sought from women between 15 and 54 years of age. Even though pregnancy is possible outside of these age limits, such cases are infrequent and should not cause a large error in the calculations. Special instructions were given to the interviewers to make certain that they approached this question carefully since questions on this topic often arouse resistance (embarrassment, shame) among the people, and may not be answered correctly. It was emphasized that the information was to be provided directly by the woman herself. This permitted comparative evaluation of the information omitted in the standard surveys of the country.

Questions regarding the deaths of infants of under five years of age were directed to the head of the household or to the individual who acted in that capacity. It was extended to this age group since it was desirable to corroborate the rates of infant mortality that were supposed to form an important subregister in the country.

Qualities and Requirements of Interviewers

A good interview requires the person who conducts it to have certain basic qualifications such as a basic knowledge of the techniques of data collection and their significance, a capacity for understanding a map, good interpersonal relations and initiative for resolving unforeseen difficulties. Besides these minimum qualifications, he should fulfill the following requirements:

Availability for traveling to any unit selected.

Possibility of finishing the task within the appointed period, including working on holidays and extra hours if necessary.

Full awareness of the importance of the job, sufficient knowledge of his future job, responsibility for its discharge, interest in it and acceptance of the work conditions.

The determination of the type of interviewer who could best handle the interviews was the subject of very careful study. The possibility was discussed of using persons of different academic backgrounds such as sociology students, social assistants, health auxiliaries and medical students. In a temporary study of this magnitude, with limited economic resources and a lack of intermediary level personnel, hiring permanent personnel as interviewers could not be considered.

Medical students were finally selected for several reasons. They already had a satisfactory basic medical preparation, were available in sufficient numbers and advantage could be taken of the instruction provided during training and an excellent opportunity would be provided for bringing future physicians into contact with families and conditions that bring about disease. Medical students in their final year were selected since they offered greater experience than those pursuing lower courses.

Training

To achieve uniformity in the information that was collected, the interviewers underwent a specific training program.

Each training period lasted for 20 hours and three basic systems were used: group training in theory, group practical training and assignment of homework. The interviewers were taught to transmit the necessary information about the procedures and techniques to produce a good quality interview and to give complete instructions about the list of families and dwellings and other procedures involved in conducting the interviews.

Since the data gathered through the interviews should be of the best possible quality and since the number of potential candidates exceeded the number required, it was decided to establish selection criteria. The following is a resumé of these procedures:

Evaluation of the results of the tests on themes that had been taught.

Evaluation of interest and participation in training sessions.

Evaluation of attendance at training sessions.

Evaluation of capacity and aptitude for conducting an interview.

Evaluation of the results of the questionnaire about the requirements that the applicant to the interviewer's post should possess.

During the first two days in the local operation, each group of interviewers was given a refresher of what had been taught and they conducted interviews with families selected for that purpose.

Quality Control of Interviews

Aside from the training program other procedures for controlling the quality of the interviews were also established.

Daily Review of the Material

The goal of the review was the identification of omissions, inconsistencies, illegible notes, erasures and so forth. As a result of the daily review of needs many errors were caught and difficulties in the tabula-

172

tion and classification with a consequent increase in costs were prevented. Also, the quality of the interview and interviewer were evaluated by this method.

The omissions, inconsistencies and illegible notes were reported in a formula so that they could be counted, analyzed and classified. If many errors were found in the questionnaires, they were returned to the interviewer for correction. This required that an additional visit be paid to the family that had been interviewed.

Observation of Interviews

The supervisor observed the interviews whenever possible for each interviewer. Observation was performed during the first days of work in each primary unit. By this means his activity could be evaluated and corrected if necessary, and erroneous interpretations rectified.

Reinterviews

Families were reinterviewed to establish the comparability of the gathered data, to determine errors and to give instructions for avoiding errors in the future.

Four reinterviews were given per segment covering a total of six segments in each prime unit. They were divided among urban and rural zones in each unit and were selected so that they would correspond, as far as possible, to one for each interviewer. The section of families and segments was made on a random basis.

To conduct the reinterviews, the supervisor sent a different interviewer who obtained information in the second interview about the composition of the family, its pattern of hospitalizations, reported chronic conditions and vital statistics.

Obtaining Cooperation

A high level of motivation was necessary to attain wide coverage and good quality of information. Different approaches were used in approaching the interviewers, those in the survey and the general public.

Interviewers

To motivate the interviewers during their training, the importance of the work they were going to perform was emphasized. The work was translated into the personal advantage that would be gained by the acquisition of knowledge about aspects of preventive medicine, the family, and environmental conditions with which they would deal later as physicians. The benefits that the data, once analyzed and published, would have for medical instruction and national health programs were also emphasized. The validity of field work as an integral part of the teaching programs the students had received was doubtless another stimulus, as were the stipend and other working conditions offered to the interviewers.

Families selected

Interviewers tried special techniques of persuasion for those families who initially refused to cooperate. For these families the following approaches were very useful: insisting on the importance of the information which they had for the family and their peers and for the health of the general population; how lucky they had been in being selected for the possibility that some of them would be chosen for a complete clinical examination. No less important was the treatment of the people during the interview and the recognition of cooperation expressed in a letter signed by the Minister of Public Health.

General Public

Health educators carried out a series of activities to inform the general public about the study.

Among the activities carried out on the national level might be mentioned the lectures delivered to different scientific and labor societies located in Bogotá, but which had national importance and influence; the inauguration ceremony for the Study of Health Manpower attended by the President of Colombia and several of his cabinet ministers, and by many distinguished national and international guests; the use of media such as press, radio, television and films and, finally, the preparation of written materials such as folders, posters and circulars.

At the departmental level, approximately the same activities were performed. These were done by the personnel participating in the study and through means of regional diffusion.

At the level of the prime unit visits were made to religious, civil and health authorities and other influential local people to request their cooperation within the community. The meeting with different groups of the population, the selection of leaders at the urban and rural levels, the use of local means of diffusion as well as informing the families constituted the chief means of persuasion. The majority of the families

174

selected for the interview had been previously informed about the impending visit of a doctor who was going to ask them for very important information, thereby motivating them and requesting their cooperation at the same time. That 97.2 per cent of the interviews scheduled were completed indicates that these efforts to obtain the cooperation of the public succeeded.

THE CLINICAL EXAMINATION

CARLOS AGUALIMPIA

OBJECTIVES

The fundamental objectives of the clinical examination in the National Health Study were:

1. To complement the information obtained during the household interviews to identify health problems.
2. To estimate certain physical and physiological averages in the general population as a basis for establishing national patterns of "biological normality."
3. To correlate the clinical findings with important social variables of the examined population.

DISEASES AND CONDITIONS STUDIED

The prevalence of disease was considered in the population (in the selection of the general conditions to be studied in the clinical examination). Procedures were selected to obtain information on conditions and diseases whose distribution was known or which were thought to be frequent, avoiding the adoption of procedures for conditions common only to limited sectors of the population whose study would have required special methods.

Table 1 shows the contents of the clinical examination in terms of the conditions specifically studied and the procedures selected according to the groups of application.

176

CLINICAL CONDUCT RELATED TO THE EXAMINATION

In developing the clinical examination, the following specific norms were adopted:

Selection of strictly random sample of patients. The resources of the study were exclusively applied to the examination of selected patients. Substitutions were not permitted, and the examination of unselected individuals was forbidden.

Personal confidential information was used only by officials of the study for the exclusive purposes of the study, and by doctors chosen and authorized by the patient.

Voluntary participation. The patient maintained the right to receive information about the procedures to which he was going to submit and to reject them if he wished to do so.

Medical attention to some patients. Although the object of the study was not treatment of the individuals who were found to be ill, measures were taken to guarantee them adequate medical attention.

Selection of informants. Anyone under 15 years of age, or whose mental condition would unfavorably affect the quality of the data, was unqualified for providing information during the examination.

SELECTION OF PATIENTS

Approximately one of every ten people interviewed was selected through a sampling procedure that simultaneously controlled for age. When the person selected agreed to be examined, the interviewer delivered the notice and attempted to resolve the patient's difficulties by repeating some fundamental recommendations: that minors or the mentally ill be accompanied by a responsible person; giving the exact location of the clinical unit; discussing the results of previous medical consultations and systems for collecting the stool sample.

Procedure of the Clinical Examination

The clinical examination was conducted with equipment and personnel in health institutions whose facilities had been adapted to the needs of the study. Each patient passed through a series of stations in a systematic procedure that lasted approximately two hours. Table 2 gives a resumé of the procedures, examiners and duration of the clinical examination.

The established sequence fulfilled the essential chronological neces-

177

TABLE I. CLINICAL EXAMINATION, TECHNIQUES AND PROCEDURES

Diseases	Medical Examination	Systematic Complementary Examinations*		Discretional Complementary Examinations**
		Type	Age Group	
1. Parasitic and infectious diseases				
Intestinal parasites	x	Corpuscle Count	All	Rectal touch
		Egg count	All	
		Tape Swab	Under 8	
Blood parasites	x	Thick Blood Smear	All	
Tuberculosis	x	Chest x-ray†	All	
		Tuberculine	Under 10	
Syphilis	x	Serological	3 and over	
Brucellosis	x	Serological	3 and over	
Chagas' disease	x	Serological	3 and over	
Poliomyelitis	x	Serological	Under 10	
Salmonellosis	x	Serological	3 and over	
Diphtheria	x	Serological	3 and over	
Histoplasmosis	x	Chest x-ray†	All	
		Histoplasmine	10 and over	
		Serological	10 and over	
Blastomicosis	x	Serological	10 and over	
Toxoplasmosis	x	Serological	3 and over	
Influenza	x	Serological	3 and over	
Arbovirus	x	Serological	10 and over	
2. Allergic diseases of the glands, endocrines and metabolism				
Diabetes	x	Blood glucose (micro)	3 and over	
		Somogy	20 and over	
3. Nutritional diseases				
Malnutrition	x	Hematocrit	3 and over	
		Hemoglobin	3 and over	
		Thin Blood Smear	All	
4. Blood and organ diseases				
Anemias	x	Hematocrit	3 and over	
		Hemoglobin	3 and over	
		Thin Blood Smear	All	
5. Diseases of the nervous system	x			Fundoscopic examination
6. Diseases of the sense organs				
Audial deficiency	x	Audiometrics	8 and over	
Visual deficiency	x	Visual acuity		
		distance	8 and over	
		near	20 and over	
7. Diseases of circulatory system	x	Chest x-ray†	All	
		Electrocardiogram	20 and over	
8. Diseases of the respiratory system	x	Chest x-ray†	All	
9. Diseases of the digestive system	x			Rectal touch

178

TABLE I. (CONTINUED)

Diseases	Medical Examination	Systematic Complementary Examinations*		Discretional Complementary Examinations**
		Type	Age Group	
10. Diseases of the genitourinary system	x			Gynecological examination, Rectal touch
11. Pregnancy, birth and puerperal complications	x			Gynecological examination, Rectal touch
12. Diseases of bone and organs of movement	x	Chest x-ray†	All	
13. All others	x			

* Examination given to all people in the respective age groups.
** Examination given to patients whose symptoms merited these additional tests.
† Excluding pregnant women.

TABLE 2. SEQUENCE OF THE CLINICAL EXAMINATION

Order	Procedure	Official	Time (min.)
1.	Identification—preliminary information—receive stool sample—wait	Receptionist	5
2.	Personal data—temperature—weight and height—visual acuity from a distance and near—Skin test	Nurses' aide	25
3.	Chest x-ray	X-ray technician	10
4.	Study of the history—questions and physical examination—Revision of chest x-ray Glucose drink—electrocardiogram—medical attention	Resident M.D.	60
5.	Hearing acuity—oral examination—dental attention revision of the history	Odontologist	25
6.	Collecting, distributing and storing blood sample	Laboratory technician	10
7.	Final interview—subsidies and provisions—special recommendations—letter of thanks	Receptionist	5
	Total		140

sities imposed by the procedure. For example, taking and developing the chest x-ray preceded the physical examination to allow for the repetition of the procedure if the print was unacceptable. This could be done before the patient had left the unit. The venipuncture should be performed one hour after drinking the glucose and at the end of the examination to avoid interfering with other procedures.

Control of Field Work

To maintain the exactness, uniformity and integrity of the information gathered, a series of control procedures was established during the field activities.

1. Daily control of the selected patients through systematic review of the interviewees and those listed for selection.
2. Observation of the procedure by supervisors. During the first days of activity, the clinical units were observed to identify difficulties and deficiencies in their function.
3. Daily review of the information gathered. Completed questionnaires, laboratory samples and special examinations were systematically reviewed with regard to their volume and quality.
4. Control of the quality of the sample. Some of the persons examined were again selected by the supervisors to verify the procedures of the clinical examination with a second test. For this control, procedures were chosen that permitted evaluation of the majority of the members of the team. The procedures produced easily analyzable results without provoking considerable disturbances in the operation by their dual realization. Table 3 shows the procedures and functionaries specifically controlled by this procedure. Comparative analysis of the duplicated results served to evaluate the quality of the work, to compare criteria when important differences were produced and to measure the variability of the information gathered.

Central Level Procedures

The collected information was sent from the prime units, preferably by officials of the study. At the central level the technical procedures remaining for some laboratory samples and special examinations were conducted by persons connected with medical schools and public service units. This provided academic and economic advantages along with greater efficiency.

180

TABLE 3. QUALITY CONTROL EXAMINATION

Procedure	Control Content	Ordinary Observer
Blood pressure	One measurement	Physicians
Audiometrics	One frequency	Odontologists
Weight and height	Complete	Nurses' aides
Visual acuity	From a distance	Nurses' aides
Oral examination	Complete	Odontologists

Processing of laboratory samples. The technical processing of laboratory samples took place in two central laboratories. This guaranteed uniformity and control of the processing, represented an economy of installations and equipment and permitted use of auxiliary personnel in the field by simplifying their duties. Nevertheless, the procedure caused the loss of some samples and variations in others when the time between the collection and the analysis was crucial.

Blood and stool samples vulnerable to damage while being stored were processed immediately after being received.

Frozen and stored specimens were divided into three factions and were processed in accordance with a scale of priorities to avoid the risk of handling and to facilitate simultaneous treatment in several laboratories. The remaining specimen fractions were classified and stored as reference controls, internal controls, for later study and for mounting in a national bank of specimens.

Interpretation of special examinations. In the planning and inauguration of techniques for the processing of the chest x-rays, electrocardiograms and blood smears, the following process was adopted before beginning the definitive work.

For each type of examination several specialists were selected who worked on material selected at random from the various units.

Three specialists of similar rank who actively participated in the planning of the work interpreted the examinations according to previously established diagnostic criteria.

All of the examinations were submitted for independent interpretations by two specialists. The reports of these two interpretations were compared to identify notable differences if they occurred. Divergent examinations were sent to a third examiner.

The findings of the first examiner were selected for the tabulations when the first two reports agreed. The findings of the third examiner were used if differences occurred between the first two.

Final Diagnosis

Final diagnoses integrated all the results of the medical and complementary examinations to produce a definitive diagnosis of the patients examined. This stage of work has hardly begun, and, as yet, precise methodological recommendations have not been obtained.

LONGITUDINAL STUDY OF THE HEALTH INSURANCE PLAN OF GREATER NEW YORK . NEVA R. DEARDORFF

T O understand the Special Research Project on which the HIP is now embarked, it is necessary to know somewhat in detail (1) the setting for the observation of family health experience provided by the HIP program, (2) the type of records which are routinely kept, (3) the specific objectives of this inquiry, (4) the methods of study which are being employed, and (5) the problems encountered thus far.

This inquiry began officially on July 1 of this year and is scheduled for completion within a three-year period. It is hoped that some preliminary findings will begin to emerge by the end of the second year. Pilot operations, intended solely to facilitate the conduct of the study, have already produced data which in themselves are enlightening.

THE HIP OPERATION AS A SETTING FOR THE STUDY OF THE HEALTH OF FAMILIES

I take it that everyone present knows that the HIP program rests upon four major policies; family coverage for comprehensive care, prepayment by subscribers for physicians' and auxiliary services, group medical practice, and the payment of capitations by HIP to medical groups as their full compensation and reimbursement for the services that they render to subscribers and their dependents.

There are few barriers to enrollment so that the covered families range in age from newly married couples, through those with young children, those with older children up to 18 years of age, and on to the older couples whose children are no longer in the parental home. But there are some families on the HIP rolls with some members not covered. For health insurance purposes the New York State law defines a family as a group composed of spouses and unmarried children under the age of 18 years. This means that households composed of related persons who are neither spouses nor parents and children, are ruled out as insurable families, and that children over 18 are excluded, as are many other kinds of relatives, such as dependent parents. Some of the excluded persons may be able to enroll independently, but they are recorded as separate units and their experience is not a part of the family history as it accumulates in the records of the insurance organization. However, from the standpoint of the study of health in families, the part within the legal definition is a large and important segment of the family population.

A second point of significance for studies of the families served by HIP is its insistence upon their having family physicians chosen after the medical group has been selected. The same physician gives the family members their initial physical examinations and their subsequent check-ups, attends many minor and some serious illnesses and accidents and when advisable, refers patients to the specialists on the staff of the medical group. This assignment of responsibility to the general physician is somewhat attenuated by the modern requirements of specialist care for children and maternity cases. All of the medical groups provide routine care of babies by pediatricians and many carry this to the age of 5 or 6. About a third of the HIP children are enrolled in medical groups that continue this care to the age of 13. Almost all of the medical groups assign all of the pre and post-natal care to their obstetricians as well as the deliveries. The extensive use of specialists tends, of course, to erode the field of the general physician but he still is, in theory, at least, the doctor who sees the family as a whole. Insofar as that system contributes to a better understanding of the health problems of families, the HIP data reflect that advantage.

As you know, there are no deterrents upon families in seeing their doctors or in referrals to specialists. Moreover, almost all of the medical groups, with the aid of the central organization, systematically ply their enrollees with bulletins instructing them to see their physicians early and regularly and with excellent health educational materials. Apart from his own inclinations, there is no reason why every HIP subscriber should not immediately upon enrollment present himself and his eligible dependents for the receipt of all that

184

the medical profession has to offer for the improvement of his health and that of the other family members, and should not thereafter receive all needed services. While hospitalization is not provided by HIP, all enrollees are expected to have insurance for it so that no barriers will be imposed in respect of that; HIP physicians render the services to hospitalized as well as to ambulatory and home-bound patients.

The HIP Records

Because the originators of HIP had found so little recorded or compiled by the earlier prepayment plans on the subject of utilization of medical services, they resolved that if HIP ever achieved actual operation, records of what occurred would be kept and reports currently issued. Accordingly, from the beginning every medical group has been required by contract to see that every physician on its staff returns a brief notation on every visit of a patient to him and every visit by him to a patient at home or in the hospital. This record on the now familiar "Med 10" form allows but one line to report such contact but on this line appears the date, the family identification number, the sex, family status and age of patient, the insured group to which the family belongs, the status of the case as new or old, the place the patient was seen—office, home, or hospital—the nature of the service—health examination, preventive service, surgery, delivery, or diagnosis and/or treatment —and what the diagnosis was. The report, of course, shows the medical group and the physician who returned it. These reports come into the HIP headquarters on a monthly basis, with the medical groups keeping carbon copies.

Of the array of items on the "Med 10" the common identification number for the family distinguishes this record from those ordinarily in effect in clinics and hospitals, even when they concern themselves with family factors in health. At first thought this may seem an unimportant matter, but without it the data for all of the members of a family can be assembled only with great difficulty and expense and in some instances can hardly be assembled at all, as in the case of duplicating names without clear means of family identification.

185

All physicians' returns are carefully checked for completeness and internal consistency upon their receipt at the HIP office and the necessary corrections secured from the reporting groups. During 1947, the year in which the HIP opened on March 1, a total of 160,000 visits were reported; in 1948 the number rose to 500,000; in 1949 to 850,000, and in 1950 to 1,140,000. Physicians' reports are now flowing in at the average rate of 100,000 per month. Visiting nurse services are similarly reported by the nursing agencies.

After these returns have been edited, an IBM card is punched for each service report so that at the end of the year it is possible to list all of the medical services received by the family with each service assigned to the member who received it.

The utilization data are paralleled by equally good materials on the enrollment, that is, on the base population. Not only does the Registrar have complete files of the initial enrollment with cards well filled out, but all subsequent changes have been promptly recorded on a history card and every month tabulations analysing these changes have been made. Periodically, as of a given day, the data on the age and sex of the base population are tabulated and size of family groups ascertained. These current analyses set the stage for sampling procedures which can be properly tested and supported. Table 1, made for one of the Project's pilot studies, will

Table 1. Persons in a sample of two-tenths of one per cent of the HIP enrollment to January 15, 1951, classified by date of entry into the Plan, status on July 31, 1951, and interruption in coverage.

DATE OF ENTRY	Total	COVERED, 7/31/51			NOT COVERED, 7/31/51					
		Total	Uninterrupted	Interrupted	Uninterrupted	Interrupted	Length of Coverage			
							Less than 1 Year	1 to 2 Years	2 to 3 Years	More than 3 Years
TOTAL	638	512	504	8	122	4	49	30	36	11
Before 1/15/48	241	177	175	2	60	4	15	13	26	10
During 1948	47	31	30	1	16	0	5	4	6	1
1/1/49–1/15/49	26	19	19	0	7	0	3	4	0	0
During 1949	219	194	189	5	25	0	15	6	4	0
1/1/50–1/15/50	3	3	3	0	0	0	0	0	0	0
During 1950	101	87	87	0	14	0	11	3	0	0
1/1/51–1/15/51	1	1	1	0	0	0	0	0	0	0

illustrate the kind of longitudinal enrollment data that the HIP record system makes easily available. It also throws some light on population changes with which longitudinal studies of this kind must cope.

These data on the HIP population and its utilization have been widely used for a great variety of administrative purposes. Several series in service accounting parallel the records of the dollar transactions. They are HIP's contribution to the actuarial basis of comprehensive prepaid medical care. As such, the collection and compilation of these data at HIP's expense has justified itself. But these uses by no means exhaust the possibilities of these materials for enlightenment on the broader subjects of health conditions and the use of medical care. It was to exploit the supererogatory possibilities that a special research project was set up this year with the substantial aid of the Commonwealth Fund and the Rockefeller Foundation and the indispensable assistance of a distinguished advisory committee.

THE OBJECTIVES OF THE HIP SPECIAL RESEARCH PROJECT

It must be clear to anyone acquainted with materials bearing on public health that here is a large and unique vein to be worked. However, if the ore extracted is to test high, the mining processes must be planned with great care. The financing was given by the two foundations with the explicit understanding that the Special Research Project would be directed toward broad interests in public health and medical care, and need pay no attention to the administrative concerns of HIP itself.

The general areas of inquiry initially laid out included

1. The analysis of the utilization experience of HIP for a four-year period in rendering medical care to its enrollees of various types with the factors of age, sex, education, occupation, length of enrollment, etc. taken into consideration.

2. Appraisal of that experience in the light of the medical care received by comparable families in the general population.

3. The enhancement of understanding of health conditions and problems of individuals and families both inside and outside of HIP.

187

4. Exploration of the preventive aspects of the HIP program.

5. Some contribution to the methodology of surveys of (a) sickness, (b) "health experience," and (c) medical care received.

Within each of these broad areas specific questions are now being formulated. The very able and hardworking Steering Committee and staff[1] are now actively engaged in this process.

While everyone agrees in theory that in statistical studies precise lines of inquiry should be laid out in advance and all of the methods and processes shaped to the end of arriving at unequivocal answers to the questions posited, even to the drafting of the statistical tables ultimately to emerge, there is good reason to believe that this practice is not invariably followed even by the advocates of this procedure. But in the case of this study, a valiant effort is being made to exemplify it. The members of the Steering Committee have been urged by the Chairman to send in the questions to which they wish attention addressed. The staff of the Project is at this time in the throes of that phase of the advance planning. We are now drafting statistical tables conceived as the end results of our study and are then testing each step in the procedure to see that it contributes to those ends. No one is so naive as to believe that the anticipated questions will exhaust the possibilities for rewarding exploitation of these materials, but it is hoped that no major opportunity will be missed.

Within the broad areas listed above, these tables are undertaking to set forth (1) the experience, viewed longitudinally, of the persons and families in HIP, (2) the extent to which HIP sub-

[1] It consists of the following persons: Dr. Lowell Reed, Chairman; Dr. W. Thurber Fales, Vice-Chairman; Dr. Dean A. Clark; Dr. Selwyn D. Collins; Dr. Paul Densen; Miss Jean Downes; Mr. Morris H. Hansen; Dr. Philip Hauser; Dr. Forrest E. Linder; Dr. Robert Reed; Dr. Theodore Woolsey as a special consultant.
Besides these persons, the HIP's permanent staff includes Dr. George Baehr, Dr. Edwin S. Daily, Dr. George Rosen, and Mr. Morton Miller, the consulting actuary, who serve as ex-officio members of the Steering Committee. Dr. Henry Makover, author of the report on the quality of medical care provided by the HIP medical groups and now the medical director of one of them, also serves as a special consultant.
On the staff are: Mr. Jerome Cornfield, on loan from the National Cancer Institute; Mr. Nathan Goldfarb; Mrs. Eva Balamuth.

188

scribers rely for their medical care solely upon HIP medical groups, and (3) a comparison of conditions of health and medical care in HIP families with similarly circumstanced families not in HIP.

THE LONGITUDINAL STUDIES

Longitudinal studies of family health conditions and of the unobstructed use of medical care are of great potential significance from several points of view. Aside from the possibility of adding to our meager fund of knowledge about the incidence and prevalence of many troublesome conditions, not hitherto reported, it is of great importance to see what, if any, relation exists between the illnesses of family members that spring neither from transmissible nor hereditary diseases. Clues to other factors of mental and physical environment may become more visible when we are able to examine systematically over a period of years the illness experience of large numbers of families. Following cohorts of families with specified conditions through a series of years should help to bring out such associations as exist.

The longitudinal aspects of the health and sickness experience of a group of people observed over a period of time can be approached from at least two directions. On the one hand the happenings to this group, *as a group,* can be reported from year to year and the changes noted in the *group's* pattern of experience, irrespective of the sequence of changes experienced by any one person or family. On the other hand, the *movement* of persons and families from one category to another over the years may be the question toward which the analysis is primarily pointed. Was there any discernible pattern in the changes for persons and families variously characterized? Both types of questions have their uses but the second seems to me to be considerably more penetrating than the first.

There are important longitudinal aspects to demand for medical care. How is that demand distributed among families of various types in a given year? How over a series of years? Is there a fairly random distribution among all families or is there a hard core of families who year after year have substantially large needs? If there is such a core, what diseases and conditions create this demand?

What kinds of families, in terms of age of parents and of children, of economic level, of number of children, are associated with high and low demand for medical services of the several types i.e., preventive care, maternity service, treatment of minor illness, care for serious conditions?

For the purpose of planning and promotion of health services, and of health education, the impact of illness from year to year upon breadwinners, homemakers, and upon children needs to be more clearly seen.

From the point of view of those concerned with the *prevention* of illness and injuries, reliable longitudinal data for defined population groups would seem to be of great usefulness, as they are, of course, to those concerned with the financing of medical care.

Once pertinent and significant questions have been formulated, there remains the job of aligning the data to answer them. Any comparison of health experience from year to year of large numbers of families would seem to require some type of standard classificatory description of that experience. Obviously, the family's experience derives from the experience of its members. So the first job is in some way to characterize each person's health experience for a year. At first it was thought that this could be done for the HIP enrollees by combining several items of experience—total utilization of physician's services, days in the hospital, and episodes of illness which were judged by the concentrations of medical services within defined periods of time. It was found that sheer volume of medical services reflected the other conditions so directly as to make it as definitive an index as would the use of the several kinds of factors. With primary classifications on the basis of utilization, the next step is to see what diagnoses are associated with each class with due regard, of course, to age and sex.

These data are limited to persons who have come under medical observation. Naturally, we shall know nothing of the health conditions of the persons who sought no care during a given year except as we learn about them through experience in prior and subsequent years and through the household survey to be described later.

190

Once having characterized all of the *persons* as to their health experience, it will then be necessary to devise a classification of families in respect of their size, composition, and inclusion of persons who are heavy, medium, or light users. It should be possible to see how constant over a series of years, the respective factors are for each of the members and for the family as a whole. Distinctions will have to be made between utilization for illness and for maternity and preventive service, including pediatric care. While these are not simple statistical analyses, they can be made and are of great importance in the understanding of and the planning both for family service in health and medical care and for insurance against its costs.

By reason of the size of the HIP operation, the initial advisory committee, composed in large part of the same persons who are now on the Steering Committee, recommended that for the longitudinal study, the HIP population be sampled. The records currently kept as well as the detailed pilot study referred to above, indicate that 319,000 different persons were enrolled in HIP prior to January 15, 1951. Persons enrolled since that time are not to be included in the study since they could not have had a year's experience before the end of the study period which has been put at December 31, 1951. Of all the persons ever enrolled, about 75 per cent will have been retained as of that date. In terms of person-years, 19 per cent are for enrollees covered by one-person certificates, 23 per cent by two-person certificates, and 58 per cent by certificates covering three or more persons. A given person may during the four-year period have been covered in all three categories.

After due consideration it has been decided to draw for the longitudinal studies a straight 10 per cent sample of all families and single persons enrolled prior to January 15, 1951. Such a sample should yield approximately 32,000 different persons who will have had 72,000 full calendar years of coverage and enough additional coverage in fractions of calendar years to add 12,000 more person-years to the experience. Almost 8,800 persons will have been covered for four years; these will account for approximately half of the full calendar years of coverage studied.

The selection of these subjects can be made on the basis of the final digit in their certificate numbers, since the enrollment in HIP has been serially numbered as it was accepted. Care has been exercised in the Registrar's Division from the beginning to make sure that this procedure could be safely followed now. This greatly simplifies the checking of the sample and aids in many other procedures connected with the study.

A single statistical summary is being made of all of the enrollment data on every subject in the sample, that is, date of birth, sex, family status, address, contractor group membership, medical group enrollment, and the dates of all changes in the mutable items on the one hand and of all of the reported utilization data. Thus, there are available the observations reported by physicians on these people over a period of years as well as for each year of coverage. It is possible so to relate date of birth to each year's experience of each person that his age in his first, second, third, and fourth year of coverage will be available. While for adults this may not be of prime importance, for children, adolescents, and for those advanced in years, the exact age contemporaneous with the experience is necessary for proper presentation of materials.

In the management of the data on diagnoses, great care is being exercised first to code the reported material intelligently and then to attach to each diagnosis the number of services rendered in connection with it and to indicate whether the diagnosis was reported by a general physician or by a specialist. A nice point arises in connection with the use of hindsight in coding the diagnoses in the earlier phases of a patient's care. But it has been decided to code each year's diagnoses as if they alone were available to the coder. The analysis of the total experience over a period of years should bring out the course of a person's experience, and the character of his earlier diagnoses.

Both in the establishment of the health status of persons and of the categories of health conditions, the HIP materials will present some new problems. Because the benefits provided are comprehensive, the data on diagnoses ramify through all kinds and degrees of illness and injury, obstetrical and pediatric care, preventive

192

services, such as health examinations and immunizations and includes such subjects of remedial services as birthmarks, malformations, and a wide variety of physical defects, obesity, sterility, postural defects, and taper off with minor health problems which for the great mass of people, would be brought to the attention of private physicians only under the conditions of prepaid comprehensive care, aided by an active campaign of health education. This means that in any plan of analysis of the health conditions of the HIP enrolees, the conventional concept of illness itself and of illnesses to be counted as units must be carefully reviewed. Because of this widened range in the nature and seriousness of the conditions for which care is given, comparisons between the experience of different groups of persons and between the experience of the same groups from year to year, cannot be handled as they are when sickness is taken to mean only attacks of well-defined disease. It is becoming evident that in the absence of a precise definition of illness or sickness, comparisons of incidence and prevalence can be safely made only in terms of specific diagnoses and even then considerable allowance must be made for the factors of heightened awareness and attention to minor conditions which characterize different population groups.

Longitudinal studies of this character present many other knotty problems of methodology and presentation of findings. The sheer passage of time brings conditions which increase or decrease the resort to medical care. A somewhat predictable cycle of health conditions underlies the unpredictable occurrence of disease. The two should be disentangled. Even within a four-year period babies grow up, girls enter the child-bearing period, women enter or complete the menopause, boys pass through the hazardous period of accidents, young men reach the peak of health and vigor, the degenerative diseases begin to appear in the middle aged and for their control require medical vigilance, older men enter the period of urological difficulties, both old men and old women reach their terminal illnesses. Some statistical skill will be required to dissect the *expected* from the unpredictable needs for medical services of persons and families. This is, of course, bound up with the interpenetration of preventive and remedial services.

The portrayal of family conditions will not be a simple task. Families are differently composed in respect of members with these varying needs and the composition itself of families changes over the years. Sometimes it changes with startling suddenness as when one of our HIP subscribers divested himself of a childless wife in April and by October had taken unto himself a new wife with two children. Such a domestic turnover brings statistical, if not other kinds of embarrassment. The ways of handling such statistical problems in longitudinal studies require thought and ingenuity if the findings are to be precise and definitive. Groupings of families that are meaningful for health analyses and that facilitate orderly presentation of data remain to be developed. We shall be looking to the sociologist for help and guidance in setting up these groups.

All of these and many other problems assail us as we set out to tell what happened to our HIP families over a four-year period.

The other half of the Special Research Project is an attempt to learn the extent to which the HIP service was augmented by other medical service and to see how the service rendered the HIP families compares with what they otherwise would have received.

THE USE OF OUTSIDE PHYSICIANS BY HIP SUBSCRIBERS

Obviously, the first problem is to test the assumption that the families in HIP rely solely upon it for all of their medical care. It is known that some do not. Some people do not immediately transfer to a new family doctor. For some people HIP membership with its basic medical security makes possible the use of the specialist whom they might not otherwise have. The proportion who continue to use their former physicians or to indulge in having some "eminent" man or otherwise use outside medical services is not known. We are inclined now to believe that the amount of such service cannot be a substantial factor since few people would be willing to go on paying both their HIP premiums and doctors' bills in these times of pressure on family budgets. But it is necessary to know about this situation; speculation about it is not enough. Only a field inquiry will provide the answer. For the ascertainment of this and other facts it has been decided to visit 5,000 HIP families who were enrolled prior to 1951. In this field inquiry the

194

names and addresses of all physicians serving the family for any purpose on the day before the visit, during the eight weeks prior to the visit and for hospitalized illness and disabling conditions lasting seven days or more in the year 1951, will be recorded. This will at once bring out the volume and type of outside medical care that HIP subscribers are using. This can also be related to the length of the period of enrollment and the economic level of the subscriber. Parenthetically, it may be worth noting that the use of outside physicians, if widely followed, would reduce the general utilization rate. We have been inclined to believe that this deficit was more than offset by the conditions of medical neglect encountered in these early years of the Plan's operation. But we have had no way of checking this. The Special Project should help to clear up this question.

Comparison of HIP and Other Families for Medical Care Received and for Health Conditions

Once it had been decided to visit a substantial block of HIP families—5,000—and an equal number of those in the general population, and to try to compare the health conditions found in the two groups and the medical services each group received, the planners of this study were beset with great temptations as well as serious problems of methodology. The temptations were those common to such enterprises. New York City has not had a general health survey of this magnitude since 1935–1936 and badly needs new light on many phases of public health. If families were to be visited in such numbers, the most should be made of the opportunity to learn about their social and economic environment as well as about their health and their experience with medical care. Obviously, their medical care has meaning only as it is related to health conditions and need for it. Moreover, here is an opportunity in the case of the HIP population, to check what respondents to a field inquiry will report about their illnesses and their medical care against what the HIP physicians routinely reported about them. This is heady wine to a group of research people and the natural consequences promptly ensued. Proposals burgeoned for items that

195

it would be well to collect to illuminate the general subjects of health and medical care and that would make the data comparable with studies previously made or now being conducted. But sober second thought has prevailed and it has been agreed that the inquiry must concentrate upon its major objective, that is, of examining the volume and character of medical care received by the two groups of families with a general sickness survey serving as the background against which to assess the adequacy of that care.

Reference has been made above to the likelihood of differences between the HIP and the non-HIP population in awareness of the need for medical care. One device to be employed to measure the effect of the free availability of medical care upon the users of it is the comparison of the length of time that HIP and other persons waited before calling a physician in the case of illness. Another is the extent and nature of unattended illness. Data on the character of prenatal care of all women who have pregnancies within the last year is also to be sought.

The schedule, still subject to pre-testing and revision, to be used in the single-visit survey of households, has enjoyed the benefit of the advice and suggestions of the highly experienced members of the Steering Committee and the staff. It is set up in such a way as to standardize the process of questioning and to pre-code the answers.

While a good many proposed items were finally rejected, we believe that, as it now stands, the schedule and the sickness memorandum will secure data of genuine public health significance and that it will provide an adequate basis for the comparisons toward which this study is primarily pointed.

In the case of 5,000 families, there will be available not only the data collected in the field survey but also all of the materials prepared for the longitudinal study. Thus both the longitudinal picture will be enriched with the additional data on income, education, housing, employment, and the other socio-economic data not reported on the regular HIP records, and the cross-section view will have the benefit of the longitudinal data on these families. The possibilities in the case of these families for testing survey methods are very substantial.

196

Alfred Politz Research, Inc. has been engaged to gather the data from the field, that is,, to secure schedules on approximately 10,000 families. The field work is to be carried through in two months, March and April, 1952.

Let us summarize by saying that in its external aspects the HIP Special Research Project can be said to consist of an analysis of the experiences in health and medical care, as reflected in the HIP records, of about 32,000 persons who have been covered by HIP at some time during the period from January, 1948, to January 15, 1951, with about 8,800 of them covered for four years by the end of 1951. A total of approximately 84,000 person-years of experience will be examined, with 72,000 of them full calendar years.

To bring perspective to this account of the experience of the HIP subscribers, a field survey will be conducted to secure additional data on 5,000 HIP families and comparable data on 5,000 families in the general population of New York City. By means of this survey it is hoped to establish the extent and character of the use of outside physicians by HIP enrollees and to compare the medical services they received in the prevention and the treatment of disease, injury, and defect, with those received by similarly circumstanced families outside of HIP.

Both the longitudinal study and the household survey are expected to make substantial contributions to knowledge of the extent and character of illness and health problems in the families of New York City. Full advantage is to be taken of a situation in which a base population can be described, in which the health data and medical care information comes from physicians reporting currently, and in which the population was free of economic deterrents to the full use of physicians' services for all medical needs.

Viewed from the inside, this inquiry presents many problems of method and technique in the longitudinal study of persons and families with their ascending ages, lengthening periods under comprehensive care, the definition of illness itself, multiple diagnoses, the shifts in family composition, together with all of the issues involved in the completion of a one-interview field survey of a large number of households in two populations, one of which has been

197

subjected to systematic stimulation to pay attention to health problems and to seek medical care for the prevention and early detection of disease. This is but a partial list of the complexities with which the study must deal. But under the guidance of its highly competent Steering Committee, its staff now has considerable confidence that it will come through on time and in good form.

This paper originally appeared in *Research in Public Health,* the proceedings of the 1951 Annual Conference of the Milbank Memorial Fund.

EVALUATING THE COMMUNITY PSYCHIATRIC SERVICE IN CHICHESTER: RESULTS

JACQUELINE GRAD
AND
PETER SAINSBURY

We wish to describe how far the aims of the Chichester and District Psychiatric Service have been achieved in practice.

To do this we will examine referrals to this service and to the control psychiatric service in Salisbury. Next we will compare the patient populations referred to the two services in 1960–1961 to see if they were sufficiently well matched to meet the design of our research. Then we will describe the differences in admissions to hospital in the two services and draw some conclusions about which factors favored community care and which hospital admission. Finally we will summarize initial findings on the effects on the family of looking after a mentally ill person.

Data were gathered to compare the clinical outcome of patients in the two services after two years, to see whether community care was as effective as hospital care and what happened to the families of patients in the community care service. Unfortunately the data-processing machinery to which we entrusted the analysis of our work last year did not prove adequate to the task and these results are not yet available.

WHO IS REFERRED FOR PSYCHIATRIC TREATMENT?

The first question we asked about the Chichester community service was: Who is referred to it, that is, for whom must it provide? An examination of the referral rates in Chichester and Salisbury enabled us to study two aspects of this problem and consider a third (Table 1).

199

TABLE I. POPULATIONS ON WHICH REFERRAL RATES ARE BASED*

TABLE I. POPULATIONS ON WHICH REFERRAL RATES ARE BASED*

Age Group	Chichester		Salisbury	
	Males	Females	Males	Females
15–24	6,797	7,132	6,720	7,402
25–34	6,141	6,507	6,877	7,047
35–44	6,639	7,528	7,155	7,715
45–54	7,602	9,063	7,447	7,839
55–64	6,887	8,853	6,267	7,228
65–74	5,168	7,923	4,378	5,724
75+	2,870	5,396	2,314	3,932
Total population aged 15+ yrs.	42,104	52,402	41,158	46,887

* These figures are taken from the Registrar General's 1961 Census; the populations of military establishments within the two areas have their own psychiatric facilities and have therefore, been deducted.

TABLE 2. REFERRAL RATES PER 1,000 POPULATION FOR MEN AND WOMEN IN 10-YEAR AGE GROUPS FROM CHICHESTER AND SALISBURY SERVICE DISTRICTS

Age Group (yrs.)	Males		Females		Total	
	Chichester	Salisbury	Chichester	Salisbury	Chichester	Salisbury
15–24	5.3	3.3	4.9	4.5	5.1	3.9
25–34	6.0	5.1	10.3	8.4	8.2	6.8
35–44	5.9	3.4	10.2	7.5	8.2	5.5
45–54	4.6	4.8	5.0	5.4	4.8	5.1
55–64	5.1	3.5	6.8	6.1	6.0	4.9
65–74	5.6	4.6	7.1	5.9	6.5	5.3
75+	8.4	5.6	12.8	6.6	11.3	6.2
Total	5.6	4.2	7.8	6.3	6.8	5.3

First, what kind of people are being referred to a psychiatrist, irrespective of the type of service provided? Referral rates will tell us more about the incidence of psychiatric illness in a community than the more commonly reported admission rates do; but the lack of information on who is referred to psychiatric outpatient clinics, day hospitals, and other community services is striking. This omission is becoming increasingly evident as extramural treatment is substituted for the mental hospital. In what follows, therefore, we will attempt to draw some inferences about the characteristics that referrals to Chichester and Salisbury have in common.

Second, what kinds of patients are being selectively referred to a community service? That is, has the introduction of community care affected who is sent for treatment? To answer this question we compare referral rates from Chichester and Salisbury.

Third, the analysis of referral rates provides some clues about the etiology and natural history of mental illness. This epidemiological approach is particularly suitable in communities, such as those we are studying, where psychiatric treatment is freely available, and where every person is registered with a general practitioner and consequently has an equal chance of being referred for psychiatric consultation if he needs it.

FINDINGS

The referral rate for the population aged 15 years and over is 6.8 per 1,000 in Chichester and 5.3 in Salisbury (Table 2). The significantly higher rate in the community service raises a number of questions. Does it, for instance, mean that the service is tapping a larger proportion of the mentally ill in the area? In other words, does the easy access to the psychiatrist, his ready availablity to the family doctor, and the wider range of services offered encourage referral? Or does it only imply that there is more mental illness in the Chichester area for which provision is demanded?

One may also ask whether the higher rate in Chichester is due to more of all kinds of patients being referred, or due to certain types of patients who would not have been referred now coming because of the special facilities of the community service. These problems were examined further by analyzing referral rates by age, sex, marital status, mode of living, district, social class, diagnosis, and duration of illness.

In both services the rate of referral was highest for the age groups 25–44 and 75 and over (Figure 1). Thus referral rates to a service are in marked contrast to the more familiar admission rates to a hospital, which show a steady increase with age.

There were, however, interesting differences between community care and control service. The referral rates to the community service were relatively higher for the two age groups mentioned above. When these differences were further examined by sex, it was seen that the higher community care referral rate was due to the high rate for *women* under 44 and over 75, especially the latter. So far, then, we may say that the younger and the older women have a

201

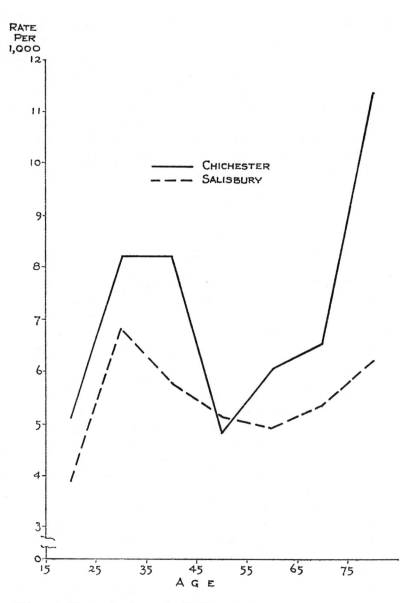

Figure 1. Total referral rates for 1960.

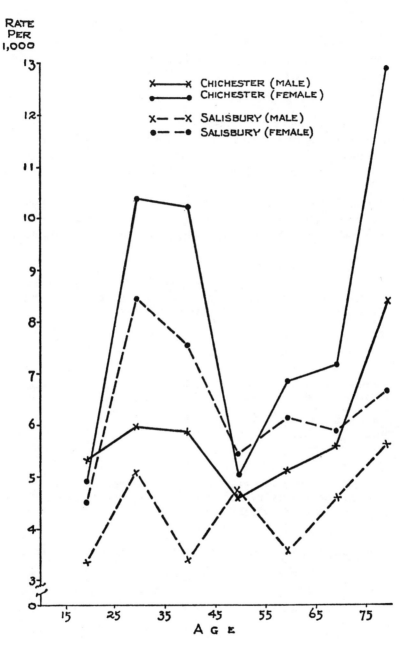

Figure 2. Male and female referral rates for 1960.

greater chance of being referred if there is a community service.

The lowest referral rates to both services are at the ages 45–64 years, the involutional period—a finding which may surprise the clinical psychiatrist.

Age and Sex

In both Chichester and Salisbury the referral rate for women was significantly higher than that for men. As the ratio of the Chichester rate to the Salisbury one was the same for both sexes, sex did not account for the higher referral rate in Chichester (Figure 2).

Marital Status

In both services the rank order of referrals was first divorced and separated, then widowed, next single, lastly the married (Table 3).

TABLE 3. REFERRAL RATES PER 1,000 POPULATION FOR MEN AND WOMEN OVER 15 YEARS BY MARITAL STATUS FROM CHICHESTER AND SALISBURY SERVICE DISTRICTS

Marital Status	Males		Females		Total	
	Chichester	Salisbury	Chichester	Salisbury	Chichester	Salisbury
Single	7.1	5.7	7.0	5.6	7.0	5.6
Married	4.7	3.5	7.2	6.2	5.9	4.9
Widowed	6.9	3.5	9.9	6.6	9.3	5.9
Divorced or separated	45.5	35.5	25.9	23.3	30.5	27.4
Total	5.6	4.2	7.8	6.3	6.8	5.3

TABLE 4. MARITAL STATUS AND AGE: REFERRAL RATES PER 1,000 POPULATION IN THREE AGE GROUPS FOR MARRIED AND SINGLE MEN AND WOMEN, CHICHESTER AND SALISBURY

Age and Marital Status Group*	Males		Females	
	Chichester	Salisbury	Chichester	Salisbury
15–44 yrs., single	7.0	5.2	5.6	4.9
45–64 " "	4.7	8.0	6.8	7.7
65+ " "	14.4	6.7	10.6	5.8
15–44 yrs., married	4.4	3.0	9.3	7.3
45–64 " "	4.4	3.4	5.3	4.8
65+ " "	5.7	5.1	5.8	6.1

* Divorced, separated, and widowed patients are excluded from this table.

204

When marital status rates were broken down by sex the high referral rate for the widowed applied only to women. The high rate in all the single groups suggests that living alone may increase the likelihood of being referred to a psychiatrist.

Table 4 shows that three groups were preferentially referred to the community service, i.e., their rates were markedly higher in Chichester. These were elderly widowed women, young married women (under 44 years), and elderly single men and women.

We have seen that sex alone did not account for the higher referral rate found in the community service, but clearly part of the difference can be accounted for when the age, sex, and marital specific rates are examined.

Living Alone

The higher referral rates for patients without a husband or a wife suggests that social isolation may increase the chance of referral. We, therefore, examined the referral rates for patients living alone, a presumably socially isolated group. We used the tables given in the 1961 National Census[1] to calculate rates for people living alone and for people in two-person households. Table 5 shows that in both services the rates for people living alone were significantly higher and

TABLE 5. REFERRAL RATES PER 1,000 POPULATION BY HOUSE-HOLD SIZE, CHICHESTER AND SALISBURY

Household Size	Chichester	Salisbury
1 person alone	12.3	9.5
2 persons	7.2	5.5
3–4 persons	4.4	3.5
5+ persons	3.6	2.8
Total private households	5.2	3.9
Hotels, boardinghouses, and institutions	23.5	22.5

TABLE 6. REFERRAL RATES PER 1,000 POPULATION OF EM-PLOYED AND RETIRED MALES BY SOCIAL CLASS

Social Class	Chichester	Salisbury
Upper I and II	10.4	8.8
Middle III	4.3	3.9
Lower IV and V	5.0	2.7

so they have a greater chance of being referred to a psychiatrist. The exceptionally high rates for people living in hotels, boardinghouses, and other nonprivate households bear this out. These are general findings and not peculiar to the community service.

Social Class

Table 6 shows that in both services the referral rate for males was highest for Social Classes I and II. This high rate in the professional and managerial classes is of special interest because it is the reverse of what has been found for mental hospital admission rates. Admission to hospital is highest in the lower social classes[2]. This excess of high social class referrals in Chichester is found mainly in the elderly.

The second highest rate in Salisbury was in the middle class group (III), but in the lower ones (IV and V) in Chichester. Moreover, the two services differed significantly in the rates of referral from Classes IV and V. We conclude that there is a relatively greater tendency for nonskilled manual workers to be referred in the Chichester area.

Urban and Rural District Rates

In both services the urban referral rate was higher than the rural. This was especially evident in Chichester. Table 7 shows that the urban referral rate was significantly higher in Chichester, but the rural one is not. This higher urban rate was maintained when age, sex, and marital status were taken into account, so one of the factors contributing to the higher rate in Chichester is the urban rate.

When subdistricts were analyzed separately, we found that the highest referral rate in the Salisbury district was from the city of Salisbury itself (5.6 per 1,000). In the Chichester district the highest rate was in the seaside town of Bognor Regis (8.5 per 1,000) which is seven miles from Chichester City. Chichester had the next highest rate (7.3 per 1,000). The high rate in Bognor implies that proximity to the hospital is not the only factor determining high urban rates.

While a brief acquaintance with the cathedral cities of Salisbury and Chichester would dispel any notion that the higher referral rates are attributable to the stress of city life, the high rate in Bognor may well be related to its ecology which is typical of a holiday resort and one to which the elderly retire. In fact, when Bognor was compared with other administrative areas we saw it had the highest rates for those groups already found to be at risk: the widowed, the single, the aged, and the young married women.

206

Diagnosis

In a preliminary study on the reliability of diagnosis, we found good agreement between the Chichester psychiatrists on broad diagnostic categories. We would also expect reasonable agreement with Salisbury psychiatrists, but have realized in the course of working in the two areas that they differed in the use of detailed diagnostic categories, especially within the functional psychoses.

In both areas referral rates were highest for the functional psychoses, next were the neuroses, then organic psychoses, and lastly personality disorders. With the exception of personality disorders, more women were referred in all diagnostic categories, and this was most marked for depressive illnesses (Table 8).

On comparing the two services, the rates for functional and organic psychoses were found to be significantly higher in the community care service. The two services had very similar referral rates for neuroses (1.9) and for personality disorders (0.5). The higher rate in Chichester is, therefore, confined to the more serious disorders.

With few exceptions patients over 65 were diagnosed as having an organic or depressive disorder. Table 9 shows that the referral rate in

TABLE 7. AREA OF RESIDENCE: REFERRAL RATES PER 1,000 POPULATION AGED 15+ YEARS FROM URBAN AND RURAL AREAS OF CHICHESTER AND SALISBURY SERVICES

District	Rate per 1,000 Population
Chichester urban districts	8.0
rural districts	5.0
Salisbury urban districts	5.4
rural districts	4.5

TABLE 8. REFERRAL RATE PER 1,000 POPULATION BY DIAGNOSTIC GROUPS FROM CHICHESTER AND SALISBURY SERVICE DISTRICTS.

Diagnosis	Males Chichester	Salisbury	Females Chichester	Salisbury	Total Chichester	Salisbury
Organic psychoses	1.2	0.6	1.4	1.0	1.3	0.8
Functional psychoses	2.2	1.5	3.5	2.7	2.9	2.1
Neuroses	1.4	1.5	2.3	2.3	1.9	1.9
Personality disorders and other	0.9	0.6	0.6	0.3	0.7	0.5
Total	5.6	4.2	7.8	6.3	6.8	5.3

TABLE 9. REFERRAL RATE PER 1,000 POPULATION AGED 65+ YEARS FOR ORGANIC DISORDERS AND DEPRESSIONS FROM CHICHESTER AND SALISBURY SERVICE DISTRICTS

Diagnosis	Chichester	Salisbury
Organic disorders	3.9	2.9
Depressions	3.8	2.1

TABLE 10. REFERRAL RATES PER 1,000 POPULATION AGED 15+ YEARS BY DURATION OF PRIOR ILLNESS.

Duration of Illness	Chichester	Salisbury
Less than 6 months	3.8	2.4
6 months to 2 years	0.8	0.8
2 or more years	2.1	2.1

the population 65 and over for organic disorders and depression was higher in Chichester. The rate for depression in this age group was 3.8 in Chichester and 2.0 in Salisbury; the rates for organic disorders were 3.9 and 2.8, respectively. In the age group 15–44 the most obvious difference was the higher rate for depression in Chichester (3.1) compared with Salisbury (2.3). Depressive illness appears to account for the greater part of the relatively high referral rate at this age. When referral rates by diagnosis were examined in the sub-districts, the most striking finding was the high rate for depressive illnesses in Bognor Regis.

Duration of Illness

On referral the psychiatrist recorded on the research schedule how long the patient had been ill. Table 10 compares referral rates of patients with illnesses of durations of less than six months, of six months to two years, and over two years in the two services; it shows that Chichester had a much higher rate for patients with illnesses of short duration, but the rates did not differ for illnesses which had lasted for longer than six months. Therefore, we concluded both that the introduction of a community service encouraged referral at an earlier point in the illness, and that some patients with recent illnesses were being referred who were missed by the hospital-oriented service.

The pattern of referral rates was similar in the two services in the following ways: Women were more likely to be referred than men; the peak age groups for referral were 25–44 years and 75 and over, and the first of these was mainly due to the referral of young married women. Referral rates dipped at the age group 45–64 years. Rates for married men were low, but young married women had a higher rate than single ones. Other marital status rates were highest for the divorced and separated, and for other groups likely to be living alone. The importance of this last is further borne out by the exceptionally high rate of people living in one-person households and hotels.

People from the highest social classes and town dwellers were referred more commonly whatever the type of service, and, finally, the diagnostic group with the highest referral rate was the functional psychoses. The majority of these were endogenous depressions.

All the above mentioned are, we infer, high risk groups for referral for psychiatric treatment.

The higher referral rate in Chichester can probably be ascribed to the introduction of community care. That this may be so is supported both by the finding that the rates were higher in all categories of referral with very few exceptions, and that they were higher for illnesses of short duration.

The referral rates which distinguished the community service were those for elderly widowed women, particularly those living alone in towns; for young married housewives; for the lower social classes, and for people suffering from depression and organic disorders.

Finally, there is some suggestion, both from the analysis of these rates and from the known figures for suicide, that there are some social configurations which predispose to mental breakdown. One of these may well be the solitary mode of living that retirement to a seaside resort away from one's family and previous community imposes. This is a hypothesis we will be able to explore further in the more detailed follow-up study of a cohort of these patients.

MATCHING THE PATIENT POPULATIONS
IN CHICHESTER AND SALISBURY

The design of this study to evaluate the community service by contrasting it with a hospital-centered one, required that the two popula-

| | Per cent Referred | | No. Referred | |
	Chichester	Salisbury	Chichester	Salisbury
Patients Referred	100	100	823	585
Sex				
men	38	38	309	220
women	62	62	514	365
Age: men				
15–24	15	11	47	24
25–34	15	21	46	47
35–44	18	13	55	29
45–54	16	21	48	47
55–64	15	14	47	31
65+	21	19	66	42
Age: women				
15–24	9	10	46	38
25–34	16	21	82	75
35–44	20	19	102	68
45–54	12	15	62	53
55–64	14	14	72	52
65+	29	22	150	79
Marital status				
single	24	24	199	140
married	57	62	468	363
widowed	15	10	120	60
divorced or separated	4	4	36	22

tions referred should be comparable; or at least we should know in
what respects they are dissimilar, so that any differences could be
allowed for in the analysis.

Since the referral rates to Chichester and Salisbury differed, the
matching of the two populations on those clinical and social characteristics which might affect disposal and outcome, are important,
especially as regards age, sex, and severity of illness.

Tables 11 and 12 and Figure 3 show how the two populations re-
semble each other on the most relevant variables. The social and
demographic characteristics are well matched. The one respect in which
they differ is in the higher proportion of elderly women patients referred to Chichester. Although this difference does not reach statistical
significance, its effects are evident in the slightly higher proportion of
widows and retired housewives in the community service.

To see how the two populations matched clinically we assessed

210

TABLE 12. PER CENT DISTRIBUTION OF REFERRALS TO CHI-
CHESTER AND SALISBURY SERVICES COMPARED FOR SOCIAL AND
CLINICAL VARIABLES

| | Per Cent Referred | | No. Referred | |
	Chichester	Salisbury	Chichester	Salisbury
Patients Referred	100	100	823	585
Social class				
I and II	36	34	296	197
III	38	40	310	229
IV and V	25	26	206	151
Employment status: men				
working	42	38	130	83
off sick	20	25	61	54
unemployed	15	18	47	39
retired	22	20	69	44
Employment status: women				
working	13	12	69	42
off sick	5	8	25	29
unemployed	10	9	53	33
retired	16	11	84	40
housewives	55	61	283	221
Previous illness				
with	47	45	387	264
without	53	55	436	321
Diagnosis: men				
organic psychoses	21	15	65	34
functional psychoses	40	36	123	79
neuroses	23	34	71	74
other	16	15	50	33
Diagnosis: women				
organic psychoses	18	16	90	58
functional psychoses	45	43	233	157
neuroses	30	35	152	128
other	8	6	39	22

severity of illness in both services; we also compared the broad diagnostic categories and amount of previous illnesses referred to each.

Severity was described in two ways. First we ranked the frequency with which the 28 symptoms were recorded in both services. They ranged from such disabling symptoms as delusions and aggression to milder ones such as loss of concentration and insomnia. A high rank correlation (0.88) implied that the two populations had a similar range of mild and severe symptoms referred.

Despite the hazards of recording diagnosis reliably, when broad categories were used no significant difference was found in the

211

diagnoses of women referred. The only difference in the men was that more than the expected number of neuroses were referred in Salisbury. This was significant at the 5 per cent level.

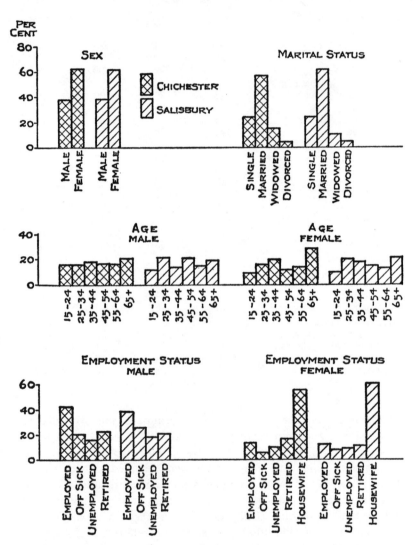

Figure 3. Matching: referrals to Chichester and Salisbury, compared for social, demographic, and clinical factors.

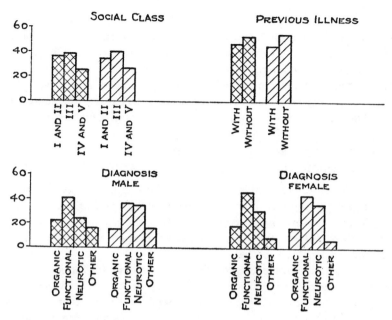

Figure 3. (Continued)

Secondly, severity was independently measured by the effects the illness had had on the family at the time the patient was referred. This measure was chosen as one particularly appropriate to an inquiry intended to assess community care. A rating of burden on the family was obtained on a random sample (of approximately one-third) of the referrals. The effect of the illness on the family in the two services did not differ significantly (Table 13).

TABLE 13. EFFECTS ON FAMILIES WHEN PATIENTS ARE FIRST REFERRED TO THE PSYCHIATRIST

| | | Per Cent of Families Rated | | |
	No Burden	Some Burden	Severe Burden	
Chichester N = 271	40	42	18	100
Salisbury N = 139	29	46	25	100
Total sample N = 410	36	44	20	100

213

We concluded, first, that although Chichester had more patients referred they were clinically similar to those in Salisbury. Secondly, more patients in all diagnostic categories were being seen in Chichester.

Thirdly, such differences in the referred populations as have been found suggested that the Chichester service tended to receive relatively more elderly patients and organic disorders and fewer neurotics. Any bias, therefore, is toward more severe cases in Chichester.

THE EFFECT OF COMMUNITY CARE
ON ADMISSION TO HOSPITAL AT REFERRAL

Whether a service of this kind affects the number of hospital beds that a community must provide for its mentally sick has been a topic of current concern in Britain ever since the Minister of Health published a Hospital Plan which predicted that our need for psychiatric beds in 1970 will be halved.

The original purpose of the Chichester community service, it will be remembered, was to reduce admissions to an overcrowded hospital, and Dr. Morrissey's paper gives figures to show that this was soon achieved. Our own findings confirm this. Despite the similarity of the populations referred to the two services, the proportions of referrrals admitted to the hospital in the Chichester district and in the Salisbury district were very different. Admission was recommended (and carried out within three days) for 14 per cent of all patients referred to the Chichester community service and for 52 per cent of those referred to the Salisbury hospital service.

TABLE 14. DETAILED DISPOSAL IN THE TWO SERVICES AT REFERRAL

| | Per Cent Referred | | No. Referred | |
	Chichester	Salisbury	Chichester	Salisbury
Admitted to				
mental hospital	14	52	117	303
other institution	8	5	72	30
Total admitted	22	57		
Not admitted				
day hospital	15	—	120	1
home care	16	3	129	20
outpatient	34	35	278	205
discharged to G.P.	13	4	107	26
Total not admitted	78	43		

214

In Table 14 the disposal of patients after they had first seen the psychiatrist is set out in more detail, and it is seen that in Chichester 78 per cent of the patients remained with their families, being treated at home (16 per cent), at the day hospital (15 per cent), as outpatients (34 per cent), or discharged to the care of their general practitioner (13 per cent). In Salisbury, 43 per cent remained with their families. The same proportion as in Chichester attended outpatient clinics but only 3 per cent were treated in their homes.

DISPOSAL RELATED TO CLINICAL
AND SOCIAL CHARACTERISTICS

These differences in disposal between Chichester and Salisbury led us to ask which clinical and social considerations determine admission and which favor home care. It can be seen in Table 14 that 22 per cent of referrals to the community service were thought to need a bed, either in the mental hospital or some alternative institution (usually a geriatric ward or nursing home), whereas in the hospital-oriented service this need applied to 57 per cent, a ratio of 2.6 admitted in Salisbury for every one admitted in Chichester.

It would be reasonable to expect the lower proportion admitted in Chichester to be consistently maintained in all groups of patients and any marked departure from the expected ratio (1:2.6) occurring in

TABLE 15. PROPORTION OF REFERRALS ADMITTED RELATED TO DEMOGRAPHIC FACTORS

| | Per Cent Admitted | | No. Referred | |
	Chichester	Salisbury	Chichester	Salisbury
Patients referred	22	57	823	585
Sex				
Men	22	54	309	220
Women	23	59	514	365
Age				
15–44	13	46	378	281
45–64	21	62	229	183
65+	42	76	216	121
Marital status				
married	16	48	468	363
single	26	67	199	140
widowed	44	84	120	60
divorced or separated	31	68	36	22

any group will be of interest as indicating that the characteristics of that group affected disposal differently in the two services. By comparing proportions of referrals admitted in the two areas in this way we were able to discover which types of patients were preferentially admitted and which were treated outside the hospital.

TABLE 16. PROPORTION OF REFERRALS ADMITTED RELATED TO CLINICAL FACTORS

| | Per Cent Admitted | | No. Referred | |
	Chichester	Salisbury	Chichester	Salisbury
Patients referred	22	57	823	585
Diagnosis				
organic psychoses	47	89	155	92
functional psychoses	24	64	356	236
neuroses	8	36	223	202
personality disorders	21	54	42	41
other	9	36	47	14
Previous illness				
with	20	58	387	264
without	26	56	436	321
Duration of illness				
<6 months	29	61	451	264
−2 years	14	48	112	89
2+ years	16	55	246	226
Symptoms				
suicidal	60	68	40	56
aggressive	60	69	50	65
confused	59	88	114	113
unable to care for self	60	94	74	107
deluded	48	87	73	106
hallucinated	43	89	49	56
overactive	54	71	43	62
insomnia	22	53	367	284
loss of concentration	19	52	218	210
phobias	5	38	43	47
anxiety	9	46	205	286

Tables 15, 16, and 17 show that whichever category of patients was considered the community service always had lower, and usually very markedly lower, proportions of referrals admitted. However, the proportion admitted in the various groups often differed considerably from the expected 22 per cent in Chichester and 57 per cent in Salisbury.

216

TABLE 17. PROPORTION OF REFERRALS ADMITTED RELATED TO SOCIAL FACTORS

| | Per Cent Admitted | | No. Referred | |
	Chichester	Salisbury	Chichester	Salisbury
Patients referred	22	57	823	585
Social class				
I and II	25	55	296	197
III	16	54	310	229
IV and V	30	62	206	151
Household size				
living alone	34	82	83	57
wih 1 other	22	62	226	163
with 2–3 others	18	46	304	219
with 4 or more	15	50	144	111
hotel or institution	59	82	58	34
Household composition				
living alone	34	82	83	57
with spouse	16	48	436	352
with children	32	69	53	29
with parents	14	53	99	68
with relatives or friends	30	80	70	35
with others	46	77	78	43
Employment status				
employed	8	31	199	125
off sick	27	63	86	83
unemployed	32	72	100	72
retired	45	76	153	84
housewives	18	57	283	221

Sex, Age, and Marital Status

Both services admitted referred men and women in roughly equal proportions. Although more women were referred than men, sex did not affect disposal in either service. Age, however, was a factor differentiating the services. The community service admitted more than the expected aged referrals, and fewer of the expected younger ones than did the hospital service; though again, of course, the actual proportion admitted was consistently less. The Chichester service, therefore, is prepared to cope *in the community* with the needs of younger patients more readily than those of older ones (Figure 4).

In both services proportionately fewer married than single referrals were admitted; but this preference for treating married patients in the community was more evident in Chichester. Whereas Chichester favored the extramural care of the married, the converse was found with widowed referrals.

217

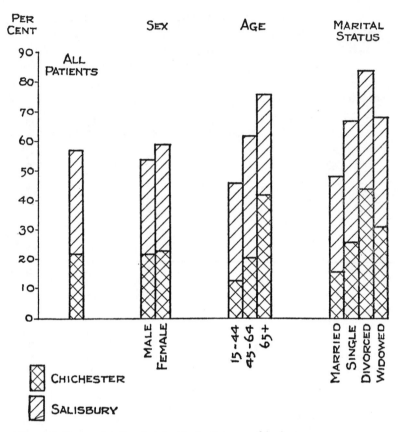

Figure 4. Per cent referrals admitted: demographic factors.

Diagnosis

Neurotics and other referrals with minor conditions who were discharged to the general practitioner following consultation were those least often admitted to hospital in both services. But the ratio of admission of neurotics was one in Chichester to every four in Salisbury (cf. 1:2.6 for all referrals). In contrast, the senile and organic psychoses were preferentially admitted whatever the service, but the readiness to admit was more marked in the community service, the ratio now changing from 1:2.6 to 1:1.9. The functional psychoses were admitted in about the expected proportion in both services. The com-

218

munity service, in spite of a low admission rate, selectively encouraged the admission of organic psychoses and discouraged the admission of neuroses by comparison with the hospital service.

Previous Illness and Duration

A history of previous illness was not clearly related to admission in either service, though there was some tendency for patients with a history to be admitted in Chichester in preference to those without a history.

Illnesses of short duration tended to be admitted in both services, while those of longer duration were excluded from hospital to a relatively greater extent in the community service (Figure 5).

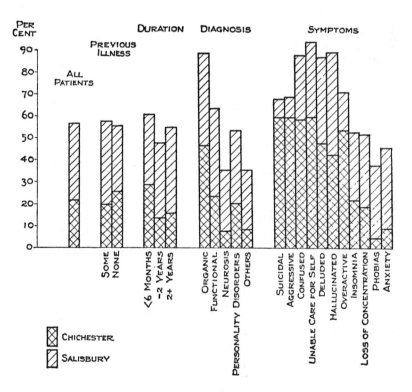

Figure 5. Per cent referrals admitted: clinical factors.

219

Symptoms

It is of interest to see which symptoms are least well tolerated in the community. Referrals with the most socially conspicuous and disturbing symptoms were admitted nearly as readily in the community service as the hospital one. For example, about 60 per cent of those clinically judged as suicidal, aggressive, or unable to care for themselves at referral were admitted in both services. In no other categories did the proportion of referrals admitted in the services so closely approach one another. The community service was apparently sufficiently alert to these significant conditions to recognize them and respond appropriately (Figure 5).

Social Class and Occupation

Both services admitted proportionately more patients referred from the lower socio-economic classes. A distinctive feature of the community service was that patients in Social Class III (skilled manual and white collar workers) were preferentially treated outside hospital. Whether the patient was currently working also influenced admission. The community service rarely admitted any patient who was employed at referral, and a much less marked trend in the same direction was evident in the hospital service. Similarly the community spared active housewives from admission to a greater extent than did the other service. Unemployed and retired people in both services had a higher likelihood of admission. Compared with Salisbury, Chichester preferentially admitted the retired as they did the aged and widowed (Figure 6).

Household Size and Composition

Patients who lived apart from their families at referral, either alone or in hotels, were those most likely to be admitted in both services. Living in a hotel was a factor notably affecting admission in the Chichester service. People living with a husband or wife were relatively unlikely to be admitted in both services. This also applied in Chichester to young people living with their parents, though not in Salisbury. Living in social isolation increased the probability of admission, especially in the community service (Figure 6).

In conclusion, all clinical factors were found to affect admission markedly, whatever the service. Those operating differentially in that they were more powerful in the Chichester community service were:

220

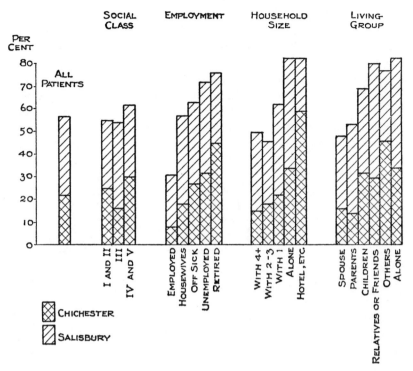

Figure 6. Per cent referrals admitted: social factors.

a diagnosis of organic psychosis, a recent onset of illness, and the presence of clinically severe and socially disabling symptoms.

Similiarly, most social factors affected admission in both services. Those more operative in the community service were old age and social isolation. Married patients, young people, those in Social Class III, and those living with a near relative were selectively treated in the community.

Table 18 and Figures 7 and 8 show what happens to the patients in Chichester and which extramural facilities are most likely to be recommended *at referral* for the various groups of patients.

Nursing homes and other institutions are alternatives to the mental hospital for the disposal of old and widowed patients, but unlike the mental hospital they are rarely used by patients in Social Class II.

221

The day hospital, on the other hand, is used least for the elderly. Affective psychoses predominate, whereas organic disorders are eschewed; otherwise this disposal is not especially selected for any category.

Domiciliary care was used for widowed *women* with senile psychoses and seldom for referrals under 35 years, for men, and for those who were divorced or separated. It was used more for the married than the single, and contrary to prediction, home care showed no clear association with social class.

TABLE 18. DETAILS OF DISPOSAL IN THE CHICHESTER SERVICE

	22% Admitted			*78% Not Admitted*		
	14	8	15	16	34	13
	Grayling-well	*Other Institutions*	*Day Hospital*	*Domicili-ary Care*	*Outpatient Clinics*	*Discharged to G.P.*
Age						
15–24	12	3	10	4	45	26
25–34	6	5	19	7	48	14
35–44	10	3	17	13	43	14
45–54	15	6	17	8	43	11
55–64	15	8	19	14	32	12
65+	23	19	8	32	10	7
Sex						
Men	16	7	14	4	36	7
Women	13	10	15	18	31	12
Marital status						
single	18	8	13	11	36	15
married	10	6	18	15	40	12
widowed	23	21	6	31	6	13
divorced or separated	22	8	14	8	31	17
Social class						
I	17	11	12	17	35	9
II	17	6	12	18	35	12
III	9	8	18	17	35	14
IV	17	15	14	12	28	14
V	24	3	14	14	35	11
Diagnosis						
senile	21	31	—	39	1	7
other organic	28	15	6	11	31	9
schizophrenic	22	3	14	11	35	16
affective	18	5	24	15	34	3
reactive	5	10	10	21	42	13
anxiety	2	1	16	10	50	21
personality disorder	7	14	5	10	38	26
other	2	6	4	7	17	63

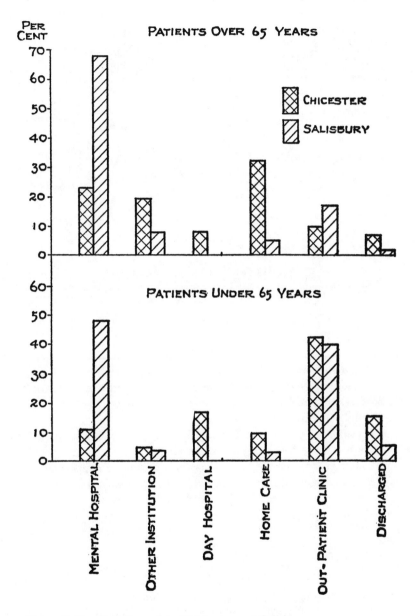

Figure 7. Detailed disposal in Chichester and Salisbury.

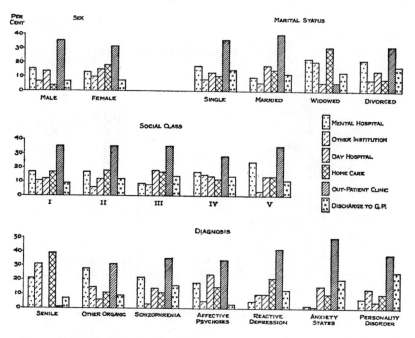

Figure 8. Detailed disposal in Chichester.

Outpatient clinics, like the day hospital, are used least for the old and widowed. Whereas the day hospital cares for those with affective disorders, outpatient clinics are more likely to be used for treating neurotic patients.

Discharge of patients to the family doctor following a single consultation is more frequently recommended for patients under 25 than any other group, and for those diagnosed as having a personality disorder and those with no psychiatric abnormality. It was least often recommended for men, for the aged, and for people in the highest social class.

EFFECTS ON THE FAMILY

One of the principal ways we chose to evaluate the community care service was by estimating whether community care placed an undue burden on patients' families. Although data on the long-term

224

effects on the families of patients in Chichester and Salisbury are not yet available, some interesting findings have emerged regarding the burden of mental illness to the family both at the time the psychiatrist is first called in (the most acute stage of the illness) and in the month after the patient was referred.

We have seen that in Chichester many people with mental illnesses of all degrees of severity are living in the community. Were it not for the introduction of the community care service they would have been admitted to a mental hospital. If you lived in Salisbury during the year 1960–1961 and were sent by your family doctor to see a psychiatrist, you were more than twice as likely to go to the mental hospital as you were if you lived in Chichester. If it were true that community care placed a heavier burden on families than mental hospital care, then you would expect to find that patients' families in Chichester had more problems to bear than families in Salisbury.

Four hundred and ten patients, a random sample of approximately one in three of all referrals to both areas, were chosen for detailed study and an estimate of the effect they had on their families was made (*see* Table 13).

By the time these 410 patients first saw the psychiatrist for advice, nearly two-thirds of their families were facing problems that were marked enough to be recognized by the fairly crude measures we used, and in one-fifth of them this burden was rated as being severe. At that time—before referral to mental hospital or community care had been made—there was no difference between the problems incurred by families in Chichester and Salisbury (*see* Table 13).

More than one-half of our informants ascribed symptoms of emotional disturbance to worrying about the patient, and one-fifth of them attributed neurotic symptoms such as insomnia, headaches, excessive irritability, and depression to concern about the patient's behavior. Social and leisure activities were restricted in a third of the families, and children were adversely affected in a third. Twenty-nine per cent had had their domestic routine, housework, shopping, etc., upset. A quarter of the families had had their income reduced by at least 10 per cent, and in 9 per cent the family income had been cut to less than half its usual level. These figures represent a serious amount of social disability, especially when one recollects that mental illnesses of all degrees of severity are catered to in the National Health Service, so that mild cases sent for consultation and advice only were included in our sample.

225

The behavior popularly associated with insanity, such as violence, disturbing the neighbors, and embarrassing acts, was not that which caused the greatest concern, rather it was the importunate patient who made excessive demands that disturbed families most.

The type of behavior most frequently referred to as troublesome, for example, was the patient's preoccupation with and harping on various bodily complaints. Second in importance was the family's fear that the patient might harm himself—commit suicide or meet with an accident in traffic or at home. Another group of patients whose behavior was particularly disturbing to their families were those who needed nursing care or supervision at home. Thirty per cent of the sample required attention of this sort and half of these (15 per cent of the 410) were bedfast or required such constant attention that the relatives said the patient could hardly ever be left alone. It was the elderly patients and those with organic psychoses who restricted other family members in numerous ways and caused the most severe burden.

Those families who had other problems besides the patient found him the more difficult to cope with. They are likely to be hardest hit by any type of psychiatric service that places more of the care of the patient on them. Any schemes for home care and the treatment of patients outside the mental hospital will need to make some provision in the community for those social, health, and economic peculiarities of families shown to be especially liable to hardship when they have a patient at home. Similarly, allowances need to be made for interpersonal stresses within a family in deciding whether treatment within or out of a hospital is to be preferred.

Effects on the Family Compared in the Two Services

The main purpose of the study was to evaluate the community care service by comparing the effect it had on families with the effect that a hospital-centered service had. The second rating of family burden was made three to five weeks after referral when the decision to admit the patient, or not, had been implemented. The burden on families in both areas had now decreased significantly.

Table 19 shows that when just those families who had a *severe* burden were considered separately, both services were equally effective. Chichester reduced severe burden in 62 per cent, and Salisbury in 61 per cent, of the families. But when the whole sample was analyzed, 44 per cent of the families in whom any adverse effect had been recorded were relieved in Salisbury and 35 per cent in Chichester. Although the

TABLE 19. PERCENTAGE OF RELIEF ONE MONTH AFTER RE-
FERRAL

| | Families Relieved | | | |
| | Chichester | | Salisbury | |
Burden Rating	%	Number	%	Number
Some	24	109	36	64
Severe	62	47	61	33
Total (any burden)	35	156	44	97

TABLE 20. PERCENTAGE OF RELIEF ABOUT "WORRYING"
BEHAVIOR

| | Families Relieved | | | |
| | Chichester | | Salisbury | |
Type of Behavior	%	Number	%	Number
Frequent complaints about bodily symptoms	22	93	41	58
A danger to himself	67	86	76	49
Importunate and demanding	40	80	61	54
Behaving oddly or expressing peculiar ideas	51	65	63	40
Unco-operative and contrary	56	82	95	20
Restless or overtalkative	66	71	82	22
Troublesome at night	75	59	75	24
A danger to others	67	33	65	17
Objectionable, rude, or embarrassing	57	28	80	5

greater relief afforded by Salisbury was not statistically significant, the
trend was consistently maintained in all clinical and social groups. For
example, the relief in the different diagnostic groups was not significantly greater in one service than in the other; nevertheless, in all
diagnoses the relief was a little greater in Salisbury, notably in organic
cases which were the most difficult for families to cope with.

None of the psychiatric symptoms previously found to be related to
family burden was relieved more in one service than in the other.
However, one other symptom, depression, related significantly to the
family burden in the two services. Patients with depression caused
more hardship if they were treated in the community service than if
they were treated in the hospital service. Patients with depression
were not usually admitted in Chichester.

We found also that families who had patients with more socially
serious symptoms—being troublesome at night, dangerous to themselves and others, or behaving peculiarly—tended to be equally relieved in the two services; but families dealing with patients who

227

displayed less socially conspicuous behavior were relieved significantly more in Salisbury than in the Chichester community service (Table 20).

The community care families were relieved more than the Salisbury ones when the patient was under 40 years old. In the higher age groups, previously found to present most problems, however, Salisbury families were relieved significantly more. An allied finding was that the Salisbury services relieved the families of widowed patients more. In both services the families of the women patients were helped more than those of men.

A significantly greater relief in anxiety in the closest relative, and reduced interference with social and leisure activities, was obtained in Salisbury. On the other hand, there was a decided tendency for Chichester families to be relieved if the patient's employment situation had been a cause for concern. Perhaps if the patient remained out of the hospital, the threat of losing his job because of illness was less (Table 21).

Again, the ways in which the patient's illness disrupted family life were helped in Chichester as much as in Salisbury if they were conspicuously disturbing, such as loss of income or employment or quarrels with neighbors, but where the private anxiety or leisure time of the family was concerned the Salisbury service helped more (Table 21).

The comparison of the effects on the family in the two services was designed to find out whether too heavy demands were made on families in the home-care service. The most definite conclusions we have been

TABLE 21. PERCENTAGE OF RELIEF IN SELECTED FAMILY PROBLEMS

| | Families Relieved | | | |
| | Chichester | | Salisbury | |
	%	Number	%	Number
Health of closest relative:				
mental	10	217	20	108
physical	42	83	45	29
Social and leisure activities of family	34	89	63	51
Children affected	18	33	18	17
Domestic routine	65	63	81	52
Income of family	6	69	8	25
Employment of others than patient	63	38	62	26
Patient's employment affected	11	27	6	17
Patient's job lost	18	17	8	12
Difficulty with neighbors caused by patient	68	22	50	6

228

able to draw is that in spite of the community service admitting 50 per cent fewer patients, the over-all burden on the family one month after referral was not reduced *significantly* more in one service than in the other. Contact with the psychiatrist had an equally impressive effect in reducing family burden after one month in *both* services. This was too soon for treatment to have played a large part and suggested that it was either admission to the hospital or the feeling that help was now available and that something was going to be done that accounted for the relief.

The services were most similar in the degree to which they relieved *severe* burden. Whereas the community service responded to severe burden as well as did the hospital-centered service, it was not so effective in helping families where problems were less marked. The Chichester community service tends to leave families to cope with the less severe problems.

The way that the service seems to operate is by selecting for admission those patients whose families had most problems. This, of course, requires very careful selection for admission. It seems that to be as effective as a hospital-centered service in reducing family burden, a community care service must be *more* sensitive to family and social problems. In Chichester this extra awareness of the psychiatrists to the effect that a patient has on his family and the careful judgment of the family's level of tolerance is probably achieved by the practice of frequent domiciliary visiting and close contact with the general practitioners. The ready availability of the psychiatrist in the community also means not only that he is subject to more social pressure and closer to the family situation but that more families and general practitioners are *prepared* to cope with their patients out of hospital. This is a peculiarity of the setup of the service in Chichester and possibly of the personalities of the psychiatrists there. It would not necessarily apply to all types of community care service.

In conclusion, we should like to add a word about the implications of social psychiatric investigations of this kind for social planning.

The controversy over community care that has waged since Tooth and Brooke[3] published their article on psychiatric bed needs has provided some nice examples of incomplete bits of information being used to support unsubstantiated beliefs about the value of one or the other type of care.

The effect that increased extramural treatment of psychiatric patients has on the community is only one aspect of a complex problem

229

of social planning which must include a regard for the therapeutic and administrative efficiency of this treatment. Little will be known about outcome, for example, until more follow-up studies are done.

To concentrate, however, on the aspect we have looked at in most detail—effect on the family—individual hard cases have been widely quoted in the press and at meetings to show that community care is harmful. Certainly you could also take our findings to mean that families have a greater burden to bear where this policy prevails.

However, it would be improper to condemn a policy on insufficient evidence. All our figures show is that for *certain types of patients* and in *certain social circumstances* home care, as it is provided at Chichester, leaves the family with more problems than mental hospital care does.

Psychiatric patients are not a homogenous group and it is essential to find out what types of psychiatric service organizations are appropriate for what types of patients. The most compelling and best substantiated warnings about the harmful effects that community care may have on families of patients come from the work of Wing and Brown[4] of the Medical Research Council's Social Psychiatry Research Unit. They have looked at the effect of chronic schizophrenic patients as presenting the most intractable psychiatric problem, and it is important that their extremely valuable contribution should not be generalized as a condemnation of community care for all psychiatric patients. Similarly, although Tizard and Grad[5] found that families who cared for an idiot or imbecile at home were heavily penalized, this did not lead them to the conclusion that institutional care was to be recommended.

All that these findings can do is to point to problems implicit in the present situation and suggest possible remedies. They are never the complete test of the efficacy of a system.

REFERENCES

[1] Census 1961, England and Wales, London, Her Majesty's Stationery Office.

[2] The Registrar General's Review of England and Wales for the Year 1960, London, Her Majesty's Stationery Office.

[3] Tooth, G. C., and Brooke, E. M., Trends in the Mental Hospital Population, *Lancet,* 1, 710–713, April 1, 1961.

[4] Wing, John, et al., Morbidity in the Community of Schizophrenics Discharged from London Mental Hospitals in 1959, *British Journal of Psychiatry,* 110, 10–21, January, 1964.

[5] Tizard, Jack, and Grad, Jacqueline, THE MENTALLY HANDICAPPED AND THEIR FAMILIES, Maudsley Monograph, No. 7, London, Oxford Press, 1961.

231

Interview Techniques and Problems Associated with Health Surveys

SOME PROBLEMS IN THE COLLECTION AND ANALYSIS OF MORBIDITY DATA OBTAINED FROM SAMPLE SURVEYS

ANN CARTWRIGHT[1]

THIS is a discussion of problems considered in formulating questions to elicit information about ill-health. The biases of different methods are considered and a method of analyzing the data collected in an inquiry utilizing a particular set of questions is described. A comparison is made between the results obtained in this inquiry and those from the Survey of Sickness (1), and the probable effects of the two different methods on the results are discussed.

SCOPE OF THIS SAMPLE SURVEY

This survey was part of a larger research program that was undertaken by the Public Health Department of the London School of Hygiene and Tropical Medicine. The broad aim of the whole project was to study people's use of the different parts of the National Health Service. The study was carried out in a relatively small area so that material could be collected from several sources about the different aspects of the problem. The area chosen was a post-war housing estate just outside London. The estate had a population of about seventeen thousand. As in many other new housing estates, the population was relatively young with a high proportion of children and few elderly people (2).

A family morbidity survey was designed as part of this research project. Its aims were to supplement information obtained from various records, and also to present a picture of the problems of ill-health and the success of the health services in solving these problems, as seen from the viewpoint of the individuals and families concerned. The sample for this study was composed of the families and individuals living in a

[1] Department of Public Health and Social Medicine, University of Edinburgh. Formerly in the Department of Public Health, London School of Hygiene and Tropical Medicine.

randomly selected three-sixteenths of the dwellings on the estate. We aimed at interviewing, personally, all the adults[2] in this sample of dwellings on two occasions (3), at an interval of four weeks.

In addition, mothers of school and pre-school children were to be interviewed about their children on two other occasions, also at an interval of four weeks.

The morbidity survey was conducted during the period from May, 1954 to February, 1955.

AIMS AND DIFFICULTIES IN FORMULATING THE QUESTIONS

At the first interview we wanted information about people's health at that point in time. We thought of this as including not only illnesses which were present at the time, but also recurrent conditions to which people believed they were subject. For each of these conditions, we wanted to know such things as when it first started, whether it caused much pain or discomfort, what treatment and advice had been received for it, and whether the individual was satisfied with the treatment received. At the second interview we concentrated on events that had occurred between the two interviews: new illnesses, and incapacities and also the consultations, and any medicines which had been taken during that time. The various consultations and medicines were related to particular illnesses by asking what illnesses they were for, and any condition disclosed at this stage that had not been reported previously was recorded.

At the first interview, however, we were anxious to avoid formulating any criteria of illness based on incapacity, or consultation, or medication in asking about people's health at that time. We wanted to obtain an index of morbidity that did not depend on people's use of the health services or on whether they had spent time in bed or stayed away from work.

It is perhaps worth expanding this point so that we can consider the advantages and disadvantages of the methods we ac-

[2] This we defined simply as people aged 15 or more who had left school.

236

tually used against those of other possible methods. If, for example, we had asked only about illnesses for which a general practitioner had been consulted, that measure of morbidity would have been open to the objection that some people will consult a doctor about an illness for which other people would not. Whether or not a person consults his doctor about a particular complaint will depend on such things as his estimate of what the doctor can do for his illness, his fear of what he may be told, his dislike of treatment, his need of a certificate, his past experience of general practitioners, his relationship with his present physician, the time he has to wait in the surgery, his estimate of the severity of possible consequences of his illness, his tolerance of pain or discomfort, etc. All these factors mean that the amount of use made of general practitioners may not be directly related to the existence of morbid conditions.

Again, if we had taken as our criteria certain degrees of incapacity, staying in bed or stopping away from work or school or not going out of doors, this would mean in effect very different things for the housewife with young children, the elderly retired man living on his own, the adolescent girl in her first job, and so on.

In addition, if we had taken either of these criteria—consultation with a doctor or a certain degree of incapacity, we would not have been told about a number of conditions in which we were, in fact, interested. We wanted to compare the varicose veins for which people consult the doctor with those they do not, and we wanted to compare the people who acted in these different ways.

Once we rejected these various objective criteria for defining an illness we were confronted with other problems and difficulties. Whether a person reports an illness to an interviewer will be influenced by such things as his impression of the purpose of the inquiry, his relationship with the interviewer, his attitude toward ill-health, his ability to express his opinions, and of course, on the actual questions asked.

237

Our aims in formulating the questions to be asked at the first interview in order to elicit illnesses were, then, first of all to indicate the level of ill-health in which *we* were interested, and, thus, to minimize, we hoped, the effects of people's different ideas and expectations about health and disease on the way in which they reported illnesses here, then to stimulate people to think about their own health in these terms, and finally to overcome some of the difficulties which people experience in expressing their ideas about illness.

In attempting to do this we decided to ask first about chronic illnesses and complaints to which the person had been subject at some time during the preceding twelve months. Secondly, we asked about physical disabilities. (We asked about these specifically because we felt that people with such conditions might not regard them as an illness and would otherwise not have mentioned them.) After that we asked about other illnesses, injuries, or minor complaints which were present at the time. Finally, we read out a list of forty or forty-one conditions and asked if they had any of these at the time or if they were subject to them. We varied the order in which these conditions were presented in four different ways, alphabetically, then top to bottom and ends to middle, so that the first order was 1, 2 . . . 40; the second order was 40, 39 . . . 1; the third was 20, 19 . . . 1, 40, 39 . . . 21; and the fourth order was 21, 22 . . . 40, 1, 2 . . . 20.

The conditions listed were: backache, breathlessness, catarrh, colds, constipation, coughing, depression, diarrhoea, dizziness, eyestrain or other eye trouble, faintness, fever, fits, headaches, indigestion, kidney trouble or trouble passing water, loss of appetite, loss of weight, nerves, night sweats, painful or swollen joints, pains in the chest, palpitations or thumping heart, paralysis or weakness in any limb or other part of the body, piles, rashes or itches, rheumatism, running ears or earache, running sores or ulcers, sleeplessness, stomach pains, swelling of the ankles, swelling or lump in any part of the body, trouble with teeth or gums, undue irritability, undue tiredness, unusual

238

bleeding from any part of the body, varicose veins, vomiting, weak or painful feet and for women, women's complaints. This list provides a fairly clear indication of the level of ill-health in which we were interested. It is also fairly comprehensive in that most symptoms come under one of the items and there are not very many morbid conditions which are not generally associated with one or more of these items. Such symptoms as headaches, indigestion, or undue tiredness might be regarded by some people as relatively minor, but apart from the fact that we wanted information about such things, there is also the problem that if we had not asked about such things specifically, some people would have reported them and others, who also had them, would not. We would have obtained an index of "willingness to talk about illness" rather than an index of morbidity. However, by asking directly about certain selected diseases and symptoms, we have created other difficulties, principally a bias towards reporting those particular conditions.

It seems relevant here to discuss what other methods we could have used to stimulate people to think about their ill-health.

One of the possibilities was to list, not diseases or symptoms but different parts of the body. This was done to a certain extent on the Survey of Sickness (1). People were asked "Have you anything wrong in the way of colds, catarrh, or nose or throat troubles or anything wrong with your eyes, ears, teeth, headpains, chest, heart, stomach or indigestion, liver, kidneys, bowels or constipation, legs, feet, hands, arms or rheumatism, skin complaints, infectious diseases or anything wrong with your nerves?" Women were also asked whether they had anything wrong in the way of women's complaints. So many actual conditions were introduced that the avoidance of bias by not asking about particular conditions was lost, and this was the main advantage of the method, from our point of view. It seems likely that if a "pure" list of parts of the body were to be tried out, it would be found that people do not think in those terms. A cold is not something wrong with their nose or throat but a cold.

The way people think about their illnesses was the reason for discarding another suggested solution to this problem—that we should ask only about symptoms not about specific diseases. This had the attraction that symptoms such as pains, lumps, itches, etc., are things that an individual should be able to report reliably, whereas when it comes to reporting say rheumatism the informant is making a diagnosis which may or may not be justified. But here again we found that the neat theoretical solution did not work out in practice. When asked whether they had or were subject to painful or swollen joints, some of the people who said "no" later reported rheumatism, and, when asked how this affected them, said "my knee is swollen" or "my wrist is painful." Now it may be that they did not understand what a joint is, but it may also be that once a complaint has been diagnosed and labelled medically it ceases to be thought of as a symptom. People fail to recognize their rheumatism in a question about swollen and painful joints.

THE CLASSIFICATION OF SELF-REPORTED ILLNESSES

One of our main interests was in the actions people had taken or not taken about their various complaints, and, to some extent, this would depend on whether they felt the various conditions they had reported were related. What people do about a cough that is associated with bronchitis is likely to be rather different from the action they take about a cough which is not associated with any other symptoms and is attributed to smoking. In addition it might often be unrealistic to ask about the action taken for each component of a composite condition. Therefore, we decided that our unit of illness would be any group of conditions which the informant regarded as being related. So, when the informant reported a second or subsequent condition, the interviewer asked whether it was connected with anything mentioned before, and if the informant thought it was, it was recorded as being part and parcel of that illness.

240

In addition, for each reported condition the informant was asked first "how does it affect you?", and any symptoms mentioned here were recorded as part of that illness. Then he was asked, "what do you think is the cause?", and occasionally, when the initial response had been to a symptom on the check list, an informant mentioned at this time what might be called a major disease.

Some examples of conditions which informants associated together and which we therefore treated as a single illness were:

(a) Undue tiredness associated with headaches which made the person irritable and was attributed to the journey to work.
(b) Coughing causing breathlessness and attributed to asthma.
(c) Piles associated with constipation and said to be causing stomach ache and attributed to having children.
(d) Weak and painful feet associated with rheumatism which also caused backache and was attributed to living in a damp house.

From this type of information, we coded three things for each illness:

1. *The Main Diagnosis.* This could have been reported initially as a condition or as an associated symptom or as a cause, but each illness could have only one diagnosis, and the selection of the appropriate one was based on a system of priorities which is described below. A modified version of the International Statistical Classification of Diseases and Injuries and Causes of Death was used.

2. *Certain Associated Symptoms or Conditions.* These were the 41 items on our check list, and as many of these as were mentioned were coded here. (We multi-coded 4 columns of a Power-Samas card.)

3. *The Cause,* for which a code was devised from the answers given. It covered 21 different things, including the weather, the war, work, and childbearing, and one code indicated when the reported cause had in fact been coded as the main diagnosis.

241

Where a single condition was reported, the problem was straightforward. Where two or more conditions were related, and were therefore regarded as a single illness, the system of priorities adopted for selecting the main diagnosis was as follows:

1. If only one condition was classifiable under disease groups 1–15 or 17 in the International Classification the others falling in group 16, symptoms and ill-defined conditions, the defined condition was taken as the main diagnosis.

2. Where two conditions were associated and both fell in groups 1–15 or 17 the criteria as to which should be taken as the main diagnosis were:

a. If one condition was included in our check list and the other was not then the condition not on the check list was taken as the main diagnosis. In this way both conditions were included in the description of the condition, one as the main diagnosis and the other as an associated condition.

b. If one condition, in the general concensus of medical opinion, could be considered as causing the other or as being more severe than the other, then it was taken as the main diagnosis. Examples of this were:

Associated Conditions	*Main Diagnosis*
Bunions and Corns	Bunions
Blood Pressure and Menopause	Menopause
Overweight and Thyroid	Thyroid
Conjuctivitis and Hayfever	Hayfever

c. If neither 1 nor 2 applied then the condition which appears first in the International Classification list was coded as the main diagnosis.

3. Where an illness consisted of two or more conditions all of which fell in the group of "symptoms and ill-defined conditions" we used an order of priority which corresponded in general to the order of the International list.

With these questions, and this definition of an illness, an average of 2.9 illnesses per person was reported by adults at the first interview of the survey. Nearly three-quarters of these illnesses were elicited only after the question listing 40 or 41 symptoms or diseases. (Table 1.) Nearly half of the illnesses which were reported at this question were recurrent but not present at the time of interview. They tended to be chronic illnesses, in that 55 per cent first occurred over

Table 1. Certain characteristics of illnesses reported by adults at different questions at the first interview.

	Q1. Chronic Illnesses and Recurrent Complaints	Q2. Physical Disabilities	Q3. Other Illnesses Injuries Minor Complaints Present at Time	Q4. Check List of 40 or 41 Items	Reported Later at Interview or Not Known When Reported	All Illnesses
	Per Cent	Per Cent	Per Cent	Per Cent	Per Cent	Per Cent
Nature						
Continuous	48	87	61	36	35	41
Recurrent, Present	16	3	32	14	14	14
Recurrent, Not Present	34	5	5	48	39	42
Don't Know. No Answer	2	5	2	2	12	3
When First Had It						
All Life	4	12	2	5	9	5
20 Years Ago or More	16	30	8	15	9	15
10 Years Less Than 20 Years	20	26	5	17	9	18
5 Years Less Than 10 Years	17	15	7	18	9	17
1 Year Less Than 5 Years	27	8	11	29	25	27
6 Months Less Than 1 Year	6	1	2	7	10	7
1 Month Less Than 6 Months	7	—	7	5	9	5
Less Than 1 Month	2	1	56	3	4	4
Don't Know. No Answer	1	7	2	1	16	2
Pain or Discomfort						
A Lot	51	20	34	25	22	30
A Little	34	24	53	46	38	43
None	12	42	11	27	23	24
Don't Know. No Answer	3	14	2	2	17	3
General Practitioner Consulted						
Yes	83	51	36	46	48	53
No	15	29	62	52	35	44
Don't Know. No Answer	2	20	2	2	17	3
Number of Illnesses (100 Per Cent)	858	137	130	3,102	102	4,329

five years before the interview, and only 15 per cent in the previous year and 3 per cent in the previous month. It should be remembered however that all these had been present at some time during the previous year. A quarter of them were said to cause a lot of pain or discomfort and a general practitioner had been consulted about nearly half of the conditions reported at this stage of the interview.

Each illness was associated with an average of 1.6 conditions on the check list and adults reported an average of 4.7 of these check list conditions per person. Examples of the effect of associating conditions together in this way are given in Table 2 which shows the proportion of various conditions on the check list which were (a) reported and (b) classified as the main diagnosis.

Two-thirds or more of the reported cases of breathlessness, cough, sleeplessness, and backache were associated with other more serious conditions, in that the other condition became the

Table 2. Proportion of various conditions on the check list which were coded as the main diagnosis and the most frequent diagnoses in other cases.

	Per Cent of Adults Reporting This Condition	Per Cent of Reports of This Condition Coded as Main Diagnosis	Most Frequent Diagnoses in Other Cases
Nerves	22	67	Mental, Psychoneurotic & Personality Disorders, Menopause, Skin Conditions
Varicose Veins	14	92	Obesity
Piles	7	95	Complications of Pregnancy, Puerperium
Colds	22	72	Bronchitis, Sore Throat, Tonsilitis, Hay Fever
Catarrh	26	53	Colds, Bronchitis, Deafness, Sinus
Cough	20	33	Colds, Bronchitis, Catarrh, Tuberculosis, Asthma
Diseases of Teeth	12	93	——
Constipation	13	69	Piles, Ulcer of Stomach or Duodenum
Rheumatism	24	80	Arthritis, Neuritis, Heart Trouble
Headaches	31	47	Nerves, Menstruation, Menopause, Colds, Catarrh
Sleeplessness	12	31	Nerves, Menopause
Breathlessness	19	27	Heart Trouble, Tuberculosis, Bronchitis, Asthma, Obesity, Menopause
Backache	23	32	Rheumatism, Menstruation, Kidney Trouble
Indigestion	17	65	Ulcer of Stomach or Duodenum, Nerves, Constipation

main diagnosis under our system. The most frequent diagnoses when the condition on the check list was not taken as the main diagnosis is shown in the final column of the table. This illustrates our system of priorities. If a cold was associated with bronchitis, tonsilitis or hay fever, one in the latter group became the main diagnosis but if it was related to catarrh or cough then the main diagnosis was a cold. Similarly piles were subordinated to complications of pregnancy or the puerperium but became the main diagnosis when only associated with constipation.

In 5 per cent of the illnesses, the main diagnosis as coded had been reported initially as the cause of associated conditions. In this group the most frequent diagnoses were the menopause, disorders of menstruation, obesity or overweight, complications of pregnancy and blood pressure.

COMPARISON WITH THE SURVEY OF SICKNESS

The illness rates obtained on our inquiry appear relatively high and it therefore seemed worth while to make a comparison with another somewhat similar survey in an attempt to see how far this higher rate can be explained by the different methods used.

The Survey of Sickness was carried out from 1943–1952 and during this period monthly samples of adults in England and Wales were questioned about their health in recent months.[3] We can thus compare the number of illnesses reported as being present during a particular month in this Survey with the number of illnesses present during the four weekly periods in our Family Health Survey. Our figures are based on information supplied by adults who were interviewed twice and include all illnesses reported at the second interview as well as those illnesses which were reported at the first interview and said to have been present at any time between the first and second interviews.

[3] Up to 1951 the sample was drawn from the National Register and included adults aged 16 years and over. The size of the monthly sample varied from 2,500 to 4,000. A multi-stage sample was used, the details of which are given in Reference 1.

245

The main differences in the methods of the two inquiries are set out in Table 3, and the illness rates for different age and sex groups in each survey in Table 4.

The illness rates on the present inquiry were greater than those on the Survey of Sickness for all age and sex groups, even though on the latter inquiry all conditions and symptoms are said to have been treated as separate illnesses. How far this happened in practice may perhaps be questioned. Interviewers are more likely to do the practical and apparently reasonable thing than to obey instructions from Headquarters implicitly especially if they regard these as being rather theoretical and divorced from reality, and especially also if they

Table 3. Summary of main differences in method between Survey of Sickness and this inquiry.

	SURVEY OF SICKNESS	PRESENT INQUIRY
Period Studied	People Were Interviewed during the First Fortnight of a Month, and Questioned about their Sickness during the Previous Two Calendar Months.	People Interviewed and Asked about Illnesses Present at Time and Conditions to which They Were Subject.
		People Re-interviewed 4 Weeks Later and Asked about Illnesses Reported at First Interview and Other Illnesses Occurring during Four Weeks.
Questions Asked	Check Questions Asked about Colds, Catarrh, Nose or Throat Trouble, Eyes, Ears, Teeth, Head, Pains, Chest, Heart, Stomach or Indigestion, Liver, Kidneys, Bowels or Constipation, Legs, Feet, Hands, Arms, or Rheumatism, Skin Complaints, Infectious Diseases, Nerves, Women's Complaints.	40 or 41 Specific Diseases or Symptoms Listed at First Interview. At Second Interview People Were Asked about Illnesses, Consultations, Incapacity and Medicines Taken since Previous Interview, and about the Illness to which Any Incapacity, Consultation, Medicine Was Related.
Unit Coded and Analysed	All Conditions and Symptoms Mentioned Were Treated as Separate Illnesses.*	People Asked if Conditions They Reported Were Related, and Connected Conditions Were Treated as a Single Illness.
Person Interviewed	Proxies Allowed after Three Calls. No Figures Available of Numbers Involved.	Proxies Only Accepted if Otherwise No Information Would Have Been Obtained for that Individual. 93 per cent of Adults Interviewed Personally.
Type of Sample	Individuals Aged 16 and Over on The National Register.	All Adults (People Who Had Left School) in a Sample of Dwellings.

* Registrar General's Statistical Review of England and Wales for 1950–51.

246

	1950 Survey of Sickness Monthly Prevalence Rates (Spells) per Individual Interviewed	Present Inquiry Average Number of Illness Present During Four Weeks Period	Ratio Present Inquiry Rate Survey of Sickness Rate
Males			
16–44	1.00	2.22	2.2
45–64	1.32	2.63	2.0
65 and Over	1.79	3.47	1.9
Females			
16–44	1.38	2.88	2.1
45–64	1.82	3.39	1.9
65 and Over	2.30	3.83	1.7
Males 16 and Over	1.20	2.35	2.0
Females 16 and Over	1.66	3.01	1.8

Table 4. Comparison of illness rates on Survey of Sickness and on present inquiry.

involve extra work. The temptation to regard running noses, catarrh, and coughs as all part of a cold and not to record them as separate conditions must be very great and in many ways eminently reasonable.

The difference in rates was greater for males than for females, and for the youngest age group, 16–44 than for the other age groups. These differences in the *ratios* for the age and sex groups may be due to a greater number of "proxy" interviews on the Survey of Sickness, but the substantial difference between the rates in the two inquiries remains to be explained.

It is possible to make only rather limited comparisons of the diseases reported on the two studies because of the groups which have been used, but some comparisons of the frequency with which various diagnoses were recorded are given in Table 5. The condition showing the greatest difference, with the excess in our survey was tuberculosis and this probably can be explained in terms of the actual incidence of the disease. The area in which our inquiry was carried out was a post-war housing estate and since people with tuberculosis were given priority on the housing list, this estate initially contained an unduly high proportion of people with this complaint.

The other conditions with an excess approaching this magnitude were disorders of menstruation and menopausal symptoms. Here part of the explanation for the difference may be that in a third of our cases, these conditions were only mentioned when we asked about the cause of some related symptoms. Another part of the explanation of the different frequency with which disorders of menstruation were reported may be in the age distribution of our adult population which contained a relatively high proportion of adults under 45. Other conditions with a marked excess for the present inquiry were varicose veins and piles each of which was mentioned specifically on this study but not on the Survey of Sickness.

Three conditions, diseases of the teeth, constipation, and

Table 5. Comparison of certain disease rates on Survey of Sickness and present inquiry.

	RATE PER 1,000 INDIVIDUALS				RATIO Present Inquiry Survey of Sickness	
	Survey of Sickness		Present Inquiry			
	Males	Females	Males	Females	Males	Females
Rheumatism	116	195	110	157	0.9	0.8
Bronchitis	43	38	48	47	1.1	1.2
Arthritis	13	28	15	26	1.2	0.9
Ulcers of Stomach	7	3	}21	}8	}1.2	}1.6
Ulcers of Duodenum	10	2				
Nerves	54	148	74	139	1.4	0.9
Mental, Psychoneurosis and Personality Disorders	11	16	15	21	1.4	1.3
Asthma	8	9	12	16	1.5	1.8
Colds	126	120	185	185	1.5	1.5
Constipation	26	71	61	125	2.3	1.8
Headaches	65	146	168	232	2.6	1.6
Diseases of Teeth	50	52	110	143	2.2	2.8
Varicose Veins	14	37	82	155	5.9	4.2
Piles	7	7	46	49	6.6	7.0
Menopausal Symptoms		}27		56		}6.5
Disorders of Menstruation				120		
Tuberculosis—All Forms	4	3	31	34	7.8	11.3

* These figures are not compa·able to those in Table 2 as these are based on illnesses present during a particular four week period while those in Table 2 refer to all illnesses reported at the first interview.

248

headaches, were recorded as diagnoses about twice as frequently on our study as on the Survey of Sickness although they were mentioned specifically in the questions on both inquiries. Over a third of our cases of constipation were reported because we asked about medicines taken during the period between the two interviews, and a number of people had taken laxatives for constipation but they had not previously reported constipation as an illness. Similarly, 30 per cent of the headaches were reported because of the aspirins which had been taken for them during the period. These factors only account for some of the discrepancy between the rates on the two inquiries. There is other evidence that incidence of these three conditions, diseases of the teeth, constipation, and headaches, is particularly high on the estate where our inquiry was carried out. An analysis of the General Practitioner's records shows that in each case the rates are 2, 3 or 4 times as high as the average rates on other studies of General Practitioner's records.

Finally, the rates on the two inquiries for nerves, colds and rheumatism did not show a very great difference and each was mentioned specifically on both studies. The other conditions showing relatively little difference, bronchitis, asthma, ulcers of the stomach or duodenum, and mental psychoneurosis, and personality disorders are all fairly major complaints.

These comparisons suggest that differences in method make it difficult to reach any definite conclusions about the relative morbidity in the two populations.

Summary

Various objective criteria for defining an illness and the reasons for not using them in this inquiry have been discussed. In the questions finally adopted a list of 40 or 41 separate conditions was included. In the analysis of the results these specified conditions were incorporated into the description of illnesses and the unit of illness was the group of diseases and/or symptoms which informants regarded as being related.

Some comparisons with the Survey of Sickness illustrate the different ways in which the questions asked and the method of analysis can influence the nature of morbidity data collected on this type of inquiry.

ACKNOWLEDGEMENTS

The program of research of which this study formed part, was directed by Professor J. H. F. Brotherston, formerly Reader in Public Health at the London School of Hygiene and Tropical Medicine, whose advice has been invaluable. I am grateful also to Professor J. M. Mackintosh, Margot Jefferys, F. M. Martin and other colleagues at the London School of Hygiene and Tropical Medicine for their helpful interest in this work.

REFERENCES

1. Logan, W. P. D., and Brooke, E. M.: General Register Office Studies on Medical and Population Subjects. No. 12, The Survey of Sickness, 1943 to 1952.

2. Brotherston, J. H. F., Chave, S. P. W. and others: General Practice on a New Housing Estate. *British Journal of Preventive and Social Medicine*, 10, No. 4, October, 1956.

3. Cartwright, Ann: The Effect of Obtaining Information from Different Informants on a Family Morbidity Inquiry. *Applied Statistics*, VI, No. 1, 1957.

INTERVIEWS HARDEST-TO-OBTAIN
IN AN URBAN HEALTH SURVEY

REGINA LOEWENSTEIN
JOHN COLOMBOTOS
AND
JACK ELINSON

Survey researchers are necessarily concerned about possible bias in their survey data resulting from inability to interview all persons selected by the sampling plan. The proportion of persons in the sample with a particular socioeconomic characteristic, for example, may be under- or overrepresented among those interviewed. Measuring bias caused by nonresponse is the responsibility of the statistician. The staff of the Master Sample Survey in the Washington Heights Health District undertook to study nonresponse bias by investigating the characteristics of a "hard-to-obtain" subsample.

PROCEDURE

Between November, 1960, and April, 1961, interviews were sought from a two-stage stratified cluster sample of 4,500 dwelling units. By the first cut-off date, interviews had been obtained in 3,300 (77 per cent of eligible dwelling units, allowing for sampling losses). Of the 1,000 households not represented in these "early" interviews, 550 (12 per cent) had refused to be interviewed and the remaining 450 (11 per cent) had either not been successfully contacted or not interviewed for reasons other than direct refusal.

To study the characteristics of this "hard-to-obtain" group, a sample of one-third, or 340, of these households were selected for intensive field efforts over a ten-week period (May 1 to July 15) by specially selected staff members. By the final cut-off date, interviews had been obtained in 210, or about 60 per cent, of these dwelling units,

251

including about one-half of the previous refusals and three-fourths of the previous nonrefusals. Of the remaining 130 households with no interviews obtained, almost 80 per cent had refused at least once and only 20 per cent had never been contacted.

To study the characteristics of persons in dwelling units with no interviews but whose names were known, tabulations from the 1960 United States Census were obtained. Census tables gave data on age, sex and race of about 200 persons, as well as size of family, in the 94 dwelling units that could be identified and matched. It was then possible to estimate the distributions of these four characteristics for 98 per cent of the dwelling units eligible for interview from the sum of (1) the early cases, (2) the triple-weighted late cases, and (3) triple-weighted noninterviews in the late subsample. The characteristics of the remaining two per cent (nonidentified and nonmatched names) were assumed to be the same as noninterviews. The resulting estimated

TABLE I. FIELD STATUS OF DWELLING UNITS, FAMILIES AND PERSONS IN ESTIMATED SAMPLE; BY SIZE OF FAMILY AND AGE OF PERSONS

	Estimated Sample	Interviewed Early*	Interviewed Late**			Not Interviewed**		
			Total Late	Previous Refusals	Previous Non-Refusals	Total Not Interviewed	Previous Refusals	Previous Non-Refusals
Dwelling units								
Estimated number	4,343	3,329	630	294	336	384	258	126
Per cent distribution	100	77	14	6	8	9	6	3
Size of families								
Estimated number of families	4,803	3,705	687	312	375	411	273	138
Per cent distributions								
all families	100	77	14	6	8	9	6	3
1 person	100	73	16	6	10	11	6	5
2 persons	100	73	16	7	9	11	7	4
3 persons	100	82	13	8	5	5	3	2
4 or more persons	100	85	12	5	7	3	3	
Age of persons								
Estimated number of persons	11,527	9,196	1,563	741	822	768	525	243
Per cent distributions								
all persons	100	80	13	6	7	7	5	2
Under 15 years	100	85	12	5	7	3	2	1
15–44 years	100	84	12	5	7	4	3	1
45–64 years	100	76	14	6	8	10	7	3
65 years and older	100	73	17	12	5	10	6	4

* Interviewed in November, 1960, through April, 1961.

** The results of the second phase of interviewing on a one-third sample of cases not completed in the first phase, weighted by 3, were completed in May through July, 1961.

252

TABLE 2. SIZE OF FAMILIES AND AGE OF PERSONS OF THE WASHINGTON HEIGHTS HEALTH DISTRICT, OF THE ESTIMATED SAMPLE, OF INTERVIEWS RECEIVED BY FIELD STATUS, AND ESTIMATE OF NONINTERVIEWS

	Washington Heights Health District*	Estimated Sample	Marginal Distributions**	*Interviews Received* Early***	*Late†* Total Late	Previous Refusals	Previous Non-Refusals	Not Interviewed††
Size of families								
Total number of families	100,987	4,804	4,392	3,705	229	104	125	
Per cent distribution all families	100	100	100	100	100	100	100	100
1 person	30	30	29	29	34	26	40	35
2 persons		33	32	32	34	38	31	47
3 persons	70	17	18	18	16	21	11	10
4 or more persons		20	21	21	16	15	18	8
Age of persons								
Total number of persons	269,277	11,529	10,759	9,196	521	247	274	
Per cent distribution all persons	100	100	100	100	100	100	100	100
Under 15 years	18	18	19	19	17	15	18	9
15–44 years	38	37	38	39	33	30	36	22
45–64 years	31	31	29	29	32	29	36	48
65 years and older	13	14	14	13	18	26	10	21

* Based on data by Census Tracts in United States Censuses of Population and Housing: 1960, Final Report PHC (1)—104, Part 1.

** The results of the second phase of interviewing on a one-third sample of cases not completed in the first phase are weighted by 3. Marginal Distributions = Early Cases + 3 (Late Cases)

*** Interviewed November, 1960, through April, 1961.

† Interviewed May through July, 1961.

†† Based on tabulations by the United States Bureau of the Census of a sample of not-interviewed cases matched with 1960 census records.

final response rate was 91 per cent of families and 93 per cent of persons eligible for interviews.

FINDINGS

Table 1 summarizes the results of this procedure. The sample sought was estimated to be 4,800 families with 11,500 persons.[1] The 3,300 early interviews gave information about 3,700 families and 9,200 persons. With the addition of the triple-weighted late interviews, the tabulations of this survey are based on 4,000 interviews with 4,400 families[2] comprising 10,750 persons.

Table 2 shows the distributions of persons by age and families by size for the early and late cases, with late cases classified also as previ-

253

ous refusals and previous nonrefusals according to their status as of the first cut-off date. Although the early and late cases differ both in size of family and age of persons, the distributions of all interviewed cases ("marginal distributions") and of early cases are almost identical because, even after weighting, the 229 families represented in the late cases are only 16 per cent of the total interviewed.

Nonresponse bias will be examined by comparing early and late interviews; also, previous refusals and previous nonrefusals among the late interviews. All differences mentioned are statistically significant at the .05 level, usually implying an absolute difference of from five to 15 per cent.

Demographic and Socioeconomic Characteristics

No differences were found between early and late cases, or between previous refusals and nonrefusals, with regard to sex, race, religion, occupation, family income and many other characteristics. Late interviews, however, contained fewer families with children under 16 or any adult under 35 but more with at least one person over 65. Many other characteristics that had different distributions among early and late cases stem from the larger proportions of small families and older persons among the late cases. Differences between previous refusals and previous nonrefusals are also associated with differences in family size and age. The previous-refusal group had more families with all members over 65 years, more adults keeping house, fewer adults working full time, and fewer adults with a high-school education. The late cases, and particularly previous refusals, were more often families who had been living at the same address for at least 15 years. The larger number of one-person families among the previous nonrefusals reflects interviewers' difficulties in finding them at home.

Reported Chronic Conditions and Symptoms

Early and late cases, like previous refusals and nonrefusals, did not differ with regard to reported presence during the previous year of 29 specified chronic conditions, 12 out of 13 impairments, four symptoms of cardiovascular disease, drinking problems, institutional care, or limitations on ordinary activities as a result of illness. These findings did not reflect the preponderance of older persons in the late cases and especially among the previous refusals. Further analysis of 12 age-sex groups reporting at least one chronic condition, however, failed to change the overall picture. In fact, late cases and previous refusals were more likely to report no chronic conditions than their age-sex counterparts in the early cases and previous nonrefusal groups. (Were persons in the late cases, especially previous refusals, healthier or more laconic in the interview?) Similarly, on the 22 Midtown psychophysiologic symptom questions,[3] the four field-status groups showed no differences either in average score or in distributions of scores. Nor did they differ in their responses to a supplementary series of psychological symptom questions concerning disturbances of mood, thought and feeling.[4]

Reported Medical Care During Past Year

Early and late cases did not differ in the proportions who reported one or more attended conditions during the previous year nor in the average number of reported visits for medical care (whether per person interviewed or per person reporting at least one attended condition). No early-late or refusal-nonrefusal difference was found in the proportions of persons reporting that all ambulatory medical care was from doctors in private practice. However, late cases and especially previous refusals had fewer persons with one or more hospital stays. Previous nonrefusals more often reported at least 20 days of disability, had more visits to the outpatient department and made more use of a number of different ambulatory care facilities in the course of the study year. No differences were seen by previous field status as to reported dental care, eye examinations, periodic checkups, polio shots or expressed need for additional health services.

SUMMARY OF FINDINGS

The previous refusals and previous nonrefusals differed from each other on more of the 200 characteristics investigated than did the early and late cases; in many respects the previous nonrefusals were more like early cases than like previous refusals.

To measure the effect on the final results of the intensive interviewing effort, distributions on the 200 variables were compared with and without the late cases. Only 15 variables had distributions that differed by as much as two or three per cent in even one category. In other words, very few characteristics would have been affected if field work had stopped at the first cut-off with no intensive effort to obtain interviews from a sample of the noninterviewed.

255

DISCUSSION

Most comparisons discussed in this report are first-order relationships; i.e., two pairs of field-status groups compared without controlling for other variables. Analyses of second- and third-order relationships should yield further understanding about the types of persons who refused to be interviewed in this health survey or who were hard to interview for other reasons.

Findings in other surveys—with different interviewees, interviewers and interview content—would not necessarily be the same. Frequent comparisons of distributions of important characteristics while a survey is in progress would inform the field staff what groups need more intensive effort. Decisions regarding additional field work would depend on the nature and magnitude of nonresponse bias, available funds and whether the major emphasis of the survey is to estimate the characteristics of a community or to study the interrelationships of these characteristics.

REFERENCES

[1] According to the United States Censuses of Population and Housing, the Washington Heights Health District in 1960 had 100,000 housing units and 270,000 persons.
[2] The number of families is larger than the number of households because some dwellings units were occupied by more than one family.
[3] See Appendix for questionnaire.
[4] *Ibid.*

ACKNOWLEDGMENT

This paper was adapted from the 1962 Proceedings of the Social Statistics Section of the American Statistical Association.

SOURCES OF REFUSALS IN SURVEYS

BARBARA S. DOHRENWEND

AND

BRUCE P. DOHRENWEND

Although research workers would like to reduce the number of potential respondents who refuse to participate in survey interviews,[1] they disagree about where responsibility for the problem lies. For example, Pomeroy stated that ". . . poorly trained interviewers and faulty interviewing create more reluctance on the part of respondents than any other factor."[2] His position is supported by Cannell and Axelrod's finding, in a follow-up of survey respondents, that the complaints of critical respondents generally concerned the interviewer rather than the content of the survey.[3] In contrast, Schwartz inferred, on the basis of an exploratory follow-up of both participants and nonparticipants among respondents selected for a sample survey, that ". . . with nonparticipants it actually isn't the interviewers who are being criticized, but the process of being interviewed . . ."[4] Schwartz suggested that at least a portion of refusals are due to the personality and values of the nonparticipants. An issue for those concerned with reducing refusals is, therefore, to determine relative responsibility of interviewers and respondents for refusals.

PROCEDURE

The data for this study of interviewer and respondent responsibility for refusals come from a probability subsample of 94 married couples and 26 single household heads, 214 individuals in all, chosen for reinterviews from a previous survey carried out in the Washington Heights section of Manhattan an average of two years earlier.[5] The subsample is limited to Irish, Jews, Negroes and Puerto Ricans between the ages

257

of 21 and 59, living in households headed by a male. Interviews were completed with the designated respondents in 69 per cent of the households; 12 per cent were lost because they were ill, had died, had moved out of the state or could not be located; respondents in the remaining 19 per cent of the households refused to be interviewed after repeated call-backs.

The study started with ten teams of interviewers, each composed of a man and a woman. Most of the interviewers were initially inexperienced in survey interviewing. They were given intensive training for this study by the study director and an experienced field director for an average of 15 hours. Of the original ten teams of interviewers, three were Negro and three were Puerto Rican. The aim was to match, as nearly as possible, interviewers and respondents on ethnic background.[6] Within ethnic groups, households were assigned at random to one of either two or three teams of interviewers. The procedure with married couples was to conduct the interviews separately but simultaneously in different parts of the home.

Each household in the sample was sent a letter explaining the purpose of the study (to investigate the public's ideas about mental health) before an interviewer telephoned for an appointment. If the potential respondent refused over the phone, or had no phone, the interviewer team (or team member for single respondent) visited the home with the aim of securing the interview on the spot. If this attempt was unsuccessful, the household was assigned to another interviewer team for a repeated attempt, in person, to obtain the interview. Because this approach permitted the more able member of each team to take major responsibility for contacting potential respondents, it may have reduced the extent to which interviewers determined respondent re-

TABLE I. RELATION BETWEEN UNCOOPERATIVE BEHAVIOR ON THE FIRST WAVE AND REFUSAL ON THE SECOND WAVE

| | First Wave | |
| | No Uncooperative Contacts | One or More Uncooperative Contacts |
Second Wave	%	%
Interview completed	81	62
Refusal	19	38
(Number)*	(81)	(21)

* These numbers are smaller than those in Table 2 because data on contacts in the first wave were missing for four cases.

$X^2 = 5.80$, P $< .02$.

258

fusals below what it would have been if each interviewer had functioned independently.

The interviewer's report, prepared after completing an interview, included his judgment as to whether the respondent was hostile, suspicious or guarded rather than friendly or solicitous.

The panel approach permits the comparison of current respondents and nonrespondents on a much larger number of characteristics than would be possible with the more usual procedure of comparing some demographic characteristics of one's completed sample with similar characteristics reported in the census, but it excludes from investigation those persons who have never agreed to be interviewed. Thus a question arises about the generalizability of the findings to the more usual situation, which focuses on refusals in the first (and usually only) wave of a survey.

If respondents who refused on the second wave were as cooperative as others on the first wave of the study, no justification would be found for drawing generalizations about initial refusals from the data on second-wave refusals. If, on the other hand, second-wave refusals turn out to be respondents from whom interviews were obtained on the first wave only after resistance was overcome, it would be a basis for suggesting that results from the second wave are relevant to first-wave refusals.

Table 1 shows the relation between uncooperative contacts on the first wave, in which the respondent refused to give an interview or failed to keep an appointment before finally consenting to be interviewed, and refusals on the second wave. Because respondents who were uncooperative at some time before giving an interview on the first wave were twice as likely as others to refuse on the second wave, it appears that refusal on the second wave is related to the inclination to refuse the first interview. Furthermore, the consistency of some of the findings with those of two other studies—one having data on cases of complete refusals[7] and the other concerned with respondents who were interviewed only after having refused when first approached[8]— also suggests continuity in the refusal phenomenon. At the sime time, the fact that 19 per cent of those who were cooperative throughout the first wave refused to cooperate on the second indicates that respondent predispositions may not provide the entire explanation of refusals.

Do Interviewers Contribute to Refusals?

Table 2 shows the disposition of each interviewing team's randomly

TABLE 2. COMPLETION STATUS OF HOUSEHOLDS CLASSIFIED ACCORDING TO ORIGINAL RANDOM ASSIGNMENT TO INTERVIEWING TEAMS

Ethnicity	Interviewing Team	Completion Status				N*
		Completed by Originally Assigned Teams	Completed by Alternate Team	Refusal	Out of Sample Because of Illness, Moves, Out of State, Fail to Locate, etc.	
Irish	I-1	9		6		15
	I-2	8		7		15
	All teams	17		13		30
Jewish	J-1	12	1	2		15
	J-2	8	4	2	1	15
	All teams	20	5	4	1	30
Negro	N-1**	4	1	2	3	10
	N-2	9			1	10
	N-3	6		1	3	10
	All teams	19	1	3	7	30
Puerto Rican	P-1***	5		2	4	11
	P-2	7		1	2	10
	P-3	3	6			9
	All teams	15	6	3	6	30

* A married couple is tabulated as a single unit because the two interviewers on each team worked together to secure their respondents' participation, and in only two cases did one spouse participate and the other refuse; these two cases are classified as refusals.

** A male interviewer quit after attempting five interviews. (One of these, in a sample drawn from another Negro population, was completed.) Another male then substituted in this team. The outcome of these interviews is, therefore, the combined performance of two male and one female interviewers.

*** One male substituted for another about half-way through the assignment; the first was forced to leave because of other commitments.

assigned interviews. Although refusal rates differ markedly between ethnic groups, with the Irish showing the highest rate, rates are remarkably similar for equivalent samples of respondents within ethnic groups. Final refusal rates are in some respects misleading, however, because many interviews were reassigned after the original team failed to secure them. The clearest evidence of interviewer responsibility for noncompletion of interviews, therefore, is the number of cases completed by a second team after the first team was unsuccessful. In cases where both teams were unsuccessful, it is more difficult to infer that the interviewer, rather than the respondent, is primarily responsible for the ultimate refusal.

Table 3 shows that a significant difference exists among the Puerto Rican teams in the number of randomly assigned cases completed by an alternate team. Two teams had no cases completed by an alternate, but P-3 completed only three of the nine cases originally assigned to them. To what extent the six noncompletions were due to actual refusals and to what extent they were due to lack of persistence by the interviewers in following up initial contacts cannot be determined from the records. However, inasmuch as all of the six cases were successfully completed by an alternate team, it appears that P-3's failures were not attributable to determination on the part of the respondent not to cooperate.

A further indication of interviewer responsibility is provided by the results of the interviewers' ratings of respondent hostility shown in Table 4. In two ethnic groups, Negro and Puerto Rican, the number rated "hostile" varied among respondents randomly assigned to different interviewing teams. One possibility is that this difference between teams is the result of a stronger tendency on the part of some interviewers to project hostility onto their respondents. Some evidence,

TABLE 3. COMPARISONS OF PERFORMANCE OF TEAMS WITHIN ETHNIC GROUPS

Teams Compared	Number of Assignments Completed by Original Team as Against Number Reassigned			Number of Assignments Completed by any Team as Against Number of Refusals		
	X^2	d.f.	P	X^2	d.f.	P
Irish		*		0.14	1	n.s.
Jewish	1.91	1	n.s.	0.006	1	n.s.
Negro		*		2.93	2	n.s.
Puerto Rican	11.00	2	<.01	1.22	2	n.s.

* No assignments or only one assignment completed by alternate teams.

Ethnicity of Respondents	Originally Assigned Team	Total Number of Respondents	Respondents Rated Hostile, Suspicious or Guarded		X^2	d.f.	P
			N	%			
Irish	I-1	16	2	12			
	I-2	14	1	7	0.24	1	n.s.
Jewish	J-1	25	1	4			
	J-2	23	4	18	1.05	1	n.s.
Negro	N-1	9	5	56			
	N-2	14			9.77	2	< .01
	N-3	9	2	22			
Puerto Rican	P-1	9					
	P-2	13	2	15	5.76	2	< .10
	P-3	18	7	33			

however, suggests that this is not the case. Of the seven Puerto Rican respondents rated hostile in P-3's original random assignments, six had been reassigned to three interviewers who found not a single hostile respondent among their own original assignments. A similar pattern appears among the five Negro respondents rated hostile in N-1's assignments; two of these respondents were reassigned to other interviewers who had not rated any of their own initial respondents hostile.

The tendency for reassigned respondents to be rated hostile may be caused by selective projection of hostility by some interviewers onto respondents who have been reassigned to them. However, in view of the fact that some of these respondents were also rated hostile when interviewed by the original team (particularly in the case of N-1), the more parsimonious explanation is that these respondents actually expressed hostility. The fact that initial interviewer assignments within ethnic groups were randomized leaves little reason to believe that one team originally faced more inherently hostile respondents than did another team interviewing in the same ethnic group.

The implication of these results is, therefore, that interviewers whose randomly assigned respondents were disproportionately rated hostile tended to generate hostility and must be considered responsible for their respondents' tendency to refuse to cooperate. Interviewers in the present study probably did not contribute substantially to ultimate refusals only because more competent interviewers were able to compensate for less competent ones.

Do Respondents Contribute to Refusals?

A striking fact (see Table 2) is that the Irish respondents, whose interviewing teams showed least variation in performance, had a refusal rate over three times that of any of the other ethnic groups.[9] Although this outcome could be due to incompetence on the part of both interviewing teams assigned to the Irish, the alternate explanation that the high refusal rates could be attributed to the respondents seems more reasonable in view of the fact that I-1 was also a back-up team for Jewish respondents, where they were successful in obtaining a number of interviews previously not obtained by another team.

If respondents are sometimes responsible for refusals, what motives underlie these refusals? The importance of culturally defined values is suggested by the finding that among the Irish respondents on whom background data were available,[10] 13 of 17 born in Ireland (76 per cent) refused the second interview, compared with eight of 28 (28 per cent) second- or third-generation Irish. Although refusals were not characteristic of immigrants in other subcultures—of 38 Puerto Ricans born in Puerto Rico, only three (eight per cent) refused—the result with Irish immigrants fits Robins' finding that refusals were significantly higher among respondents whose parents were born outside the United States than among children of native-born parents.[11] Although Robins' study differs from this one in that she does not specify the ethnicity of her respondents and classifies them according to their parents' rather than their own migrant status, the two findings together suggest the optimistic hypothesis that refusal to cooperate in survey research is a deviation from behavior dictated by the dominant norms in United States culture.

Although this study did not confirm Robins' findings that education and occupation were significantly related to refusals,[12] the finding of a significant relation between refusal rate and age, shown in Table 5, is consistent with the results of the earlier Washington Heights study, which found interviews with persons over 45 years of age harder to obtain than interviews with younger respondents.[13]

The nonsignificant difference for neuropsychiatric scores shown in Table 5 is particularly interesting because researchers have tended to assume that refusal to be interviewed is to some degree correlated with psychopathology.[14] The results of the present study are, however, consistent with an earlier report of no difference in either the average or distribution of neuropsychiatric scores between respondents who were difficult to obtain and others.[15] Nor do the data disclose a dis-

263

TABLE 5. RELATION OF RESPONDENT CHARACTERISTICS TO REFUSALS

Personality Factors	N^*	Per Cent Refusing	X^2	d.f.	P
Whether often angry					
Yes	24	4⎫	4.63	1	< .05
No	150	23⎭			
Don't know	1				
Direction of anger					
Self	85	21⎫	0.50	1	n.s.
Others	55	16⎭			
Total	140	19⎫	0.71	1	n.s.
Don't know	35	26⎭			
Whether show anger					
Show	75	23⎫	0.12	1	n.s.
Keep to self	93	20⎭			
Don't know	7				
Whether often guilty					
Yes	53	13⎫	2.02	1	n.s.
No	117	25⎭			
Don't know	5				
Whether often afraid					
Yes	19	11⎫	1.25	1	n.s.
No	154	21⎭			
Don't know	2	50			
Number of friends					
Less than 3	24	21			
3 or more	151	21			
Psychophysiologic Symptom score**					
Less than 4	137	23⎫	1.63	1	n.s.
4 or more	38	13⎭			

Demographic Factors

Education of head of household					
Less than high school	80	25⎫	1.77	1	n.s.
High school or more	95	17⎭			
Age					
Under 40	82	12⎫	11.91	1	< .05
40 or older	93	28⎭			
Occupation†					
White collar	9	22			
Blue collar	83	23			
White and blue combined	92	23⎫	0.19	1	n.s.
Professional and managerial	46	23⎭			
Income††					
Less than $3,000	19	16⎫			
$3,000–4,999	38	24⎬	0.66	3	n.s.
$5,000–7,499	72	21⎪			
$7,500 or more	37	24⎭			

FOOTNOTES FOR TABLE 5.

* Excluding respondents lost from sample because of illness, death, etc., and wives interviewed on the second but not the first interview.
** A 22-item index developed by the Midtown Study on which a score of 4 or more was found to discriminate between persons rated impaired as against those rated unimpaired by psychiatrists; see Langner, T. S., A Twenty-two Item Screening Score of Psychiatric Symptoms Indicating Impairment, *Journal of Health and Human Behavior*, 3, 269–276, 1962.
† N = 138 because of exclusion of housewives with no other occupation.
†† N = 166 because of loss of cases in which no answer was given to the income question.

tinct personality type associated with refusals. Even the one significant chi square shown in Table 5 indicates that refusers tended, like the great majority of respondents, to say they are not angry often. Furthermore, as the only significant result among eight personality factors tested, it may be simply chance.

CONCLUSION

Partly as a tactic to encourage interviewer persistence, field researchers have generally worked on the assumption that refusals are almost wholly attributable to poor interviewing. Because refusals can be precipitated by the wrong approach on the interviewer's part, he must be encouraged to think and act as if every respondent can be persuaded to cooperate. This necessary "set" in the field should not, however, blind the survey analyst to the fact that potential respondents who refuse to cooperate with competent interviewers probably differ in some respects from those who do cooperate. Inasmuch as demographic differences between interviews obtained and refusals present a serious problem for the survey analyst, further investigations are needed to determine whether and under what conditions such differences can be expected to occur. The results of the assessment of interviewer, as against respondent, responsibility for refusals indicate that it is possible to identify cases for which each is responsible.

REFERENCES

[1] *See*, e.g., the editorial, Public Relations and Research Interviewing, *Public Opinion Quarterly*, 28, 118, 1964.

[2] Pomeroy, W. B., The Reluctant Respondent, *Public Opinion Quarterly*, 27, 287–293, 1963.

[3] Cannell, C. F. and Axelrod, M., The Respondent Reports on the Interview, *The American Journal of Sociology,* 62, 177–181, 1956.

[4] Schwartz, A., Interviewing and the Public, *Public Opinion Quarterly,* 28, 135–142, 1964.

[5] See Appendix for sampling plan of Master Sample Survey of Washington Heights Health District, 1960–1961.

[6] Exceptions were a team of white Protestant interviewers assigned to Irish respondents (I-1) and a woman of Protestant background who interviewed Jewish respondents with her Jewish husband. These assignments do not seem to have had any special effects.

[7] Robins, L. N., The Reluctant Respondent, *Public Opinion Quarterly,* 27, 276–286, 1963.

[8] Loewenstein, R., Colombotos, J. and Elinson, J., Interviews Hardest-to-Obtain in an Urban Health Survey, in this volume.

[9] $X^2 = 11.58$, d.f. $= 3$, $P < .005$.

[10] Data were not available for some wives interviewed in the second, but not the first, study.

[11] Robins, *op. cit.,* p. 280.

[12] *Ibid.*

[13] Loewenstein, *et al., op. cit.*

[14] See, e.g., Robins, *op. cit.,* pp. 277–278.

[15] Loewenstein, *et al., op. cit.*

ACKNOWLEDGMENTS

This work has been supported in part by Grants OM-82, MH 07327–01, MH 07328–01 and MH 10328–01 from the National Institute of Mental Health, United States Public Health Service.

Adapted by permission from Public Opinion Quarterly, 32, 74–83, Spring, 1968. Copyright by Princeton University Press, 1968.

SOCIAL DISTANCE AND INTERVIEWER EFFECTS

BARBARA S. DOHRENWEND

JOHN COLOMBOTOS

AND

BRUCE P. DOHRENWEND

What kind of relationship between interviewer and respondent minimizes interviewer biasing effects? To answer this question, a model has been developed in terms of social distance between interviewer and respondent. That is, the model focuses on the question: Which types of interviewers bias which types of respondents? With respect to the problem of the direction of bias, respondents are assumed most likely to make their answers conform with what they believe to be the norms and expectations of the interviewer.

THE PROBLEM OF TOO MUCH SOCIAL DISTANCE

Much of the available evidence concerning which types of interviewers affect which types of respondents suggests that bias is found where disparity exists in the social status of interviewer and respondent. In his groundbreaking study, Katz[1] demonstrated that social-class disparity produced bias in responses; and, later, Hyman and his colleagues[2] showed that disparities in race, religion or sex also produced such effects. A recent study by J. A. Williams, Jr.,[3] however, showed that white interviewers biased the responses of high-status Negro respondents less than those of low-status Negroes. His finding suggests that these effects are related to degree of status dissimilarity or, as Williams terms it, social distance.

Williams assumed that the effect of social distance is mediated by interviewers' and respondents' perceptions of each other.[4] In his work to date he has dealt only with mediation of Negro respondents' perceptions of white interviewers by the relevant status indicator of color. It is possible, however, that Negro respondents do not perceive white interviewers so indiscriminately, but instead see some as hostile and others as friendly, and respond accordingly. The same argument can be made for white lower-class respondents, who would generally be expected to perceive middle-class interviewers as socially distant, but could also be expected to differentiate between those who seem more friendly and those who seem less friendly. In the present study the first analysis of interviewer effects was designed, therefore, to test the hypothesis that white middle-class interviewers with a negative attitude toward persons of lower status bias the answers of Negroes and of white lower-class respondents more than do white middle-class interviewers without this negative attitude.

PROCEDURE

Investigation of this hypothesis was based on a community health survey of a sample of 1,713 adults in the Washington Heights Health District of New York City.[5] Respondents were drawn from a population that is ethnically, economically and educationally heterogeneous. They were classified into three income levels: less than $3,000, $3,000 to $5,999, and $6,000 or more.[6]

The 57 interviewers included both men and women, but were relatively homogeneous with respect to class background, age and education—all being from middle-class backgrounds, under 40 years of age and at least high-school graduates. The 26 interviewers included in the analysis of interviewer effect (16 men and ten women) are the white, non-Puerto Rican members of the interviewing staff who completed at least 15 interviews. Interviewers completing fewer interviews were eliminated to reduce the variability among interviewers attributable primarily to differences among their respondents. Two-thirds of the respondents were randomly assigned to interviewers, with the remaining one-third assigned according to administrative convenience—usually based on location of an interviewer's residence. To give equal weight to each interviewer despite differences in the number of interviews completed, the basic datum used in this analysis was the mean of the scores obtained by an interviewer from respondents in a designated category.

The Indicator of Interviewer Effect

The data used for the test of interviewer effects were 22 psycho-physiologic symptom questions developed as an index of psychopathology by the Midtown study.[7] Higher scores indicate a presumed greater probability of the presence of psychopathology. The direction of the interviewer effect on this score can be predicted from the *Social Desirability*[8] of the items. On a scale from one—representing extremely undesirable—to nine, representing extremely desirable, the average rating given these items by a subsample of 27 Irish, Jewish, Negro and Puerto Rican respondents[9] was 3.2, with individual item ratings ranging from 2.2 to 4.1. Thus, all items were rated undesirable. A respondent attempting to present a favorable image of himself to the interviewer could be expected, therefore, to tend to reject these items, thereby lowering his psychophysiologic symptom score. Distortion in the opposite direction seems unlikely, because it would require that the respondents be motivated to present an unfavorable picture of themselves to the interviewers.

Measurement of Interviewer Attitude

At the completion of their assignments, the interviewers answered the following question concerning their preferences for respondents:[10]
Did you prefer to interview: (Circle one of each line)

men	women	no difference
poor people	rich people	no difference
whites	Negroes	no difference
old people	young people	no difference

Because the answer "no difference" was offered in each case, choice of the higher status clearly implies rejection of the lower one. Preferences for respondents who were male, rich, white or young were scored positive in building an index of rejection of persons of low status. These responses formed a Guttman scale, with the order from most to least popular being young people, whites, rich people and males.[11]

Among the 26 interviewers included in this study, 14 expressed no preferences for any type of high-status respondent, six expressed only the most popular preference (for young respondents), and the remaining six scored higher on the scale by expressing at least two preferences. An empirical split on the scale argued, therefore, a cutting point between the interviewers who expressed no preference and those who expressed at least one preference. This division yielded two groups of nearly equal size, closely matched with respect to sex of interviewer. Among the 14 interviewers without preferences, eight were male and six female; among the 12 with preferences, eight were male and four female.

Would such a division between interviewers who expressed no preference and those who expressed at least one preference make sense conceptually? It implies something that is not self-evident: That interviewers who only expressed a preference for young respondents tended to reject not only the old but also Negroes and poor people. Yet a number of considerations support this inference. The fact that the questionnaire items form a Guttman scale implies that they are related to a general attitude of rejection toward lower-status persons. Rejection of Negroes and poor people has, however, become increasingly unpopular and hence less likely to be expressed openly. Thus, it is possible that interviewers who admitted only the attitude of rejection of old people would covertly express rejection toward Negroes and poor people even though unwilling to state this feeling overtly.

Because the interviewers expressed their preferences after completing their interviews, a finding that interviewers' attitudes are related to their respondents' answers could mean that the respondents' answers produced these attitudes. Fortunately, however, this alternative interpretation appears implausible in the case of positive results, inasmuch as the prediction is that interviewers with preferences will obtain lower scores from low-status respondents than will interviewers without preferences. If this prediction is confirmed, it would hardly seem reasonable to infer that those who interviewed the relatively "well" Negroes and low-income whites responded with rejecting attitudes, whereas those who interviewed the relatively "sick" respondents in these categories did not. Multiple t-tests were used to test the hypothesis about the effects of interviewers' rejecting attitudes on Negro and lower-class white respondents.[12]

RESULTS

The mean symptom scores shown in Table 1 indicate that the results for all categories of respondents except low-income Negroes were in accord with the hypothesis. Among whites, as predicted, only low-income respondents were influenced by the interviewer's attitude. Con-

TABLE I. PSYCHOPHYSIOLOGIC SYMPTOM SCORES OBTAINED BY INTERVIEWERS WITH AND WITHOUT PREFERENCES FROM WHITE AND NEGRO RESPONDENTS IN THREE INCOME GROUPS

| | | Interviewers | | | | | | |
| | | Without Preferences | | | With Preferences | | | |
Respondent Race and Income	(n)	Mean Score	(N)	(n)	Mean Score	(N)	Difference in Means	t
White								
Less than $3,000		3.62			2.29		+1.33	1.73[a]
	(13)		(82)	(9)		(83)		
$3,000 to 5,999		2.26			2.25		+0.01	0.02
	(13)		(150)	(12)		(194)		
$6,000 or more		1.25			1.72		−0.47	1.50
	(13)		(168)	(12)		(204)		
Negro								
Less than $3,000		2.14			1.86		+0.28	0.14
	(8)		(31)	(8)		(38)		
$3,000 to 5,999		2.63			1.07		+1.56	1.90[a,b]
	(10)		(41)	(7)		(57)		
$6,000 or more		2.46			1.11		+1.35	1.51[c]
	(7)		(30)	(8)		(53)		

(n) = number of interviewers, (N) = number of respondents.

[a] $P < .05$, one-tailed test.

[b] Because of heterogeneous variances, d.f. were reduced according to Welch's formula in Winer, B. J., STATISTICAL PRINCIPLES IN EXPERIMENTAL DESIGN, New York, McGraw-Hill Book Company, 1962, p. 38.

[c] $P < .10$, one-tailed test.

sistent with the prediction for Negroes, middle-income Negroes reported fewer symptoms to interviewers with preferences than to interviewers without preferences and high-income Negroes showed a trend in the same direction. Contrary to expectation, however, no difference is found among the low-income Negroes by type of interviewer.

These results pose two problems of explanation: (1) How to integrate findings concerning the status-related attitudinal variables with results from other studies concerning the effects of status dissimilarity? (2) The finding of no effect among low-income Negro respondents, the group most dissimilar in status from the white middle-class interviewers, seems to contradict J. A. Williams' proposition that the greater the dissimilarity the greater the probability of effects. Before attempting to deal with these problems, however, consider a direct challenge to the notion that status homophily minimizes the probability of interviewer biasing effects.

271

This challenge was presented by Hyman, who hypothesized that some interviewers, whom he labeled intrusive, tend to develop too much rapport with their respondents, because of ". . . a tendency to want to enter deeply into the respondent's affairs, which naturally increases the orientation of the respondent in the direction of the interviewers."[13] These interviewers, Hyman suggested, tend to bias their respondents' answers. To illustrate this position, Hyman described an interview that sounded like a "hen party," in which two women of similar background engaged in a friendly social visit,[14] thus suggesting that an interviewer's intrusive tendencies are activated by a respondent of similar status who can be treated as a friend. This hypothesis implies that status similarity is likely to produce biased answers, but dissimilarity—particularly if it is a type that would ordinarily preclude close friendship —raises a barrier against biasing effects caused by interviewer intrusiveness. Dissimilarity in race or socioeconomic status seems especially likely to raise such a barrier, but age or sex differences might also interfere with the easy intimacy that, Hyman suggested, is developed by the intrusive interviewer.

PROCEDURE

The procedure used to test for effects of interviewer intrusiveness is the same as that used to test for effects of interviewer's social preferences, except in the following respects.

The Indicator of Interviewer Intrusiveness

At the completion of their assignments, interviewers answered questions concerning whether they had been embarrassed by certain topics in the interview.[15] Of the 11 topics included, six formed a Guttman scale.[16] Ordered from most to least likely to be found embarrassing, these topics are:

> Why women cannot have children
> Income
> If families get public assistance
> Religious affiliation
> Who a person's friends are
> Age of adult women

Because embarrassment about asking such questions implies a personal rather than a professional relationship between interviewer and respondent, this scale was used to indicate an underlying intrusive attitude on the part of the interviewer. For the purpose of testing Hyman's hypothesis, the 26 interviewers in this investigation were divided into two equal groups, 13 who did and 13 who did not report embarrassment on at least one item. An alternative interpretation of these scores as indicative of differences in general level of interviewer competence would be supported only if it were shown—contrary to the prediction concerning intrusiveness—that interviewers who reported embarrassment performed less well than others with all types of respondents.

The intrusiveness hypothesis was tested for white respondents by analysis of variance.[17] To determine the effect of intrusiveness on Negro respondents, mean scores obtained by embarrassed and by unembarrassed interviewers were compared at different income levels and so forth as in the analysis for effects of preference shown in Table 1.

RESULTS

The two interviewer attitudes, embarrassment and preference for high-status respondents, were uncorrelated in the sample of 26 interviewers.[18] Moreover, neither attitude was distinctly characteristic of male or female interviewers.

No evidence was found that embarrassed interviewers obtained more biased answers from respondents of like sex or age than from respondents of different sex or age. The results of the analysis of variance shown in Table 2 indicate, however, that the interaction of interviewer embarrassment and respondent income was a significant source of

TABLE 2. ANALYSIS OF VARIANCE OF INTERVIEWER ATTITUDES AND RESPONDENT INCOME FOR WHITE RESPONDENTS*

Source	SS	df	MS	F	
Interviewer intrusiveness (I)	5.07	1	5.07		
Interviewer preferences (P)	0.12	1	0.12		
IP	0.42	1	0.42		
Error (interviewers)	50.04	20	2.50		
Respondent income (R)	32.42	2	16.21	10.73	$P < .01$
IR	13.37	2	6.68	4.42	$.01 < P < .05$
PR	6.27	2	3.14		
IPR	8.84	2	4.42	2.93	$.05 < P < .10$
Error (respondents)	60.46	40	1.51		

* Interviewer is unit of analysis.

273

variation in white respondents' symptom scores. In contrast, but as expected, the analysis for Negro respondents according to income level did not show any effects associated with interviewer embarrassment.

The mean scores describing the effects of interviewer embarrassment on the answers of white respondents in different income groups are shown in Table 3. As predicted from Hyman's intrusiveness hypothesis, unembarrassed interviewers obtained higher symptom scores from the middle-income respondents than did embarrassed interviewers.

The lowest-income respondents also reacted very differently to embarrassed and unembarrassed interviewers—but in the opposite way from respondents in the middle-income group. The finding that these low-income respondents were also affected differently by interviewers with and without preferences, as shown in Table 1, raises the question of how they responded to combinations of the two attitudes. The most striking effect suggested by the mean scores shown in Table 4 is that interviewer embarrassment tended to ameliorate the adverse effects on low-income respondents of an interviewer's preference for high-status respondents.

TABLE 3. MEAN PSYCHOPHYSIOLOGIC SYMPTOM SCORES* OBTAINED BY EMBARRASSED AND BY UNEMBARRASSED INTERVIEWERS FROM WHITE RESPONDENTS AT THREE INCOME LEVELS

Respondent Income	Interviewers	
	Embarrassed	Unembarrassed
Less than $3,000	3.72	2.52
$3,000–5,999	2.02	2.62
$6,000 or more	1.62	1.29

* Interviewer is unit of analysis.

TABLE 4. MEAN PSYCHOPHYSIOLOGIC SYMPTOM SCORES* OBTAINED FROM WHITE LOW INCOME RESPONDENTS BY EMBARRASSED AND UNEMBARRASSED INTERVIEWERS WITH AND WITHOUT PREFERENCES FOR HIGH-STATUS RESPONDENTS

	Interviewers With Preferences	Interviewers Without Preferences
Embarrassed interviewers	3.42	4.70
Unembarrassed interviewers	1.36	3.36

* Interviewer is unit of analysis.

DISCUSSION

Although the findings concerning the effects of interviewer embarrassment, and those reported earlier concerning interviewer preferences, tended to confirm expectations on a number of counts, they also pose several challenges for explanation:

1. To relate effects of interviewers' preferences for high-status respondents on middle-income Negro and low-income white respondents to effects of interviewers' embarrassment on middle-income white and low-income white respondents.

2. To reconcile the finding that white middle-class interviewers' preferences for high-status respondents have no effect on low-income Negro respondents with Williams' finding that large status-dissimilarity increases the probability of interviewer effects.

3. To integrate findings concerning the status-related effects of attitudinal variables with previous theory and findings concerning the effects of interviewer and respondent status-dissimilarity.

It has been implied that the status-dissimilarity hypothesis and the intrusiveness hypothesis are opposing points of view about the sources of interviewer effects. If, however, these two views are related to the idea of social distance, no reason is seen why they should be opposed. In this frame of reference, they combine to imply the very simple and powerful idea that in the interaction of interviewer and respondent either too much or too little social distance can be present. At either extreme of social distance, the probability is high that the respondent's answers will be biased by interviewer effects. Conversely, an optimal middle social distance can be found to minimize interviewer effects.

How can this optimal middle range of social distance be identified? The attempt to solve this problem led to the development of a model that predicts interviewer effects from hypothetical relationships among three factors: (1) objective difference in the social status of interviewer and respondent, (2) the interviewer's attitudes and (3) the social distance the respondent perceives between himself and the interviewer. The aim was to construct the model in such a way that it would be consistent with the empirical results on interviewer effects and with the organizing hypothesis that these effects are due to either too much or too little perceived social distance between interviewer and respondent.

Figure 1 describes the respondent's perception of the social distance between himself and the interviewer as a function of the objective difference in their status and of the attitudes of the interviewer. It suggests, moreover, that the importance of the interviewer's attitudes varies with the amount of objective difference between the interviewer's status and that of the respondent.

On the low end of the perceived social distance scale (the left side of the diagram), the objective difference between the status of the interviewer and that of the respondent is small. The results suggest that

FIGURE I. INTERVIEWER BIASING EFFECTS PRODUCED BY INTERVIEWER ATTITUDES AND RESPONDENT-INTERVIEWER STATUS RELATIONSHIP AS MEDIATED BY RESPONDENT'S PERCEPTION OF SOCIAL DISTANCE

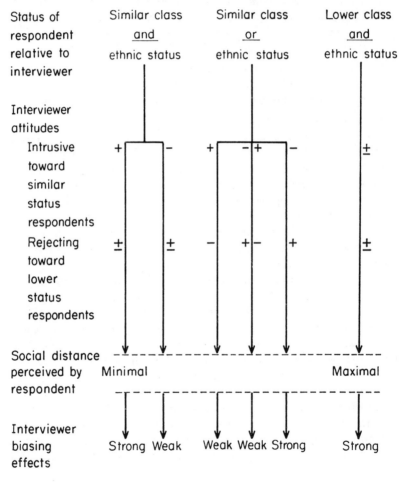

in this situation it is not the objective relationship, but the interviewer's attitude, presumably reflected in his behavior, that is critical in determining whether or not the respondent perceives the interviewer as so close that he biases his answers. The diagram indicates that the interviewer who tends to be embarrassed is most likely to be perceived as too close by a respondent whose status is like his and to get biased answers from such a respondent.

On the high end of the perceived social distance scale (the right side of the diagram), the objective difference between the status of the interviewer and that of the respondent is large. In this situation the white middle-class interviewers' status preferences were found to have no effect on lower-class Negro respondents' answers. This result appeared to be inconsistent with J. A. Williams' finding that white interviewers obtained more biased answers from low-status Negro respondents than from high-status Negroes. The discrepancy disappears, however, if one assumes that when the objective difference between the interviewer's status and the respondent's is large, it is this objective difference, rather than interviewer attitudes, that determines the respondent's perception of the interviewer.

This assumption of the critical role of a large objective status difference is supported by a number of research findings relevant to the case of white middle-class interviewers and Negro lower-class respondents. For example, Robin Williams[19] has presented evidence in his study of intergroup attitudes that lower-status Negroes, particularly those with less education, perceive extreme social distance between themselves and the white middle class. Considered in this light, it is not surprising that white middle-class interviewers' preferences for high-status respondents were not related to the answers of lower-class Negro respondents, for when a group is perceived as being at a great social distance the ability to discriminate subtle differences among members of that group is minimal. This point is supported by Pettigrew's[20] observations concerning lower-class Negroes' perceptions of whites.

Therefore, absence of effects on lower-class Negroes' responses associated with white middle-class interviewers' attitudes does not indicate lack of interviewer effects. Rather, it is more consistent with previous findings concerning the interaction of these two groups to infer that white middle-class interviewers tend to bias the answers of lower-class Negro respondents regardless of the interviewers' attitudes toward these respondents.

Finally, what about the case where the objective distance between the interviewer's and respondent's statuses is intermediate? The results suggest that the interviewer who is unembarrassed and prefers high-status respondents is most likely to bias respondents' answers in this situation; the interviewer who is embarrassed and has no status preferences is least likely to bias answers. Furthermore, because embarrassment can be consistently interpreted as indicating a tendency to seek a close relationship with respondents and preference for high-status respondents as a tendency to reject lower-status respondents, the unembarrassed interviewer with preferences probably is seen as markedly more distant than the embarrassed interviewer without preferences by respondents at this objective social distance. Thus, the model suggests that where objective social distance is intermediate, the probability of interviewer biasing effects is least when the interviewer's attitudes tend to minimize the perceived social distance.

This model is suggested as a framework for dealing with questions about the locus of interviewer effects, particularly in the difficult areas of cross-class and cross-race interviewing. For example, Paul Sheatsley has asked, "Which is the lesser evil: to have an uneducated colored woman interviewed by a white woman more nearly approaching her own socioeconomic status, or to have her interviewed by a Negro, who has an M.A. in sociology?"[21] The model is in agreement with the implication underlying Sheatsley's question—that interviewer and respondent should share either ethnic or class status, so that the objective status difference is not too great.

Given such an objective status difference, in the intermediate range, the model indicates two lines of investigation to answer Sheatsley's question. First, the model suggests that attempts be made to measure lower-class Negro respondents' perceptions of social distance in the two types of relations, that is, with lower-class-white and with middle-class-Negro interviewers, to determine whether the perceived distance in one relation is markedly less than in the other. If the difference in perception is not large, the model indicates that their attitudes would be an important criterion for recruiting interviewers. That is, one would select either middle-class-Negro or lower-class-white interviewers who do not reject persons of lower status. Furthermore, inasmuch as the danger here is that social distance will be perceived as too large, not too small, the model suggests—contrary to survey research folklore— that interviewers who are embarrassed should be recruited as added insurance against respondents' perceiving too much distance between themselves and the interviewers.

278

REFERENCES

[1] Katz, D., Do Interviewers Bias Polls?, *Public Opinion Quarterly*, 6, 248–268, 1942.

[2] Hyman, H. H., *et al., Interviewing in Social Research,* Chicago, Chicago University Press, 1954, pp. 159–167.

[3] Williams, J. A., Jr., Interviewer-Respondent Interaction: A Study of Bias in the Information Interview, *Sociometry,* 27, 338–352, 1964.

[4] *Ibid.,* p. 340.

[5] See Appendix for description of sampling plan for Master Sample Survey of Washington Heights Health District, 1960–1961.

[6] The first cutting point was dictated by the Bureau of Labor Statistics' estimate that $3,000 per year is the poverty line for a family in New York City. The second cutting point was set at $6,000 so as to be able to secure a reasonable number of Negro respondents in the "high" income category.

[7] Langner, T. S., A Twenty-Two Item Screening Score of Psychiatric Symptoms Indicating Impairment, *Journal of Health and Human Behavior,* 3, 269–276, Winter, 1962.

[8] Edwards, A. L., THE SOCIAL DESIRABILITY VARIABLE IN PERSONALITY, ASSESSMENT AND RESEARCH, New York, Dryden Press, 1957.

[9] These respondents are the ones in a sample survey of 151 community members who completed their interviews in a short enough time to permit administration of the Social Desirability measures.

[10] A choice between sick and healthy people was also included, but it was not used in identifying interviewers with preferences, because this scale was designed to test the effect of interviewer attitudes toward their respondents rather than possible effects of their feelings about a specific topic such as health.

[11] The coefficient of reproducibility of the scale is .95 and the Borgatta error ratio is .67. *See* Borgatta, E. F., An Error Ratio for Scalogram Analysis, *Public Opinion Quarterly,* 19, 96–100, Spring, 1955.

[12] Although an analysis of variance involving respondent's race, respondent's income and interviewer's preferences would have been an appropriate first step, it was not possible because not enough interviewers were available who had interviewed Negro respondents in all three income categories.

[13] Hyman, H. H., *op. cit.,* p. 48.

[14] *Ibid.,* pp. 46–47.

[15] The question was, "Here are some topics or questions that embarrassed some interviewers. How embarrassed were you in asking questions on the following topics?" The response alternatives were: very embarrassed, somewhat embarrassed, not too embarrassed, not at all embarrassed. The first three responses were counted as positive.

[16] The coefficient of reproducibility of this scale is .96 and the Borgatta error ratio is .34. *See* Borgatta, E. F., *loc. cit.*

[17] Interviewer embarrassment and preferences were combined with age and with income in each of two three-way analyses of variance. Because of the necessity for controlling interviewer sex in the analysis involving respondent sex,

not enough cases were available to control preferences simultaneously with embarrassment in the analysis according to sex. A separate analysis determined that preferences yielded no significant interaction effects with interviewer or respondent sex.

[18] $X^2 = 0.15$ with (one) 1 degree of freedom.

[19] Williams, R. M., Jr., STRANGERS NEXT DOOR, Englewood Cliffs, New Jersey, Prentice-Hall, Inc., 1964, pp. 259–263.

[20] Pettigrew, T. F., *A Profile of the Negro American*, Princeton, New Jersey, D. Van Nostrand Co., Inc., 1964.

[21] Sheatsley, P. B., An Analysis of Interviewer Characteristics and Their Relationship to Performance, *International Journal of Opinion and Attitude Research*, 4, 487, 1950–1951.

ACKNOWLEDGMENTS

This paper was adapted by permission from Public Opinion Quarterly, *32, 410–422, Fall, 1968. Copyright 1968 by Princeton University Press.*

This work was supported in part by Grants OM-82 and MH-10328-02 from the National Institute of Mental Health.

EFFECT OF INTERVIEWERS' SEX
ON INTERVIEW RESPONSES

JOHN COLOMBOTOS

JACK ELINSON

AND

REGINA LOEWENSTEIN

The homogeneity of interviewing staffs in sex, age, socioeconomic status and education has been of concern to survey researchers for some time. Some years ago, in a summary of the composition of the field staffs of various survey research organizations, Sheatsley noted:[1]

> The composition of most national field staffs has dangerous implications for survey bias arising out of the interviewing situation. We have a condition in which the great bulk of market and opinion research interviewing today is conducted by women talking to men, by college graduates talking to the uneducated, by upper-middle-class individuals talking to those of low socioeconomic status, by younger people talking to the increasingly larger old-age groups, by white persons talking to Negroes and by city dwellers talking to rural folk.

One reason for the predominance of women on interviewing staffs is undoubtedly their greater availability for part-time work such as interviewing. A methodological justification for the selection of women interviewers is based on the assumption that "homophily" between interviewer and respondent—in this case with respect to their sex—facilitates communication between them.[2] The rationale for using women interviewers in family health surveys is made explicit by Trussell and Elinson:[3]

> Previous studies suggested that the sex of the interviewer has something to do with the yield of reported illnesses. While the data were relatively meager, the evidence was in the direction of supporting the thesis that interviewers of the same sex as the respondent elicited more reports of illness.

281

Since the preferred respondent was the female head of the family, female interviewers were indicated.

But other researchers studying other health-related problems have developed an equally plausible rationale for using male interviewers. Cisin, for example, in a study of drinking practices, notes:[4]

> Public opinion poll interviewers are usually middle-aged housewives who look the part. Since male respondents, especially, might be reluctant to discuss the details of their drinking with a lady who subtly reminded them of the village gossip (or, worse yet, of their mothers), the California study made maximum use of male interviewers, selected largely for their studious, academic appearance, an appearance that was supposed to reflect a high level of academic interest and an equally high level of personal disinterest. The manner and attitude of these interviewers were modeled after those of Kinsey's interviewers. Their training reflected the need to give the impression that they had heard everything, that nothing the respondent might reveal could surprise them.

What, in fact, is the effect of the interviewers' sex on health survey data? Studies comparing responses obtained by male and female interviewers are relatively rare and their findings, for the most part, have been inconclusive.[5] An opportunity to investigate this question with respect to one kind of health interview data, reports of psychiatric symptoms, was provided by the Washington Heights Master Sample Survey of 1960–1961.[6]

PROCEDURE

The total sample of 2,300 housing units was divided into three subsamples of equal size. In two of these, sets of geographically close housing units were randomly assigned to the interviewers. However, because some female interviewers refused to accept assignments in low socioeconomic areas, it was not possible to carry out strictly random assignments throughout the area.[7] In this analysis, it was nevertheless decided to include all interviews, whether or not they were randomly assigned; and to control for respondent's race and education in examining differences in the responses obtained by male and female interviewers.

The analysis presented here is based only on the work of 31 white interviewers, 21 men and ten women, who completed 15 or more respondent forms.[8] Their work accounts for 1,479 such forms, or 86 per cent of the total of 1,713. The distributions of the number of respondent forms completed per interviewer are roughly the same among male and female interviewers.

282

The sex composition of the interviewing staff was not the result of any deliberate policy, but rather reflects the main sources used to recruit interviewers; that is, college placement offices and the state employment service. Both the men and women were relatively young (only two were over 45), but the men were younger. All but two interviewers (both women) had had at least some college, but the men had a little more education. More than a third of the men, in fact, were students in college or graduate school during the field work. Of the ten women, four were housewives.[9]

The effects of interviewers' sex is examined with respect to two measures of respondents' self-reported symptoms. One measure—called the "psychiatric screening" score—is based on the number of positive responses to a battery of 22 items developed by researchers in the Midtown Study to discriminate between psychiatrically impaired and "well" persons.[10] The second measure is based on the number of positive responses to eight items asking about disturbances of mood, thought or feeling.[11] This measure is called the "supplementary psychiatric" score.

FINDINGS

The differences between the average scores obtained by male and female interviewers from all respondents are negligible: 2.17 and 2.04, respectively, on the psychiatric screening score; and supplementary psychiatric scores of 1.12 and 0.99, respectively.

Controlling for the respondents' race and sex, Table 1 shows a tendency for male interviewers to obtain higher scores on both measures from all groups of respondents, male and female, white and Negro;[12] but these differences are small and none is statistically significant. It is possible that their youth and their student status account for the male interviewers' obtaining higher scores. The data do not support this interpretation, however, when both age and main activity of interviewer are controlled and Negro respondents are excluded because of the small number interviewed by women. The tendency for male interviewers to obtain higher scores among white respondents persists when the following controls are introduced: age and education of interviewers; sex, age and education of respondent; and geographic location of respondent's residence. But it is somewhat unstable because of small numbers of cases in many cells, nor does it appear to be concentrated among any specific groups of respondents.

TABLE I. PSYCHIATRIC SYMPTOM MEAN SCORES ACCORDING TO SEX
OF INTERVIEWER AND RACE* AND SEX OF RESPONDENT

Respondents	Psychiatric Screening Score		Supplementary Psychiatric Score	
	Male Interviewers	Female Interviewers	Male Interviewers	Female Interviewers
All respondents	2.17 (925)	2.04 (410)	1.12 (884)	.99 (375)
White				
Male	1.80 (277)**	1.49 (148)	.94 (266)	.78 (138)
Female	2.62 (365)	2.44 (201)	1.42 (354)	1.21 (183)
Negro				
Male	1.90 (113)	1.81 (27)	.84 (108)	.78 (23)
Female	1.99 (170)	2.29 (34)	.94 (156)	.84 (31)

* Respondents of Puerto Rican origin are excluded from this table.

** Figures in parentheses are the numbers of persons in that category. For example, the 277 white male respondents interviewed by men reported a mean average of 1.80 symptoms on the psychiatric screening score.

If one wished to examine the relationship between sex of respondents and self-reported psychiatric symptoms, one would also want to know whether a staff of male interviewers produces different results from a staff of female interviewers. Table 1 shows that female respondents report higher scores than male respondents regardless of the interviewers' sex. Furthermore, the magnitude of sex-linked differences in scores is generally similar whether the interviewers are men or women.

SUMMARY

There is essentially no difference in the reporting of psychiatric symptoms to male and female interviewers in a community survey. The question as to whether responses obtained by male and female interviewers differ in other types of health surveys—for example, when respondents report about other family members, about acute or chronic physical illness, about sex and drinking practices—requires further analysis for a more complete picture of the effects of using male or female interviewers in health surveys. Differences in response patterns according to the interviewers' sex may depend on subject matter and specific questions asked as well as on the composition of respondent populations and other characteristics of the specific survey situation. What the finding reported here suggests is that the rationales commonly presented for hiring either male or female interviewers need to be critically reexamined.

284

REFERENCES

[1] Sheatsley, P. B., An Analysis of Interviewer Characteristics and Their Relationships to Performance, Part I, *International Journal of Opinion and Attitude Research,* 4, 487, 1950–1951. *See* also Lazarsfeld, P. F. and Thielens, W., Jr., THE ACADEMIC MIND, Glencoe, Illinois, The Free Press, 1958, pp. 343–355; Stember, C. H., *The Effects of Field Procedures on Public Opinion Data,* unpublished Ph.D. dissertation, Columbia University, 1955.

[2] *See* Hyman, H. H., INTERVIEWING IN SOCIAL RESEARCH, Chicago, University of Chicago Press, 1954, pp. 153–170.

[3] Trussell, R. E. and Elinson, J., CHRONIC ILLNESS IN A RURAL AREA, CHRONIC ILLNESS IN THE UNITED STATES, Volume III, Cambridge, Harvard University Press, 1959. p. 61.

[4] Cisin, I. H., Community Studies of Drinking Behavior, *Annals of the New York Academy of Sciences,* 107, 610, 1963.

[5] *See* Hyman, *op. cit.,* pp. 165–166; Benney, M., Riesman, D. and Star, S. A., Age and Sex in the Interview, *American Journal of Sociology,* 62, 143–152, 1956; Hanson, R. H. and Marks, E. S., Influence of the Interviewer on the Accuracy of Survey Results, *Journal of the American Statistical Association,* 53, 635–655, 1958; Horvitz, D. G., Sampling and Field Procedures of the Pittsburgh Morbidity Survey, *Public Health Reports,* 67, 1003–1012, 1952; Kirsch, A. D., Newcomb, C. H. and Cisin, I. H., An Experimental Study of Sensitivity of Survey Techniques in Measuring Drinking Practices, Social Science Research Project, George Washington University, Washington, D. C., March, 1965, pp. 18–20 (mimeographed); United States Department of Health, Education and Welfare, A HEALTH STUDY IN KIT CARSON COUNTY, COLORADO, Washington, Public Health Service Publication No. 844, 1962, pp. 49–50.

[6] *See* Appendix for description of sampling plan for Washington Heights Master Sample Survey of 1960-1961.

[7] The experience with random assignments involving female interviewers points to a dilemma for studies of the effects of interviewers' sex. On the one hand, it indicates that such studies are not normally possible in slum areas. On the other hand, if women are recruited who do agree to accept assignments in these areas, questions may be raised about the degree to which these women are typical of female interviewers.

[8] *See* Appendix for questionnaires.

[9] Any decision regarding the desirability of recruiting male or female interviewers must, of course, be prepared to take into account other differences between them—although not necessarily the same differences found in this study. It is not surprising that survey interviewing, generally an intermittent, part-time job, is likely to select different types of people from among men and women in the population. For a discussion of the factors affecting the composition of interviewing staffs, *see* Sheatsley, *op. cit.,* pp. 487-491.

[10] *See* Appendix for questionnaires.

[11] *Ibid.*

[12] Puerto Rican respondents, who make up about ten per cent of the population in the district, were excluded from this analysis because the vast majority (102 out of 108) were interviewed by men.

285

ACKNOWLEDGMENT

This paper was adapted from Public Health Reports, 83, 685–690, August, 1968.

286

EDUCATION REPORTED IN INTERVIEWS
An Aspect of Survey Content Error

PAUL W. HABERMAN

AND

JILL SHEINBERG

This paper examines differences in level of educational attainment reported for the same individuals in two questionnaires administered at approximately a three-year interval. Certainly the importance of respondent's education as a research control variable and as an indicator of socioeconomic status needs no amplification, nor does the objective of improving interview data reliability to which this paper is addressed.

BACKGROUND

In the 1960–61 Master Sample Survey of Washington Heights[1] (Study A), information about level of education was obtained for 7,000 adult residents (aged 20 and over). Approximately three years later (1963–1964), 430 of these persons were reinterviewed for a National Council on Alcoholism study, "Distinctive Characteristics of the Alcoholic Family,"[2] (Study B). The composition of this subsample is indicated in Table 3.

In Study A, one family informant, usually the wife, was asked the following questions about educational achievement for all family members over the age of sixteen: "What is the highest grade you attended in school? Did you finish the — grade (year)?" All 430 persons interviewed in Study B were asked the following questions about their own educational attainment: "What was the highest grade you went to in school?" (If eight, 12 or 16 years of school:) "Did you graduate grammar school (high school) (college)?" Consistency of responses between the two studies was compared in terms of eight educational levels (see Table 2) rather than number of years of schooling completed.

FINDINGS

Table 1 compares consistency of educational level reported for all 430 persons in Studies A and B. Whether respondents reported for themselves in both studies or only in Study B, response discrepancies were almost equal. Educational level was inconsistently reported for nearly two-fifths of the sample studied. However, because inconsistencies were rather evenly divided in both directions (upgrading and downgrading), the overall frequency distributions of reported educational level for the two studies showed little response bias.[3]

The majority of the inconsistencies were discrepancies of only one level, primarily involving "some grammar school" and "grammar school graduate" or "some high school" and "high school graduate," as indicated in Table 2.

Inconsistent responses occurred somewhat more often among males and older respondents. The response variance[4] by age indicated steadily declining consistency from the twenties through forties, leveling off after 50 (see Table 3). This seems to reflect diminishing accuracy of recall over time.

Allowing for the time interval between interviews, age was much more reliably reported than education; 87.7 per cent of respondents in Studies A and B consistently reported age. Misstatements of age, unlike education, were more likely to come from women. Differing masculine and feminine values might be a factor in the sex-differentials of misreported age and education, because men generally place more

TABLE I. CONSISTENCY OF EDUCATIONAL LEVEL REPORTED IN STUDIES A AND B BY SAME AND DIFFERENT RESPONDENTS

Consistency of Educational Level Reported	Total (430) %	Same Respondent (282) %	Different Respondent (148) %
Studies A and B consistent*	62.1	62.4	61.5
Study B higher	20.5	20.2	20.9
Study B lower	17.4	17.4	17.6
Total	100.0	65.6	34.4

* Includes respondents who reported attending school during the interval between interviews, if their responses were otherwise consistent.

288

TABLE 2. EDUCATIONAL LEVEL REPORTED IN STUDY A AND STUDY B:* PERCENTAGE DISTRIBUTIONS

Educational Level Reported in Study A	Educational Level Reported in Study B								
	None	Some Grammar School	Grammar School Graduate	Some High School	High School Graduate	Some College	College Graduate	Graduate or Professional School	Total**
None	0.9	0.5	0.2			0.2			1.9
Some grammar school		12.3	4.0	2.1	0.5				18.8
Grammar school graduate		3.3	10.0	2.3	1.4				17.0
Some high school		1.6	3.5	16.0	3.7	0.9			25.8
High school graduate		0.2	1.4	3.3	14.2	2.8	0.9		22.8
Some college			0.2	0.2	2.1	4.7	0.9		8.1
College graduate			0.2	0.2	0.2	0.2	2.1		3.0
Graduate or Professional school						0.2	0.5	1.9	2.6
Total**	0.9	17.9	19.5	24.2	22.1	9.1	4.4	1.9	100.0

* Study A educational level also used in Study B for those respondents who reported attending school during the interval between interviews.
** Sum of component percentages may not equal totals because of rounding.

importance on their educational attainment, whereas women tend to be more concerned about advancing age.

COMPARISONS WITH FINDINGS OF OTHER STUDIES

In another family research project making use of the Washington Heights community Master Sample Survey, conducted by the Community Service Society of New York,[5] 82 married women between the ages of 20 and 44 who participated in Study A were reinterviewed about three years later. With questions similar to those asked in Study A about their own and their husbands' education, consistency of responses for these women was 72.6 per cent (compared with 62.1 per cent for Studies A and B). To make the two reinterview studies more comparable, self-reports by the 110 Study B women under 45 and the 82 Community Service Society wives were examined for consistency. These two groups had identical consistency rates (74.5 and 74.4 per cent, respectively). About the same percentages of inconsistencies were discrepancies of only one educational level and the division between upgrading and downgrading in the reinterviews was also similar. Thus, the Community Service Society study findings confirm the degree of response variance between Studies A and B.

Two additional and unrelated studies measuring reliability of ob-

TABLE 3. CONSISTENT RESPONSES ON EDUCATIONAL LEVEL IN STUDIES A AND B BY SELECTED RESPONDENT CHARACTERISTICS

Respondent Characteristics	N	Per Cent Consistent Responses*
Sex		
Male	200	56.5
Female	230	67.0
Race		
Negro	155	63.2
White**	275	61.5
Age group (in Study A)		
20 to 29	57	73.7
30 to 39	108	67.6
40 to 49	90	58.9
50 to 59	99	56.6
60 and over	76	56.6

* Includes respondents who reported attending school during the interval between interviews, if their responses were otherwise consistent.
** Including 32 Puerto Ricans.

TABLE 4. CONSISTENCY OF EDUCATIONAL DATA REPORTED OVER
AN INTERVAL OF TIME IN VARIOUS STUDIES

Study	N	Number of Educational Levels	Per Cent Consistent Responses
A/B	(430)	8	62.1
"Cincinnati"*	(410)	7	67.0
"Baltimore"*	(470)	6	54.0

* See Hyman, H. H., INTERVIEWING IN SOCIAL RESEARCH, Chicago, University of Chicago Press, 1954, pp. 247–248.

jective data over a six-month interval also had results comparable to those of Studies A and B, as indicated in Table 4.[6]

As part of the 1960 Cenusu of Population, a reinterview survey was conducted shortly after completion of the census interviews.[7] The estimated bias (i.e., the difference between census and reinterview survey distributions of reported educational attainment) was similar to, although smaller than, the Studies A and B differences. The census response bias by educational group ranged up to 1.0 percentage points, with a median of 0.7 percentage points; the comparable figures for the current study were 2.5 and 1.0. The longer interval between Study A and Study B interviews might account for the larger response bias.

DISCUSSION

Inconsistencies in this and other comparable studies seem rather large. It is not known, moreover, how many persons may have made consistent misstatements. But educational attainment reported by a family informant and by a personal respondent was equally reliable and, because the response bias was relatively small, the overall distributions in Studies A and B were similar. By reducing the number of educational levels to three—grammar school graduate or less, some high school or high school graduate only, and some college or more—the response variance in this sample could have been reduced from 37.9 to 21.1 per cent.

Reduction in survey-content error for reported educational level might be accomplished by using the following interview techniques. First, a question such as, "Did you have a chance to get as much education as you wanted?," used in at least one previous survey,[8] should precede the questions on actual attainment. This may alleviate feelings of inadequacy the respondent may have concerning his education and thereby minimize a tendency to overstate his formal schooling.

A question about the age at which the highest-grade-attended was completed should lessen the possibility for misinterpretation. Despite the apparent clarity of the question, some answers seemed to refer rather to the respondent's age when he left school or to number of calendar years of attendance. The additional question would enable the interviewer to probe when obvious inconsistencies appeared between years of schooling and age at school-leaving.

Finally, some attempt should be made, especially in doubtful cases, to ascertain if courses taken after completion of high school are formal education. A question about the name of the school or the courses taken undoubtedly would have reduced the 12.9 per cent of Studies A and B discrepancies involving high-school graduation and "some college."

REFERENCES

[1] See Appendix for description of sample design.

[2] Bailey, M. B., Haberman, P. W. and Sheinberg, J., The Alcoholic Family, in this volume.

[3] Response bias is measured by *net* content error, that is, the number of persons with higher reported educational levels in Study B *minus* the number of persons with lower reported educational levels in Study B.

[4] Sample response variance is measured by *gross* content error, that is, the number of persons with higher reported educational levels in Study B *plus* the number of persons with lower reported educational levels in Study B. This definition and the one above are derived from Bureau of the Census, Procedural Report on the 1960 Censuses of Population and Housing, Working Paper No. 16, Washington, D. C., 1963, pp. 125–146.

[5] *See* Mayer, J. E., Disclosing Marital Problems, in this volume.

[6] Hyman, H. H., INTERVIEWING IN SOCIAL RESEARCH, Chicago, University of Chicago Press, 1954, pp. 247–248.

[7] Procedural Report on the 1960 Censuses, *op. cit.*

[8] Columbia University School of Public Health and Administrative Medicine, FAMILY MEDICAL CARE UNDER THREE TYPES OF HEALTH INSURANCE, New York, The Foundation on Employee Health, Medical Care and Welfare, Inc., 1962.

ACKNOWLEDGMENTS

This paper was adapted by permission from Public Opinion Quarterly, 30, 295–301, Summer, 1966. Copyright 1966 by Princeton University Press, Princeton, New Jersey.

This study was supported by Grant OM–664 from the National Institute of Mental Health and Contract U–1254 from the Health Research Council of the City of New York.

Statistical Techniques for

Design and Analysis

A NEW SURVEY TECHNIQUE AND ITS APPLICATION IN THE FIELD OF PUBLIC HEALTH

BERNARD G. GREENBERG

JAMES R. ABERNATHY

AND

DANIEL G. HORVITZ

Surveys that collect information of a confidential or private nature are plagued by both nonrespondence and untruthful reporting. Warner[1] developed a randomized response technique that enables respondents in personal interview surveys to provide truthful information on sensitive or highly personal questions and yet retain their privacy. The technique is based upon the idea that the respondent selects, on a probability basis, one of two (or more) questions using a random device. The respondent answers "Yes" or "No" to the question, which has been selected by chance, without revealing to the interviewer which question was actually being answered.

Previous papers[2,3] attempted to improve the efficiency of the randomized response technique for collecting data about qualitative characteristics and to assess its applicability in field studies of public health interest. Another paper[4] extended the method for use in measuring quantitative responses as well. A recent survey was done in several urban centers in North Carolina designed to evaluate the procedure and to obtain estimates of certain sensitive qualitative characteristics of the population, such as abortion rates, oral contraceptive use and emotional problems. Preliminary estimates of illegally induced abortion

297

have been reported elsewhere.[5] The present paper discusses further findings from this study.

METHODOLOGY

The randomized response device consisted of a small, transparent plastic box with two statements printed on the front side of the cover, easily legible to the respondent. The first printed statement had a small red ball in front of it and the second statement had a blue ball in the same location. Inside the box were 35 red and 15 blue balls. The respondent was asked to shake the box of balls thoroughly, and tip the box allowing one of the balls to appear in a "window" which was clearly visible to the respondent. The color of the ball that appeared in the window determined which of the two questions the respondent was supposed to answer. If a red ball appeared, she answered the statement that had a red ball beside it; if a blue ball appeared, she answered the statement with a blue ball beside it.

The interviewer was some distance away from the respondent and, of course, was unable to view which question was selected. The respondent's reply was simply "Yes" or "No" without specifying to which question the answer referred. The box was shaken again before returning it to the interviewer to prevent her observation of the ball color.

The purpose of this series of experiments was to estimate (1) the proportion of women who had experienced an induced abortion during the past year, (2) the proportion of women taking oral contraceptives, (3) the proportion of women who had experienced an induced abortion at some time during their lifetime, and (4) the proportion of women who had had an emotional problem requiring professional help.

The set of statements pertaining to abortion during the past year was administered to a sample of 1,300 women in the childbearing ages, 18–44. The statements were as follows:

"I was pregnant at some time during the past 12 months and had an abortion which ended the pregnancy."

"I was born in the month of April."

The women who were asked about abortion during the past year were also queried about use of the contraceptive pill. The set of statements pertaining to oral contraceptive use was printed on another box whose cover was as follows:

"I am now taking the "pill" to prevent pregnancy."

"I was born in the month of April."

A pair of statements relating to abortion over a lifetime was administered to a different sample of 1,600 women who were 18 years old or over. The statements were:

"At some time during my life I had an abortion which ended the pregnancy."

"I was born in the month of April."

Women in this sample were not queried about use of the contraceptive pill since some were over 45 years of age.

In a third sample designed to obtain information on the prevalence of emotional problems, the following set of questions was used with 750 married women 31 years old or over:

"At some time during my life I had an emotional problem which caused me to seek help from a professional person, such as a psychiatrist, doctor, clergyman, psychologist, or social worker."

"The color of the ball in the window is blue."

The "emotional problem" trial was different from the others in that it used three colors of balls: red, white and blue. After shaking the box in the usual fashion and causing a ball to roll into the window, respondents with a red ball in the window answered the emotional problem statement. Those with *either* a white or blue ball in the window answered the other statement. Rationale for this modification will be discussed later.

The three independent samples of women involved in the four experiments described were stratified cluster samples, randomly selected from five metropolitan areas in central North Carolina with populations ranging from 100,000 to 250,000.

The randomized response procedure was thoroughly explained to each respondent prior to her participation. To familiarize her with the device, she practiced with and participated in a trial use of the box with an entirely different set of statements immediately preceding the test situation. The definition of the word "abortion" as used in this study[8] was explained to the respondent during the interview. In addition, the interviewer explained the reasons for using the randomized approach rather than asking direct questions. Respondent opinion on the latter approach in obtaining abortion data was elicited through the following question:

"If an interviewer, like myself, asked one of your friends if she had ever had an abortion, do you think that person would answer truthfully?"

Later in the interview, after the randomized response procedure had been completed, the respondents were asked:

"Do you believe other people will think that there is a trick to the box and that we really can figure out which question they answer?"

"When you played the game, were you convinced that I would not know which question you were answering?"

The purpose of this set of questions was to measure the success in convincing the respondents that survey motives were legitimate and above reproach, and that the interviewer had no veiled intent to trick or mislead.

Calculation of Estimates

Derivation of the formulae used in calculating maximum likelihood estimates of the various parameters of interest under the assumption of simple random sampling has been reported.[3] In computing estimates of the proportion of women in the childbearing ages having an abortion in the past year $(\hat{\pi}_1)$, and the proportion taking oral contraceptives $(\hat{\pi}_3)$, it was assumed that the proportion of this group of women born in April (π_Y) was known in advance. This assumption was also made in determining estimates of the proportion of women 18 years of age or older who had had an abortion at some time during their lifetime $(\hat{\pi}_2)$. The estimate of π_Y used in the calculation of $\hat{\pi}_1$, $\hat{\pi}_2$ and $\hat{\pi}_3$ was .0826, obtained from a weighted distribution by month of birth of all live births filed with the North Carolina State Board of Health, 1924–1950. The formula for calculating these estimates (using $\pi_1|\pi_Y$ as an example) was:

(1)

$$\pi_1|\pi_Y = \frac{\lambda - \pi_Y(1-P)}{P}$$

and

$$\text{Var}\,(\pi_1|\pi_Y) = \frac{\lambda(1-\lambda)}{nP^2}$$

where

λ = the probability that a "Yes" answer will be reported.

= $P\pi_1 + \pi_Y(1-P)$

P = the probability that the abortion question is selected by the respondent. (This is equivalent to the ratio of red balls to total balls in the plastic box.)

n = sample size.

Estimates of $\pi_1|\pi_Y$, $\pi_2|\pi_Y$, $\pi_3|\pi_Y$, and their variances assuming simple random sampling) are obtained by substituting the proportion of "Yes" responses $(\hat{\lambda})$ for λ in the formulae.

Estimates of the proportion of women with an emotional problem $(\hat{\pi}_4)$ were also computed under the assumption that π_Y was known in advance. In this sample, the neutral statement was, "The color of the ball in the window is blue." The parameter π_Y was related to ball color rather than to month of birth and will be referred to as π'_Y to distinguish it from π_Y used in calculating π_1, π_2 and π_3. It was defined as follows:

$$\pi'_Y = \frac{\text{Number of women drawing a blue ball}}{\text{Number of women drawing a non-red ball}}$$

The exact value of π'_Y could not be determined from the sample because both the numerator and denominator were unknown quantities. However, the expected value of this proportion would be the ratio of blue balls to non-red balls in the plastic box, and this was known. The expected value of π'_Y was considered to be a reasonable estimate of π'_Y and was used in calculating $\hat{\pi}_4$. Making the second question a function of the distribution of balls used in the experiment obviates the necessity of searching for a neutral question with low frequency whose value is known in advance. Both methods are subject to error, particularly with small sample sizes, but π'_Y as a function of the distribution of balls would likely yield a more accurate estimate.

When the distribution of balls is not used to fix an expected value for the neutral question, the precise value of π_Y may not be known in advance and it may not be amenable to *a priori* estimation. Under these conditions the sample design can be altered to permit estimation not only of the sensitive characteristic but π_Y as well. In the sample designed to estimate the proportion of women having an abortion during their lifetime, provision was made for estimating both π_2 and π_Y. This was accomplished by selecting two independent subsamples of women. The proportions of red balls, P_1 and P_2, used in these two subsamples of sizes n_1 and n_2 were not the same and the proportions of "Yes" responses, $\hat{\lambda}_1$ and $\hat{\lambda}_2$, were also different. Estimation formulae assuming π_Y not known in advance were

$$\hat{\pi}_2 = \frac{\hat{\lambda}_1 (1 - P_2) - \hat{\lambda}_2 (1 - P_1)}{P_1 - P_2} , \quad \hat{\pi}_Y = \frac{\hat{\lambda}_1 P_2 - \hat{\lambda}_2 P_1}{P_2 - P_1}$$

$$\text{Var} (\hat{\pi}_2) = \frac{1}{(P_1 - P_2)^2} \left[\frac{\lambda_1 (1 - \lambda_1)(1 - P_2)^2}{n_1} + \frac{\lambda_2 (1 - \lambda_2)(1 - P_1)^2}{n_2} \right]$$

$$\text{Var} (\hat{\pi}_Y) = \frac{1}{(P_2 - P_1)^2} \left[\frac{\lambda_1 (1 - \lambda_1) P_2^2}{n_1} + \frac{\lambda_2 (1 - \lambda_2) P_1^2}{n_2} \right].$$

Under this sampling design where two subsamples are used, one may decide later to assume an advance knowledge of π_Y. If so, a single estimate of $\pi_2 | \pi_Y$ may be obtained from each of the two subsamples using formula (1), and a combined estimate may also be calculated. Using invariance as the weighting

302

factor for each subsample, the combined estimate of $\pi_2|\pi_Y$ would be

$$\hat{\pi}_2|\pi_Y = \frac{[\hat{\lambda}_1 - \pi_Y (1 - P_1)] A + [\hat{\lambda}_2 - \pi_Y (1 - P_2)] B}{AP_1 + BP_2}$$

where

$$A = n_1 P_1 \hat{\lambda}_2 (1 - \hat{\lambda}_2)$$
$$B = n_2 P_2 \hat{\lambda}_1 (1 - \hat{\lambda}_1)$$

Assuming simple random sampling, the variance of this combined estimate is one-half the harmonic mean of the two individual variances.

In this study a stratified cluster sample was used rather than simple random sampling. The estimated variances of the estimates to follow were computed consistent with this design, and also under the assumption of simple random sampling. The cluster sample variances were generally eight to ten per cent higher than the simple random sample variances.

DISCUSSION OF RESULTS

In the presentations to follow, estimates and variances of the proportion of women with the several characteristics (oral contraception, emotional problems, abortion) are shown by race, marital status, age, education and number of pregnancies. Data concerning the opinion questions are also shown in the same detail. Variances of the estimates are rather high for some of these subgroups, particularly those involving small n's. In interpreting the estimates, therefore, the magnitude of the variances should be taken into account.

Oral Contraceptive Use

The estimates and variances of the proportion of women taking oral contraceptives are shown in Table 1. It is estimated that one-fourth of the women 18–44 years of age were taking oral contraceptives at the time of the survey. A higher estimate

303

TABLE I. ESTIMATES AND VARIANCES OF THE PROPORTION OF WOMEN TAKING ORAL CONTRACEPTIVES ($\hat{\pi}_3$), AND PROPORTION WITH EMOTIONAL PROBLEMS ($\hat{\pi}_4$), BY RACE, MARITAL STATUS, AGE, EDUCATION AND NUMBER OF PREGNANCIES, URBAN NORTH CAROLINA, 1968

Characteristics	Oral Contraceptive Use*				Emotional Problems**			
	Sample Size	$\hat{\pi}_3$	$\sqrt{Var\ \hat{\pi}_3}$	Confidence Limits (95%)	Sample Size	$\hat{\pi}_4$	$\sqrt{Var\ \hat{\pi}_4}$	Confidence Limits (95%)
Total	1,251	.2510	.01616	.2193–.2827	754	.2283	.02365	.1819–.2747
White	782	.2310	.01988	.1920–.2700	546	.1987	.02718	.1454–.2520
Nonwhite	469	.2844	.02750	.2305–.3383	208	.3059	.04712	.2136–.3984
Never Married	236	.1886	.03381	.1223–.2549				
Ever Married	1,015	.2655	.01827	.2297–.3013	754	.2283	.02365	.1819–.2747
Age (in years)								
Under 31	447	.3823	.03070	.3221–.4425	312	.3151	.03864	.2394–.3908
31–44	538	.1713	.02165	.1289–.2137	431	.1694	.02982	.1110–.2278
45 and over								
Education (years of school completed)								
Under 9	108	.2424	.05440	.1358–.3490	167	.2306	.05033	.1319–.3293
9–12	606	.2517	.02324	.2061–.2973	342	.2584	.03582	.1882–.3286
13 and over	301	.3027	.03506	.2340–.3714	237	.1791	.04057	.0996–.2586
Number of pregnancies								
0–4	830	.2796	.02056	.2393–.3199	583	.2157	.02665	.1635–.2679
5 and over	181	.2079	.03981	.1299–.2859	167	.2819	.05195	.1801–.3837

Note: Estimated variances shown are based upon simple random sampling. These variances should be increased approximately ten per cent to approach the correct estimates under the cluster sample design used in this study.

* Sample comprised women 18–44 years of age.

** Sample comprised ever married women 31 years of age or over.

was found for nonwhite (.284) than for white women (.231). With regard to marital status, oral contraceptive use was estimated to be 40 per cent greater among the ever married than the never married, .266 and .189, respectively.

In the ever married population, contraceptive use declined with age, and increased as education level increased. Little difference in contraceptive use was found for women with fewer than three children as compared with women with three or four children. Among women with five or more children, contraceptive use was lower than in women with less than five children.

In a national sample of married women in the childbearing ages surveyed in 1965, Ryder and Westoff[6] reported that the proportion of women currently using oral contraceptives declined as age increased. They also reported an increase in their use as educational level advanced. Regarding parity, they found the proportion of oral contraceptive users was lower among women who had had five or more live births than among those who had had less than five. Similarities in the findings of the two studies are striking.

Two major differences are found in the Ryder-Westoff findings and those reported here. The former was a national study and showed 15.5 per cent of married women under 45 years of age using oral contraceptives, compared with 26.6 per cent in the present study. They also showed oral contraceptive use to be approximately 25 per cent higher for whites than non-whites. These differences may be explained by the fact that the North Carolina study was done three years later than the national study and a higher proportion of users might be expected. Moreover, the present study was carried out in large metropolitan areas where family planning clinics are abundant and are promoted by municipal health authorities for the disadvantaged and welfare groups. A high proportion of those attending these clinics are nonwhite. A slightly higher proportion of users among nonwhites was expected in the sample and these estimates would, therefore, appear to be reasonable.

Kunin, *et al.,* in a 1967 study conducted among employed women of both races in Charlottesville and Albemarle County, Virginia, found oral contraceptive use in women of childbearing ages to be approximately 31 per cent for whites and 25 per cent for nonwhites.[7] These results are quite similar to those reported here and are a further indication that the randomized response estimates are credible.

Emotional Problems

As shown in Table 1, the proportion of ever married women 31 years old or over who, at some time during their life, had sought professional help for an emotional problem was estimated as .228. The proportion was higher for nonwhites than whites, .306 and .199, respectively, and this difference was statistically significant.

Emotional problems requiring professional help were more prevalent in ever married women 31–44 years of age (.315) than among those 45 years old or over (.169). This may be a reflection of a number of factors, such as selective mortality, greater availability of counselors and increased popularity of counseling among the younger group, removal of taboos on learning about emotional illness in recent years, menopausal problems in younger group, economic differentials between the two groups and the like.

Ever-married women with a high school education or less were more likely to have had an emotional problem requiring professional help than were those with one or more years of college. The proportions in the education categories seeking help were .231 among those with less than ninth grade education, .258 in the group with 9–12 years of school and .179 in the college group.

Ever-married women with five or more pregnancies were more susceptible to emotional problems leading to professional assistance than were those women with less than five. The proportions were found to be .282 for women with five or more pregnancies compared with .216 for those with fewer.

306

The emotional problem findings are generally in the direction expected, and the estimated magnitude of the condition appears plausible.

Abortion

Estimates and variances of the proportion of women having an induced abortion in the past year and during a lifetime, assuming π_Y known in advance, have been reported.[5] The lifetime estimates are repeated here for purposes of comparison with those made under the assumption that π_Y was completely unknown. Values of $\hat{\pi}_Y$ were calculated from the data under the latter condition. The three sets of estimates are shown in Table 2.

Both estimates of $\hat{\pi}_2$ indicate a higher proportion of the nonwhite population having had an induced abortion during their lifetime than the white population. With regard to marital status, the estimates were the same for the ever married and the never married populations when π_Y was assumed to be known. Estimates were higher for the never married group when π_Y was assumed unknown.

Estimates pertaining to age and education were similar under both π_Y assumptions. Of the three age groups considered among the ever married population, women 31–44 years of age recorded the highest proportion having had an induced abortion over their lifetime. Of the three educational levels, the highest proportion having had an abortion was found among women with less than nine years of school. When π_Y was assumed known, the estimated proportion of women having had an induced abortion was higher for those with five or more pregnancies than for those with fewer pregnancies. The opposite was found when π_Y was assumed to be known.

If π_Y were known in advance without error, or could be fairly accurately estimated, the corresponding estimates of $\pi_2|\pi_Y$ would be more accurate and less variable than the estimates obtained when π_Y is unknown. This increase in precision arises not only through lack of error of π_Y in computing

307

TABLE 2. ESTIMATES AND VARIANCES OF THE PROPORTION OF WOMEN HAVING AN ABORTION DURING LIFE-TIME ($\hat{\pi}_2$), AND THE PROPORTION BORN IN APRIL ($\hat{\pi}_Y$) BY RACE, MARITAL STATUS, AGE, EDUCATION AND NUMBER OF PREGNANCIES, URBAN NORTH CAROLINA, 1968

| | Sample Size | | Abortion During Lifetime* | | | | | |
| | | | Assuming π_Y Known | | | Assuming π_Y Unknown | | |
Characteristics	n_1	n_2	$\hat{\pi}_2\|\pi_Y$	$\sqrt{Var\ \hat{\pi}_2\|\pi_Y}$	π_2	$\sqrt{Var\ \hat{\pi}_2}$	$\hat{\pi}_Y$	$\sqrt{Var\ \hat{\pi}_Y}$
Total	1,015	576	.0412	.01020	.0622	.01520	.0597	.01633
White	672	415	.0164	.01308	.0508	.01911	.0405	.01703
Nonwhite	343	161	.1028	.01724	.0917	.02590	.0943	.02678
Never married	134	82	.0410	.02828	.1538	.04370	−.0245	.03162
Ever married	881	494	.0410	.01136	.0471	.01676	.0756	.01408
Age (in years)								
Under 31	172	143	−.0033	.01809	.0387	.02876	.0456	.01964
31–44	242	129	.0529	.01982	.0510	.02899	.0850	.03448
45 and over	446	210	.0441	.01621	.0352	.02393	.0969	.02858
Education (years of school completed)								
Under 9	215	103	.0670	.02199	.0887	.03389	.0619	.03221
9–12	431	221	.0252	.01589	.0287	.02304	.0846	.02247
13 and over	221	161	.0226	.01458	.0509	.02269	.0563	.01617
Number of pregnancies								
0–4	697	406	.0376	.01332	.0486	.01948	.0692	.01719
5 and over	180	82	.0547	.02339	.0265	.03393	.1206	.03310

* Sample comprised women 18 years old or over.

TABLE 3. PERCENTAGE DISTRIBUTION OF RESPONDENTS' OPINIONS CONCERNING FRIENDS' RESPONSE TO DIRECT QUESTIONS ON ABORTION, WHETHER FRIENDS WOULD SUSPECT A TRICK IN RANDOMIZED TECHNIQUE, AND WHETHER RESPONDENTS WERE CONVINCED THAT NO TRICK WAS INVOLVED, BY RACE, MARITAL STATUS, AGE, EDUCATION AND NUMBER OF PREGNANCIES

Characteristics	Sample Size	*Would friends respond truthfully to direct question on abortion?			**Would friends suspect a trick in randomized technique?			***Were you convinced that no trick involved in randomized technique?		
		Yes	No	Not Sure	Yes	No	Not Sure	Yes	No	Not Sure
Total	4,571	16.9	65.8	17.3	20.8	60.7	18.5	76.3	15.4	8.3
White	3,047	17.1	64.8	18.1	18.6	65.6	15.9	79.6	13.5	6.8
Nonwhite	1,524	16.5	67.8	15.7	25.4	50.7	23.9	69.5	19.3	11.3
Never married	517	15.3	73.5	11.2	28.0	53.9	18.0	73.1	20.4	6.5
Ever married	4,054	17.1	64.8	18.1	19.9	61.5	18.6	76.7	14.8	8.5
Age (in years)										
Under 31	1,104	14.3	74.5	11.2	28.1	57.3	14.6	75.0	18.6	6.4
31–44	1,656	18.2	65.7	16.1	22.5	61.2	16.3	76.7	15.6	7.7
45 and over	1,708	17.3	60.5	22.2	14.5	62.4	23.1	76.7	13.0	10.3
Education (years of school completed)										
Under 9	894	19.2	60.3	20.5	15.8	55.8	28.4	74.7	13.5	11.8
9–12	2,258	15.7	67.7	16.6	22.2	59.9	17.9	76.4	15.4	8.2
13 and over	1,343	17.3	66.6	16.0	21.7	65.4	12.9	77.1	16.8	6.1
Number of pregnancies										
0–4	3,200	16.8	65.1	18.1	19.7	61.6	18.6	76.9	14.6	8.5
5 and over	832	18.5	63.2	18.3	20.3	61.4	18.3	76.1	15.3	8.5

Exact wording of questions:

* If an interviewer, like myself, asked one of your friends if she had ever had an abortion, do you think your friend would answer truthfully?

** Do you believe other people will think that there is a trick to the box and that we really can figure out which question they answer?

*** When you played the game, were you convinced that I would not know which question you were answering?

$\hat{\pi}_2|\pi_Y$, but also through an increase in sample size attained by combining the two subsamples. As seen in Table 2, the standard error of the estimate is about one-third smaller in this study when the computations were based on a priori estimates of π_Y.

In assuming π_Y to be .0826, it is known that even if this value were correct for the total sample, it would be subject to error when applied to various subdivisions (such as age, education, race, marital status and number of pregnancies) that involved relatively small sample sizes. An alternative would have been to design the study such that π_Y was a function of the distribution of balls.

It will be observed that the estimates of π_Y calculated from the data are not constant. The value from all replies was .0597, but it ranged from zero in the never-married population to 12 per cent in the ever-married group of women with five or more children. It will also be noted that when $\hat{\pi}_Y$ is less than the assumed value (.0826), the $\hat{\pi}_2$ values are greater than $\hat{\pi}_2|\pi_Y$ and, conversely, when $\hat{\pi}_Y$ is greater than .0826, the $\hat{\pi}_2$ values are less than $\hat{\pi}_2|\pi_Y$. The importance of an accurate estimate of π_Y is obvious.

Opinions of Respondents

In addition to the three samples selected to obtain data on abortion, contraception and emotional problems, a fourth sample of 975 persons was selected for other purposes. The data in Table 3 represent data collected over all four samples, viz. these 975 persons plus those reported in Tables 1 and 2. Only 16.9 per cent of the respondents in this study believed that their friends would truthfully respond to a direct question as to whether or not they had ever had an induced abortion. Almost two-thirds of the women in the study population believed that their friends would not respond truthfully to such a question.

Little variation was found in the response to this question over the various subgroups. A slightly lower proportion of non-whites believed their friends would respond truthfully as compared with whites. The never-married women seemed more adamant in this attitude than did the ever-married group. With regard to age, those under 31 had the lowest proportion of women who believed their friends would respond truthfully. These three groups are those most likely to have had an abortion, and yet they had the lowest proportion who believed their friends would respond truthfully to a direct question as to whether or not they had ever had an induced abortion.

Although most respondents felt that their friends would not answer truthfully to a direct question, 60.7 per cent expressed the opinion that people would not suspect a trick in the randomized procedure. Although this result may indicate a high degree of faith in the technique, some concern centers on the 20.8 per cent who felt that their friends would suspect a trick. A means is being sought to close this gap.

The nonwhite population, the never married and those under 31 years of age were the most pessimistic about the acceptance of the technique by other individuals.

When the proportion of respondents was calculated who said they themselves were convinced that the technique assured anonymity, 76.3 per cent were in this category. This apparent increase in confidence toward the randomized response procedure may have represented the respondent's desire to please the interviewer. The nonwhite, never married and the young were still the ones most skeptical about the procedure.

SUMMARY

A survey in five metropolitan areas of central North Carolina using the randomized response procedure in obtaining data on induced abortion, oral contraceptive use, emotional problems and opinions of respondents toward this new interviewing technique has been described. Findings of this survey are reported.

The proportion of women taking oral contraceptives was found to be 25.1 per cent in the study population. Estimates of contraceptive use were slightly higher for nonwhites than whites and, in the ever-married population, declined with age and increased with education.

The proportion of women having an emotional problem at some time during their life was estimated as .228. The estimated proportion was greater among nonwhites (.306) than whites (.199). The estimates were also higher in women 31–44 years of age than in women 45 years old or over.

Estimates of the proportion of women having an abortion during the past year among women 18–44 years of age have been reported elsewhere.[5] Estimates of the proportion of women 18 years old or over having an abortion during their lifetime are presented by race, marital status, age, education and number of pregnancies. A comparison of abortion estimates when the proportion of respondents born in April is assumed known and when it is not known is discussed. Under the latter condition, estimates of the proportion born in April are calculated and compared with the assumed estimate.

Most of the respondents reported that they were satisfied that the randomized response approach was legitimate and that it would not reveal their personal situation.

As is true with most survey results, an absolute and unequivocal validation of the findings presented in this paper cannot be made. To do so would require accurate knowledge of the sensitive characteristics of the populations in advance. If such data were available, or could readily be obtained, there would be no reason for conducting this survey. The authors are in the process of trying to construct a population with known sensitive characteristics to more precisely evaluate the randomized response procedure results by comparing them with the known parameters.

Some of the areas investigated in this study are not as sensitive as others and, in those instances, we have compared our findings with those reported in the literature. In the highly sensitive areas, such as induced abortion, our only recourse was to apply the subjective test of "reasonableness" to the results.

312

In both areas we were generally satisfied with the findings, and are confident that, when properly used, the randomized response technique can provide answers to a number of sensitive questions in the field of public health.

REFERENCES

[1] Warner, S. L., Randomized Response: A Survey Technique for Eliminating Evasive Answer Bias, *Journal of the American Statistical Association*, 60, 63–69, 1965.

[2] Abul-Ela, A.–L. A., Greenberg, B. G. and Horvitz, D. G., A Multi-Proportions Randomized Response Model, *Journal of the American Statistical Association*, 62, 990–1008, 1967.

[3] Greenberg, B. G., Abul-Ela, A.–L. A., Simmons, W. R. and Horvitz, D. G., The Unrelated Question Randomized Response Model: Theoretical Framework, *Journal of the American Statistical Association*, 64, 520–539, 1969.

[4] Greenberg, B. G., Abernathy, J. R. and Horvitz, D. G., Application of the Randomized Response Technique in Obtaining Quantitative Data, Proceedings of the Social Statistics Section, American Statistical Association, 1969.

[5] Abernathy, J. R., Greenberg, B. G. and Horvitz, D. G., Estimates of Induced Abortion in Urban North Carolina, *Demography*, 7, 19–29, 1970.

[6] Ryder, N. B. and Westoff, C. F., Use of Oral Contraceptives in the U.S., 1965, *Science*, 153, 1199–1205, September 9, 1966.

[7] Kunin, C. M., McCormack, R. C. and Abernathy, J. R., Oral Contraceptives and Blood Pressure, *Archives of Internal Medicine*, 123, 362–365, April, 1969.

[8] An abortion is an operation of some kind that a pregnant woman has to end her pregnancy and keep from having a baby, or something she might do to herself to end the pregnancy and keep from having a baby.

ACKNOWLEDGMENT

This research was supported under Research Grants HD 03461-01 and HD 03441-01 from the National Institute of Child Health and Human Development.

ON THE PERSON YEARS CONCEPT
IN EPIDEMIOLOGY AND DEMOGRAPHY

MINDEL C. SHEPS

The need to estimate a risk of some kind in a sample of individuals who are followed for a period of time is common to many different kinds of studies. This paper will report an investigation into the behavior, under defined conditions, of the "exposure time" or "person years" indices that are often used to estimate risks in such studies. One example, the Pearl Index[1], has been common in studies of the effectiveness of contraceptives.[2] Analogous indices are not infrequently calculated in therapeutic and epidemiological investigations. It will be the contention of this paper that the use of this type of index should be confined to rather limited circumstances. In particular, if the individuals in a sample cannot be assumed to experience constant and equal risks, this class of indices does not constitute an appropriate measure.

The particular form of the Pearl Index to be discussed here, the *conception rate,* may be defined as the number of women in a group who conceive for the first time during a period of observation, divided by the total number of months during which they are exposed to the risk of pregnancy.[3] Similarly, in some medical follow-up studies, the number of years during which each patient is observed are added together and the observations expressed as the number of deaths or of relapses per person-year of observation. The pur-

315

pose of the calculation in each case is to estimate a risk, i.e. the probability of an occurrence per unit time, while allowing for the time during which the risk has operated on each person.

Clearly, such estimates are important in many situations. Thus, the conception rate is intended to estimate an important component of reproduction rates, namely, the monthly chance of conception (fecundability). Estimates of this risk may be crucial to evaluation of contraceptive methods and of family planning programs. Similarly, comparisons of death rates, of morbidity rates, or of relapse rates may be crucial in epidemiological investigations and in evaluations of therapy.

It seems desirable to investigate the properties of an index that is often used for important purposes and that apparently has considerable appeal. The calculations obviously treat 20 years of observation in one person as equivalent to one year in 20 persons or to six months in 40 persons. Intuitively, such an assumption seems unrealistic; its effects under different circumstances merit some study.

An alternative method of measuring risk, the actuarial or life table method, is in the opinion of many a better way of studying events that may occur during a period of time.[4,5,6] The focus here is, however, the behavior of the exposure-time index under several sets of assumptions. Interest will be directed to the expected value of the index and its sampling distribution under those assumptions, with particular attention to:

1. The changes effected in the index by increasing the duration of observation or increasing the number of subjects.

2. The effect of unequal durations of observations for individual subjects. Often, subjects are under observation for unequal periods of time: they enter at different times but the study has a set closing date, they move away, or cease to report for other reasons.[4] Subjects not available for observation throughout the complete period of the study will be referred to as withdrawing from observation or as losses.

3. The effects of heterogeneity among the subjects, i.e. of unequal

316

risks with respect to the occurrence being studied, and also of unequal probabilities of withdrawing for different subjects.

The report will be presented in three parts: a statement of the problem and a summary of previous work, a description of the methods used in this investigation, and a report of the findings with numerical illustrations. An appendix summarizes some of the theoretical results whose derivation is presented elsewhere.[7] For concreteness, most of the ensuing discussion will be in terms of conceptions and the conception rate, although it applies equally well to many rates calculated in the same fashion. For more general purposes, we may refer to an occurrence-time index, an occurrence rate or an occurrence probability.

THE INDEX

Definition

The index may be calculated in a number of different ways. With respect to fecundability, for example, the numerator may be defined variously as all first conceptions occurring during the period of observation,[2] as all first conceptions that lead to live births,[8] or otherwise. In the presence of varying periods of observation for individuals in the sample, questions arise as to the best method of allowing for losses in both the numerator and the denominator.[4, 9, 10] In the particular example of the conception rate, what is known as the anniversary method is often used. Thus, if the maximum period of observation for an individual is x months plus a fraction, the risk is estimated during x months only. In effect, losses are considered to occur at the beginning of a month and not to be "at risk" during the month. This rule is applied equally to persons who do experience the event (such as conception) during their last fractional month of observation and to those who do not. If other assumptions are made, leading to modifications in the calculations, the model to be presented would also have to be modified,[7] with corresponding but nonessential changes in details of the results.

317

Review of the Problem and Previous Work

Since the index amounts to an average over time, an inherent assumption is involved that the risk being measured remains constant for any subject during the time of observation. This assumption may be very far from the truth in epidemiological or medical studies and in studies of contraceptive effectiveness. In the latter case, for example, a group of women may be followed for a number of months after they first start using a new contraceptive. Learning may produce more effective use, or, on the contrary, the desire to avoid conception may weaken as the months go by. This fact alone might be considered a sufficient reason for discarding the index in favor of a method (such as a life table) that is better adapted for observing changes in risk with time.

Even if we make the assumption of constant risk per individual, however, (which does not seem unreasonable in some circumstances), all the difficulties do not necessarily disappear.[11, 12] First, it is necessary to distinguish between a hypothetical homogeneous population, with an identical risk for each subject, and the more likely situation where the population is heterogeneous, i.e. with fecundability varying among couples, or mortality risk varying among different individuals.

In a homogeneous sample, the index is a consistent maximum likelihood estimator of the occurrence probability. The estimator is positively biased, the bias decreasing with increased sample size.[7, 10] Furthermore, under defined circumstances, an analogous exposure-time estimator of the probability of survival for the total duration of a study was found by Littell[13] to have some advantages, in a homogeneous sample subjected to a constant risk of mortality, over the usual actuarial (life table) estimator.

The behavior of the index in samples of moderate size has received little study even for homogeneous samples. For example, it has at times been assumed that the important determinant of the reliability of the index is its denominator, the exposure time. Thus this quantity is the denominator in Pearl's equation for the variance of the index, derived by treating it as a binomial variable and equating the number of woman-months with sample size in the formula.[14] It can be shown[7] that this formulation is consistent with large sample (maximum likelihood) theory for homogeneous samples. Several questions then arise: Since the exposure-time can be increased by increasing either the duration of observations or the sample size, do these two procedures have the same effect on the index and its distribution? In general, what are the small sample properties of the index and the variance in homogeneous populations?

The behavior of the index when applied to heterogeneous populations has received some study for the case of conception rates. Thus, it has been shown that, given constant fecundability per couple, but variation from one couple to another, the proportion of those remaining at risk expected to conceive in any month decreases with the duration of follow up.[15,16] The value of the index has been shown to decrease as the period of observation grows longer, both empirically and theoretically.[17,18] In fact, after a sufficiently long period, the mean time to conception or, more generally, the mean exposure time, is expected to equal the reciprocal of the harmonic mean of the risk,[15] and hence the index will approximate the *harmonic* mean of the probability rather than its *arithmetic* mean. Accordingly, as Gini[11] and Potter[18] have emphasized, comparisons of rates calculated for groups followed for different periods of time become highly questionable.

Studies have also been made of the index in artificial sampling experiments on real data. Thus, on sampling from a set of histories, Beebe[19] found that the observed variance of the index in his samples exceeded the variance estimated from Pearl's formula. Potter and Sagi,[20] in similar sampling experiments, extended the examination of the observed variance to include comparison with an estimate calculated according to the well known approximation to the variance of a ratio. They concluded that this approximation was fairly satisfactory and Pearl's formula less so for their sampling scheme. They also found appreciable departures from the normal distribution, the index tending to be skewed to the right. Since

319

there is no reason to assume that the data sampled in these studies were generated by homogeneous populations, the findings apply to heterogeneous groups in particular.

The sampling schemes described assumed an infinite population in which each woman had a fixed exposure time and a fixed outcome. The variation that they estimated, therefore, consisted of differences among repeated samples from this fixed population. We might also consider, however, that for any individual, the outcome and the exposure time are random variables. A scheme of this kind, using random numbers, was reported by Littell[13] for a related problem in the paper already cited.

METHODS

The Model

For the present report, the following model is postulated. In conformity with the definition of the anniversary method given earlier, it is assumed that all conceptions or events under study occur in mid-month and all losses from observation exactly at the end of a month (i.e. at the beginning of the following month).

Assume that N individuals are followed for a maximum of m months (from the beginning of month 1 to end of month m). The sample is composed of k indistinguishable subgroups. The ith subgroup (where i refers to any value 1, 2, . . . , k) consists of n_i individuals (or couples) who are characterized by two probabilities that remain constant over time for each individual, while varying among subgroups:

1. The risk or conditional probability of the occurrence, e.g. the probability that a woman in the ith group will first conceive in any month, given that she is still under observation. The risk experienced by an individual in the ith group is denoted by p_i.

2. The conditional probability that an individual in the ith group will be lost from observation at the end of any month, given that she is still at risk, denoted by λ_i.

In the "fixed sample" case to be discussed first, the numbers n_i

320

are considered fixed and the subject of study is the behavior of the index in identical samples. In the "fully stochastic" case, the model is extended to include also the sampling variation involved in choosing a sample, by considering an infinite population of whom the proportion P_i is characterized by the probabilities p_i and λ_i. A random sample of size N is drawn from this population and the index calculated.

Derivation of Results

Four principal approaches were used to derive the results:

1. Under the model described, the exact probability distribution of the number of losses, occurrences (A), and exposure times (B) in homogeneous and heterogeneous populations was derived, leading to the exact distribution of the index $R = A/B$.[7] Numerical results for a few homogeneous parameters were obtained with a computation program on an IBM 7090. For heterogeneous samples, however, these computations quickly become very time consuming, and have not at present been pursued to any extent.

2. In addition to these exact results, the cumulants of the ratio in small samples from homogeneous populations were obtained according to the methods of Haldane and Smith,[21] and the behavior of the cumulants studied from the results.

3. A Monte Carlo program was written to simulate the process on an electronic computer for samples of fixed composition. In the simplest case, for example, it was assumed that a homogeneous sample of individuals (or couples) all with risk p, and no losses was followed for a maximum of m months. A random number was selected and its value determined whether the event (conception) was considered to have occurred to the first individual during month t, where t could equal 1, 2, . . . , m. The result was stored and the process repeated. This sampling scheme thus allowed a random process to act separately in each hypothetical woman, her particular exposure time and the absence or presence of conception being a sample of the values that could be obtained for her.

After all members of the hypothetical sample had been taken through the process, the index was calculated for the sample. A total of 1000 samples were drawn for various combinations of N,

m and p and the results were analyzed. Extensions to include losses and heterogeneous samples are easily made. The results obtained included the distributions and moments of the number of conceptions, the exposure time and the conception rate.

4. A computer program was written to calculate, from formulas given in the appendix, expected values for the number of occurrences, the total exposure time and the variances and covariance of these variables. With these results, values for approximations to the mean and variance of the index could be calculated in the same program.

FINDINGS

Homogeneous Samples Without Losses

Theoretical results show[7] that in *homogeneous* samples without losses, under the model described, the small positive bias of the index *increases as the period of observation (m) is prolonged* and decreases with increasing sample size (N). As m becomes very large, the absolute value of the bias is expected to approach $p(1-p)/N$, and its relative value $(1-p)/N$. For a moderate value of p such as 0.2, the bias may therefore approach .8/N and for small values such as 0.001, it may approach .999/N. Even in this case, however, the bias is not large, unless N is quite small.

The variance of the index is reduced by increases in either m or N. The rate of decrease with increasing duration of observations (m) depends on the risk (p). On the other hand, the reduction with increasing sample size is more consistent, since it does not depend on the value of p.

The index, in small samples, is skewed to the right for the usual levels of risk (i.e. $p<0.5$), the coefficient of skewness varying as $1/\sqrt{N}$. For fixed values of N, prolonging the duration of the study frequently tends to increase the skewness of the index and hence its departure from the normal distribution. This tendency also varies with p. The kurtosis is an even more complex function of the parameters and of the duration of observations, the coefficient of kurtosis varying as $1/N$.

Numerical values for exact probability distributions of the index were calculated for small samples without losses. Examples of such results for homogeneous samples of 25 persons are shown in Table 1. In these samples, the bias in the index is under four per cent but, as expected, it increases with increasing duration of observation (m). Considerable increases are shown in the coefficients of skewness and kurtosis as m grows larger.

The reduction in the bias and the coefficients of variation, skewness, and kurtosis that is associated with increased sample size may be illustrated by comparing the values in the first part of Table 2, where N = 50, with the first part of Table 1.

TABLE I. EXACT RESULTS FOR INDEX IN HOMOGENEOUS SAMPLES WITHOUT LOSSES ($N = 25$)

| | Duration of Observation in Months | Mean | Characteristics of Index Coefficients of: | | |
			Variation	Skewness*	Kurtosis*
Fecundability (p)					
0.20	1	.2000	.40	.30	.01
	4	.2034	.23	.41	.32
	8	.2048	.24	.43	.60
	12	.2056	.19	.61	.75
	16	.2060	.18	.65	.82
	20	.2063	.18	.67	.85
	∞	.2064	.19	.67	.85
0.15	1	.1500	.48	.40	.13
	6	.1530	.24	.47	.45
	12	.1540	.20	.59	.74
	18	.1546	.20	.67	.90
	24	.1549	.19	.70	.97
	30	.1551	.19	.72	.99
	∞	.1551	.20	.72	.91
0.10	1	.1000	.60	.53	.31
	6	.1019	.28	.47	.42
	12	.1025	.23	.56	.65
	18	.1029	.21	.64	.91
	24	.1031	.20	.69	.97
	30	.1033	.20	.72	1.06
	∞	.1036	.20	.74	1.04

(The values for $m \to \infty$ were calculated from approximate formulas.[7,11])
* The measure of skewness is μ_3/σ^3, and of kurtosis, $\mu_4/\sigma_4 - 3$.

Simulation Program (The values given for finite m were obtained from a simulation program.)

Duration of Observations in Months	Mean	Characteristics of index		
			Coefficients of	
		Variation	Skewness	Kurtosis
Monthly probability of loss = 0				
1	.2000	.283	.21	< .01
4	.2012	.167	.29	.16
8	.2017	.142	.31	.30
12	.2020	.135	.43	.38
16	.2025	.132	.44	.41
20	.2026	.132	.47	.42
∞	.20320	.130	.47	.42
Monthly probability of loss = 0.1				
1	.2000	.283	.21	< .01
4	.2028	.165	.22	+ .06
8	.2027	.143	.31	− .21
12	.2032	.135	.38	− .10
16	.2035	.133	.41	− .08
20	.2038	.132	.43	− .06
∞	.20316	.132	.46	+ .45
Monthly probability of loss = .05				
1	.2000	.283	.21	< .01
4	.2007	.169	.24	.23
8	.2015	.151	.43	.72
12	.2018	.147	.45	.85
16	.2023	.144	.50	.99
20	.2024	.144	.50	1.00
∞	.20304	.140	.43	+ .39

The Effect of Losses on Homogeneous Samples

The effect of losses on estimates made for homogeneous samples was studied both in theoretical results and by means of the simulation program. For moderately long periods of observation, the effect of introducing losses or making them more frequent (i.e. of increasing λ) may vary with the levels of p, λ and m. As m becomes very large, however, the bias in the index is expected to be decreased by the presence of losses, the relative bias approaching the value $(1-\lambda)(1-p)/N$. The effect of losses on the higher moments of R is also not a simple, monotonic function of λ. For large m, however, and small p, the presence of losses will usually increase the relative variation.

Table 2 presents some illustrative numerical results of the simulation program, for samples of size 50 with fecundability equal to 0.20, the monthly probability of loss taking on values of 0, 0.01 and 0.05. With a monthly probability of loss equal to 0.01, the bias in the mean, i.e. in $E(R)$, was increased for moderate values of m. The coefficients of variation and skewness showed little change, the former tending to be a little higher and the latter a little lower than in the cases without losses. The coefficient of kurtosis became negative, then decreased in absolute value with increasing m, and was expected to be positive as m became very large.

In the simulation experiments with a monthly probability of loss equal to 0.05, the mean value of R was lower, showing a smaller bias than when $\lambda = 0$, at all values of m calculated. The variance and the coefficients of variation and kurtosis were all greater than in the case without losses. The coefficient of skewness in this case showed an inconsistent relation to that in the case without losses. For very large m, however, and p = 0.2, the skewness is expected to be reduced by losses.

Heterogeneous Samples (Fixed Sample Case)

The expected value of the index in heterogeneous samples is a complex function of the degree of heterogeneity, the various probabilities, and the duration of observations.[7] As already mentioned, *in a heterogeneous group without losses* the *expected value decreases* with increasing *m:* from the arithmetic mean fecundability of the group in the first month toward the harmonic mean. If the sample is small, however, the tendency for the index to decrease in value is counteracted in part by positive terms in the expected value of the ratio, such as are responsible for the positive bias of the index in homogeneous samples.

Before turning to small samples and to other complications, it should be emphasized that even for large samples without losses and with equal periods of observations, occurrence-time indices may not serve as valid comparisons, because arithmetic and harmonic

325

means do not necessarily vary in the same direction. Thus, it is easy to imagine that one of two samples has a higher arithmetic mean risk but a lower harmonic mean than the other. In such a case, indices calculated after a short period of observation would indicate that this first sample had the higher risk; after a longer period of observation, the conclusion would be reversed.

Almost all the numerical calculations performed for heterogeneous groups utilized approximate formulas for $E(R)$ and its variance.[22] Comparison between these approximations and exact results, in a few instances, showed that the approximations gave lower values than the exact results, the agreement improving with increasing sample size. In general, the approximations are therefore conservative, that for the variance being more so than that for the mean.

TABLE 3. THE EFFECT OF SAMPLE SIZE ON THE EXPECTED VALUE OF THE INDEX [E(R)] IN A HETEROGENEOUS MODEL WITHOUT LOSSES

m	Ratio of the Expected Number of Occurrences to the Expected Exposure Time	Approximate $E(R)$ Sample Size	
		$N = 15$	$N = 300$
1	.1667	.1667	.1667
2	.1655	.1681	.1656
3	.1643	.1680	.1645
4	.1632	.1675	.1634
5	.1621	.1669	.1624
6	.1612	.1662	.1614
7	.1602	.1656	.1605
8	.1594	.1650	.1597
9	.1586	.1644	.1589
10	.1578	.1639	.1581
11	.1571	.1634	.1574
12	.1565	.1629	.1568
13	.1559	.1625	.1562
14	.1553	.1622	.1557
15	.1549	.1618	.1552
∞	.1500	.1598	.1505

Arithmetic mean p = .1667
Harmonic mean p = .1500
Variance p   = .002222

A numerical example of the effect of sample size on the expected value of the index for heterogeneous groups without losses is shown in Table 3, where it is assumed that the occurrence probability for two-thirds of each sample is equal to 0.2 and for the remaining one-third it is equal to 0.1. The first column in Table 3 shows the ratio of the expected cumulative number of occurrences (conceptions) to the expected cumulative exposure time at each month. This ratio, which is not affected by sample size, decreases with time, from the initial value of 0.1667 toward 0.1500 (the harmonic mean probability). For a sample of size 15, even the approximation for $E(R)$, which is a little lower than the exact value, is considerably higher than the ratio just discussed. In fact, from months two to five inclusive, it is higher than the first month's value of 0.1667. It remains well above the ratio of the two means at all times. This positive discrepancy increases with m, the asymptotic value for very large m being more than six per cent higher than the ratio of the expectations. When the sample size is increased to 300, however, as in the last column, the expected value of the index closely approaches the ratio of the two means in the first column.

If probabilities of loss are included in the model, the Pearl Index for a heterogeneous sample can take on a rather wide range of values depending on the postulated probabilities of this outcome, even if they be equal for all subgroups. This phenomenon is to be expected since, at any time after the beginning of the study, the composition of those remaining is a function of time, the occurrence risks, and the probability of loss. In the context of conception rates, for example, a larger proportion of the more fecund women than of the less fecund ones will have conceived at any time after the beginning of the study, but the relative proportions change from one time to the next. Consequently, the composition of the remaining sample keeps changing and the composition of the losses must change as well. Late losses will include relatively more of the less fecund women than will early losses. Naturally, the effect of losses on the composition of the group depends also on the rate at which they are lost, i.e. on the value of λ.

Numerical examples of these effects are seen in Figure 1, for

327

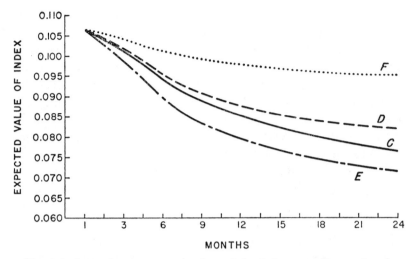

Figure 1. Approximate expected values of the Index according to duration of the study. Samples consisting of 250 individuals with monthly risk equal to 0.05 and 150 with monthly risk equal to 0.20. Monthly probabilities of leaving study are:

	Set C	Set D	Set E	Set F
Less fecund	0	.05	.01	.10
More fecund	0	.05	.10	.01

heterogeneous samples with N = 400. The composition of the samples for these four sets of calculations was identical with respect to fecundability. In Set C, the probability of loss was put equal to zero, and in Set D this probability was assumed equal to 0.05 for all individuals in the sample. This assumption produces an increase in the expected value of R, the increment increasing with the passage of time. When individuals from the more fecund group are lost at a higher rate than those from the less fecund (Set E), the expected values of the index fall below those in Set C. Conversely, if the rate of loss is higher for the less fecund group, the expected value of the index is relatively high (Set F). While these results are not surprising, they demonstrate the problems involved in using the index for heterogeneous samples containing individuals followed for unequal periods of time.

328

The index behaved more erratically in the examples of Figure 2, which relate to samples of 1000 consisting of a mixture of four subgroups, in all of which the distributions of fecundability were again identical. The expected values cannot be characterized consistently for different assumptions about the probabilities of loss. Again, if this probability is assumed to be identical for all individuals in the sample, the expected value of the index is higher than in the absence of losses (Set H versus Set G). For Set J, it was assumed that individuals in the sample were subject to unequal probabilities of loss, which were positively correlated with fecundability. The expected values of the index in the earlier months were below the corresponding values in Set G, from which losses were excluded. During the third year, however, the values in Set J became higher than those in Set G. Consequently, comparisons between two such samples (which have identical distributions of fecundability) would indicate higher conception rates for Set G if both samples were followed for two years or less, and lower rates for

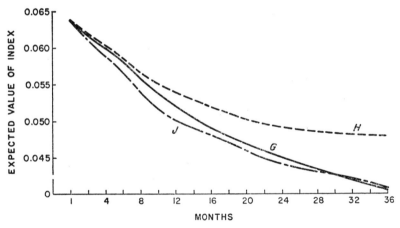

Figure 2. Approximate expected value of the Index according to duration of the study. Heterogeneous samples consisting of 4 subgroups. In all cases, the mean risk is .0645, its variance .0027, and the harmonic mean is .0214. The probability of loss is zero for set G, equal for all individuals in set H and positively correlated with risk in set J.

Set G if both samples were followed for more than three years. Thus, even keeping the duration of follow-up equal for two such samples would *not* provide a valid comparison of their fecundabilities.

Heterogeneous Population (Fully Stochastic Case)

The foregoing has been concerned with the effects of stochastic variation only in samples of fixed composition. If we add to our assumptions by providing for variation among samples drawn from a heterogeneous population in the way described earlier, it is found that both the index itself and its variance may be expected to be higher than in the fixed sample case.[7]

A numerical example is shown in Table 4, where the fixed sample has a composition identical with that of the population in the stochastic case. The example is relatively simple in that it excludes the possibility of losses and specifies only two subgroups in the population. It can be seen, however, that the variance of the index is considerably higher if the formula is based on the more appropriate assumption that includes sampling variation. More important than the variance, however, is the related effect on the expected value of the index, which departs increasingly from the changing values of the ratio of the two expectations in column 1.

Provision for losses in this model would result in values even more discouraging than those shown in Figure 2.

TABLE 4. A COMPARISON OF THE "FIXED SAMPLE" MODEL AND THE "FULLY STOCHASTIC" MODEL IN A HETEROGENEOUS POPULATION* WITHOUT LOSSES

Month of observation (1)	Expected No. of Occurrences/ Expected Exposure Time (1)	Approximations for Ratio			
		N Times the Increment to be Added to Column (1) for the Expected Value of the Ratio		N Times the Variance	
		Fixed Sample	Stochastic Case	Fixed Sample	Stochastic Case
1	.04375	0	0	.0399	.0418
4	.04093	.0137	.0164	.0088	.0105
8	.03760	.0136	.0192	.0037	.0053
12	.03473	.0124	.0200	.0022	.0036
16	.03228	.0113	.0204	.0015	.0027
20	.03020	.0106	.0206	.0011	.0022
24	.02844	.0101	.0208	.0009	.0018
∞	.01509	.0214	.0279	.00032	.00042

Arithmetic mean p = .04375
Harmonic mean p = .01509
Variance p = .001898

*P   Fecundability (p)
.625   .01
.375   .10

The behavior of the index "occurrences per person year of exposure" has been studied through a mathematical model. Numerical illustrations of the results, obtained by exact calculations, by a simulation program, and from approximate expressions, have been presented here. In all cases, it has been assumed that the risk per unit time is constant during the period of observation for any individual. Otherwise, the index is obviously not a suitable measure of risk.

In circumstances where it may be reasonable to assume that the sample is homogeneous, i.e. that all individuals have the same constant risk, the index may be treated as an estimate of that risk provided that the sample is large. Generally, the disadvantages are diminished when the size of samples is increased, but aggravated when the duration of observation is prolonged. In such homogeneous samples, the index has a small positive bias which increases with the duration of follow up and decreases with increased sample size. The variance decreases both with increasing sample size (N) and with the duration of observations (m). In general, the index is skewed, the skewness being to the right if the risk is less than $\frac{1}{2}$. This asymmetry increases with m and decreases when N is increased. The effect of changing probabilities of loss on these measures varies at different levels of risk. In many of the situations of interest, however, losses will reduce the bias and increase the variance of the index, according to the postulated model.

On the more realistic assumption that the risks or probabilities under study are not identical for all individuals in the sample, the index is of questionable value. In particular, if it is assumed also that losses may occur (this term including entry into the sample at different times), the behavior of the index may become highly erratic as the duration of follow up is prolonged. Consequently, the index cannot be recommended as a basis for comparing two or

332

more groups *even if they are observed for the same length of time,* in circumstances where it is not reasonable to assume that each sample is homogeneous. Other measures of risk that evaluate changes occurring with the passage of time, such as life table attrition rates,[6] seem clearly preferable.

The findings reported here suggest that conclusions that have been based on this index in various studies may be subject to some question. Investigators may find it necessary to re-evaluate data on which such conclusions have been based.

APPENDIX

The following symbols, some of which are defined in the paper, will be used:

N   the number in the sample

n_i the number of individuals from subgroup i in a fixed sample.

$$\sum_{i=1}^{k} n_i = N$$

p_i the risk (fecundability) of individuals in the ith group

$q_i = 1 - p_i$

λ_i the monthly conditional probability of loss for individuals in the ith group

$\gamma_i = 1 - \lambda_i$

m   duration of the study

P_i the proportion of a population that belongs to subgroup i.

$$\sum_{i=1}^{k} P_i = 1$$

$\pi_i = 1 - (\gamma_i q_i)^m$

$\nu_i = 1 - \gamma_i q_i$

A = the total number of occurrences (conceptions) observed

B = the total number of person months of observation

R = A/B = the Pearl index, i.e. the number of occurrences per person-month of exposure

E(X) and V(X) − the mean and variance, respectively, of variable X

The theoretical results, given the assumptions in the model, are:

For homogeneous samples of size N,

$$E(R) = p + p\{(1 - \nu)\pi - m\nu(1 - \pi)\}/N\pi^2 + O(N^{-2}) \tag{1}$$

$$V(R) = \frac{pq\nu}{N\pi} + \frac{pq}{N^2\pi^2}\left[1 - \gamma(1 - 2p)(1 - 3\nu)\right.$$

$$- \nu\left\{\pi + \frac{2m(1 - \pi)}{\pi}(2\nu + 3\gamma p)\right.$$

$$\left.\left. - \frac{\nu m^2 p(1 - \pi)(5 - 3\pi)}{q\pi^2}\right\}\right] + O(N^{-3}). \tag{2}$$

Generally,

$$E(R) = \frac{E(A)}{E(B)}\left[1 + \frac{\text{Var}(B)}{\{E(B)\}^2} - \frac{\text{Cov}(A,B)}{E(A)E(B)}\right] + O(N^{-2}) \tag{3}$$

$$V(R) = \left[\frac{E(A)}{E(B)}\right]^2\left[\frac{\text{Var}(A)}{\{E(A)\}^2} + \frac{\text{Var}(B)}{\{E(B)\}^2} - \frac{2\text{Cov}(A,B)}{E(A)E(B)}\right]$$

$$+ O(N^{-2}) \tag{4}$$

In heterogeneous samples, the quantities needed in (3) and (4) are found to be:

For the fixed case:

$E(A)$	$\Sigma n_i p_i \pi_i / \nu_i$
$E(B)$	$\Sigma n_i \pi_i / \nu_i$
$V(A)$	$\Sigma n_i (p_i \pi_i)(\nu_i - p_i \pi_i)/\nu_i^2$
$V(B)$	$\Sigma n_i (1 - \nu_i)[1 - (1 - \delta_i)\{1 - \pi_i + (2m - 1)\nu_i\}]/\nu_i^2$
$\text{Cov}(A,B)$	$\Sigma n_i p_i (1 - \pi_i)(\pi_i - m\nu_i)/\nu_i^2$

For the stochastic case:

$E(A)$	$N\Sigma P_i p_i \pi_i / \nu_i$
$E(B)$	$N\Sigma P_i \pi_i / \nu_i$
$\text{Var}(A)$	$N[\Sigma P_i p_i \pi_i / \nu_i][1 - \Sigma P_i p_i \pi_i / \nu_i]$
$\text{Var}(B)$	$N[\Sigma P_i\{(1 + \gamma_i q_i)\pi_i - 2m(1 - \pi_i)\}/\nu_i^2 - \{\Sigma P_i \pi_i / \nu_i\}^2]$
$\text{Cov}(A,B)$	$N[\Sigma P_i p_i\{\pi_i - m\nu_i(1 - \pi_i)\}/\nu_i^2 - \{\Sigma P_i p_i \pi_i / \nu_i\}\{\Sigma P_i \pi_i / \nu_i\}]$

REFERENCES

1 Pearl, Raymond, Factors in Human Fertility and their Statistical Evaluation, *Lancet*, 225, 607–611, September 9, 1933.

2 Tietze, Christopher and Lewit, Sarah, Recommended Procedures for the Study of Use-Effectiveness of Contraceptive Methods, *International Planned Parenthood Federation Handbook, Part I*, London, International Planned Parenthood Federation, 1962, pp. 59–72.

3 Other forms of the Pearl Index, which attempt to estimate an average lifetime risk and include more than one pregnancy per woman, will not be considered here.

4 Elveback, Lila, Actuarial Estimation of Survivorship in Chronic Disease, *Journal of the American Statistical Association*, 53, 420–440, June, 1958.

5 Chiang, Chin Long, A Stochastic Study of the Life Table and its Applications: I, II, III, *Biometrics*, 16, 618–635, December, 1960; *Human Biology*, 32, 221–238, September, 1960; *Biometrics*, 17, 57–58, March, 1961.

6 Potter, Robert G., Additional Measures of Use-Effectiveness of Contraception, *Milbank Memorial Fund Quarterly*, 41, 400–418, October, 1963.

7 Sheps, Mindel C., Characteristics of a Ratio Used to Estimate Failure Rates, in press.

8 Chandrasekaran, C. and Freymann, Moye W., Evaluating the Effects of Community Efforts to Modify Family Size, in *Public Health and Population Change: Current Research Issues*, M. C. Sheps and J. C. Ridley (eds)., Cambridge, Massachusetts, Schenkman Publishing Co., Inc., 1965.

9 Dorn, Harold F., Methods of Aanalysis for Follow-up Studies, *Human Biology*, 22, 238–248, December, 1950.

10 Seal, Hilary, The Estimation of Mortality and Other Decremental Probabilities, *Skandinavisk Aktuarietidskrift*, 37, 137–162, 1954.

11 Gini, Corrado, Sur la mesure de l'efficacité des pratiques anticeptionalles, *Revue de l'Institut International de Statistique*, 10, 1–35, 1942.

12 Sheps, Mindel C., Applications of Probability Models to the Study of Patterns of Human Reproduction, in *Public Health and Population Change: Current Research Issues*, M. C. Sheps and J. C. Ridley, editors, op. cit.

13 Littell, Arthur S., Estimation of the T-year Survival Rate from Follow-up Studies Over a Limited Period of Time, *Human Biology*, 24, 87–116, May, 1952.

14 Pearl, Raymond, On the Frequency of the Use of Contraceptive Methods, and Their Effectiveness as Used, By a Sample of American Women, *Bulletin de l'Institut International de Statistique*, 27, 208–224, 1933.

[15] Henry, Louis, Fondéments théoriques des mesures de la fécondité naturelle, *Revue de l'Institut International de Statistique*, 21, 135–151, 1953.

[16] Sheps, Mindel C., On the Time Required for Conception, *Population Studies*, 18, 85–97, July, 1964.

[17] Tietze, Christopher, Differential Fecundity and Effectiveness of Contraception, *Eugenics Review*, 50, 230–237, January, 1959.

[18] Potter, Robert G., Length of the Observation Period as a Factor Affecting the Contraceptive Failure Rate, *Milbank Memorial Fund Quarterly*, 38, 140–152, April, 1960.

[19] Beebe, G. W., *Contraception and Fertility in the Southern Appalachians*, Baltimore, The Williams and Wilkins Co., 1942, pp. 222–223.

[20] Potter, Robert G. and Sagi, P. C., Some Procedures for Estimating the Sampling Fluctuations of a Contraceptive Failure Rate, in *Research in Family Planning*, C. V. Kiser, editor, Princeton, N. J., Princeton University Press, 1962, pp. 309–405.

[21] Haldane, J. B. S. and Smith, S. M., The Sampling Distribution of a Maximum Likelihood Estimate, *Biometrika*, 43, 96–103, June, 1956.

[22] Hansen, Morris H., Hurwitz, W. N. and Madow, W. G., *Sample Survey Methods and Theory*, Vol. 2, New York, John Wiley & Sons, Inc., 1953.

ACKNOWLEDGMENTS

A large part of the investigations on which this report is based were carried out at the University of Pittsburgh. Computer programs for the results were written by Helen Chun and Joel Williamson; Lynn Doney and Florence Baseman assisted with calculation.

This investigation was supported in part by Public Health Service Research Grant GM 13436 (formerly 11134) from the National Institute of General Medical Sciences and by computer grant G 11309 from the National Science Foundation.

RETROSPECTIVE ESTIMATES OF ORPHANHOOD FROM GENERATION LIFE TABLES

IAN GREGORY

United States generation life tables have hitherto been used to estimate the frequency of orphanhood in the entire country. In the present study, actuarial estimates are developed for the state of Minnesota, and compared with those reported by a sample of 11,329 ninth-grade school children. Similar methods may be used to estimate the exact probabilities of orphanhood among individuals and groups within relatively small samples.

The loss of a parent by death may have immediate and remote consequences that are detrimental to the surviving child and to other members of society. In his monograph *Maternal Care and Mental Health,* Bowlby[1] correctly distinguished between three main classes of evidence: 1. direct studies, involving observation of the impact of separation from parents on the behavior and development of their children; 2. retrospective studies of the early histories of adolescents or adults who have already developed psychological illnesses; 3. follow-up (anterospective) studies involving the continuing evaluation of adolescents or adults previously identified as having lost (or not having lost) a parent during childhood. Bowlby was most impressed with the adverse consequences of maternal deprivation, but other authors have been equally concerned with the possible effects of paternal deprivation, which has become relatively more frequent than maternal loss, as mortality rates have declined more rapidly for women than for men.

In a previous article,[2] I reviewed a number of retrospective studies involving comparisons between frequencies of orphanhood (during specified periods of childhood) among groups of adolescents or adults with some form of psychopathology and "control" groups that had been considered representative of the general population. Methodological problems concerning such studies were discussed, and certain data were subjected to further analysis, but relationships between specific forms of parental loss during childhood and adult psychopathology remained uncertain. Further retrospective studies have appeared during the past few years, but appropriate comparisons with relevant general population data have continued to be elusive.

A number of actuarial estimates of orphanhood have in fact been made during the past 30 years, with increasingly refined techniques of estimation, but actuaries have tended to report the total numbers of orphans within a specified age range, or the proportions (percentages) of orphans among all living children within the specified age range. Behavioral scientists, on the other hand, have been more interested in the probabilities of orphanhood by the time a specified age is attained—or during a specified age period—and have tended to be unaware of the existence of the actuarial estimates, or of the multiplicity of factors entering into the computation of such estimates, or of the manner in which the actuarial data have been presented.

A direct census enumeration of orphans (maternal, paternal, and absolute) for each year of life up to age 15 was published for the year 1921 by the Registrar-General for England and Wales.[3] Similar census data on orphanhood have been obtained for Ireland, Australia, and New Zealand, but not for the United States. However, some idea of the minimum numbers of children in this country who have lost one or both parents by death may be obtained from United States census family data, concerning the numbers of children living with a widowed mother or a widowed father (who has not remarried). Somewhat more complete estimates of orphanhood in this country were obtained in a population survey of 25,000 households conducted in October 1949. However, Fisher[4] pointed to two kinds

340

of reservations regarding the accuracy of the survey estimates—the first based on sampling variability, and the second based on errors of response and nonreporting. The latter would tend to result in underestimates of orphanhood, particularly maternal and absolute orphans.

The lack of comprehensive census data on orphanhood and the limitations of data obtained from a survey sample of the population have led to increasingly sophisticated techniques of analysis based on the presumed mortality experience of the child's parents. The probabilities of a parent's dying between certain specified ages are simply the complement of the probabilities of survival, which may readily be computed from appropriate life-table survival functions (l_x), according to the age, sex, race, and residence of the parent. Lotka[5] used the mean ages of parents in the census year 1920 and the survival functions from the United States abridged life tables for 1919–1920 to estimate the frequencies of orphanhood in the United States at that time. The estimates obtained by this short method corresponded closely with those he obtained by the application of more rigorous formulas, even when the latter were increased to allow for the death of mother as a direct consequence of the birth of the child. All his estimates allowed for the possible death of father between the time of the child's conception and birth, but available data did not permit him to make adjustments for the lower mortality of married persons (or parents) than that of the total population.

Lotka was able to demonstrate a considerable reduction in orphanhood in the United States between 1900 and 1920, and a close correspondence between actuarial and census estimates for orphanhood in England and Wales. The census figures for England and Wales (1921) showed an excess of *paternal* deaths at certain ages over the actuarial figures, which was interpreted as resulting from wartime deaths in military service. On the other hand, the census figures for *maternal* orphanhood were lower than the actuarial estimates, which was considered to be the result of census underenumeration. The census data on absolute orphans (who had lost both their parents) showed a marked excess over what would have

341

been expected if the deaths of father and mother had been independent events. During the first year after the birth of the child, the observed frequency of absolute orphans was ten times as high as that expected on the basis of independence of parental deaths, but by the fifteenth year of life this ratio had gradually dropped to where the observed frequency was 1.75 times the expected frequency. When allowance was made for this gradually diminishing interdependence of deaths of father and mother, the actuarial estimates of absolute orphanhood in England and Wales corresponded quite closely with those recorded in the census data.

Estimates of orphanhood in the United States for the year 1930 were computed under the direction of Lotka,[6] and estimates for the year 1940 were provided by Spiegelman.[7] In estimating the total numbers of orphans at specified ages (in contrast to the probabilities of orphanhood by the time the child reaches these ages) it is of course necessary to take into account the mortality of the children themselves. Both Lotka and Spiegelman accomplished this by starting with the age distribution of the children as enumerated in the census year, and working backward to estimate the number of children whose fathers had died in the years before the census. Woofter[8] reversed the procedure by starting with the number of births in a given calendar year and estimating how many new orphans were created among such children in each successive calendar year. He obtained a considerably higher estimate of total *paternal* orphans for the year 1940 than Spiegelman had obtained for the same year, which may be related to Woofter's use of the age of mean mortality and mortality rates of 1929–1931, in contrast to Spiegleman's use of the mean age and mortality rates of 1930–1939 in developing his estimates.

In a theoretical article, Woofter[9] outlined two short methods of estimating probabilities of death in closed population groups, on the basis of changes occurring in the age of mean mortality over a period of time. The age of mean mortality for the fathers of newborn children is somewhat higher than the mean age of these fathers, but as time goes by the age of mean mortality advances more slowly than the mean age. In the present study, Woofter's short method B

342

will be used to develop probabilities of paternal, maternal, and absolute orphanhood for a single population of children, according to life tables for the United States and for Minnesota, for the years 1939–1941 and 1949–1951.

The problem of developing estimates of orphanhood that fully reflected changing rates of mortality in the population was not solved until accurate life tables became available for each intercensal year. The latter could then be used to construct generation life tables from which the probability of parental death may be computed for the appropriate year of birth of the child as well as the age, sex, and race of the parent. Fisher[4] reviewed earlier estimates of orphanhood, and reported the application of generation life tables in estimating the numbers of paternal, maternal, and complete orphans under age 18 as of October 1949. These estimates had been adjusted downward for the lower mortality of married persons than that of the total population, and increased by the addition of paternal orphans created by deaths of fathers in military service overseas (who were excluded from the United States vital statistics from which the life tables were computed). However, the preceding estimates reported by Fisher, as well as subsequent estimates reported by Shudde[10] and by Shudde and Epstein[11], all appear to have been based on the application of ages of mean mortality to generation mortality experience.

Oppal[12] has advised me that the current practice is to develop a series of survival functions from generation life tables for pivotal ages of fathers and of mothers, and to compute a weighted survival function for all ages of parent (father or mother) by applying the number of children born in each group of parents. This procedure is illustrated in Tables 1 and 2 of the present article. The life table mortality rates ($1000q_x$) are not required for this computation, but are included in these tables to illustrate the computation of ages of mean mortality, for use in estimates based on Woofter's short method B.

The estimates for *complete* orphanhood made by Lotka and Spiegelman (for the census years 1920, 1930, and 1940) involved an upward adjustment based on the 1921 census data for England

343

and Wales, to allow for the fact that the deaths of fathers and mothers are not always independent events. The more recent estimates have ignored this upward adjustment on the grounds that the appropriate data for the United States are not available, and that mortality from infectious diseases (especially tuberculosis) has dropped sharply in recent decades. However, both parents may well be involved in a single fatal accident, and the present article includes data reported by more than 11,000 ninth-grade school children, for whom the observed frequency of complete orphanhood was approximately 1.57 times the frequency expected if the death of both parents had always been independent of each other.

Not many behavioral scientists have traveled along this demographic pathway, and perhaps we may be excused for having occasionally stumbled or fallen by the wayside. Thus, I[7] misidentified Spiegelman's actuarial estimates for 1940 as data from a large sample of the United States population.[2] Subsequently, I attempted to develop actuarial estimates of orphanhood based on generation mortality data for the province of Ontario, relating to the period 1921–1951.[13] Unfortunately, the crude death rates from which I computed abridged life table functions (q_x and l_x) were given by place of occurrence prior to 1944 and by place of residence thereafter. Approximations were made for the age of mean mortality being slightly higher than the mean age (both absolutely and relatively higher in the case of father than mother) and also the possible death of father prior to the birth of the child. However, no adjustments were made to allow for the lower mortality of the married than that of the total population, nor for the additional deaths of fathers due to military service.

Several errors have also resulted from misunderstanding of the manner in which Spiegelman[7] presented his estimates for the frequency of orphanhood in the United States in 1940. In Table 2 of his article, estimated numbers of orphans under 18 years of age were given, and also estimated numbers of orphans within each of four age intervals (under 5, 5–9, 10–14, and 15–17 years). The corresponding numbers of total children within the population were given according to these age groups, from which may be computed

344

the percentages of paternal, maternal, or absolute orphanhood among all children within the stated age intervals. If the assumption could be made that the cumulative frequency of orphanhood showed a linear rate of increase throughout childhood, then the percentages thus obtained would correspond with the probabilities of orphanhood by the mid-point of the stated age intervals—namely, by the exact ages of $2\frac{1}{2}$, $7\frac{1}{2}$, $12\frac{1}{2}$, and $16\frac{1}{2}$ years. However, several behavioral scientists have used these percentages for comparative purposes as if they reflected the probabilities of orphanhood by the upper limit of the stated age intervals (namely, by the exact ages of 5, 10, 15, and 18 years). Thus, Barry and Lindemann[14] computed probabilities of orphanhood within three stated age intervals (0–4, 5–9, and 10–14 years) which would have been closer approximations to the probabilities of orphanhood during the intervals 0–$2\frac{1}{2}$, $2\frac{1}{2}$–$7\frac{1}{2}$, and $7\frac{1}{2}$–$12\frac{1}{2}$ years. These computations by Barry and Lindemann resulted in unduly low estimates for the general population, particularly with respect to the first five years of life, and they consequently found a supposedly significant excess of maternal deaths during the early childhood of their sample of psychiatric patients. Archibald et al.[15] obtained even lower estimates for the supposed probabilities of orphanhood in the general population, by dividing the numbers of orphans in each age interval by the total numbers of children in the population at all ages under 18. The consequent comparisons with their sample of psychiatric patients were highly inappropriate.

In a more rigorous study, Hilgard and Newman[16] compared frequencies of orphanhood among psychiatric patients and a non-patient community sample. However, they also compared probabilities of orphanhood for their community sample with percentages of orphans among all children within certain age groups, derived from the actuarial estimates of Spiegelman[7] and of Shudde and Epstein.[11] The data from Spiegelman's estimates consisted of children within the age range 15–17 years (mean age $16\frac{1}{2}$ years) and corresponded fairly closely to the probability of orphanhood by age 18 among members of their community sample. However, the data from Shudde and Epstein referred to all children within the age range 0–18 years, and amounted to only approximately 60 per cent of the probability of orphanhood by age 18 years in the authors' community sample.

Actuarial estimates hitherto have been concerned with the frequency of orphanhood in the total population of the United States, with the exception of my attempt[13] to develop estimates from generation mortality data specific to the Province of Ontario. For the behavioral scientist, however, it may be desirable to obtain accurate estimates of the probability of orphanhood among the general population of a particular state, or even for individual members of a sample that he proposes studying. The remainder of the present article will be devoted to the development of a series of actuarial estimates of orphanhood (according to various assumptions regarding the mortality experience of the parents), which are compared with the frequencies of orphanhood reported by a statewide sample of 11,329 Minnesota school children who were in ninth grade in the spring of 1954.

In a subsequent study, it is planned to compute the probabilities of orphanhood among individual members of a sample of psychiatric patients born and residing in Minnesota since 1938. The latter expected frequencies may then be accumulated and compared with the observed frequencies among various groups of patients—for example, according to diagnosis, socio-economic status, family size, and ordinal position.

In both of these studies the actuarial estimates will attempt to control for the following:

1. age of father at conception of child;

2. age of mother at birth of child;

3. race of parents—although the small numbers of nonwhite children in the Minnesota population eliminates them from the estimates developed in the present study;

4. year of birth, which is assumed to be 1939 for all estimates in the present study;

5. the lower rate of death among the married than among the total population of childbearing ages;

346

6. the additional paternal orphanhood due to wartime military service overseas;

7. the lower mortality of white Minnesota residents of childbearing ages than that of the corresponding white population of the United States;

8. the fact that the frequency of complete orphanhood reflects partial interdependence between the deaths of father and mother.

In addition, certain data will be presented on the frequencies of orphanhood reported by the large sample of Minnesota school children, according to parental socio-economic status and number of siblings.

METHODS AND RESULTS

Hathaway and Monachesi[17] presented considerable data on relationships between certain family and personal data, psychological tests of intelligence and personality, and subsequent delinquency and school drop-out, among two large samples of Minnesota ninth-grade school children. The larger of these two samples consisted of 11,329 children from 92 schools situated in 86 communities in 47 of Minnesota's 87 counties. Schools were selected to represent so far as possible Minnesota's diverse economic and geographic areas, and the sample included 28 per cent of the entire ninth-grade public school population at the time of the initial testing in the spring of 1954. Data on orphanhood, parental divorce or separation, and numbers of siblings were obtained from the responses of the subjects to a brief questionnaire that was administered at the same time as the Minnesota Multiphasic Personality Inventory. Data on parental occupation and socio-economic status were obtained from the microfilmed school records.

The mean age of all children in the statewide sample in the spring of 1954 was exactly 15.0 years. Ninety-one per cent of the boys and 96 per cent of the girls were between their fourteenth and sixteenth birthdays when the questionnaire was administered. Some data on parental socio-economic status and on number of

347

siblings were reported by Hathaway and Monachesi, but examination of relationships between these variables and orphanhood required special sorting of IBM cards and tabulations, which was undertaken by Phyllis Reynolds.

Since the children in this sample had a mean age of 15 years in the spring of 1954, it follows that their mean date of birth would have been close to the middle of the year 1939. The United States Bureau of the Census[18] published vital statistics of the United States for the year 1939 that included data on numbers of live births by age of parents according to state of residence. There were 50,121 such births listed for the State of Minnesota, all but six having the age of mother recorded, and all but 1,149 having the age of father recorded. These data were used as the populations of fathers and mothers whose frequencies of death were to be estimated (Tables 1 and 2).

In the United States census of population for the year 1950,[19] the *nonwhite* population of Minnesota at age 14 years amounted to only 479 out of a total of 42,356 of the same age (or approximately 1.13 per cent). If we consider all children in Minnesota who were aged 10 through 14 years at the time of the 1950 census, there were 2,800 nonwhite out of a total of 223,787 (or approximately 1.25 per cent) within this age group. Although the nonwhite population has considerably higher rates of orphanhood than the white population, the very small proportion of nonwhite adolescents in this particular population made it safe to restrict all subsequent estimates to the white population.

State and regional life tables for the years 1939–1941 were prepared in the statistical bureau of the Metropolitan Life Insurance Company, and published by the National Office of Vital Statistics.[20] The mortality rates $(1000q_x)$ for white males and females in the State of Minnesota were used to compute mean death rates for each parent at the birth of the child, and hence to derive the *age of mean mortality* of father at conception of the child and the age of mean mortality of mother at the birth of the child (Tables 1 and 2). Short method B, described by Woofter,[9] was used to compute the subsequent ages of mean mortality for each parent at the time the

348

TABLE I. CRUDE SURVIVAL RATES OF WHITE FATHERS FROM OCTOBER 1938 TO JULY 1954

Year of Age	Population	Initial Death Rate	Number living at conception of children (mean date Oct. 1, 1938) U.S. generation life tables, white males	Of 100,000 Alive and Aged x − 1 Years on Jan. 1, 1938 Number living at time children attained age of 15 yrs. (mean date July 1, 1954) U.S. generation life tables, white males	Of 100,000 Alive at Conception of Children Number living at time children attained age of 15 yrs. (mean date July 1, 1954)
Pivotal ages of fathers at birth of children (mean date July 1, 1939)	Number of fathers in each 5-yr. age group from ages x − 2 to x + 3 yrs., Minnesota residents, 1939	Number dying per 1000 alive at beginning of yr. of age, state life tables: 1939–41, Minnesota, white males			
x to $x + 1$	P_x	$1000 q_x$	$l_{x-1/4}$	$l_{x+16\,1/2}$	$l'_{x+16\,1/2}$
17–18	299	1.48	99,872	99,725	96,849
22–23	7,308	2.01	99,835	96,195	96,354
27–28	14,166	2.24	99,805	95,145	95,331
32–33	11,953	2.50	99,760	92,910	93,134
37–38	7,790	3.19	99,678	89,405	89,694
42–43	4,394	4.56	99,542	84,010	84,397
47–48	2,044	6.52	99,348	76,795	77,299
52–53	752	10.52	99,032	67,460	68,119
57–58	275	16.10	98,635	56,425	57,206
Total	48,981				

Mean age of father at *birth* of child $= \dfrac{\Sigma x \cdot P_x}{\Sigma P_x} + 1/2 = 32.24$ years; and at *conception* of child $= 31.49$ years.

Mean death rate at *birth* of child $\dfrac{\Sigma P_x \cdot q_x}{\Sigma P_x} = 3.007$; and age of mean mortality at *birth* of child (by interpolation) $= 36.00$ years.

Age of mean mortality at *conception* of child $= 35.25$ years; and at time child attained age of 15 years $= 35.25 + \Sigma k = 50.44$ years (*see text*).

Mean probability of survival from *conception* of child until latter attained age of 15 years $= \dfrac{\Sigma P_x \cdot l'_{x+16\,1/2}}{\Sigma P_x} = 91.70$ per cent.

child had attained an age of exactly 15 years. In the case of his short method B, the initial constant $k'_0 = 1$, and the sum of these constants was determined by linear interpolation (the top line of page 168, and footnote on page 165, of his article). In the present instance, the mean value of k for *fathers* was estimated as $\dfrac{108 - 35.25}{108 - 18}$ $= \dfrac{72.75}{90} = .8083$. Hence the annual decrement in k was estimated as $\dfrac{1 - .8083}{45} = .00426$. During the 15.75 years that elapsed after conception, the total decrement would therefore be approximately .56, and hence the age of mean mortality for fathers would have advanced by only 15.19 years. In the case of *mothers* the mean value of k was estimated as $\dfrac{108 - 28.49}{108 - 16} = \dfrac{79.51}{92} = .8642$. The annual decrement in k was estimated as $\dfrac{1 - .8642}{46} = .00295$. Hence in 15 years from the birth of the child the total decrement for mothers would be approximately .35, and the age of mean mortality for mothers would have advanced by approximately 14.65 years.

Mean survival rates were then computed from life table survival functions (l_x) at the ages of mean mortality of father at conception, and of mother at the birth of the child—and of each parent when the child had attained the age of 15 years. Four sets of uncorrected mean survival rates were obtained for father, mother, and both parents, corresponding with the survival functions obtained from life tables for the United States[21, 22] and for Minnesota[20, 23] for the years 1939–1941 and 1949–1951.

Spiegelman[24] outlined the construction of the generation life table and mentioned its application to estimates of orphanhood. Oppal[12] kindly supplied me with copies of *United States generation life tables* for each race and sex, with a starting date of January 1, 1938, and extending through 1960. The survival functions (l_x) in these tables were computed in the Social Security Administration[25] from mortality rates $(1000q_x)$ derived from United States life tables, interpolated for single years of age by the Metropolitan Life Insurance Company. In the present study, the proportion of *fathers* at pivotal

350

TABLE 2. CRUDE SURVIVAL RATES OF WHITE MOTHERS FROM JULY 1939 TO JULY 1954

Year of Age	Population	Initial Death Rate	Of 100,000 Alive at Birth of Children	Of 100,000 Alive and Aged x − 1 Yrs. on Jan. 1, 1938	Birth of Children
Pivotal ages of mothers at birth of children (mean date July 1, 1939)	Number of mothers in each 5-yr. age group from ages x − 2 to x + 3 of age, state life tables: 1939–41 Minnesota, white females, residents, 1939	Number dying per 1000 alive at beginning of yr. of age, state life tables: 1939–41 Minnesota, white females	Number living at birth of children (mean date July 1, 1939) U.S. generation life tables, white females	Number living at time children attained age of 15 yrs. (mean date July 1, 1954) U.S. generation life tables, white females	Number living at time children attained age of 15 years (mean date July 1, 1954)
x to $x + 1$	P_x	$1000q_x$	$l_{x+1/2}$	$l_{x+15\,1/2}$	$V_{x+15\,1/2}$
17–18	3,882	.97	99,820	98,100	98,277
22–23	15,062	1.11	99,730	97,460	97,724
27–28	14,428	1.44	99,675	96,615	96,930
32–33	9,500	2.07	99,610	95,340	95,713
37–38	5,237	2.51	99,505	93,390	93,855
42–43	2,006	3.50	99,350	90,405	90,996
Total	50,115				

Mean age of mother at birth of child $= \dfrac{\Sigma x \cdot P_x}{\Sigma P_x} + 1/2 = 27.82$ years.

Mean death rate at birth of child $= \dfrac{\Sigma P_x \cdot q_x}{\Sigma P_x} = 1.618$; and age of mean mortality at birth of child (by interpolation) $= 28.49$ years.

Age of mean mortality at time child attained age of 15 years $= 28.49 + \Sigma k = 43.14$ years (see text).

Mean probability of survival from birth of child until latter attained age of 15 years $= \dfrac{\Sigma P_x \cdot V_{x+15\,1/2}}{\Sigma P_x} = 96.48$ per cent.

351

ages surviving from the conception of children (mean date assumed to be October 1, 1938) until these children attained an age of 15 years (at a mean date of July 1, 1954), was computed from the formula

$$l'_{x+15\,1/2} = \frac{l_{x+15\,1/2}}{l_{x-1/4}}$$

Similarly the proportion of *mothers* surviving from the birth of the child until the latter attained an age of 15 years was estimated as

$$l'_{x+15\,1/2} = \frac{l_{x+15\,1/2}}{l_{x+1/2}}$$

These values are shown in the final columns of Tables 1 and 2, from which were computed the mean probabilities of survival of each parent until the child attained the age of 15 years, by weighting each survival function by the population of parents at the corresponding pivotal age. The complement of these mean survival functions is the probability of orphanhood, and these crude values were used in the fifth line of a work table corresponding with Table 4.

Reference has already been made to the fact that the *mortality of married persons* of each sex is lower than the mortality for the total population of corresponding ages. The National Office of Vital Statistics[26] published estimates of mortality by marital status for the years 1949–1951, which seemed to be the most relevant information available for adjusting the present estimates. Table 3 shows the development of correction factors to be applied to the crude frequencies of paternal and maternal orphanhood already computed. From this table it may be seen that the crude estimates of paternal orphanhood were multiplied by 84.35 per cent, and the crude estimates of maternal orphanhood by 90.02 per cent. The impact of this adjustment on estimates for complete orphanhood would be the product of these two figures (i.e., approximately 76 per cent) but does not need to be estimated separately.

The *wartime deaths of fathers in military service overseas* are not included in United States mortality data or life tables. War orphans must, therefore, be treated as a separate closed population, and estimates of the numbers surviving as of January 1, 1957, were obtained from Oppal.[12] The numbers of war orphans show marked

352

TABLE 3. MORTALITY RATIOS FOR MARRIED WHITE MALES AND FEMALES, 1949–51

Age	Male		Female	
Age groups of parents at birth of children, Minnesota, 1939	Numbers of fathers in each age group at birth of children Minnesota residents, 1939	Mortality ratios for married white males as percentages of mortality for total white males *at ages x + 10 yrs*, U.S., 1949–51	Numbers of mothers in each age group at birth of children, Minnesota residents, 1939	Mortality ratios for married white females as percentages of mortality for total white females *at ages x + 10 yrs*, U.S., 1949–51
x	P_x	m_{x+10}	P'_x	m'_{x+10}
15–24	7,607	78.97	18,944	87.71
25–34	26,119	83.68	23,928	91.04
35–44	12,184	87.65	7,243	92.71
45–49	2,044	90.35		
50–54	752	90.17		
55–59	275	89.82		
Totals	48,981		50,115	
Age-adjusted mortality ratios for married white persons of childbearing age, as percentages of mortality for corresponding total population		$\dfrac{\Sigma P_x \cdot m_{x+10}}{\Sigma P_x} = 84.35$		$\dfrac{\Sigma P'_x \cdot m'_{x+10}}{\Sigma P'_x} = 90.02$

variation from one calendar year of birth to the next, being particularly high for children born in the years 1941 and 1944. However, those born in 1939 and 1940 and still surviving in 1957 were estimated as approximately 3,000 and 4,000 in numbers, respectively. We may, therefore, estimate that a maximum of 3,500 war orphans born in 1939 were still surviving in the year 1954. In an estimate relating to the preceding year, Shudde[10] presented data to the effect that there were approximately 179,000 paternal orphans aged 14 years on July 1, 1953. The necessary upward revision of crude estimates on *paternal* orphanhood, to allow for war orphans born in the year 1939, would, therefore, be 3,500 per 175,000, or approximately 2 per cent.

A further adjustment was made to permit the application of *Minnesota mortality experience* to the United States generation life table data. It may be noted from studying the first four rows of Table 4 that the estimates of orphanhood based on the Minnesota life tables for 1939–1941 and for 1949–1951 are lower than the estimates of orphanhood based on the corresponding United States life tables. Each of the two Minnesota life table estimates was divided by the corresponding United States life table estimates and the mean of these ratios for each sex amounted to 78.53 per cent for Minnesota males, and 80.62 per cent for Minnesota females. The latter ratios were then applied to the corresponding estimates based on United States generation life tables (contained in row 5) to derive the corrected estimates for paternal and maternal orphanhood that are presented in row 6 of Table 4.

Estimates for *complete orphanhood* were made both on the assumption that deaths of parents were independent of each other, and also on the assumption of partial interdependence. If the deaths of father and mother were independent events, the probability of *both* parents' dying (complete or absolute orphanhood) is obtained by multiplying the frequencies of paternal and maternal orphanhood—as was done in column 3 of Table 4. When this was also done for the statewide sample of the Minnesota school children, it was found that the theoretical or "expected" frequency of complete orphanhood (if the deaths of parents had been completely inde-

354

TABLE 4. ORPHANHOOD AMONG CHILDREN ATTAINING AGE 15 YEARS IN 1954[a]

Method of Estimation	Life Tables Used in Computation	Paternal[b] including deaths of both parents	Maternal including deaths of both parents	Both Parents assuming complete independence of deaths[d]	Both Parents assuming partial interdependence of deaths[e]
				Percentages of Orphanhood by Exact Age of 15 Years	
Mean survival rates computed from life table survival functions at *ages of mean mortality* of father at conception and of mother at birth of child—and of each parent when child attained age of 15 yrs.	U.S. life tables 1939–41, white males and females	8.27	3.81	.315	.493
	State life tables 1939–41, Minnesota; white males and females	6.16	3.16	.194	.305
	U.S. life tables 1949–51, white males and females	6.76	2.32	.157	.245
	State life tables 1949–51, Minnesota; white males and females	5.58	1.81	.101	.159
Mean survival rates computed from *age-specific life table survival functions*, weighted by numbers of fathers and mothers in each age group at birth of child	U.S. generation life tables 1938–54, white males and females	7.15	3.17	.226	.354
	U.S. generation life tables 1938–54, corrected for lower mortality of Minnesota than of total U.S. white population of childbearing age[c]	5.61	2.55	.143	.224
Data reported by 11,329 Minnesota school children, in 9th grade, spring, 1954 (mean age 15.0 yrs.)	None	5.46 ± .213	1.96 ± .130	[.107] *expected frequency*	.168 ± .038 *observed frequency*

[a] Crude percentages for fathers and mothers multiplied by mortality ratios for married persons of childbearing ages, as developed in Table 3.
[b] Percentages of paternal orphans increased by 2.00 per cent to include war orphans born in 1939 (*see text*).
[c] Percentages computed from U.S. Generation Life Tables, multiplied by ratios of 78.53 per cent for Minnesota males and 80.62 per cent for Minnesota females (*see text*).
[d] Percentage of paternal orphans multiplied by percentage of maternal orphans.
[e] Estimates on assumption of independence, multiplied by ratio of observed/expected deaths in the sample of Minnesota school children (*see text*).

355

pendent events) amounted to only .107 per cent, whereas the observed frequency of complete orphanhood (actually reported by the subjects) amounted to .168 per cent—or roughly 1.57 times the expected frequency. The latter figure is slightly smaller than the ratio of observed over expected absolute orphans at age 14–15 years, computed by Lotka[5] from the 1921 census data for England and Wales. However, it is of the same order of magnitude and was felt to be an appropriate ratio by which to increase all actuarial estimates of complete orphanhood in the present study, to allow for partial interdependence of deaths of father and mother. The results of increasing the estimates of complete orphanhood by this ratio are shown in the fourth and final column of Table 4.

We are now in a position to compare the final adjusted actuarial estimates of orphanhood in Minnesota, shown in row 6 of Table 4, with the estimates obtained from direct reports of the ninth-grade school children, as shown in the seventh and last row of the same table. It may be seen that the best actuarial estimate for *paternal* orphanhood lies within one standard error of the corresponding sample estimate, and the best actuarial estimate for *complete* orphanhood lies within one and a half standard errors of the corresponding sample estimate. However, the best actuarial estimate for *maternal* orphanhood exceeds the sample estimate by more than four times its standard error, which is extremely unlikely to be attributable to chance (p < 0.001).

Lotka[5] noted a similar deficit in the observed numbers of maternal orphans recorded in the 1921 census of England and Wales, and Fisher[4] presented data showing a similar deficit in estimates based on the United States population survey of 1949. In this connection, he pointed out that underreporting would be more likely to affect the count of maternal than paternal orphans, since widowers have a higher rate of remarriage than widows, and orphaned offspring of an earlier marriage may not be reported as such. There is, however, another plausible explanation for the deficit in maternal orphans among enumerated samples—namely, that children who have lost their mothers may themselves have a higher than average mortality, and may no longer be alive at the time of the subsequent census or sample enumeration.

Marshall[27] studied the mortality experience of the brothers and sisters of a large sample of insured lives, according to whether their parents were living or dead at the time of their application for insurance. It was found that, both before and after the age of 20, those whose parents had both died had the poorest mortality, those whose parents were both alive had the best mortality, and that the mortality of those who had lost only one parent by death was intermediate.

Spitz[28] reported an unusually high frequency of death among infants separated from their mothers at the age of three months and then placed in a foundling home. These particular infants were not orphans, and only a fraction of maternal orphans are likely to be exposed to the high rates of mortality existing in some institutions. However, a considerable number of studies have shown statistical associations between high rates of both maternal and infant mortality, on the one hand, and such factors as low socio-economic status and large family size on the other—for example, Butler and Bonham;[29] Chase;[30] Taylor and Knowelden.[31]

Langner[32] provided some retrospective data on orphanhood in relationship to fathers' socio-economic status, among a sample of 1,660 residents of midtown Manhattan. The frequency of *paternal* orphanhood (including the deaths of both parents) by the age of 16 years reported by those with fathers of low socio-economic status was 17.4 per cent, and by those with fathers of high socio-economic status was 13.0 per cent. The frequency of *maternal* orphanhood (including deaths of both parents) by age 16 years reported by those with fathers of low socio-economic status was 10.2 per cent, while the frequency reported by those with fathers of high socio-economic status was 4.9 per cent. The differential with respect to maternal orphanhood appears to be more significant than the differential with respect to paternal orphanhood. However, this particular sample included adults of all ages from 20 to 59 years, inclusive, whose births were, therefore, spread over a period of four decades, so that

357

they and their parents would have been subject to greatly varying probabilities of mortality.

It is not known to what extent the latter factor might introduce systematic bias and render spurious these apparent associations beween orphanhood and father's socio-economic status. However, it is evident that premature death may prevent a young father from achieving a socio-economic status that he would otherwise have attained—and may even exert a downward influence on the socio-economic status of his survivors. While it was not entirely possible to control for the latter, the data obtained on the statewide sample of ninth-grade Minnesota school children did permit some evaluation of relationships between frequency of orphanhood, parental socio-economic status, and number of siblings. Parental socio-economic status could not be determined for 426 of the subjects— that is, for less than 4 per cent of the total sample. However, the latter included 155 out of 824 orphans—or almost 20 per cent of all orphans. The frequency of orphanhood among those for whom parental socio-economic status could be determined, according to the latter and according to the number of siblings, is shown in Table 5. In this tabulation, all the significant findings related to *paternal* orphanhood, which was most frequent among the group of lowest socio-economic status and among only children—although there is also evidence of an increasing trend in paternal orphanhood with increasing number of siblings.

Since family size has tended to be inversely related to socio-economic status, a chi-square test was undertaken to determine whether these two variables were independent of each other among the 481 paternal orphans in the Minnesota sample, for whom this information was available. Table 6 indicates an extremely small probability of their being independent in this sample. In particular, there was an excess of large families in the case of paternal orphans whose fathers had been farmers or members of the two lowest socio-economic status groups. The reverse trend is apparent among paternal orphans whose fathers had been members of the remaining socio-economic status groups.

It would appear from Tables 5 and 6 that the relationships be-

358

TABLE 5. ORPHANHOOD AMONG 9TH GRADE CHILDREN, MINNESOTA 1954*

Socio-economic Status of Parents and Number of Siblings	Observed Number of Subjects in Each Category	Percentages of Orphanhood		
		Paternal Including Deaths of Both Parents	Maternal Including Deaths of Both Parents	Both Parents
Socio-economic status				
I. Professional	265	2.26	1.51	.000
II. Semiprofessional	574	4.01	.87	.000
III. Clerical	2,230	3.90	2.24	.045
IV. Farmer	2,422	3.06†	1.98	.165
V. Semiskilled	2,592	4.90	1.62	.116
VI. Slightly skilled	1,954	4.81	1.84	.102
VII. Day laborer	840	8.33†	1.67	.119
Number of siblings				
0	677	7.83†	2.95	.295
1	2,280	4.17	1.71	.219
2	2,406	3.70	1.21	.083
3	1,932	3.83	1.97	.000
4	1,286	4.12	2.57	.156
5 or 6	1,313	4.87	1.83	.000
7 or more	983	5.39	1.63	.000
All Groups	10,877*	4.42	1.83	.101

* The total number of subjects is reduced from 11,329 (see Table 4) to 10,877 mainly because of inability to determine parental socio-economic status among 426 subjects. Expected numbers of subjects were computed for each number of siblings, according to the known distribution of the latter among the total sample. Agreement between observed and expected frequencies of subjects, by number of siblings, was tested by chi-square = 2.067, with 6 degrees of freedom, and 0.95 < p < 0.90. (Not significant.)
† Significant deviations from mean percentage of paternal orphanhood for all groups combined (p < 0.01).

TABLE 6. SOCIO-ECONOMIC STATUS AND NUMBER OF SIBLINGS FOR PATERNAL ORPHANS, MINNESOTA 1954.

Number of Siblings	Professional and Semiprofessional		Clerical		Farmer		Semiskilled		Slightly Skilled		Day Laborer		Total N	Chi-square
	Observed	Expected	Observed	Expected	Observed	Expected	Observed	Expected	Observed	Expected	Observed	Expected		
0	6	3.2	15	9.6	6	8.2	16	14.0	6	10.4	4	7.7	53	10.00
1	9	5.7	18	17.2	9	14.6	35*	25.1	14	18.6	10	13.8	95	10.17
2	5	5.4	19	16.1	7	13.7	30	23.5	19	17.4	9	13.0	89	6.97
3	1	4.5	13	13.4	6	11.4	22	19.5	16	14.5	16	10.8	74	8.26
4	1	3.2	6	9.6	9	8.2	9	14.0	13	10.4	15†	7.7	53	12.27*
5 or 6	6	3.9	11	11.6	17*	9.8	10	16.9	14	12.6	6	9.3	64	11.97*
7 or more	1	3.2	5	9.6	20‡	8.2	5*	14.0	12	10.4	10	7.7	53	27.63‡
Total N	29		87		74		127		94		70		481	
Chi-square	12.62(a)		7.20		31.04‡		16.70*		4.37		15.34*			87.27‡

(a) Not significant because of the high proportion of expected frequencies less than 5 (in this column only).

* p < 0.05.

† p < 0.01.

‡ p < 0.001.

tween frequency of orphanhood and parental socio-economic status or number of siblings are independent of the age of the child and year of his birth (since the latter are approximately the same for all these subjects). However, there is every reason to believe that these relationships between frequency of orphanhood and parental socio-economic status or number of siblings are associated with differences in the ages of parents at the birth of the child. At least half of the children born into a large family are likely to have parents of above average age at the time of their birth, whereas all of the children born into a small family may have parents who were below the ages of mean mortality at the time of the child's birth.

Hitherto, it has not been possible to control for these and other related variables (such as order of birth) in retrospective studies of samples of patients. However, generation life tables permit exact probabilities of orphanhood to be determined for each parent, according to age, sex, race, and year of birth. These probabilities can be accumulated within specified groups, adjusted for marital status and local mortality experience, and then compared with observed frequencies of orphanhood in the same specified groups, according to such variables as socio-economic status, size of family, order of birth, and psychiatric diagnosis.

SUMMARY

Orphanhood may have profound consequences for the individual as well as for society, so that estimates of its frequency have been of interest to behavioral scientists as well as administrative authorities. In the United States, no direct estimates of the frequency of orphanhood in the general population have been made by census enumeration, and frequencies estimated from survey samples have apparently reflected underreporting.

Lotka pioneered in the development of actuarial methods of estimating orphanhood, and such techniques have since become increasingly refined. The development of accurate life tables for each intercensal year permitted the construction of generation life tables, from which it is possible to determine exact probabilities of orphan-

361

hood according to year of birth, as well as age, sex, and race of the parents.

Hitherto, the estimates of orphanhood derived from generation life tables have involved the total population of the United States. However, the mortality experince of parents residing in a given state may differ considerably from that of the country as a whole.

In the present study, actuarial estimates are developed for children born in Minnesota in 1939 and attaining the age of 15 years in 1954. These estimates are compared with those reported by a sample of 11,329 Minnesota school children who were in ninth grade, and attained a mean age of 15 years in the spring of 1954. The latter data are also examined in relation to parental socio-economic status and number of siblings.

It is also possible to use United States generation life tables to compute probabilities of paternal and maternal orphanhood for individuals, which may be accumulated and adjusted to permit comparisons between expected and observed frequencies within relatively small groups, according to such factors as socio-economic status, family size, order of birth, and psychiatric diagnosis.

REFERENCES

[1] Bowlby, John, MATERNAL CARE AND MENTAL HEALTH, Geneva, World Health Organization, Monograph Series No. 2, 1951.

[2] Gregory, Ian, Studies of Parental Deprivation in Psychiatric Patients, *American Journal of Psychiatry*, 115, 432–442, November, 1958.

[3] Registrar-General for England and Wales, Census of England and Wales 1921: Dependency, Orphanhood and Fertility, London, His Majesty's Stationery Office, p. 231, table 8.

[4] Fisher, Jacob, Orphans in the United States: Number and Living Arrangements, *Social Security Bulletin*, 13, 13–18, August, 1950.

[5] Lotka, Alfred J., Orphanhood in Relation to Demographic Factors: A Study in Population Analysis, *Metron*, 9, 37–109, 1931.

[6] ———, The Diminishing Burden of Orphanhood: A Great Social Benefit, *Statistical Bulletin of the Metropolitan Life Insurance Company*, Vol. 14, no. 9, September, 1933.

[7] Spiegelman, Mortimer, One Child in Nine in a Broken Family, *Statistical Bulletin of the Metropolitan Life Insurance Company,* Vol. 25, no. 3, March, 1944.

[8] Woofter, Thomas J., Jr., Paternal Orphans, *Social Security Bulletin,* 8, 5–6, October, 1945.

[9] ————, Probabilities of Death in Closed Population Groups: Illustrated by Probabilities of Death of White Fathers after Birth of Children, *Human Biology,* 18, 158–170, September, 1946.

[10] Shudde, Louis O., Orphans in the United States, July 1, 1953, *Social Security Bulletin,* 17, 16–18, July, 1954.

[11] ————, and Epstein, Lenore A., Orphanhood—A Diminishing Problem, *Social Security Bulletin,* 18, 17–19, March, 1955.

[12] Oppal, Bertram, Personal communication to the author, 1964.

[13] Gregory, Ian, An Analysis of Family Data on 1,000 Patients Admitted to a Canadian Mental Hospital, *Acta Genetica,* 9, 72–73, 1959; reprinted in PSYCHIATRY: BIOLOGICAL AND SOCIAL, Philadelphia, W. B. Saunders Co., 1961, pp. 232–234.

[14] Barry, Herbert, Jr., and Lindemann, Erich, Critical Ages for Maternal Bereavement in Psychoneuroses, *Psychosomatic Medicine,* 22, 166–181, May–June, 1960.

[15] Archibald, Herbert C., et al., Bereavement in Childhood and Adult Psychiatric Disturbance, *Psychosomatic Medicine,* 24, 343–351, July–August, 1962

[16] Hilgard, Josephine R., and Newman, Martha F., Parental Loss by Death in Childhood as an Etiological Factor among Schizophrenics and Adult Alcoholic Patients, Compared with a Non-patient Community Sample, *Journal of Nervous and Mental Disease,* 137, 14–28, July, 1963.

[17] Hathaway, Starke R., and Monachesi, Elio D., ADOLESCENT PERSONALITY AND BEHAVIOR, Minneapolis, University of Minnesota Press, 1963.

[18] United States Bureau of the Census, Vital Statistics of the United States, 1939, Part II. Natality and Mortality Data for the United States, Tabulated by Place of Residence, p. 78, Table V.

[19] United States Bureau of the Census, Census of Population, 1950, Vol. II, Characteristics of the Population, Part 23, Minnesota, p. 45, Table 15.

[20] United States National Office of Vital Statistics, State and Regional Life Tables 1939–41, Minnesota: White Males and Females, pp. 154–157.

[21] United States Bureau of the Census, United States Life Tables and Actuarial Tables 1939–41, by T. N. E. Greville, pp. 34–37, Tables 5 and 6.

[22] United States National Office of Vital Statistics, Life Tables for 1949–51. Vital Statistics—Special Report, Vol. 41, pp. 16–19, Tables 5 and 6.

[23] United States National Office of Vital Statistics, State Life Tables: 1949–51, Vital Statistics—Special Report, Vol. 41, Supplement 22, pp. 208–211.

[24] Spiegelman, Mortimer, INTRODUCTION TO DEMOGRAPHY, Chicago, The Society of Actuaries, 1955, pp. 93–94, 150–152, 267, 279.

363

[25] United States Social Security Administration, United States Generation Life Tables, 1938–1960, by Sex and Race (unpublished).

[26] United States National Office of Vital Statistics, Mortality from Selected Causes by Marital Status, United States, 1949–51, Vital Statistics—Special Reports, Vol. 39, no. 7, p. 377, Table 2.

[27] Marshall, Edward W., Parental History and Longevity, *Transactions of the Actuarial Society of America,* 33, 395–398, 1932.

[28] Spitz, René A., Unhappy and Fatal Outcomes of Emotional Deprivation and Stress in Infancy, in Galdston, Iago (editor), BEYOND THE GERM THEORY, New York, New York Academy of Medicine, 1954, pp. 128–129.

[29] Butler, Neville R., and Bonham, Dennis G., PERINATAL MORTALITY, Edinburgh, E. and S. Livingstone, Ltd., 1963.

[30] Chase, Helen C., The Relationship of Certain Biologic and Socio-economic Factors to Fetal, Infant and Early Childhood Mortality. Part I. Father's Occupation, Parental Age and Infant's Birth Rank, Albany, N.Y., State Department of Health, 1961 (reprinted by United States Department of Health, Education, and Welfare, Children's Bureau, 1964).

[31] Taylor, Ian, and Knowelden, John, PRINCIPLES OF EPIDEMIOLOGY, ed. 2, Boston, Little, Brown and Company, 1964.

[32] Langner, Thomas S., Childhood Broken Homes, in Langner, Thomas S., and Michael, Stanley T., LIFE STRESS AND MENTAL HEALTH, New York, Free Press of Glencoe, 1963, p. 161.

ACKNOWLEDGMENTS

I am grateful to Mr. Mortimer Spiegelman, associate statistician, Metropolitan Life Insurance Company, who provided information of historical, theoretical, and practical value.

Mr. Bertram Oppal, actuary, Social Security Administration, very kindly supplied me with copies of their United States generation life tables, data on war orphans, and information on current methodology.

I am further indebted to Professor Starke Hathaway for access to the data on orphanhood among the state-wide sample of Minnesota school children, and to Phyllis Reynolds, who sorted the IBM cards and tabulated these data. This part of the study was carried out with the aid of a small research grant from the University of Minnesota Graduate School.

364

MATRIX MULTIPLICATION AS A TECHNIQUE
OF POPULATION ANALYSIS

NATHAN KEYFITZ

This paper takes advantage of the fact that the changes in numbers of a human (or any other) population may be traced by simple matrix multiplication. When an appropriately constructed matrix M is repeatedly multiplied by an age distribution it carries the numbers at the several ages into successive time periods. The age distribution n periods after the starting point is M^n multiplied by the initial age distribution. This property of the matrix has several potential uses in demography; in the present paper we confine ourselves to a few considerations regarding individual elements and columns of M^n.

While a matrix is an array of numbers, it can be treated in a manner analogous to a single number and many of the propositions of ordinary algebra apply to it. For instance, if S has the same number of rows and columns as B, then it is permissible to construct M = S + B by simply adding the elements in corresponding positions. For multiplication the convention is to take rows by columns. Thus to calculate A × B we need merely know that the jth element of its ith row is constructed by multiplying the several elements of the ith row of A by the corresponding elements of the jth column of B, and adding these products.

The usefulness of population projections as a means of demographic study does not depend on their constituting a good prediction of what will actually happen to numbers in the several age groups. This is evidently true when the projection is made on the basis of the birth and death rates of a given year, but it is true even when the rates prevailing in the past are assumed to change in the future. The point is discussed in definitive fashion by Professor Donald J. Bogue in "The Population of the United States."[1] In the present article a most abstemious viewpoint is taken in relation to prediction. The projection is considered merely as a way of regarding the fertility and mortality of a single past year. We do not think of it as estimating the population that would exist if the rates of that year were to continue into the future any more than this is brought to mind when any other rate from last year's statistics is calculated; few calculators of such rates would consider it necessary to disavow explicitly the assumption that the rates would continue into the future. The projection procedure is here considered with as little attention to prediction as the simple calculation of the increase of the population from last year to this.

THE PROBLEM: TO SUMMARIZE THE FERTILITY AND SURVIVORSHIP PATTERNS OF A POPULATION

The projection procedure is separable from the age distribution of the original population, and is considered as an operator whose elements reflect the regime of mortality and fertility of the given population in the given year, and nothing more. This is not a novel approach, for it appears in at least three papers prior to this one. Bernardelli used it to investigate what might happen in a hypothetical population of beetles.[2] P. H. Leslie worked it out for a real population of the females of a domesticated brown rat stock housed at the Wistar Institute, Philadelphia, for which a life table was available.[3] Alvaro Lopez did not apply it to actual data, but considered with its help some important problems in demographic theory.[4] The matrix, even though it has several elements, is considered in what follows as a number, and one which has a unique claim to represent the essential facts of life and death in any human population. It is a multidimensional analogue of the ratio of this year's population to last year's, differing only from this single figure in that it takes account of age and separates the effect of births from that of deaths.

The search for some simple way of summarizing the pattern of fertility and mortality to which a population is subject has been a constant preoccupation of demographers. Crude birth and death rates, standardized rates, life tables, gross and net reproduction rates, the intrinsic rates of natural increase, have been developed, applied, and their limitations pointed out. The matrix of which this paper makes use is a special combination of fertility and survivorship containing 15 non-zero elements, which is a disadvantage in that it is more cumbersome to handle 15 numbers than a single number. Our matrix is not as readily manipulated on a desk calculator as a simple net reproduction rate but, on the other hand, it gives the meaning of past rates for the trajectory of a population not only after stability has been attained, but also on the path to stability. The Net Reproduction Rate (or its refinement, the intrinsic rate of natural increase) tells us what will be the consequences for population growth if the existing rates of survivorship and maternity are continued indefinitely; the matrix enables us to deal with the practically more important question of the consequences of the present rates for the immediate future as well. In order to keep the tables here presented within reasonable length, we use five-year age groups and confine our attention to that group to which the Net Reproduction Rate refers—females under 45 years of age—the most interesting part of a population from the viewpoint of reproduction.

THE CONVENTIONAL POPULATION PROJECTION

The form of the matrix is suggested by the ordinary population projection, in which explicit assumptions are made as to future births and deaths. Whether such a projection may be best looked on as a prediction or as a mere exercise in working out the consequences of the given assumptions depends on the taste of those who are making the calculations and using them. In the present instance we choose to regard the matrix and its products as a form of analysis of the specific data referring to the immediate past from which they are constructed. The future will be referred to only as a manner of describing and summarizing data for the past.

To make the discussion concrete, consider the 1960 population of the United States as counted in the census of April 1. Excluding armed services overseas and civilians absent for extended periods of time makes the total count 179,323,175. Our first simplification is to deal only in thousands; our second, as was noted, is to confine the study to women under 45 years of age. This gives as the jumping-off point the age distribution shown in column 2 of Table 1.

TABLE 1. UNITED STATES FEMALE POPULATION, UNDER 45 YEARS OF AGE, ROUNDED TO THOUSANDS, AS COUNTED IN THE CENSUS OF APRIL 1, 1960, AND PROJECTED BY THE COMPONENTS METHOD TO APRIL 1, 1965.

(1)	1960 (2)	1965 (3)	Average 1960–1965 (4)	Age-Specific Birth Rate 1960 (5)	(4)×(5) (6)
Total	63,506,000	67,853,000			
0– 4	9,991,000	10,531,000			
5– 9	9,187,000	9,954,000			
10–14	8,249,000	9,171,000			
15–19	6,586,000	8,232,000	7,409,000	.0899	666,000
20–24	5,528,000	6,566,000	6,047,000	.2581	1,561,000
25–29	5,536,000	5,506,000	5,521,000	.1974	1,090,000
30–34	6,103,000	5,507,000	5,805,000	.1127	654,000
35–39	6,402,000	6,057,000	6,229,000	.0562	350,000
40–44	5,924,000	6,329,000	6,126,000	.0164	100,000
					4,421,000

I have placed in the same table the projection by the ordinary components method. The United States life table for 1960 was used to secure the probabilities of surviving from each age group to the following age group during the five-year period; for the girl children 0–4 in 1960 this probability was .99633; for those 5–9 it was .99829, etc. A matrix operator which would premultiply the 1960 age distribution to put survivors into the next age groups is as follows:

$$S = \begin{bmatrix} 0 & 0 & 0 & 0 & 0 & 0 & 0 & 0 & 0 \\ .99633 & 0 & 0 & 0 & 0 & 0 & 0 & 0 & 0 \\ 0 & .99829 & 0 & 0 & 0 & 0 & 0 & 0 & 0 \\ 0 & 0 & .99789 & 0 & 0 & 0 & 0 & 0 & 0 \\ 0 & 0 & 0 & .99689 & 0 & 0 & 0 & 0 & 0 \\ 0 & 0 & 0 & 0 & .99606 & 0 & 0 & 0 & 0 \\ 0 & 0 & 0 & 0 & 0 & .99477 & 0 & 0 & 0 \\ 0 & 0 & 0 & 0 & 0 & 0 & .99253 & 0 & 0 \\ 0 & 0 & 0 & 0 & 0 & 0 & 0 & .98867 & 0 \end{bmatrix}$$

where the only non-zero terms are in the subdiagonal, and these are the successive values of the life-table function $\frac{_5L_{x+5}}{_5L_x}$, i.e., $\frac{_5L_5}{_5L_0}$, $\frac{_5L_{10}}{_5L_5}$, etc.,

ending with $\frac{_5L_{40}}{_5L_{35}}$. This ability of the matrix S to "survive" the population follows from the convention of row by column multiplication. If we are interested in an operator which when applied to the original age distribution will carry it forward two periods, we multiply instead by a matrix with seven non-zero elements, located in the positions below those of the preceding matrix:

$$S^2 = \begin{bmatrix} 0 & 0 & 0 & . & . & . & 0 & 0 & 0 \\ 0 & 0 & 0 & . & . & . & 0 & 0 & 0 \\ .99463 & 0 & 0 & . & . & . & 0 & 0 & 0 \\ 0 & .99618 & 0 & . & . & . & 0 & 0 & 0 \\ . & . & . & . & . & . & . & . & . \\ . & . & . & . & . & . & . & . & . \\ . & . & . & . & . & . & . & . & . \\ 0 & 0 & 0 & . & . & . & 0 & 0 & 0 \\ 0 & 0 & 0 & . & . & . & .98128 & 0 & 0 \end{bmatrix}$$

This can be verified by multiplying S by itself. The inner product of the third row of S by its first column gives the first element in the third row of S^2, i.e., $.99633 \times .99829 = .99463$. This meets the requirement that the premultiplication of a column vector consisting of the number of persons in successive five-year age groups by S^2 will carry the first age group into the third, the second into the fourth, etc., because the non-zero elements of S^2 are in the sub-subdiagonal; these elements are products of successive pairs of the non-zero elements of S. Each higher power has one less non-zero element; after seven multiplications we have the same 9×9 matrix, but with only one non-zero element remaining:

$$S^8 = \begin{pmatrix} 0 & 0 & 0 & \cdot & \cdot & \cdot & 0 & 0 & 0 \\ 0 & 0 & 0 & \cdot & \cdot & \cdot & 0 & 0 & 0 \\ 0 & 0 & 0 & \cdot & \cdot & \cdot & 0 & 0 & 0 \\ \cdot & \cdot & \cdot & \cdot & \cdot & \cdot & \cdot & \cdot & \cdot \\ \cdot & \cdot & \cdot & \cdot & \cdot & \cdot & \cdot & \cdot & \cdot \\ \cdot & \cdot & \cdot & \cdot & \cdot & \cdot & \cdot & \cdot & \cdot \\ 0 & 0 & 0 & \cdot & \cdot & \cdot & 0 & 0 & 0 \\ 0 & 0 & 0 & \cdot & \cdot & \cdot & 0 & 0 & 0 \\ .96557 & 0 & 0 & \cdot & \cdot & \cdot & 0 & 0 & 0 \end{pmatrix}$$

The effect of operator S^8 is to transfer the age group 0–4 in 1960 to 40–45 in the year 2000, multiplying it by .96204, the probability of surviving 40 years. Matrix multiplication here is arithmetically identical with aging a population on the usual life table method.

A MATRIX FOR FERTILITY

But the study of real populations must simultaneously take account of births as well as of deaths and aging. The ordinary method of population projection would start with the fact that the average number of children born to women of 15–19 years in 1960 was .0899, and it would project this age-specific birth rate by applying it to the average number of women 15–19 exposed over the five-year period. Specifically it would multiply .0899 by the average of the first two figures opposite 15–19 in Table 1, giving the product 666,000. So continuing we obtain column 6 of Table 1. All that remains to be done is to multiply 4,421,000, the total of this column, (1) by the factor .48807 which is the fraction which girl births constitute of total births in 1960, (2) by .97612 to allow for the deaths

370

of children under five years of age between 1960 and 1965, (3) by 5 because we assume the annual rates of birth of 1960 will continue for the five years. The product of these three numbers is 2.38207 and applying this to 4,421,000 we obtain 10,531,000 as the projected female population 0–4 in 1965.

If we rearrange this calculation so as to be able to apply factors to the age distribution of 1960, we find that we must multiply the 8,249,000 girls 10–14 of that year by .1068; the 6,586,000 girls 15–19 by .4135, etc. This may be seen as a vector inner product obtainable by premultiplying the 1960 age distribution by B, a birth

$$
B = \begin{bmatrix}
0 & 0 & .1068 & .4135 & \cdot & \cdot & \cdot & \cdot & .0195 \\
0 & 0 & 0 & 0 & \cdot & \cdot & \cdot & \cdot & 0 \\
\cdot & \cdot & \cdot & \cdot & \cdot & \cdot & \cdot & \cdot & \cdot \\
\cdot & \cdot & \cdot & \cdot & \cdot & \cdot & \cdot & \cdot & \cdot \\
\cdot & \cdot & \cdot & \cdot & \cdot & \cdot & \cdot & \cdot & \cdot \\
\cdot & \cdot & \cdot & \cdot & \cdot & \cdot & \cdot & \cdot & \cdot \\
\cdot & \cdot & \cdot & \cdot & \cdot & \cdot & \cdot & \cdot & \cdot \\
0 & 0 & 0 & 0 & 0 & 0 & 0 & 0 & 0
\end{bmatrix}
$$

matrix which has only seven non-zero elements, all in the first row.

MORTALITY AND FERTILITY COMBINED

Since what we want is to find the effect of mortality and fertility simultaneously, it is convenient to add S and B to secure the single matrix M. We intend to premultiply the column vector K by M, i.e., $(S + B)K =$

$$
MK = \begin{bmatrix}
0 & 0 & .1068 & .4135 & .5416 & .3686 & .2007 & .0862 & .0195 \\
.99633 & 0 & 0 & 0 & 0 & 0 & 0 & 0 & 0 \\
0 & .99829 & 0 & 0 & 0 & 0 & 0 & 0 & 0 \\
0 & 0 & .99789 & 0 & 0 & 0 & 0 & 0 & 0 \\
0 & 0 & 0 & .99689 & 0 & 0 & 0 & 0 & 0 \\
0 & 0 & 0 & 0 & .99606 & 0 & 0 & 0 & 0 \\
0 & 0 & 0 & 0 & 0 & .99477 & 0 & 0 & 0 \\
0 & 0 & 0 & 0 & 0 & 0 & .99253 & 0 & 0 \\
0 & 0 & 0 & 0 & 0 & 0 & 0 & .98867 & 0
\end{bmatrix}
\begin{bmatrix}
9991 \\
9187 \\
8249 \\
6586 \\
5528 \\
5536 \\
6103 \\
6402 \\
5924
\end{bmatrix}
$$

and it may be verified arithmetically that this gives the same population for 1965 as we obtained in Table 1. What we have said of

371

S and B separately applies to M, i.e., it follows from the row-by-column convention of matrix multiplication that M corresponds to the projection operation because its first row generates the children in the first age group of the following time period, and its subdiagonal multiplies each age group by the proportion which survives and places the survivors in the succeeding age group. This also follows in a more general way from the distributive rule to which matrices are subject:

$$SK + BK = (S + B)K = (M)K$$

The only difference between this and ordinary algebra is that the commutative rule does not apply; in removing brackets or performing other manipulation, we must always keep the order of the factors unchanged.

POWERS OF THE MATRIX

By choosing as the top row not exactly the proportion having a child in the given age group but a kind of average of the proportions for two successive age groups, we reproduce the ordinary results of a population projection to any number of decimal places in which we may be interested. The utility of this way of expressing the projection depends on a computer being available. Our access to the University of Chicago's IBM 7094 has been through the symbolic language known as FORTRAN. The following program results in a printout of the first 21 powers of the matrix M and the product of each of these by the age distribution which represents the jumping-off point of the projection. The time required for doing this with six entirely distinct sets of data, making 126 multiplications of 9×9 matrices, as well as an equal number of matrix by vector multiplications, and including the time in which the machine compiled the FORTRAN program into machine language and wrote the results for 1,770 lines of printout, was 57 seconds. The brevity of the program is due to the fact that the computer has the capacity to repeat the same operation with different numbers, and FORTRAN has been designed to call on this capacity. Statement 105, for example, asks the machine to perform a multiplication of one row of the

TABLE 2. MATRIX TO POWERS UP TO 21 AND POPULATION PROJECTION.

```
      DIMENSION   AM(9,9),AM2(9,9),AM3(9,9),A(9),A2(9)
  1   READ INPUT TAPE 5,100,AM
100   FORMAT (9F9.8)
      WRITE OUTPUT TAPE 6,103,AM
      READ INPUT TAPE 5,20,A
 20   FORMAT (9F6.0)
      WRITE OUTPUT TAPE 6,22,A
      DO 3 I = 1,9
      DO 3 J = 1,9
  3   AM2(I,J) = AM(I,J)
      DO 200 N = 1,21
      DO 105 J = 1,9
      A2(I) = A2(I) + AM2(J,I)* A(J)
      DO 105 J = 1,9
      DO 105 K = 1,9
105   AM3(I,J) = AM3(I,J) + AM(I,K) *AM2(K,J)
      WRITE OUTPUT TAPE 6,22,A2
 22   FORMAT (9F13.0)
      WRITE OUTPUT TAPE 6, 104, N
104   FORMAT (X6HPOWER 12////)
      WRITE OUTPUT TAPE 6,103, AM3
103   FORMAT (X9F13.7)
      DO 200 I = 1,9
      AM2 (I,J) = AM3(I,J)
200   AM3(I,J) = 0
      GO TO 1
      END
```

matrix to the square power by one column of the original matrix; this line is the heart of the program. After performing for all the combinations of row and column of the original matrix, it goes on to repeat, this time putting the cube of the original matrix thus attained in place of the square which occupied the postmultiply position in the previous cycle. In this fashion the process continues to the power 21, which is to say—since each power represents a five-year evolution—for the century following the date to which the survivorship and fertility rates apply. In between raising the matrix to its successive powers the computer multiplies each power by the original (1960) age distribution of the population, and so tells us the age distribution that would appear at the end of successive five-year time intervals if the original fertility and survivorship rates are maintained.

In order to study the properties of the matrix as it approaches stability, it has been found convenient to square it repeatedly; this involves an even simpler FORTRAN program than we presented above. With the United States 1960 data we obtain for M^{64} the array

$$M^{64} = \begin{bmatrix} 153.67462 & 171.16562 & . & . & . & . & . & . & 2.70034 \\ 137.97100 & 153.67462 & . & . & . & . & . & . & 2.42440 \\ 124.11578 & 138.24242 & . & . & . & . & . & . & 2.18094 \\ 111.60715 & 124.31011 & . & . & . & . & . & . & 1.96114 \\ 100.25858 & 111.66989 & . & . & . & . & . & . & 1.76173 \\ 89.98900 & 100.23142 & . & . & . & . & . & . & 1.58127 \\ 80.66677 & 89.84810 & . & . & . & . & . & . & 1.41746 \\ 72.14744 & 80.35910 & . & . & . & . & . & . & 1.26776 \\ 64.27686 & 71.59276 & . & . & . & . & . & . & 1.12946 \end{bmatrix}$$

It is easy to satisfy ourselves of the stability of this operator which converts an arbitrary age distribution to the age distribution that would prevail in $5 \times 64 = 320$ years with the given rates of mortality and fertility. For in order to obtain any but the first row of cells of M^{65} we need only multiply a single cell of M^{64} by the appropriate survivorship factor. Thus the second element of the second row of M^{65} is given by the product of .99633 (taken from the matrix on p. 74 by 171.1656227 = 170.537445. Dividing this by the second element of the second row of M^{64}, which is 153.6746197, we have 1.1097307. Using the ratios of the third element of the third row of M^{65} to M^{64} gives us again 1.1097307. It appears that the stability applies to at least seven significant digits.

APPLICATION TO A HUMP OF BIRTHS

Having calculated these powers of M we are now in a position to study the effects of a thousand additional girls under five in 1960. In fact, the computations are contained in the powers of M, and we can simply write down the results from the first columns of the several powers of the matrix as contained in the 7094 printout. These first columns would be the only non-zero components in the

374

products M'K where K consists in 1,000, with zeros below it. I present these figures at 25-year intervals for 1960 to 2060 (Table 3). It will be seen that in 1985 the original girls are 25–29 years of

TABLE 3. NUMBERS IN THE SEVERAL AGE GROUPS RESULTING FROM 1,000 GIRLS UNDER 5 IN 1960, AT FERILITY AND SURVIVORSHIP RATES OF THE UNITED STATES IN 1960.

Age	1960	1985	2010	2035	2060
0– 4	1,000	536	641	972	1,589
5– 9		409	535	846	1,412
10–14		106	364	710	1,249
15–19			281	633	1,127
20–24			371	634	1,044
25–29		986	528	632	958
30–34			402	526	833
35–39			103	356	695
40–44				273	613
Total	1,000	2,037	3,225	5,582	9,520

age, and the distribution of their descendants is non-overlapping with the distribution of their own ages—there would have been something wrong with the calculation if it had shown such overlapping, since mothers cannot be in the same five-year age group with their own daughters. Fifty years later, in the year 2010, the original babies have passed out of the reproductive ages, and the peak of their daughters is at 25–29. The distribution of the daughters, however, is not separate from that of their granddaughters; the two overlap in the trough which appears at 15–19. The granddaughters in the 0–4 group in 2010 are 641 in number. Examination of the distribution after 75 years shows the granddaughters having their (very slight) peak of numbers at age 20–24, which is 55 years younger than the original cohort of extra births, and a new peak (of great-granddaughters) coming up as indicated in the 972,000 children 0–4 in the year 2035. Since the length of the generation is about 25 years, each of the successive columns of the table represents a new generation if one follows along any horizontal line. By 2060 the overlapping process has gone far enough so that the several generations are represented by small inflections and no peaks at all.

By how much would this result have differed with the survivorship and fertility rates of 1940? For the United States of 1940,

$$M = \begin{bmatrix} 0 & 0 & .0633 & .2199 & .2987 & .2384 & .1498 & .0737 & .0203 \\ .99093 & 0 & 0 & 0 & 0 & 0 & 0 & 0 & 0 \\ 0 & .99589 & 0 & 0 & 0 & 0 & 0 & 0 & 0 \\ 0 & 0 & .99425 & 0 & 0 & 0 & 0 & 0 & 0 \\ 0 & 0 & 0 & .99093 & 0 & 0 & 0 & 0 & 0 \\ 0 & 0 & 0 & 0 & .98861 & 0 & 0 & 0 & 0 \\ 0 & 0 & 0 & 0 & 0 & .98640 & 0 & 0 & 0 \\ 0 & 0 & 0 & 0 & 0 & 0 & .98305 & 0 & 0 \\ 0 & 0 & 0 & 0 & 0 & 0 & 0 & .97799 & 0 \end{bmatrix} ;$$

again using the first columns of its powers multiplied by 1,000 we get Table 4 corresponding to the preceding Table 3. The differences in level between Tables 3 and 4 are spectacular. The reason for the differences, as may be seen by comparison of the top rows of the two matrices, is that at the principal ages of childbearing 1960 age-specific rates were nearly double those of 1940.

TABLE 4. NUMBERS IN THE SEVERAL AGE GROUPS RESULTING FROM 1,000 GIRLS UNDER 5 IN 1960, AT FERTILITY AND SURVIVORSHIP RATES OF THE UNITED STATES IN 1940.

Age	1960	1985	2010	2035	2060
0– 4	1,000	290	203	195	201
5– 9		214	171	186	198
10–14		62	150	187	199
15–19			166	199	201
20–24			227	209	197
25–29		961	279	196	188
30–34			205	164	178
35–39			58	141	177
40–44				154	185
Total	1,000	1,527	1,459	1,631	1,724

In both Tables 3 and 4 we are approaching the stable distribution by the end of the 100-year period. At the 1940 rates this stable distribution is nearly flat as one moves from age to age, but that on the 1960 rates shows less than half the number of women at age 40–44 as at 0–4. These results are an approximation to the ultimate

376

or stable age distribution which arises from the given fertility and mortality rates. We can also make a comparison with a population which is increasing much more rapidly than that of the United States, and introduce the 1960 matrix for Mexico. We have been fortunate in securing the 1960 life tables prepared by Señora Zulma Recchini under the sponsorship of the Centro Latinoamericano de Demografía, and have combined these with the fertility and population figures given for the same year in the 1962 United Nations Demographic Yearbook. For the Mexican matrix and the 1,000

$$M = \begin{bmatrix} 0 & 0 & .1145 & .4413 & .6689 & .6384 & .5132 & .3197 & .1025 \\ .96495 & 0 & 0 & 0 & 0 & 0 & 0 & 0 & 0 \\ 0 & .99017 & 0 & 0 & 0 & 0 & 0 & 0 & 0 \\ 0 & 0 & .99234 & 0 & 0 & 0 & 0 & 0 & 0 \\ 0 & 0 & 0 & .98881 & 0 & 0 & 0 & 0 & 0 \\ 0 & 0 & 0 & 0 & .98106 & 0 & 0 & 0 & 0 \\ 0 & 0 & 0 & 0 & 0 & .98046 & 0 & 0 & 0 \\ 0 & 0 & 0 & 0 & 0 & 0 & .97649 & 0 & 0 \\ 0 & 0 & 0 & 0 & 0 & 0 & 0 & .97147 & 0 \end{bmatrix}$$

hypothetical extra population 0–4 in 1960 we have the calculations in Table 5. As before, each of the columns below is transformed into

TABLE 5. NUMBERS IN THE SEVERAL AGE GROUPS RESULTING FROM 1,000 GIRLS UNDER 5 IN 1960, AT FERTILITY AND SURVIVORSHIP RATES OF MEXICO IN 1960.

Age	1960	1985	2010	2035	2060
0– 4	1,000	627	1,001	2,235	5,245
5– 9		403	716	1,787	4,296
10–14		104	567	1,537	3,640
15–19			526	1,372	3,081
20–24			562	1,186	2,552
25–29			577	921	2,055
30–34		920	377	669	1,670
35–39			96	523	1,416
40–44				474	1,238
Total	1,000	2,054	4,422	10,704	25,193

the succeeding column by premultiplying it by M^5. Aside from the great difference in rates of increase, comparison of the United

States and Mexico shows a sharper separation between the generations in the former country. Between daughters and granddaughters of the original 1,000, for instance, as they appear in 2010 there is a trough at age 15–19 in the 1960 United States data, which is deeper both in relative and in absolute terms than that in the Mexican. This is related not so much to the level of fertility as to the shorter span of years over which women in the United States bear their children.

DESCENDANTS OF A GIVEN AGE GROUP

We draw attention to one other aspect of the survivorship-fertility matrices: the meaning of the individual cells of M^t. For concreteness in the exposition, consider the fourth cell in the eighth row of M^{15}, which is .590 with the United States 1960 data. This would be multiplied by the fourth age group of the original age distribution to secure the eighth age group 15 time periods (i.e., 75 years) later. In other words, 1,000 women 15–19 in 1960 would give rise to 590 women in the age group 35–39 in the year 2035 with the fertility-survivorship pattern of 1960. These 590 would not be the sole descendants of the original 1,000 of course, but only those who would be 35–39 in the given year; adding them to the other elements of the fourth column of the matrix 1,000M^{15} we secure the total of 7,271 for ages 0–45. It is not possible from this calculation to divide the 950 into grandchildren, great-grandchildren, etc., of the original 1,000; we could have kept the generations separate by placing successive sets of babies into ever-new matrices, but this would have greatly complicated the task. What the simple approach of this exposition provides is the statement that at the rates of survivorship and fertility of the United States in 1960, 1,000 girls aged 15–19 in 1950 would "yield" 590 women 35–39 through the several possible routes of descent, i.e., as granddaughters and great-granddaughters. At the United States 1940 rates the corresponding number is 195; at the Mexican 1960 rates it is 1,115.

To generalize this somewhat, we can find the descendants of the

378

women (on a per woman basis) in the ith age group at the initial period who are in the jth group at the tth period by noting the ith element of the jth row of M^t. Similarly if we want to know the total (to age 45) of the descendants of the initial ith age group period we add the ith column of M^t.

CONCLUSION

Out of a short experience it is already apparent along what lines machine computation will alter demographic investigation. When the writer first set out to use the computer, he fed into it a set of birth rates along with the number-living column of a life table and read out the intrinsic rate of natural increase. Apart from this, he experimented on the construction of life tables, and also on the multiplying of matrices. He put in the elements of a matrix which had been calculated by hand and read out its latent roots. Each of these steps was preceded by long work at the desk calculator, working out the data for a short problem which would occupy the computer for a fraction of a second. In short, the computer was being used like a desk calculator, disregarding its ability to carry through a long sequence of calculations.[5]

The radical change was the discovery that it was in the long run easier to program the entire sequence and have the computer at each stage prepare the data for the next stage. In the present program of 800 FORTRAN statements, there are sub-programs for reading in and checking the raw data, which consist of a mere 90 or so figures copied out of primary sources or the United Nations Demographic Yearbook, without any processing whatever. The computer then calculates a life table (checking itself by the use of three different methods) ; works out the elements of the 9×9 matrix; takes the matrix to high powers; finds the intrinsic rate of increase by four methods whose agreement is the assurance that these many parts of the program are in agreement; uses this to work out the stable population; goes on to calculate moments and cumulants of the original population distribution by age, as well as of the life table functions and the maternity function. The sequence consists of a series of sub-routines which one by one fill the cells provided as receptacles for the several 'answers. It prints out some 800 lines of results in about 12 seconds. This sequence is a kind of skeleton on which other sub-routines can be hung, written by other workers in the field. Mr. E. M. Murphy has completed a sub-routine for finding the inverse of the fundamental matrix, and for taking it to high powers; he has also worked out a way of handling the 20×20 matrix that will embrace all ages instead of being confined to ages 0–44 as is the matrix of this article. Mr. J. Palmore has worked out a standardization routine for birth rates.

These will be tied into the existing sequence, starting from raw data, as was said. So far all this takes in only the female portion of the population, but plans are under way to do the same thing for the male side. Having within the same program the trajectories of the male and female populations, it ought to be possible to program marriage rates and the reciprocal changes by which the two sexes remain in balance. We believe that this and other kinds of simulation will be attainable in the near future.

REFERENCES

[1] Bogue, Donald J., THE POPULATION OF THE UNITED STATES, New York, The Free Press of Glencoe, 1959, Chapter 26, "Future Population."

[2] Bernardelli, H., Population Waves. *Journal of the Burma Research Society,* 31, 1–18, 1941.

[3] Leslie, P. H., On the Use of Matrices in Certain Population Mathematics, *Biometrika,* 33, 183–212, November, 1945.

[4] Lopez, Alvaro, PROBLEMS IN STABLE POPULATION THEORY, Princeton, N. J., Office of Population Research, 1961.

[5] The elements of the matrices S, B, and M cited in this paper were worked out on a desk calculator with existing life tables. It is hoped that similar results secured by a computer program, which works out the elements of the matrix in the first place from raw data giving births, deaths, and population by age, will be available soon. Because of rounding off, and for other reasons, it is not to be expected that the two sets will be identical.

ACKNOWLEDGMENT

The work on which this article is based was supported by a Ford Foundation grant to the Population Research and Training Center of the University of Chicago.

BAYESIAN ESTIMATION FOR HIGHER ORDER CROSS-CLASSIFICATIONS

JEROME CORNFIELD

Table 1 gives an example of the kind of high order cross-classification with which this paper is concerned. The table shows mortality from coronary heart disease by the four variables, maximum daily amount smoked, age started, number of years discontinued and attained age. The rates are calculated from data given in Kahn's analysis of the Dorn study of the mortality of American veterans.[1] Although the table is based on over a million man years of observation and more than 10,-000 deaths from coronary heart disease, the conclusions yielded by simple inspection of the results are far from clear-cut with respect to two of the variables. If one asks whether the rates for those who had discontinued for 15 or more years had returned to the level of nonsmokers, the answer is by no means unequivocal. It may depend upon age started, maximum amount smoked and attained age, but the random variation in the data is a serious source of obscurity. Similarly, the effect of age started appears unclear. Seltzer,[2] following Kahn, concludes it is substantially without effect; other observers, inspecting the same data have reached a contrary conclusion. If analysis is confined to simple inspection, more massive accumulations of data are required and even then one may be unable to support more than the somewhat modest analysis of four variables simultaneously considered.

	Attained Age 55–64					Attained Age 65–74				
					Years Stopped Nonsmokers					
Age Began	0	1–4	5–9	10–14	15+	0	1–4	5–9	10–14	15+
<15										
15–19			$\dfrac{1218}{213,858} = 569$					$\dfrac{1587}{171,211} = 927$		
20–24										
25+										

Maximum 1–9 per Day

Age Began	0	1–4	5–9	10–14	15+	0	1–4	5–9	10–14	15+
<15	404	1250	1242	0	873	1305	0	685	1639	868
15–19	604	836	544	765	533	1161	575	805	1305	923
20–24	509	0	572	517	585	1038	1550	1434	420	1040
25+	669	364	628	360	478	1040	1437	1010	1123	1011

Maximum 10–20 per Day

Age Began	0	1–4	5–9	10–14	15+	0	1–4	5–9	10–14	15+
<15	1043	782	682	1094	777	1238	581	1011	1017	1061
15–19	912	613	809	666	523	1402	890	1392	1352	1001
20–24	872	679	842	748	488	1322	1233	1000	1650	933
25+	738	437	517	395	588	1414	202	1056	1433	1152

Maximum 21–39 per Day

Age Began	0	1–4	5–9	10–14	15+	0	1–4	5–9	10–14	15+
<15	1115	988	724	1821	736	2090	1190	2104	1037	1281
15–19	1051	854	1260	741	734	1579	1113	1363	1612	963
20–24	946	1122	784	721	557	1437	1474	1795	1162	903
25+	920	681	888	627	571	1409	1305	893	1502	1412

Maximum over 39 per Day

Age Began	0	1–4	5–9	10–14	15+	0	1–4	5–9	10–14	15+
<15	1337	389	743	816	626	1803	0	2469	1685	1261
15–19	1188	889	824	296	737	1782	866	2125	803	2139
20–24	1198	439	706	930	918	1765	581	1368	2334	800
25+	1204	1406	452	543	906	1232	599	340	1313	482

METHODS AVAILABLE

A number of techniques are used to deal with data of this
type. First, pooling: the computation of marginal rates with
each cell weighted by its own man years of exposure. As an
example, Table 2 shows the marginal rates by years discontinued
after pooling over attained age, maximum amount smoked and
age started. This is probably the most common form of analysis

used, but, as everyone knows, can be misleading. One has no assurance that the different years-stopped classes are balanced with respect to the other three variables. In fact, inspection of the original data shows serious confounding, with current smokers (0 years discontinued), for example, being a distinctly younger group than those having discontinued 15 or more years.

The usual method for handling such confounding is standardization, and in fact standardization for age (although not other variables) is a routine in most studies. Standardization has the disadvantages of supplying inefficient estimates as compared with least squares procedures[8] and of disregarding the possibility that the effect of one variable may depend upon the levels of the others. Thus the percentages effects of many risk factors in coronary heart disease are known to decrease with age[3] and for this case age standardization will produce estimates whose exact interpretation may be obscure. It is convenient to refer to such effects, when they exist, as interactions.

In least squares procedures, as applied, say, to a two-way table, one postulates each cell mean as the sum of an overall effect, a row effect and a column effect (no interaction) and estimates the effects to minimize the weighted squared difference between observed and estimated effects, the weight for each cell being the reciprocal of the sampling variance of the observation there. In higher-order classifications the restriction to no

TABLE 2. ANNUAL MORTALITY RATE FROM CORONARY HEART DISEASE X10^5, BY YEARS STOPPED, ALL ATTAINED AGES, ALL AGES BEGAN, ALL AMOUNTS SMOKED

Number of Years Stopped	Deaths/Man Years	Rate
0	6007/542,070	1108
1–4	213/28,281	753
5–9	584/58,657	996
10–14	433/43,738	990
15+	869/109,613	793
Nonsmokers	2805/385,069	728

Maximum Number of Cigarettes Per Day	0	Years Stopped			15+
		1–4	5–9	10–14	
		Number of Coronary Heart Disease Deaths/Person Years Observation			
0		1218/213,858			
1–9	66/10,920	5/598	6/1102	7/915	32/6,002
10–20	544/59,631	24/3,918	54/6,674	33/4,954	67/12,821
21–39	569/54,118	26/3,044	59/4,681	22/2,969	43/5,856
40+	170/14,306	9/1,012	13/1,577	3/1,013	13/1,763

interaction has been relaxed, but not removed,[4] and applied with great effectiveness to the National Halothane Study.[5]

An alternate route that has been investigated in recent years is the use of parametric models such as the multiple logistic.[3,6] These models also make special assumptions and investigation of their applicability may require a far from routine data-analysis.

It is clear that whatever the analysis employed for tables of this type, it has called for a choice among possible methods that requires the exercise of considerable judgment. The development of methods that reduced the judgmental component involved in application would clearly be of great interest. Bayesian procedures, which require the expression of prior judgments in mathematical form, offer a possible way of doing this and the following sections describe a Bayesian procedure.

SOME BAYES ESTIMATES

Table 3 gives the numerator and denominator values for the rates for the two-way table obtained by confining attention to one of the two age-groups and one of the four "age-started" classes. The original rates are plotted in the left-hand panel of Figure 1, and an approximation to Bayes' estimates of these rates in the right-hand panel. The original rates are erratic, largely because of the small number of deaths on which they are based. The Bayes' estimates are more orderly and appear to bring out more clearly the relations between the variables. As will be discussed, only mild assumptions have been introduced, and the absence of interactions has not been assumed.

POSTERIOR MEANS AS ESTIMATES

This section contains a brief review of the general Bayesian machinery behind the equations to be discussed under the two-way classification, which in turn lead to the right-hand panel of Figure 1.

Consider a random variable x, say an observed mortality rate, and its true value, say μ, and denote the probability density function of x, given μ by $f(x,\mu)$. This function might, for example, be normal with mean μ and variance μ/N, where N is

FIGURE I. MORTALITY FROM CORONARY HEART DISEASE BY MAXIMUM AMOUNT SMOKED AND YEARS DISCONTINUED*

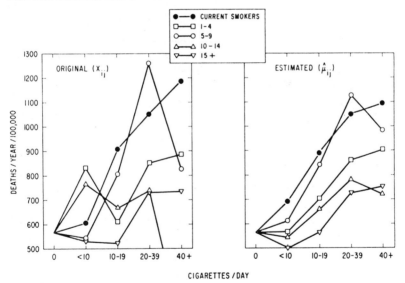

CIGARETTES / DAY

* Age started: 15–19; age attained: 55–64.

man-years of observation. The parameter μ is assigned a prior probability density function $g(\mu)$. Bayes' theorem then says that the posterior probability density function of μ, given the observation x is $f(x,\mu) g(\mu) / \int f(x,\mu) g(\mu) d\mu$. The mean of this posterior distribution, $\hat{\mu}$, may be written as

(1)
$$\hat{\mu} = \frac{\int \mu f(x, \mu) g(\mu) d\mu}{\int f(x, \mu) g(\mu) d\mu}$$

This mean supplies an estimate of the unknown parameter, μ. A suitable extension for the multiparameter case is used later. In some cases the expressions in the discussion on two-way classification lead to simple functions of x that can be easily computed; in others numerical integration is required, but this is a question of detail and not of principle.

THE ONE-WAY CLASSIFICATION

This section reviews some known Bayesian results for estimation in the one-way classification. As an example consider the 10–20 cigarettes/day smoking class in Table 3 and the estimate of the rates for each of the five "years stopped" classes. We now have 5 probability density functions $f(x_i,\mu_i)$ $(i = 1,2..5)$ and, to apply Bayesian methods, must assign a joint prior probability density function to the five values of μ. One way of doing this is to assign independent priors, that is, to express the joint prior as the product of individual priors. Thus, let

(2)
$$g(\mu_1, \mu_2, \mu_3, \mu_4, \mu_5) = \prod_{i=1}^{5} g(\mu_i)$$

If the prior functions have no parameters in common, then each μ_i will depend only on x_i. In particular if $f(x_i\mu_i)$ is normal with mean μ_i and variance V_i and $g(\mu_i)$ is normal with variance σ^2,

(3)
$$\lim_{\sigma^2 \to \infty} \mu_i = x_i$$

leading back to the estimates in Table 1. Data are available, however, that bear on the differences among the μ_i and they may be in contradiction to the assumption that σ^2 is very large. It turns out that the use of such information can result in improved estimates. Thus, in the more general case in which the $g(\hat{\mu}_i)$ are normal with mean μ and variance σ^2, where σ^2 need not be large, the mean of the posterior, $\hat{\mu}_i$ is given by

(4)
$$\hat{\mu}_i = w_i x_i + (1 - w_i) \mu$$
$$\text{where } w_i = \frac{\sigma^2/V_i}{\sigma^2/V_i + 1}$$

The parameters μ and σ^2 are unknown and the full Bayesian solution now requires assigning prior distributions to them, with the posterior means defined as multiple integrals over all unknown parameters. If a uniform prior is assigned to μ, but σ^2 is treated as known, the posterior means are still of the form (4), but with $\hat{\mu}$ substituted for μ, where

(5)
$$\hat{\mu} = \frac{\sum_i x_i/(\sigma^2 + V_i)}{\sum_i 1/(\sigma^2 + V_i)}$$

The integration over σ^2 can be performed only numerically, however. A simple approximation suggested by Lindley[7] is to compute the usual unbiased estimate of the component of variance and to treat the unknown σ^2 as equal to it. Lindley shows, for the case of equal V_i, that when this is done

(6)
$$E \sum (\hat{\mu}_i - \mu_i)^2 \leqq E \sum (x_i - \mu_i)^2$$

no matter what the μ_i; i.e., that the μ_i estimated by (4) and (5) are closer on an average to the true value than the x_i.

Table 4 illustrates the computations, for the data in Table 3 using values of V_i and σ^2 obtained in the next section. Each estimate is moved toward the mean. The magnitude of the movement is small because the variance of each x_i is small relative to the estimated component of variance. When the same method is applied to either the first or last row, the changes are of course larger.

The special feature of this method is that it provides a smooth transition between two extremes: a zero component of variance —for which case the common mean is the appropriate estimate for each class—and an infinite component of variance—for which case the individual mean is the appropriate estimate. As the order of the cross-classification increases the advantages of such an approach become increasingly manifest.

Formally, the gain from using the correct rather than an infinite value for σ^2 is given by considering the posterior variance of $\hat{\mu}_i$, defined by (4). This is easily shown to be $(1/\sigma^2 + 1/V_i)^{-1}$, which ranges in value between V_i, for σ^2 infinite, and zero, for σ^2 equal to zero. (Use of (5) adds a term to the posterior variance that is non-zero even for σ^2 equal to zero and allows for the variance of the estimate $\hat{\mu}$ defined by (5). Use of an estimate for σ^2 adds an additional term of the same type.)

THE TWO-WAY CLASSIFICATION

Consider a 2×2 table, with the four true means defined as follows:

(7)

$$\mu_{11} = \mu$$
$$\mu_{12} = \mu + C$$
$$\mu_{21} = \mu + R$$
$$\mu_{22} = \mu + R + C + I$$

Thus, C is a true column effect; R, a true row effect and I, a true interaction effect. The cell in the first row and column defined to be without row, column or interaction effects is called the reference cell. Now let the four observed means x_{ij} be independently normal about these means with known variances V_{ij}. The four unknown parameters are assigned independent prior probability density functions as follows:

(8)

μ is uniform from plus to minus infinity
C is normal with mean zero and variance σ_C^2
R is normal with mean zero and variance σ_R^2
I is normal with mean zero and variance σ_I^2

Years Stopped	Observed Rate × 10⁵ x_i (×10⁵)	Variance ×10⁷ $V_i \times 10^7$	Estimated Rate × 10⁵ $\mu_i \times 10^5$	Posterior Standard Error $(V_i^{-1} + \sigma^{-2})^{-\frac{1}{2}} \times 10^5$
0	912	1.50	909	38
1–4	613	18.04	632	119
5–9	809	12.60	792	102
10–14	666	13.34	670	105
15+	523	4.42	535	64

$$\sigma^2 \times 10^7 = 65.38$$
$$\hat{\mu} = 699$$
$$\hat{\mu}_i = \frac{65.38 x_i + V_i \hat{\mu}}{65.38 + V_i}$$

The three variances will be recognized as the column, row and interaction component of variance respectively.

It will be shown that the posterior means of the four parameters $\hat{\mu}$, $\hat{C}$, $\hat{R}$ and $\hat{I}$ are defined by the four simultaneous linear equations

(9)

$$\hat{\mu} = \frac{x_{11}/V_{11} + (x_{12} - \hat{C})/V_{12} + (x_{21} - \hat{R})/V_{21} + (x_{22} - \hat{R} - \hat{C} - \hat{I})/V_{22}}{1/V_{11} + 1/V_{12} + 1/V_{21} + 1/V_{22}}$$

$$\hat{C} = \frac{(x_{12} - \hat{\mu})/V_{12} + (x_{22} - \hat{\mu} - \hat{R} - \hat{I})/V_{22}}{1/V_{12} + 1/V_{22} + 1/\sigma_C^2}$$

$$\hat{R} = \frac{(x_{21} - \hat{\mu})/V_{21} + (x_{22} - \hat{\mu} - \hat{C} - \hat{I})/V_{22}}{1/V_{21} + 1/V_{22} + 1/\sigma_R^2}$$

$$\hat{I} = \frac{(x_{22} - \hat{\mu} - \hat{R} - \hat{C})/V_{22}}{1/V_{22} + 1/\sigma_I^2}$$

It is instructive to note that the posterior mean for any parameter is obtained by subtracting from each observed mean whose expected value contains that parameter the posterior means of all the other parameters also contained, weighting the difference by the inverse of the variance for that observed mean, and dividing the sum by the sum of the weights *plus* the reciprocal of the variance of the assigned prior for that parameter. With this insight the extension to more than two rows and columns and indeed to any higher order cross-classification can be written down at sight. Each cell mean is estimated as the sum of the appropriate constants. For example

(10)
$$\hat{\mu}_{22} = \hat{\mu} + \hat{R} + \hat{C} + \hat{I}$$

With all three components of variance infinite the estimates reduce to

(11)
$$\hat{\mu}_{ij} = x_{ij} \quad \text{for all } i \text{ and } j$$

With the interaction component of variance zero, but the other two infinite, the estimates reduce to the classical least squares estimates for a row-column table without interaction.[8] With all three interaction components of variance equal to zero, all four cell means are estimated as equal to the weighted average of the individual cell means. As in the case of the one-way classification, therefore, the general posterior means provide a continuous interpolation between various extreme cases, with the particular estimate yielded depending on the information about the three components of variance supplied by the data.

In applying equations (9) to the data of Table 3, the reference cell is the 10–20 cigarettes/day, 0 years stopped class; i.e., $i = 2$ and $j = 1$. The estimates of the components have been taken (somewhat crudely) as:

(12)

$$\text{est. of } \sigma_C^2 = \frac{1}{4} \sum_{j=2}^{5} \left[(x_{2j} - x_{21})^2 - (V_{2j} + V_{21}) \right]$$

$$\text{est. of } \sigma_R^2 = \frac{1}{3} \sum_{\substack{i=1 \\ i \neq 2}}^{4} \left[(x_{i1} - x_{21})^2 - (V_{i1} + V_{21}) \right]$$

$$\text{est. of } \sigma_I^2 = \frac{1}{12} \sum_{\substack{i=1 \\ i \neq 2}}^{4} \sum_{j=2}^{5} \left[(x_{ij} - x_{i1} - x_{2j} + x_{21})^2 \right.$$
$$\left. - (V_{ij} + V_{i1} + V_{2j} + V_{21}) \right]$$

The V_{ij} in (9) are taken as

(13)
$$V_{ij} = \hat{\mu}_{ij}/N_{ij}$$

where N_{ij} is man years of observation. This makes the equations (9) nonlinear and they have in fact been solved iteratively taking as initial approximations

(14)
$$\text{initial } V_{ij} = x_{ij}/N_{ij}$$
$$\text{initial } C_j = x_{2j} - x_{21}$$
$$\text{initial } R_i = x_{i1} - x_{21}$$
$$\text{initial } I_{ij} = x_{ij} - x_{i1} - x_{2j} + x_{21}$$

Iteration ceased when the square root of the average sum of the squared differences between the 20 values in two successive iterations became less than 5×10^{-6}; i.e., equivalent to 5 in the fourth significant digit of the nonsmoker rate of 569 per 100,-000. For the example given, 9 iterations, taking 15 seconds on the GE-265, were required.

The completely Bayesian solution requires a triple numerical integration over the posterior of σ_R^2, σ_C^2 and σ_I^2 and has not yet been investigated.

ALTERNATE PRIOR DISTRIBUTIONS

The priors assigned in (8) are, of course, not the only ones that could have been assigned and in fact are mildly contradictory to those assigned in the discussion of the one-way classification. In the former care, the priors for the μ_i are assumed independent, whereas, in the latter, the assignment implies a positive correlation between all μ_i. In view of the way in which the data overpower these priors, and the known small effect of small correlations, this choice appears without important consequences.

With other possible assignments the effects might be less than trivial, however. Rather than assigning zero means to C and R, for example, one might have made them functions of years discontinued and maximum amount smoked. The components of variance would then have become components around the assumed function values and would be greatly reduced. Nor would it be necessary to assume that the constants of these functions were known, because they too could be assigned priors and integrated out. The posterior mean in any cell would still be a weighted average of observed and fitted cell mean (for functions linear in their constants). If the row and column components were small (i.e., if the priors were in agreement with the data) the weight for the fitted mean would be large and the posterior means would assume a functional form close to that implied by the priors. If the components were large, the effect of the observed means would predominate, however. This is in contrast to frequentist procedures, such as those in Truett[3] and Armitage[6] where no smooth interpolation between data and assumed curve forms is possible.

Another generalization of the assignments (8) that might often be appropriate would be to assume that the $g(\mu_i)$ in the discussion of one-way classification were linear compounds of two or more normal distributions with different means. This would be appropriate in situations in which the true means might cluster around two or more different values, as in testing a large number of cancer chemotherapeutic agents, most of which might be expected to be ineffective, with perhaps a small number standing out from the others.

The assignment of priors is neither unique nor without important consequences, therefore, and their use requires a thoughtful and informed choice. To those who believe that any given body of data can support only one correct conclusion, this is of course a drawback.

Let $x \stackrel{d}{=} N(\mu, \sigma^2)$ stand for the statement, x is a normal variate with mean μ and variance σ^2. Then the distribution assumptions in the discussion of two-way classification can be written as

(15)

$$x_{11} \stackrel{d}{=} N(\mu, V_{11})$$

$$x_{12} \stackrel{d}{=} N(\mu + C, V_{12})$$

$$x_{21} \stackrel{d}{=} N(\mu + R, V_{21})$$

$$x_{22} \stackrel{d}{=} N(\mu + R + C + I, V_{22})$$

$$\mu \stackrel{d}{=} N(0, \infty)$$

$$C \stackrel{d}{=} N(0, \sigma_C^2)$$

$$R \stackrel{d}{=} N(0, \sigma_R^2)$$

$$I \stackrel{d}{=} N(0, \sigma_I^2)$$

The joint posterior density of the four parameters can then be written as proportional to

(16)

$$\exp\left[-\frac{1}{2}(Q_1 + Q_2)\right]$$

where $Q_1 = (x_{11} - \mu)^2/V_{11} + (x_{12} - \mu - C)^2/V_{12}$
$+ (x_{21} - \mu - R)^2/V_{21} + (x_{22} - \mu - C - R - I)^2/V_{22}$
and $Q_2 = C^2/\sigma_C^2 + R^2/\sigma_R^2 + I^2/\sigma_I^2$

But one may also write

(17)

$$Q_1 + Q_2 = \frac{(\mu - \hat{\mu})^2}{V_\mu} + \frac{(C - \hat{C})^2}{V_C} + \frac{(R - \hat{R})^2}{V_R} + \frac{(I - \hat{I})^2}{V_I} +$$

$$2\frac{(\mu - \hat{\mu})(C - \hat{C})}{K_{\mu C}} + 2\frac{(\mu - \hat{\mu})(R - \hat{R})}{K_{\mu R}} + 2\frac{(\mu - \hat{\mu})(I - \hat{I})}{K_{\mu R}}$$

$$+ 2\frac{(C - \hat{C})(R - \hat{R})}{K_{CR}} + 2\frac{(C - \hat{C})(I - \hat{I})}{K_{CI}} + 2\frac{(R - \hat{R})(I - \hat{I})}{K_{RI}} + f$$

where the V and K are arbitrary quantities. If the coefficients of $\mu,C,R,I,\mu^2,C^2,R^2,I^2,\mu C,\mu R,\mu I,CR,CI$ and RI are equated in the two expressions for $Q_1 + Q_2$, (17) and (16), equations (9) are obtained, with the function f depending on the x_{1j}, the V_{1j}, $\sigma_C{}^2,\sigma_R{}^2$ and $\sigma_I{}^2$, but not an μ,C,R or I. The posterior means of the four variables μ,C,R and I are then seen immediately, from multivariate normal theory, to be $\hat{\mu},\hat{C},\hat{R}$ and $\hat{I}$.

REFERENCES

[1] Kahn, H. A., The Dorn Study of Smoking and Mortality Among U. S. Veterans: Report on Eight and One-Half Years of Observation, in Haenszel, W. (Editor), *Epidemiological Approaches to the Study of Cancer and Other Chronic Diseases*, National Cancer Institute Monograph 19, Washington, United States Government Printing Office, 1966.

[2] Seltzer, C. C., An Evaluation of the Effect of Smoking on Coronary Heart Disease, *Journal of the American Medical Association*, 203, 193–200, January 15, 1968.

[3] Truett, J., *et al.*, A Multivariate Analysis of the Risk of Coronary Heart Disease, in Framingham, *Journal of Chronic Diseases*, 20, 511–524, 1967.

[4] Birch, M., Maximum Likelihood in Three-Way Contingency Tables, *Journal of the Royal Statistical Society*, 25, 220–233, 1963.

[5] Bunker, J. B., *et al.* (Editors), *The National Halothane Study: A Study of the Possible Association Between Halothane Anesthesic and Postoperative Hepatic Necrosis*, Washington, United States Government Printing Office, 1969.

[6] Armitage, P., *et al.*, Statistical Studies of Prognosis in Advanced Breast Cancer, *Journal of Chronic Diseases*, 22, 343–360, 1969.

[7] Lindley, D. V., Discussion to Stein, C. M., Confidence Sets for the Mean of a Multivariate Normal Distribution, *Journal of the Royal Statistics Society*, 24, 269–296, 1962.

[8] Yates, F., The Analysis of Multiple Classifications with Unequal Numbers in the Different Subclasses, *Journal of the American Statistical Association*, 29, 51–66, 1934.

ACKNOWLEDGMENT

The preparation of this paper was supported by funds made available by NIH Grant GM-15004.

396